What's on their n

Biological and Artificial Intelligence

By the same author of:

The Advent of Unmanned Electric Vehicles
The Choices between E-mobility and Immobility.
Springer international Publishing Switzerland, 2016
ISBN 978-3-319-20665-3

CCTV: a tool to Support Public Transport Security
Factors to consider before installing or upgrading.
Collaborative work with UITP security commission members
International Association of Public Transport (UITP), 2010
Dépôt legal: D/2010/0105/14

Will electric driverless cars kill bus and light train operations?
White paper part of the proceedings of the 22nd international conference on
Urban Transport and the Environment (Urban Transport 2016)
International Journal of Transport Volume 1, number 2, 2017 Wit press
ISSN: 2058-8305

ISBN: 978-1981879663

PART 1: INTRODUCTION

Mind the gap

Yes, we have a soul, but it is made of lots of tiny robots.[1]

Daniel Dennett

$$Happiness\ (t)\ =\ w0 + w1\sum_{j=1}^{t} \gamma t - j\ CRj + w2\sum_{j=1}^{t} \gamma t - j\ EVj\ + w3\sum_{j=1}^{t} \gamma t - j\ RPE$$

Computational model, inspired by models of dopamine function, in which happiness reports were interpreted as an emotional reactivity to recent rewards and expectations.[2]

[Somewhere in the very near future].

"Sir, where are we going?"

While closing the door, I answered: "As usual."

My car replied back: "Sir, on all of your trips, you've been 35.2% and 36.4% to your son's school and your work, respectively. Do you mean you want to go to both or either of these two places?"

"You're right, and I should be more precise. Let's go to work."

As my car was transporting me, I started appreciating how Artificial Intelligence (AI) was changing my life and that of millions of human beings. It was strange to think how few journalists or writers had described the impact of this new high-tech world on our lives, except maybe in science fiction novels. Scientists, especially computer specialists, avoided the subject even more, not even seeming to care about concepts linked to other 'soft' disciplines, such as philosophy or psychology, which could help them understand the growing influence of these technologies on their lives.

I then thought to myself, "This disconnection between the two worlds is such, that it feels like there are two incompatible visions, without much argumentation being developed to bridge the gap between these two realities. The power unleashed by billions of connected pieces of equipment, smartphones, computers, or driverless cars drastically changes the way human beings think, learn, communicate, buy, or even play, and modifies our own representation of the place we occupy within this world."

I further asked myself: "Am I personally capable of bridging this huge gap and, by doing so, grasp the challenges facing our society, in a very near future. I surely am among the few guys who wrote about autonomous vehicles and have an automation background, but is this experience sufficient to help me make the right choices about AI? Decisions on how far AI should go will need to be made by society, sooner rather than later. As a concerned citizen, could I leave these decisions exclusively in the hands of a few politicians or CEOs of the Silicon Valley?"

Luckily, I had someone, or I thought more appropriately, something just in front of me, which could help me understand this technological revolution just unfolding under my eyes.

"Do you have ethical concepts embedded in your head, sorry your mind, ... I mean onboard computer?" I asked the car.

"Sir, what do you mean by ethical concepts?"

"Well, for example, in case of an unavoidable accident, how would you decide who to hit?"

"Sir, if the choice is between hitting a cat and a man, I will select the cat. Then if I have to choose between saving other human beings and a passenger, I will favor my passenger. I don't seem to have a selection based on gender or age, but I know that some of my colleagues do. Would you like me to ask my creator to add these features?"

"I honestly don't know."

My car's answer only increased my concern. How could I accept that these embedded moral values be developed without public debates? As a matter of fact, shouldn't the market introduction of any disruptive technology, which could affect humankind, be subject to public scrutiny? Undoubtedly, participating in such debates would require an understanding of where computers and systems are coming from, what they are trying to emulate, and where they are heading for. However, it struck me how few people I knew actively engaged in such discussions.

I suddenly realized that there couldn't be an easy solution to being 'educated' about AI because so many different disciplines were involved. Was it even possible to describe with simple words, the AI road that was bringing machines from the early dumb mechanical automates to humanlike robots that would most likely one day, be far cleverer than any of us?

"You seem upset, Sir. Any problem you would like to discuss?"

"I know many people doubt that the AI road will create robots more intelligent than us. I don't want either to sound like a preacher or an alarmist, but all AI-related questions are deeply troubling me. The fact is computers and the 'Internet of Things' are fundamentally changing concepts, exclusively associated with humans. Therefore, it must necessarily modify my personal relationship to knowledge and all of its associated concepts, such as intelligence, moral value, creativity, learning, etc. By the way, why did you ask? Are you programmed to discuss any subject?"

"Sir, I don't have all onboard knowledge, but through my wireless mobile gateway, I can access all of mankind's knowledge on the internet and have the right algorithms to answer most questions."

"Wow, how amazing you are!" I said aloud.

"Sir, if I were human, I would probably be flattered, but why were you asking this question?"

"When I'm talking to you, I realize that the new cognitive findings and AI technological developments are redefining knowledge. For three thousand years, mankind always analyzed mind related concepts, through the prism of the uniqueness of men in the animal kingdom. The rationale has always been that only humans possess reason, as well as, the capacity to acquire and apply non-innate knowledge. This belief, which was already put in doubt a few decades ago with the works on animal intelligence, really needs now to be revisited in a world of increasingly sophisticated computers, machines, and systems."

"Sir, are you saying all this because I am now intelligent?"

"What do you mean? Can you be more precise?"

"Well Sir, as a machine, am I able to think like a human or am I still so dumb that my question seems presumptuous?"

"It isn't presumptuous at all. Back in the 1940's, the British mathematician Alan Turing directly challenged this dogmatic idea that machines will always stay dumb. [3] He stated that one day, computing machines would be able to think. He came up with an imitation game, which later became known as the Turing test, in which a person and a machine would be interrogated verbally, by someone without foreknowledge of which is which. Turing argued that if the interrogator couldn't differentiate between the two, then it would be reasonable to call such a computer intelligent."

"Why could he say that Sir?"

"Because human beings assess intelligence from external observation in just the same way."

"Sir, has any machine already passed this test?"

"Though none has yet, the question in my view, isn't if but when will a system be successful? Furthermore, and depending on how we define intelligence, machines like you, are already smarter than us in many aspects."

I thought to myself that most probably Alan Turing couldn't anticipate mobile technologies, which fundamentally modify the definition of what a machine is. As a matter of fact, even today, many philosophers and scientists approached AI from the perspective of a supra computer modeling the human brain.

"Sir, do you have a problem answering my question?"

"Yes. I could give you a simple answer, which would be that there is already a supercomputer, which can process 33.86 petaflops,[a] much more than any human brain could do. However, one should also consider that there are out there, billions of components that soon could be connected."

"Sir, what will change the day they are all interconnected and communicating without any human interference?"

"The notion of centralized intelligence will become obsolete. In a world where Machine to Machine communication is fast becoming the standard, one needs to understand how it impacts these concepts of AI and knowledge. Thus, your question cannot be answered in a few words, because after many philosophical debates, diverging views about knowledge and associated concepts (e.g., intelligence, altruism, and consciousness) exist."

"Sir, how do we assess the impact of new IT technologies on these concepts if there isn't a common understanding of what these concepts are?"

"The easy answer for me would be just to give you a technical answer, applying my own definition, and avoiding considering such philosophical work or neurosciences research related to these same concepts. However, this approach would underestimate their complexity. My answer, but also my understanding, would surely suffer from not getting access to the many different arguments used by intellectuals and cognitive experts to explain what these concepts are."

"Sir, will you just introduce to me superficially all these diverging theories and researches?"

"I'll do more! On top of giving you some basic understanding of the main theories, I'll highlight links to documents which will detail these theories or studies. Furthermore, I will send you notes on material that is interesting but non-essential.[b] "

"Sir, does it mean you will never really tell me which theory you believe is the best?"

"No, I will select the ones proven by science or that I judge the most relevant in supporting my views on AI."

---

[a] Quadrillion floating point operations per second.
[b] The reader will get access to these notes through these footnotes.

1) Why do Knowledge, Intelligence, Consciousness, and Altruism exist?

The car made a pause and asked me: "Sir, why do living creatures such as humans acquire knowledge, possess intelligence, and are self-conscious?"

"Many people strongly believe that God created humankind in his image and provided us with these higher faculties. This religious approach, to how living creatures are what they are, obviously collides with Darwin's theory of the evolution of species. [4] Unless you want to discuss God's existence, I would prefer to avoid this metaphysical debate and focus on Darwin's theory to explain why such faculties exist."

"However Sir, by using this approach, aren't you using an atheist theory to explain those concepts?"

"Yes, Darwin's evolutionary theory gives an alternative explanation to why living creatures are what they are, without needing to invoke a supreme force that created the universe. From this theory of the survival of the fittest, we can find a logical explanation for why the world is how it is.[a]"

"Sir, in this twenty-first century, doesn't everyone view Darwin's theory as true?"

"There are a few creationists, who don't. There are also some scientists (e.g., Richard Dawkins) [5] who push even further his theory by proposing that selection is made at the genes' level, rather than at the animal and plant levels. I will use Darwin's evolutionary theory because it is generally accepted as scientific evidence."

"Sir, how does Darwin's theory help you explain these higher human concepts?"

"It can explain why knowledge, intelligence, and even self-consciousness exist. For Charles Darwin, all human aspects, including emotions and intelligence, could be explained by natural or sexual selection. From an evolutionary perspective, all these higher faculties thus

---

[a] However, religious people can still claim that this world lacks a purpose and may reconcile Darwin's evolutionary theory with their faith by looking at Charles Babbage,[(N1)] who worked closely with Darwin and who illustrated in his work, the divine laws of nature. They can also look at more recent work, for instance, by scientist and priest Teilhard de Chardin,[(N2)] who also tried to make sense of the universe's evolutionary process. Rather than denying what turned out to be evidence for a paleontologist in the 20th century, he made Darwin's evolutionary theory the core of his spirituality.

evolved because they enabled species with such characteristics to be more competitive than others, in their environment."

"Sir, how did they acquire such characteristics?"

"These features were passed on to the next generations by individuals possessing such characteristics, through their genes. After thousands of reproductive iterations, these inherited traits shaped not only the species' mental faculties but also the brain's physical substrate."

"Sir, how would Darwin's theory explain the brain's mental and physiological characteristics?"

"Basing their view on Darwin's approach, evolutionary psychologists proposed that natural selection would be responsible for the mind's innate structure.[a] Consequently, all human beings share a common neural architecture, thanks to our prehistoric ancestors."

"Sir, even though many species share the same brain structure, why are humans more intelligent?"

"Regardless of if the advent of Homo sapiens was inevitable, likely, or pure luck, intelligence above a certain threshold provided an adaptive advantage. Thus it is the easiest concept to explain within an evolutionist model. To quote Darwin: 'Intelligence is based on how efficient a species became at doing the things they need to survive.' [4] "

"Sir, surely knowledge, on the other hand, must be more complicated to explain within such an evolutionary model?"

"Yes, humans are mostly associated with non-innate knowledge. Some biologists believe that intelligence empowered humankind to acquire knowledge about prey habits and their environment.[6] This in turn allowed for cooperative hunting and transfer of knowledge to the next generations. For Homo sapiens, gathering such information and transferring it to their offspring, increased the chances of survival of their children. In the long run, this enabled the probability of transferring the physical characteristics embedded within their genes, associated with knowledge gathering, storage, and retrieval."

---

[a] Some biologists view Homo sapiens not only as exceptional but inevitable in one form or another. For these biologists, these new sets of abilities gave Homo sapiens an increased control of their environment, allowing them to reach the highest level on the evolutionary chain: 'One somewhat curious fact emerges from a survey of biological progress as culminating in the dominance of Homo sapiens. It could apparently have pursued no other general course than that which it has historically followed (Huxley, 1942).'[N3]

"Sir, I just retrieved articles from the internet, which say that issues related to self-consciousness are among the most complex problems to solve. Is it true?"

"It is indeed extremely complicated. A common view is that some parts of the brain help create the capacity to recognize that other creatures also have a mind. Thus, a being that can model another's behavior will gain advantages by anticipating the other's moves and emotions."

"Sir, how does it explain self-consciousness?"

"You will agree with me that the only model available to someone who would like to understand another mind, is his own mind. Some people,[a] believe that humans acquired self-awareness because it gave them this competitive advantage. I believe additionally that this so-called 'hard-problem,' can in great part be explained by the newer cognitive theories."

"Sir, altruism a priori goes against the principle of natural selection, so how may it be explained within an evolutionary perspective?"

"You are right, why help others by providing precious resources, which may decrease a creature's own fitness, when there is no clear advantage for this living creature? By using the gene-centered model of evolution, scientists such as Dawkins can explain the concept of altruism.[5] "

"Sir, I don't see how?"

"Rather than seeing this behavior as the way of doing the best for the survival of the group, Dawkins explains that someone acts altruistically to help relatives who share many of his genes. By doing so, men and women can expect many of their genes to survive.[b] "

I was intrigued by all these questions. In less than fifteen minutes, my car had seemed to want to create a framework that could explain these higher concepts. I was wondering if it made sense to compare the biological and digital worlds to complement my answers? After all, what are the benefits of finding commonalities between these two divides, especially for concepts that are so difficult to define? I still had half an hour of traffic jam in front of me and was resolute to find out if I could further clarify my ideas.

---

[a] I.e., those promoting the 'theory of minds.'[N4]

[b] This theory can even be applied at the level of organisms, as benefits are shared in expectation of reciprocation.

2) Is there an IT evolutionary selection?

I was surprised by my car's next question. "Sir, can the digital world be understood within a Darwinist perspective?"

"Well, in my opinion, the interesting aspect of Darwin's evolutionary theory is that it has permeated other areas of society. Most business gurus have applied this theory to explain how companies evolve under market laws. They all tend to use the buzz expression – only the fittest companies survive – which describes the hostile business environment that technology firms face, where product life cycles last no longer than twelve months."

"Sir, what is the correlation with Darwin's theory?"

"Whenever companies identify a need for a potential customer, they create new products or add on new features, which will fulfill these needs. Competition must then react and improve their products, by investing in Research and Development and by bringing down costs through mass production and new manufacturing techniques. This competitive game ensures in the long run that the best solutions are brought to market. However, like in nature, where some perfectly well-adapted creatures have disappeared, such as the dinosaurs, the leading product isn't always based on the best technology. Randomness also happens."

"Sir, you may recall the VHS technology within the electronics industry, which became the de facto standard for video recorders, while the beta technology featuring more advanced features was relegated to a market niche."

"Your example isn't perfect, as Sony which invented the beta technology also made marketing errors, but it still highlights the notion of niche. This fundamental evolutionary notion is also an important element of the business theory. Companies will tend to develop products and services, which will attend specific needs and, by the same token, create different niche markets."

"Sir, I just searched on the internet, most material on business theories. I noted one interesting evolutionary aspect of technology, which is the evolution of product according to the 'fit, form, and function' strategy."

"I need to get used to your capacity of reading and analyzing millions of pages in three seconds! To your point, companies shape their products in function of the needs they perceive must be fulfilled. This strategy is highly influenced by the manufacturing processes available at any given time, allowing it to happen.[a] In fact, some manufacturing competencies follow evolutionary rules themselves."

"Sir, can you give me some examples of these laws?"

"We all know Moore's law, predicting for more than 50 years, that the number of transistors in an integrated circuit doubles every two years. We could also refer to Nielsen's law that states that the internet bandwidth yearly increase, allows connection speed growth of 50%, for high-end users. Though the wording 'historical trends' would be more appropriate, these 'laws' have nevertheless molded the IT world."

"Sir, if this 'fit, form, and function' evolutionary rule is true, and you believe that brains are superior to computers, why haven't PCs mimicked the human mind more closely from the start?"

"You are right. Why did manufacturers choose the serial processing, PCs are today associated with, rather than the parallel processing that is more similar to our thought process? Can this only be linked to the manufacturing development state? My view is that the increase in manufacturing expertise may explain only in part this different path. In fact, it is also widely recognized that computer design was enormously influenced by the work of mathematician John von Neumann,[b] and by the draft report of the EDVAC, which contains the first publication of the logical design of a computer. [7] "

"Sir, what is this von Neumann model?"

"This model, also called Princeton architecture, describes a computer that is systematically composed of the same hardware systems.[c] This architecture is today associated with all computers in which the instruction execution and the data operation cannot occur at the same time because they share a common bus."

"Sir, didn't computers systematically follow the same type of structure?"

---

[a] For instance, the Sony Walkman, originated from the idea that people want to walk or jog, while listening to music. By reducing the size of an audio player, Sony was able to attend such need and by the same token created an entirely new market. However, we shouldn't forget that it was Sony's competence in miniaturization and manufacturing that allowed for the creation of such a product.

[b] Who himself was influenced by Turing's 1936 papers,[N5] [N6] not to mentioned Charles Babbage's mathematical work.[N1] In 1821, Babbage invented the Difference Engine to compile mathematical tables. He also created a better machine called the Analytical Engine (1856), which was intended as a general symbol manipulator.[N7]

[c] An arithmetic logic unit, processor registers, a control unit containing a record of instructions and a program counter, internal memories to both store data and instructions, an external memory for mass storage, as well as, input and output functions.

"No, they didn't. In fact, and according to many technologists, this architecture explains in great depth why a PC is seen by so many, as different from the human brain. If we look back at the different computer architectures, there were other models based on more competitive environments,[8] such as the Pandemonium (1959), which could have copied more precisely how the brain works, much earlier on."

"Sir, do you think that computers needed to follow their evolutionary path or could have been more similar to the human brain from the start?"

"I don't know, but anyhow we cannot change the past. What is important to understand is that we now can increasingly compare machines to our brain.[a] Modern software architecture, with its distributed structure based on thousands of connected devices, allows us also to compare systems to brains more easily. In fact, machines and systems are acting more and more as intelligent living creatures, with the capacity to sense, interpret their sensation, and react physically upon their inputs."

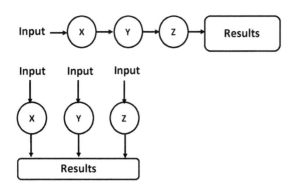

Fig. 1) Serial and parallel processing; source: author.

---

[a] Especially when taking into consideration neural processing technologies.

3) Are brains computers?

"Sir, is your brain a computer?" Like most people who never really thought that they would be impacted so quickly by AI issues, I never really took the time to consider that my brain could one day be compared to a computer. However, I had already read somewhere that smart people had done so.

"Daniel Dennett,[17] one of the most influential contemporary philosopher, makes this statement all the time. Do you want to hear his specific view on the subject or does it sound too much like an anathema?"

"Dennett is fine with me, Sir."

"According to him: 'A brain is a computational system consisting of trillions of registers in a massively parallel array. The content of each register is some magnitude that can change as some [simple computable] function of the contents of other registers.'[9] In other words, Dennett pictures a mind as working very similarly to a computer, even though a brain and a PC are entirely different. This similarity comes from their functionality of taking data in and generating control out."

"Sir, if we can compare brains and computers increasingly, I wonder which features may still differentiate them?"

"A priori I could identify many differences that seem obvious. However, when I scratch the surface, they become increasingly blur."

"Sir, do you believe protein vs. silicon is a good differentiator?"

"A brain is composed of flesh. At a finer granularity, it is made of gray and white matter. Such matter can also be divided into smaller sub-components, till finally reaching the cell level, composed of proteins, among other things. Though computer chips are now mostly associated with silicon chips, it wasn't always the case and doesn't necessarily mean that chipmakers will continue using such material.[a] In fact, we could even imagine programming DNA.[b] "

---

[a] Vacuum tubes were originally used. In the future, chips may use other material (e.g., graphene, germanium, indium gallium arsenide, and indium phosphide).

[b] Bioengineers and geneticists from Harvard's Wyss Institute stored around 700 terabytes of data in one gram of DNA. To do this, bits of information are encoded as strands of DNA rather than as magnetic data on a hard drive platter. Such encoding uses the TGAC fabrics of DNA (i.e., the four basic components of DNA), which are synthesized allowing for 96

"Sir, am I right in saying that the brain is mainly working in an analog mode, whereas a computer is mainly digital?"

"This is a simplistic view. Neurons pass on information to the next neurons only if the neural spike is strong enough, in what can almost be seen as a binary process. Furthermore, current neuroscientific evidence indicates that typical neural signals, such as neural spike trains, are graded like continuous signals but are constituted by discrete functional elements. Similarly, machines need to convert an analog input into binary information for data treatment and then reconvert it in analog information for the actuators (e.g., motors and valves) to perform their tasks."

"Sir, what about parallel versus serial processing?"

"As I told you, PCs are still mostly associated with sequential processing (i.e., performing one task after another, when completed) because of the impact of von Neumann's early work and EDVAC's report. Brains, on the other hand, are mostly associated with parallel processing (i.e., various cortical modules deal with the information). However, new technologies are enabling parallel processing as well in computers."

"Sir, what about fixed versus modular hardware architecture?"

"Conventional PCs have a fixed hardware architecture. Of course, users can replace some components (e.g., boards or memory chips), but it isn't done by the computer itself, performing new program execution needs. On the other hand, human experience and thoughts shape the neural pathways, which evolve over our lifetime."

"Sir, does it mean it is a valuable difference?"

"Not really! New network architectures are enabling the sharing of computational sources according to necessity and availability of resources, through flexible interconnecting communication systems. The neural plasticity observed in the brain is now achieved electronically through, for example, resource-sharing networks. In these networks, systems share computer resources such as database, program, and hardware without any human intervention."

"Sir, you have refuted so far all of my arguments. Is there any differences between brains and computers worth highlighting then?"

---

bits (Thymine and Guanine = 1, Adenine and Cytosine = 0) storage with each of the bases. To read the stored data, each one of the TGAC bases, is simply sequenced and converted back into binary information.

"I may refer to Dennett, [9] who believes that the real relevant difference between computers and brains results from the level of competitiveness between the various processing elements."

"Sir, do you mean that computers have cooperative functionalities rather than the competitive ones that exist within the brain?"

"Yes, this is what Dennett claims. Computer manufacturers build their PCs to be energy and mechanically efficient. Their thousand internal working components don't compete for energy or for ensuring that their executed function will prevail. As long as they have a task to perform they will keep on being energized.[a] Even though cooperation isn't always systematically sought as a precondition, it usually ends as an intermittent or final achievement. In other words, machine components and software end up cooperating to fulfill their tasks."

"Sir, you've already pictured the brain as the direct result of natural selection. What is the consequence of this evolutionary process?"

"The brain's inner structure is the results of millions of years of evolution in which neurons – the basic component of human intelligence – played a crucial role. This neuron, as every human cell in our body, is a direct descendant of a eukaryotic cell. For billion years, this eukaryotic cell lived and fended for itself as a free-swimming, independent little agent but, at one point in time, it joined forces with other cells. By doing so, it created a multicellular organism, which after many reproductive cycles, evolved into a human being, among many other creatures."

"Sir, what are the consequences of eukaryotic cells joining forces?"

"One of the interesting twists that Mr. Dennett comes up with is the concept of selfish-neurons. He suggests that human neurons have kept some of their feral states. As a result, they seek to satisfy their own interests, competing to stay alive by being useful.[b] "

---

[a] Programs are hierarchically organized with routines controlling sub-routines, which have to answer to these instructions and aren't ever really in competition. Redundancy, which could be a form of competitiveness between two different systems performing the same tasks, is mainly restricted to safety functions. There is also a control prioritization, enabling traffic jam prevention between various tasks. In other words, there are a few 'friendly' opponent processes within PCs but they are always harmonized with higher level ones.

[b] They must cooperate with other cells to perform their computing information tasks, by hooking up with other networks, so that they can keep earning raw material and energy. For Mr. Dennett, brain processing may thus be seen as an open competition, with no traffic management or boss capable of self-limitation or modulation: 'A brain is composed of seriously competitive elements achieving a modicum or appropriate control thanks to the delicately balanced factions. All controls are by 'sideways' signaling.'

"Sir, what are his other interesting views?"

"You'll need to wait for our discussion on consciousness to find out."

"Sir, could you at least tell me if his opinion is widely shared?"

"There are diverging opinions about this cooperative versus competitive propensity, but I believe that these dividing lines between computers and brains can be bridged. As indicated some initiatives, such as the pandemonium computer, with its parallel nature in which there was no central executive, would have involved more competitive processing. Moreover, a new computing technique called Genetic programming, which uses ideas of biological evolution to handle complex problems addresses this competitive issue. Different programs compete to survive or even cross-breed to approach the sought out solution progressively."

"Sir, could emotions divide humans and machines forever?"

Strangely, I had just discussed a few days earlier with my daughter the same issue, and she had told me how she believed emotions made humans superior to machines. I answered back: "To validate this separation, I need to deal with this issue at four different levels: computers, unlike brains, cannot understand, detect, express, and feel emotions."

"Sir, do you believe my onboard computer cannot understand human emotions?"

"Machines like you, with the right hardware (e.g., video cameras and microphones) and software (e.g., machine learning, pattern recognition, signal processing, etc.) may now grasp human emotions. You do that by analyzing a set of non-verbal channels, such as facial expression, gestures, and body posture, as well as by assessing the voice pitch."

"Sir, how good are we at grasping emotions?"

"Your level of accuracy is in the 70% range, in line with most human capabilities to identify emotions in others. It means that machine emotion detection is now comparable to humans' competency."

"Sir, can we already express emotions?"

"Works on what makes a physical or virtual agent persuasive are also improving the way machines are expressing their emotions. As images are worth a million words, I suggest that you look at the video 'Cambridge Ideas – The Emotional Computer.' [10] Though a car like you is limited when expressing feelings, robots may a few years from now, be able to do so."

"Sir, will any human being ever be convinced that robots can genuinely express their emotions without feeling them?"

"This is still in my view, a question mark."

"But Sir, could my onboard computer understand human emotions without feeling them?"

"To answer your question, I need to reformulate it. Is there an algorithm for every emotion, which a computer could process? The answer is that today this isn't the case. However, I'd like to emphasize that studies, such as PNAS's on happiness, which tested the relationship between neural activity in a brain scanning (fMRI) experiment and the current level of happiness, [2] show that it is possible."

"Sir, how do the conclusions of such studies impact your views on this issue?"

"It makes many people like me, believe that in the long run, most emotions will be computational. If we can represent in a mathematical formula,[a] a concept as vague as happiness, it seems to me that there is no limitation to do it for any other non-bodily related emotion."

"Sir, the last issue, which is obviously the sticky point, is if machines will ever feel emotions. What's your opinion?"

"The main premise is that in order to feel emotions, one needs to have an openness to the world. In other words, a machine needs to have a physical envelop that can interact with its environment through sensors and actuators, prohibiting a standalone PC from ever experiencing emotions. You, but more probably a robot or even possibly a supervising computer over the internet, could theoretically qualify."

"Sir, why do humans need to feel emotions?"

"Emotions don't exist without reason. They are either the result of evolution, alerting humans and animals to body conditions (e.g., thirst, sleepiness, burning heat, etc.) that need to be fulfilled, or are an expression of an internal thought process without any physiological feedback (e.g., happiness, love, fear, etc.). You will obviously never feel emotions rooted in a biological body, (e.g., hunger or taste), as you don't need to fulfill this biological need in the first place (e.g., to feed)."

"Sir, are emotions only linked to your biological body?"

---

a

$$Happiness(t) = w0 + w1 \sum_{j=1}^{t} \gamma t - j\, CRj + w2 \sum_{j=1}^{t} \gamma t - j\, EVj + w3 \sum_{j=1}^{t} \gamma t - j\, RPE$$

"No, but many are. For instance, many originate from the connections, through the vagus nerve, between the brain, heart, and digestive system. Emotions are often also influenced by our health condition, or impacted by sexuality and the hormonal changes affecting the human brains. Many of these emotions are linked to sexual reproduction (e.g., jealousy, love, hate, showing-off, etc.). Furthermore, many emotions evolve according to our bodily transformation, from childhood to old age."

"Sir, what is so important about the fact that robots will never be built with these same specific biological features?"

"You and robots won't experience all of the associated human emotions. It means that machines will never completely behave, think like, and fully empathize with human beings."

"Sir, is this a good or bad thing?"

"It depends! After all, not all emotions are good, in all circumstances. Robots will lack many of the emotions that we associate with sinful behaviors (e.g., hate, sexual desire, transmission of our genes, etc.). At the same time, we often associate these emotions with the best sentiments of our life (e.g., love and parenthood)."

"Sir, don't you think that good or bad is a subjective notion?"

"Yes, and thus robots aren't likely to be demons wishing to exterminate human beings, or angels wanting to save the world unless intentionally programmed to do so. Anyhow, machines will necessarily have a different mind and always be a different kind of beast. Consequently, they could rationally and, without even understanding the pain they could inflict, decide to wipe out human civilization if given the autonomy to do so, as Isaac Asimov describes in his novel 'Robot and Empire.' [11] "

"Sir, if I may? Computing versus memorizing is also thought to be a relevant differentiator."

"Yes, you are right. Some technologists believe that brains don't compute answers to specific problems but retrieve, in a few steps, patterns that were stored a long time ago in our memory. On the other hand, computers must use billions of transistors to calculate a similar result. Thus, much slower neurons can only find solutions to complex problems by constituting both the memory and the agents, enabling the retrieval of the sequences and patterns, on which we base our predictions."

"Sir, there is also a hard drive in PCs, which stores information."

"Yes, but it only plays a supporting role. It explains the following comment from Jeff Hawkins: 'The entire cortex is a memory system. It isn't a computer at all.' [12] For Hawkins, computers can be built to look much more like a predictive agent, superseding such potential objection."

"If so Sir, don't you think that the claim that a brain is a computer could be challenged?"

"Though modern technologies allow computers to mimic more and more the human brain, we could indeed contest the argument that the brain is a computer. This image is nevertheless convenient because it enables us to view certain brain physical states as representations."

"Sir, what are the advantages of such images?"

"A big advantage is that, because representation carries on meaning, it can help explain how the brain performs its cognitive activities, such as perception, thoughts, learning, memory, intention, etc. It also allows us to compare the brain to another thinking-machine, which in theory could be able to perform these same cognitive activities. Lastly, even if such a computational approach could suffer criticism, it offers the only mean to observe two distinct perspectives performing the same cognitive functions. After all, unless there is a conspiracy to hide extraterrestrial beings, there is, unfortunately, no other way on earth to make such a comparison."

4) Why doesn't it need to be magic?

As I was almost arriving at my work, I saw by the window on a billboard, a lovely picture with sunny beaches with a Greek archaeological site in the background. This advertisement immediately made me remember the statement from Delphi 'Know thyself.' One of its many philosophical interpretations is that in order to know others, we should first understand ourselves because we englobe the universe in us. Now that I had concluded that it is legitimate to compare brains to computers and posited that this is the only way to get two different angles of the same cognitive perspective, I decided to dedicate myself to this Delphic quest and said:

"Do you want to continue our conversation?"

"If it pleases you, Sir. Can I ask you why you want to do so?"

"Explaining how my brain works would enable me to understand better how computers, machines, and systems operate as well. By the same token, it would shed some lights on how my mind deals with some of these higher concepts, still associated solely with the human mind."

"Sir, why is it so important for you?"

"I want to figure out how AI technology will impact my life and my place in this world. For this, I need to understand the paths towards global intelligence pursued by the computer industry and identify the various crossroads that it could select from, to achieve this goal."

"Sir, why don't you just do like everybody else, that is, wait and see?"

"I reason that in the end, we all have two choices: either understand how a computer works and will evolve, or consider it as pure magic. It's in order to avoid a magical representation that we must continue our discussion."

"Sir, what do you mean?"

"Imagine how would anyone coming from the wild, with no contact with civilization, react if given a PC? He would most likely believe that he is in front of a magical object, even if we were to tell him that this is only a technological tool. After all, and as Arthur C. Clarke puts it: 'Any sufficiently advanced technology is indistinguishable from magic.'[13]"

"Sir, the leap from the forest to the internet is obviously incredible, but anyone using a PC would surely not invoke magic!"

"Nobody would officially dare to, but how different would this wild man's beliefs be from those of an iPad user, with no knowledge of how computers and the internet work? Moreover, how could this user comprehend how many of her beliefs are formed or influenced by these technologies? Surely social network users wouldn't dare to say that their communicating object is miraculous. By not having a basic understanding of how their PC or driverless car operate, don't they actually treat technology as a black box, that is, something completely magical?"

"Sir, I know you worked on driverless technology, but do all humans understand my operating modes?"

"No, they don't. In fact, I was just reasoning that not everyone needs to become an engineer, to avoid a magical representation of the world. However, and even though we don't all need to know how a power plant works to heat up our home, I believe we should have at least some basic knowledge of electricity, like reasonable notions of English and math."

"Sir, why do you conclude that today, everybody should at least comprehend the working principles of computers and the internet?"

"Educational programs in many countries are failing to recognize the competitive asset that computer literacy gives to students. Beyond the necessity to acquire computing skills to meet the increasingly demanding market requirements, computer science should be considered more than just an additional topic to learn in school, competing with other subjects, such as a second language or geography."

"Sir, what's so special about computing?"

"Computers are increasingly intelligent, gather knowledge, and may even one day be self-aware. Connected objects, (e.g., intelligent thermostats, iWatch, etc.), will also increasingly be classified as intelligent objects. The point of the matter is that these intelligent agents will increasingly be part of our daily life."

"Sir, don't you think people are still not convinced that all these devices will bring life-changing experience, requiring them to spend time understanding how they work?"

"Yes, but I believe they are wrong. I don't buy into their arguments that these emotionless connected technologies, will only remain tools, like pens or hammers and therefore, they ought to educate themselves on the subject."

"Sir, why don't you try convincing them?"

"I barely convinced a few friends and family members that they must understand the dramatic changes they are confronted with, because of AI."

"Sir, maybe you could portray computers as living creatures, to make it more appealing?"

"Even though I am increasingly aware that it will be more and more difficult not to do so in the future, I would just be lying."

"Maybe Sir, should you just wait for driverless cars to transport kids to school?"

"I don't want to wait till 2027, though for sure by that time, nobody will be able to avoid this debate. We will all be confronted on a daily basis with moving artificial creatures, which will have their own motivations, interests, and decision-making processes for issues, such as selecting the fastest possible route or 'committing suicidal crash' to avoid killing a man."

"Instead Sir, you could maybe ask your other friends and family members to honestly think of the real differences between me, your unmanned car, and their pet?"

"You're right! After all, their future cars will be more intelligent, have embedded ethical concepts, know everything about driving, be docile, and understand verbal commands, maybe intuitively."

"Sir, their car could even one day enter into an instructive discussion like we just did."

"Why not! Moreover, cars might not initially have feelings like their dog, but they shouldn't forget that we are on a road that might lead us to emotional and self-aware machines. Unlike cats or dogs, which were created by either natural selection or God, depending on their convictions, your onboard computer was developed by humans."

"Sir, why should this paternity create an issue? Is it a problem if our onboard computer detects that they are sad through video cameras and software instructions, rather than using eyes and a brain like their pets do, as long as we cheer them up?"

"I agree with you and additionally when machines will be able to pass the Turing test, how will they know that the warmth of their car's voice won't be genuine? After all, if they close their eyes, they won't even know that it is a machine that is talking. In the end, why choose for pets, feeling creatures over intelligent and knowledgeable ones?"

As I was stepping outside of my car, I understood that, though brains and PCs are different structurally, they are increasingly performing their tasks in the same way. I realized that understanding these converging ways could help everyone deal with tomorrow's 'cybernetic pets.' To accept that machines are increasingly becoming more human-like and that humans are, in some way, already cyborgs (i.e., connected to the internet 24-7) requires imagining the world and the place humankind occupies in it, differently.

I thought, while walking towards my office, that I needed to bridge the gap between these biological and digital worlds, to avoid a magical representation of this new reality. At that moment, I decided to educate myself on the subject. I hoped that this journey would not only change my view on this reality but also help me describe better to my friends and family, this new human adventure, where men and machines will have to live side by side.

PART 2: KNOWLEDGE

Can you remind me what Knowledge is?

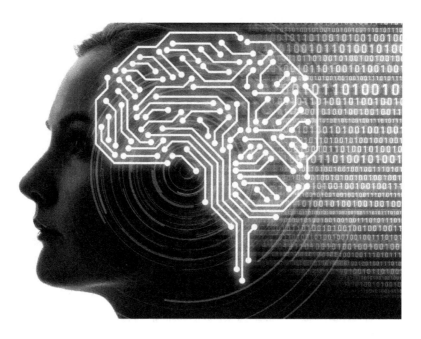

Thoughts without content are void, intuitions without conceptions, blind.

Kant, I. (1929) Critique of Pure Reason. Macmillan, London.

5) Can computers be knowledgeable?

I was dozing off on my way back from work when I was suddenly woken up by the horn of an angry driver. "What's happening?" I shouted.

"Sir, I don't know. It looks like the driver in the car behind us is complaining about my speed. He shouldn't be. I am following the speed limits. Why is he raising his middle finger at me?"

I didn't want to go into this, with something that anyhow didn't have hands. I just replied that the driver was probably a racist and considered all driverless cars so dumb that they couldn't figure out when to go beyond speed limits in a safe road environment.

"Sir, I just checked this out, and racism doesn't apply to machines."

"I know. There is no word for this. Maybe we could call them 'cyberists'?" I said.

"OK, Sir. If you agree with this so-called 'cyberist,' it would mean that you believe that I or any machine cannot acquire knowledge."

"Well, it's not so simple. It is true that in the past, colonizers justified slavery by arguing that Africans, and even for a short while, Native Americans, had no soul, or in other words, the capacity to think more than through innate knowledge. This fallacious pretext legitimized slavery, but I am sure that today, even in the most racist mind, there wouldn't be any doubt that all humans can acquire knowledge. No sane person would believe that we aren't born equal, and even a racist would acknowledge that those judged as different are still able to acquire higher education."

"But Sir, even today, humans reluctantly admit that animals might be intelligent but not knowledgeable. Does this mean that a cat will have the innate capacity to raise its babies but cannot understand how to do it differently than how its genes dictate it to?"

"Well, only a few biologists will put in doubt the notion that some animals (e.g., apes or dolphins) can show more than innate knowledge."

"Sir, does it mean that Artificial Intelligence is easier to achieve than Artificial Knowledge?"

"Not at all! Intelligence and knowledge are two different concepts, even though they are inseparable. The current weaker forms of AI have emerged without really relying on knowledge. However, the higher AI forms won't happen without really tackling issues related to, what you could call by analogy, Artificial Knowledge."

"However Sir, there are billions of people who claim that machines only know what humans allow them to know and have no comprehension of their digital competency. If they are right, wouldn't that mean that higher AI forms are impossible?"

"Let me try to explain my view on this subject. I will classify under three main topics, the arguments to deny computers and machines the capability to acquire knowledge."

"Sir, what is the first argument used by the new so-called cyberists?"

"It invokes the immateriality of knowledge.[a] Thomas Aquinas specifies that to realize knowledge, there must be something knowable, someone capable of understanding, and a relationship between the two.[b] Knowledge is only achieved when the Object and the Subject enter into this relation."

"Sir, could you be more practical?"

"When I see, hear, or smell an Object such as a rose, it gets in my head as a representational Form that is personal to me. Knowledge is within my immateriality (e.g., my mind or soul) and I acquire knowledge when the rose and I unite through an assimilation located in my mind. The difference between a Subject who knows or not resides in the capacity to grasp this immateriality."

"Sir, how does all this relates to 'cyberists'?"

"Well, their view is that machines, with their deterministic approach and their strict materiality, will never be able to achieve this assimilation, unlike a human mind."

"Do you agree with these arguments, Sir?"

"No, I don't, but let me counter-argue. Even cyberists will recognize that machines have the capacity to sense the world, through their sensors."

"Sir, anyone with a scientific background should know that machines do it much better than human beings."

"Yes, so I will focus my discussion on the intellectual Form of knowledge. Thomas Aquinas argues that things are knowable in function

---

[a] There are two forms of knowledge: sensory and intellectual. The senses receive the 'Forms' of the material Object, while the intellect assimilates and recombines more abstractly, the Object's material conditions. This assimilation between the Object and the Subject isn't done according to the nature of the Object but rather to the Subject's nature: 'Everything received is done so according to the nature of the receiver.'[N9]

[b] All knowledge or every cognition is in the 'knower through an assimilation of the knower to the known.'[N8]

of their immateriality and the Subject knows of it, in proportion to his own immaterial nature.[14] If we agree on this scale of immateriality, a vegetal will have less knowledge than a cat, which will be less knowledgeable than a human being."

"Sir, the interesting question is where do you position computers and machines on this scale? Between the vegetal and cat, between the cat and man, or beyond humans' limits?"

"Well, saying that PCs are purely material is fundamentally not knowing computers. Software, which runs these computers, is an abstract representation of a set of rules and thus, surely should deserve some marks on this immateriality scale. However, according to the advocates that a deterministic approach cannot generate such property, it doesn't."

"Sir, what's wrong with this view?"

"New software technologies are now resorting to problem-solving solutions, which end up in non-deterministic processes. Artificial Neural Networks (ANNs) for instance, are using this approach to mimic the human brain, allowing computers to detect abstract patterns or create strategies. It enabled a computer in 2016 to beat the best human GO player.[a] Thus, and sharing the view of many scientists, I believe we would still grade computers on this scale of immateriality between cats and humans. However, we would slowly approach the moment when PCs would be at par with us."

"That's great news for AI Sir, but what about the second argument?"

"It is what I would call the paternity issue. Manufacturers and programmers build in or write the set of rules, which allow computers to perform their tasks. Therefore, 'cyberists' believe that whatever the program does, men enable the computers to know. Though ANNs can learn all by themselves to detect patterns or solve problems, it is still a human being that creates the algorithms allowing them to do so."

"Why is that argument wrong, Sir?"

"New programming techniques (e.g., genetic programming), which I won't describe now, but I promise to do later, allow programs to recombine some of their instructions and coding, not only in function of the results achieved but also on a random basis. In other words, the end resulting program is different from its original state."

---

[a] Moreover, modern software architectures are increasingly decoupling the application (e.g., game) from the connected object (e.g., iPhone). As a result, information becomes abstracted from the physical object, enabling its assimilation by other apps running on other connected devices, without any human interference.

"But Sir, wouldn't that kill only partially the cyberists' paternity argument?"

"Indeed, a human being could still claim the paternity of the original program, which enabled such genetic recombination. However, how different is it from humans' own learning process paternity? For religious people, this paternity comes from God that created man in its image and gave us the capacity to learn. Thus, another being or entity also provided the set of rules that allows us to acquire knowledge."

"On the other hand, non-believers think the natural selection process created the favorable conditions enabling humans to acquire knowledge."

"You're right. A process isn't another being and is thus fundamentally different in its nature.[a] However, even within a Darwinian world, it is only because other men or women (e.g., parents or teachers) give us the set of rules (e.g., moral, musical, scientific, syntax, etc.) that we can become a knowing Subject. Therefore, if the paternity argument is true for human beings, it may surely also be applied to computers.[b] "

"Sir, I am not sure your arguments will convince 'cyberists'."

"Well, this one seems to me irrefutable. Google within its AutoML project, designed an AI application that builds other AI applications. This piece of software was able in 2017 to develop alone a computer vision system, which outperformed all man-made models.[c] "

"Fair enough Sir. You still need to show that competency can exist without comprehension."

"Humans create the rules by which computers perform their functions but don't give them the key to understanding why they do it. As a consequence, you or any other machine will never understand why you must know something, even if you could perform the function. Thus,

---

[a] Genetics, which is the result of this natural selection, not only constitutes our innate knowledge but also gives us the potential to acquire new knowledge. The available neurons within our brain's inner structure are there to connect and form neural networks, supplying us with the capacity to acquire higher mental functions, such as communication. However, the potential of such higher mental functions will just materialize if, and only if, the conditions are favorable. For instance, we will become a musician or be able to speak if, and only if, exposed to such capacity. In other words, without the teaching of other human beings, there cannot be any real knowledge.

[b] Furthermore, connected PCs or devices in a Software Oriented Architecture will acquire knowledge from other computers without foreknowledge of the other devices' program. In other words, any connected device can learn automatically without access to the other devices' inner set of rules and programs.

[c] AutoML acts as a neural network controller, which develops new AI networks for a specific task (in this case announced in May 2017, this child AI was called NASNet).

advocates in the superiority of humans could righteously claim that competency without comprehension doesn't allow us to consider machines as knowledgeable."

"Sir, this is a tough argument to fight."

"Yes, but let me introduce two inversions of reasoning, which were formulated by two scientists I've already presented:

- Charles Darwin: 'To make a perfect and beautiful machine, it is not requisite to know how to make it.' [4]
- Alan Turing: 'To be a perfect and beautiful computing machine, it is not required to know what arithmetic is.' [3] a "

"Sir, what do these inversions bring within this context of higher concepts associated with the mind?"

"Mr. Dennett uses them to conclude that knowledge, intelligence, and consciousness are, in fact, the effect and not the cause.[15] It's because of the billions of 'small robots' within our brain performing their tasks independently and competitively, without comprehension of the resulting thought, that we can gather knowledge."

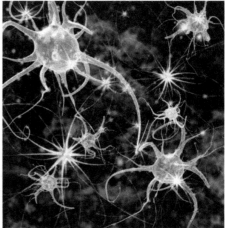

Fig. 2) Millions of small robots within the brain, in this case, mirror neurons.

---

a These two statements are very closely aligned and sustain that there can be competence without comprehension. Darwin's evolutionary theory explains that out of chaos, living creatures as sophisticated as humans can emerge through randomness. Turing explains that an ability that might seem obvious for a computing machine, such as knowing how to do math is in fact not necessary for computers to perform arithmetic operations.

"Sir, could you be more explicit?"

"It isn't because we are inherently knowledgeable, intelligent, or self-aware that we understand why we do things, but rather because our brain performs millions of operations through our neurons, that we acquire understanding and become knowledgeable. So if we agree that competence can exist without comprehension within the brain (or in nature, as Darwin rightly puts it), why refuse that it may also happen within PCs? After all, a beautiful computing machine doesn't need to know what arithmetic is."

"Sir, what are these millions of tiny robots and how do they perform within your heads these tasks that allow understanding?"

"I will explain it in due time. I wish now to demonstrate that with modern software architecture, out of randomness and chaos, machines are able to create structured data, information, and knowledge. I'll use the similarities between the biological and digital worlds, to do that."

What are the differences between Data, Information, and Knowledge?

"Sir, in the various websites and web posts, people seem to mix these three concepts you just referred to, especially outside of computer sciences. Could you give a precise definition of data and information?"

"Yes, I need to, as these concepts reside at the heart of what machines are. Data is the concrete physical proprieties or facts found in the real world, which are used to describe the environment. Our senses first perceive raw data, which we then process in our brain. This creates issues, as perception through our senses and brain processing can be different from one person to the other."

"What kind of issues, Sir?"

"For instance, a colorblind person will have a reduced sensibility to red (called protanomaly), green, or blue lights. Normal and colorblind people will thus, see the same object but describe it differently. To avoid such errors of interpretation, we've established for all physical representation of the world, measurable units, such as meters, kilograms, feet, or pounds."

"Sir, are these units universal?"

"Yes, a meter will be the same in Canada or Brazil. However, all these units are based on conventions. If I go back to my example of colors, the universal physical units to describe colors are the wavelength (in nm) and the frequency interval (in THz). For instance, we define the color around the light spectrum of 635 to 700 nm and 430 to 480 THz."

"Sir, why do humans give such a range?"

"Because we know, through our senses, that there are different tones of red. The point is that any colorblind person who's suffering from protanomaly, using a measuring system to assess the color of an object, will be able to read the same data as a normal person would. He'll know for sure that the object is red, though he cannot perceive it."

"Sir, if data is an abstract, non-physical, universal, and standardized representation of the world, what is then, information?"

"It is the structured and organized way of presenting data. Data is thus intrinsically part of information but is only a portion of it. For instance, 80 kg isn't information but data. There needs to be at least a few additional elements to classify this mass as information, such as the Object's weight, a physical unit (e.g., kilograms, tons, or pounds), a time, and a location of measurement."

"Sir, are these few elements sufficient?"

"You must also consider the media where we present the information and the language used both by the sending and receiving ends, for such representation. In other words, there is no information without the language and the form used (e.g., graphical, sound, or waves) to represent it."

"Sir, is that all?"

"No, there is still one important feature missing. All the previous elements must be tagged together in a coherent manner, usually by time. This tagging notion is fundamental for data to become information."

"Sir, could you give me an example of information based on weight measurements?"

"If I use my weight as an example, information in English will look like: my mass measured at 18:35 on the 6/3/2018, in Berlin, is 80 kilograms."

"Sir, but without data and information, wouldn't we still get an impression of your weight?"

"Yes, but it would be vague (e.g., I look fit). The point is that with information, we get data, process it mentally, and can pass it along easily to others who may access it at a different time. In fact, we transform data into other physical patterns, such as graphics and letters, sound, or even signs, to communicate and share this information.[a] "

"Sir, information and data are surely the two sources that brains or computers use to build knowledge. However, what are the differences, if any, between knowledge and information?"

"Before answering your question, I must first explain what knowledge is, and this requires introducing several new concepts. Intelligence and knowledge are mental phenomena, which per consequence cannot be explained by simple physical description, due to their immaterial nature. They can only be correlated by physical evidence such as exams, IQ tests, and behaviors, or described by a philosophical representation of the world."

"Sir, how will you explain knowledge to me?"

"I will first define through the 'soft disciplines' what knowledge is and how technology impacts it. In a second step, I'll describe the learning process within the brain using the most recent findings in neurosciences. Finally, I will describe how PCs, machines, and systems get access to knowledge and store it. By doing this, I'll highlight both similarities and differences between the cyber and biological worlds."

---

[a] There is more than just a physical dimension to information, which science and technology only deal with. Besides it, there are the mental and social aspects of information that cannot be underestimated. This is why, linguistic patterns of a text, must be grasped mentally to be shared socially. There are other significant differences between data and information. Information allows us to expand our knowledge beyond the range of our senses. Data can't be wrong – if obviously the measurements were done correctly – but information can. This is especially true, as information captures data at a specific moment in time and, as we all know, data changes over time. Furthermore, a mistake people often make is thinking that the analyzed information is always an accurate reflection of data, but the tagging of information can be done erroneously.

6) What is Knowledge and how is it impacted by technology?

Is there a universal definition of Knowledge?

"Sir, what is knowledge and how different from intelligence is it?"

"I realize that answering that question can be complex and engineering chats very often tend to use shortcuts. For instance, they just say knowledge is what we know, intelligence is observable, and tend to pass on to other subjects."

"Sir, there must be some specialists?"

"Yes, they are philosophers, some of whom are extremely famous (e.g., Plato, René Descartes, Immanuel Kant, etc.). There is even a specific discipline, called Epistemology. Though I am not a specialist myself, I will try to present a definition of knowledge that we may extend to computers and machines. I'll treat intelligence later on."

"Sir, why don't you want to talk about intelligence now? Everybody speaks about Artificial Intelligence, and there is never any mention of knowledge. Don't you think that what makes the buzz should be more relevant?"

"I don't. Intelligence is easier to grasp than knowledge because you can measure it through IQ tests. It probably feels also less subjective, and this could explain the buzz. However, we cannot understand AI outside of a broader context regrouped under this notion called knowledge. Furthermore, epistemic debates have raised issues about knowledge, which we probably must solve before any higher forms of AI can be reached. In fact, recent epistemological debates have already discussed if AI is even possible, though they don't usually make any reference to intelligence."

"Sir, by using Epistemology to explain problems about knowledge, which must be solved for the higher forms of AI to happen, don't you think there is a risk you may denature these debates since it never really tackled intelligence issues?"

"I will try not to, by applying a segmentation that isn't commonly used in Epistemology. I'll discuss the 'knowledge that' now and in a later conversation, describe the 'knowledge of.' However, I won't discuss issues about the 'knowledge how.' You are programmed to speak many languages, so you must know that in French, for instance, two words exist (i.e., 'Savoir' and 'Connaissance') to express these knowledge types, but even then, not all French philosophers will give the same definition to these ideas.[a] Thus, I'll resort to Umberto Eco's definition,[16] which associates the 'knowledge that' with Epistemology and the 'knowledge of' with Gnoseology."

"Sir, what does it mean?"

"To simplify this knowledge distinction, Epistemology will treat mostly about the possibility of creating the foundation of true propositions on Objects, while Gnoseology will deal mainly with the conditions of knowledge, starting from the Object's denomination."

"Let me just check if I've understood, Sir. In the first case, you analyze why humans know that a cat is a mammal with four legs, fur, whiskers, that eats meat, etc., while in the second, you define how humans know a cat is a cat, or Maxime is your son Maxime, and nobody else."

"Correct! In Epistemology, knowledge is a series of conditions or opinions about an Object, shared by a community of people. On the other hand, in Gnoseology we must refer to a Subject's intelligibility to understand that a specific cat is a cat or John is John, and thus the knower and the known-object are both positioned at the individual level, through his experience. This intelligibility explains why I'll deal with Gnoseology later on when we discuss intelligence."

"But Sir, don't you think that the knowledge that a cat is a mammal with whiskers, also requires this capacity?"

"Yes, but knowledge can be seen as the strict analysis of the relations made between different Objects (e.g., cat, whiskers, and mammal) already intellectualized. In other words, on top of understanding what a cat, whiskers, and a mammal are, you must consider the links between them that form a pattern."

"Sir, I'm OK with you associating knowledge with Epistemology and intelligence with Gnoseology. As you wish to focus on knowledge initially, could you tell me what is its main philosophical starting point?"

"It is called the 'tripartite' because it is based on three conditions, which need to be met for someone to say he or she knows that something is true. Some people also refer to the anachronism 'JTB' or 'Justified True Belief,' which represents these three conditions. This definition of knowledge is credited to Plato:[b]

---

[a] French philosophers tend to describe these concepts slightly differently than Eco. 'le Savoir' usually belongs to a community, which has ruled on a 'Connaisance' and defined it as a 'Savoir.' On the other hand, 'Connaissance' is described as being inside and unique to an individual. In other words, the active process of producing called 'Connaissance' is to be opposed to this process' result, called the 'Savoir.'

- A person 'Believes' the statement to be true.
- The statement is in fact 'True.'
- The person is 'Justified' in believing the statement to be true.[17] "

"Sir, there is something I don't understand. It seems to me that beliefs and justifications are internal processes, while the truth is on the outside, proven by facts."

"You rightfully point out the controversy of such a well-known definition. Linking these inner and outbound notions has proven problematical and is part of the historical debate of Epistemology. Before analyzing the issues, I would like to start by showing the JTB limitations. In 1963, the American philosopher Edmond Gettier proposed two scenarios where these three criteria apparently seemed to be met,[18] but where we could debate that the result was knowledge due to elements of luck involved, thus proving that the JTB approach was incomplete."

"Sir, what happened since then?"

"Philosophers have taken different approaches to try to solve this problem: finding a fourth condition, which would solve the Gettier dilemma; attempting to reject the problem by showing that Gettier's scenarios are not really cases of justified true belief; or proving that Gettier's scenarios are cases of knowledge after all. Though the search for a bullet-proof definition of knowledge is still ongoing, I will show other limitations of this JTB theory. To do so, I need to define more precisely these concepts and present succinctly the different issues raised by them."

"Sir may I? Belief: according to Stanford's encyclopedia of philosophy: 'The term 'belief' refers to the attitude we have, whenever we take something to be the case or regard it as true. To believe something, in this sense, needn't involve actively reflecting on it.'[19] "

"Indeed, beliefs are basically in the head and can be viewed as the way we see the world. For most philosophers, it also means that it is just what humans think it is and thus implies that they recognize implicitly that this representation of the world could be wrong. Furthermore, beliefs are convictions we hold to be true, mainly without relying on any evidence or tangible proof. These beliefs grow from what we see, hear, experience, read, and think about."

"Sir, could you help me understand by giving me examples?"

---

b However, Plato rejected the JTB concept because for him,[N10] any justification must already be knowledge to be qualified as true belief, producing a circular definition. To his credit, this fact didn't raise any real problem for him, as he believed humans are born with innate knowledge. Indeed, Plato thought that we grasp the essence of things thanks to our soul and thus don't need to justify it as a true belief.

"Beliefs (e.g., if someone works hard she will be successful) are basic assumptions that we make about the world, and our values (e.g., hard-work is good) originate from those beliefs. Values are ideas we deem important. From these ideas, we develop an opinion, which we hold to be true and mostly unchangeable. From our beliefs, we derive values, which can be true or false when compared with evidence, but nonetheless, hold true for us."

"Sir, according to the same Stanford Encyclopedia of Philosophy: 'The problem of truth is in a way easy to state: what truths are, and what (if anything) makes them true. But this simple statement masks a great deal of controversy. Whether there is a metaphysical problem of truth at all, and if there is, what kind of theory might address it.'[20] "

"Here also, there are various theories (e.g., Correspondence, Coherence, and Pragmatism theories) addressing this problem. They have in common to answer questions about the nature of truth directly.[a] "

"Sir, what's your opinion on these theories?"

"I am well aligned with Pragmatism, which considers the scientific approach of viewing truth as a continuous process, where something is true until proven wrong. To quote the American philosopher Peirce, 'The opinion which is fated to be ultimately agreed to by all who investigate is what we mean by the truth.'[21] Furthermore, something is true, if, through the inquiry, the world really is that way. Truth is not in our head but can be found or demonstrated in the real world."

---

[a] This is how they address it differently:

- **Correspondence theory**: What we believe or say, is true if it corresponds to the way things are, that is, to the facts.
- **Coherence theory**: A belief is true if, and only if, it is part of a coherent system of beliefs.
- **Pragmatism**: True beliefs are guaranteed not to conflict with subsequent experience and will remain settled at the end of a prolonged validation inquiry.

"Sir, this a summary of what I could found on justification: If beliefs are at the base of knowledge, what turns beliefs into knowledge? It seems that this is where the notion of justification comes in. Human beings know something if they're justified in believing it to be true."

"As can be expected, there are several competing justification theories (e.g., Inferential justification, Foundationalism, Coherentism, and Reliabilism) and no consensus on which is the right one.[a] "

"Sir, which theory is then better adapted to describe systems and new IT technologies?"

"Reliabilism, unlike the other theories, is based on external factors. If the method used is known to be reliable (e.g., the right measurements), then beliefs are justified."

What are the differences between Information and Knowledge?

"Now that I have created a framework to explain what knowledge is, I can go back to your initial question on differences between knowledge and information and check if these two concepts may exist one without the other. By doing this, I'll show the limits of the JTB approach to knowledge."

"Please do so, Sir."

"Information refers to tagging several data together, to better describe an object or concept by way of this relational connection. For instance, and going back to my weight example, the problem with such information is that nobody really cares about it. Even though it could be considered a Justified True Belief, it wouldn't be thought of as knowledge since it would lack two important characteristics. It wouldn't be considered meaningful by a community of people."

- [a] **Inferential justification:** For a belief to be justified, three conditions must be met: there must be some other idea that supports it and makes the belief plausible; we must trust that this supporting idea is accurate; we must have good reasons to believe that this idea is true.
- **Foundationalism:** This theory integrates the notion that justification of our beliefs is ultimately derived from basic beliefs, which act as the foundation for all that we know.
- **Coherentism:** It's based on the principle that coherence justifies the whole system of beliefs. This coherence is ensured by the fact that the set of beliefs is consistent, cohesive, and comprehensive.
- **Reliabilism:** Beliefs are justified if they are formed based on a reliable mechanism or methodology.

"Sir, why are the notions of meaningfulness and community of people important?"

"It transforms information into knowledge and underlines the notion that it should be thought of as useful. Furthermore, a group of people should grant this information, this characteristic of meaningfulness, to complete this transformation. From this, we can see that, though there cannot be knowledge without information, the opposite isn't true."

"Sir, is this the only knowledge specificity worth highlighting?"

"No. What creates knowledge is the deterministic process by which patterns, within a given set of information, may be found. It means that whenever we memorize information on a topic (e.g., by heart), we don't necessarily acquire knowledge about it. To do so, one needs some cognitive and analytical ability to establish or interpret such patterns.[a] "

What are the issues about Knowledge in the age of the internet?

"Sir, there is still something I don't understand. In order to become knowledge, information must pass the JTB test. The problem with this concept is that it is centered on a person's knowledge and doesn't focus on the ideas or concepts themselves being justified."

"Correct! There is an inherent subjective nature of knowledge, partly based on the idea that beliefs, justified or not, are things that individuals have. I've also indicated that information must be meaningful and useful to a group. It shows that knowledge must be considered at the conceptual level and not the individual one."

"Sir, by considering meaningfulness, haven't you introduced other issues?"

"Yes, this notion is intrinsically biased and depends on our values and interests, which are influenced by the social-economic environment in which we live.[b] Even our moods and genetics can influence our view of

---

[a] To make an analogy, tomography views (i.e., body scans) resulting from the data processing supplied by various scanning technologies, can be considered information. However, it requires the knowledge of a cancer specialist learned over years of studying and experience, to detect the patterns indicating whether there is a tumor or not.

[b] In the early 1900s, a conservative society tried to convince the middle-class women to take care of their husband and family and not pursue a career of their own. This was even published knowledge with books detailing how to become the perfect housewife.[N11] Obviously, today such knowledge wouldn't be judged meaningful in many occidental societies, or at least not for the same reasons (e.g., it could still be useful knowledge in the context of the history of the emancipation of women).

what is a meaningful justified true belief. The point is that universal knowledge, – something that would be known by everyone and accepted by all as such – is rare especially for non-scientific topics, even though the truth on which such knowledge relies is always universal. This notion of truth is another characteristic of knowledge that raised huge epistemic debates."

"Sir, I don't understand why. I thought that sciences like mathematics were always accepted by all, as true knowledge. For instance, adding two plus two will always give four (at least in base-10) whether you are in the United States, in France, or on the moon."

"Correct, but even though mathematical operations are now widely seen this way, we cannot extend it to all scientific theories. You just need to look at Darwin's theory of the evolution of the species, which is still today challenged by revisionists, to understand the power of beliefs on our appreciation of what knowledge is. The problem with truth is that it cannot always be proven, because we don't have the right information or technical know-how to prove it yet or, for some topics, never will."

"Sir, even if we validate a theory at one point in time, couldn't new ideas or technologies prove such a theory wrong?"

"Exactly! Truth can only be considered as such until proven false. Hence, the notion of truth is time-based. In fact, the truth must be seen as a quest and in this sense is coherent with Pragmatism for which new theories challenge established ideas till they replace the old knowledge or are themselves proven to be wrong."

"Sir, there is no truth then."

"Not at all! The fact that a theory might be supplanted in the future doesn't make it any less true today."

"Sir, your representation of knowledge is starting to be quite different than a justified true belief. If knowledge is biased and time-based, how can we define it?"

"In fact, the answer to such a question looks a lot like what post modernistic philosophers think. They don't claim that truth doesn't exist but reject the idea that any individual's belief about what is true can be certain, because of all our individual biases. In some way, they introduce the notion of probability of certainty."

"Sir, you are saying that probabilities would best describe Objects?"

"Kind of, but I don't want to discuss this now. I promise to develop this concept of probability in the future, but will need before that to introduce Immanuel Kant's critical philosophy."

"Sir, if you come back to my question, what is the best way of reducing such uncertainty?"

"It is to make sure that the truth is accepted by a community of people, with credible knowledge on the topic. We would fulfill the condition for justification if this community of people agreed that the methods used to prove that a belief is true, have been met and such true belief has been enduring the test of time. Furthermore, this reviewing process would ensure that the provided information is meaningful to more than just one person."

"Sir, by claiming that we achieve the justification of a true belief through a consensus of recognized experts, aren't you in fact simply transferring the problem, especially in an era where knowledge is widely accessed through the internet?"

"You are raising the issue about the limitations of peer review. It would mean that to know if a belief is true, someone would need to know if the peers having reviewed the information on which such belief is founded, have the right know-how to corroborate or refute such truth. Furthermore, in the case of scientific truth, using the pragmatic approach I favor, we would need to know if the methodology used to confirm the truthfulness of such a belief, was also done adequately."

"Sir, isn't it always obvious?"

"Before the internet, we easily knew who the knowledge providers were. An author would sign a book, and a professor would present herself in front of the class. We could quickly identify their methodology by questioning them or reading their bibliography."

"Sir, does it mean you believe knowledge provided on the internet isn't credible?"

"No, but with websites such as Wikipedia or the Stanford Encyclopedia of Philosophy, this becomes much trickier.[a] To be fair, a few scientific results have recently been shown to be wrong even if they had already gone through a thorough classical peer-reviewing process and been validated. Though peer reviews by scientific magazines, such as 'Nature,' should be able to spot mistakes, they haven't systematically done so."

"Sir, does this imply that the peer review process isn't impartial?"

---

[a] In the case of Stanford, everybody assumes that people who worked on the website of such a prestigious university, have the philosophical skills to write on the matter. But we don't know for sure if professors or first year students have performed the work. In the case of Wikipedia and as work is performed by volunteers without any possible mean of checking their competency level, we have no way of telling if the belief is truly justified, unless a note indicates that the information hasn't been checked.

"Currently, individuals are asked to perform reviews by editors, for magazines, newspapers, etc. Their reviews can be perceived as intrinsically flawed, as the few peers who often work on rival theories or technologies, are expected to do the job quickly, without often even being paid. Open peer review on the internet is changing this process, probably for the better. Within such process, any person may appoint herself to scrutinize the publication."

"Sir, do these new IT-enabled processes work?"

"Yes, they spotted a few errors that the usual process didn't. This new reviewing approach challenges the usual top-down methodology, which has been around since the middle of the twentieth century."

"Sir, is this approach in line with the evolution of scientific knowledge?"

"Yes, in his essay 'All life is problem-solving,'[22] Karl Popper identifies the evolution of sciences due to the selective pressure of eliminating errors about scientific theories.[a] This evolutionary approach to scientific progress suggests that the interplay between conjecture and refutation is key to advancement in acquiring scientific knowledge and must be checked using these new reviewing processes."

"Sir, do you consider the resulting benefits of such a bottom-up control systematically positive? For instance, some internet fans are suggesting that control by a crowd is better than that of the experts."

"You are right about raising the issue of internet filtering. James Surowiecki in his theory of the 'Wisdom of crowds' claims that it is better to have more eyes checking than less,[23] especially if we take into account the four following parameters: diversity of opinion, independence, aggregation, and decentralization."

"Sir, don't you think it is better to have an expert reviewing than ten neophytes?"

"Mr. Surowiecki indicates that groups are often smarter than the brightest people in them and thus, there is no need to get advice from experts. Decisions made, based on the aggregation and consolidation of information found in groups, are usually better than the ones made by specialists."

"But Sir, what do you think about the many articles claiming the internet cannot be trusted?"

"The interesting aspect of Mr. Surowiecki's opinion is that it goes against the criticism made of the internet, that there are many errors on

---

[a] What is now called the scientific method.

websites such as Wikipedia and, as a consequence, cannot be considered a reliable source of knowledge. For these critics, books or white papers are less prone to mistakes and should be considered more truthful. However, I could give thousands of counterexamples. An obvious one would be Hitler's 'Mein Kampf' but I could also refer to Hegel and Schopenhauer's books that justified science-based racism."

"Sir, are you saying that with the internet, there should be fewer errors?"

"I am. In fact, the Italian semiologist Umberto Eco, in an interview on Wikinews,[24] says that such a bottom-up approach can protect from the control of the 'expert idiots,' as he bluntly puts it. He recognizes that errors may still occur under the 'wisdom of the crowds' principle but much less so if the control is done by motivated people, which he calls the 'wisdom of the motivated crowd.' He argues that such wisdom can only work when reviewers are motivated to do peer review."

"Sir, do you share that vision?"

"I do and would even add that such a control is the only way to maintain an updated knowledge in an era where technologies and information are changing so fast. Mr. Eco also identifies in this interview, one important additional issue about knowledge in the era of the internet. It is the problem of filtering information on websites or even identifying the wrong sites if someone has no foreknowledge at all of a subject.[a] "

"Sir, students and basically anybody with questions or problems, use the internet to solve their issues. By doing so, aren't these search engines changing the relation humans have with learning?"

"Internet queries can be problematical. In the past, the identification of potential problem-solving sources would come from a teacher or an expert. Today, mathematical models will search instantly in millions of books or newspapers, and select the most pertinent information based on the search criteria. Therefore, understanding which model we use for performing such queries is fundamental. If you look at Google, the prominent worldwide

---

[a] Not only is there an issue about the exactitude of the information featured on a web page, but there is also an issue about the readers' capacity to understand if this information, or even the web page itself, can be trusted as reliable. If we go back to the 'Mein Kampf' example, the question is if this book could have been published online today without immediately being ridiculed by people. It is true that the web contains thousands of hate sites or blogs, but looking at them through the prism of Mr. Surowiecki's four parameters should immediately help identify trustworthy sites. Nowadays, the issue isn't so much about identifying hate sites but being quick enough to close them faster than they are rebuilt.

search engine, it uses around 200 ranking factors to determine a page's popularity."

"Sir, what are these models?"

"Google ranking methodology is intellectual property and consequently inaccessible. My partial understanding is that a few parameters play a more important role in the search than others.[a] On top of searches already performed, keywords are the main selection criteria. Their density, prominence, and proximity are especially important filtering elements.[b] "

"Sir, isn't there a risk that knowledge becomes tributary of fashion and fake news?"

"Yes, these search models create a quality issue as websites full of misinformation can increase their rankings, if enough people link to them. Furthermore, and all things being comparable, the most read articles will usually appear first. In other words, the risk of acquiring knowledge in this internet era is that information, rather than being based on the most accurate or pertinent documents, will often rely on the ones that generated the most buzz or on the better marketing techniques used to generate such buzz. It is quickly becoming an increasing risk, which we've seen recently, may even influence Presidential elections."

What are the sources of Knowledge?

"Sir, you've indicated that humans need cognitive and analytical abilities to establish or interpret patterns. How are they acquired?"

"The obvious answer would be through experience, books, media, or from other people at school and at home."

---

[a] According to many experts, Google's 'Pagerank' is their most important selection criterion, though Google has recently introduced other factors to reduce its impact on the result (e.g., Google Panda is a filter that can prevent low-quality sites and pages from ranking well in the research). It works by counting the number and quality of links to a page to estimate how important the site is. The underlying assumption is that more important websites are likely to receive more links from other websites.

[b] Keyword key filtering feature:
- **Keyword density**: how many times the search word appears in the document, in regards to the overall number of words in this document.
- **Keyword prominence**: it relates the word in regards to the position it holds near the beginning of the document.
- **Keyword proximity**: the closer the keywords are located from each other, the more relevant they are.

"But Sir, in order to do that, wouldn't it be mandatory to know already how to read, think, or speak? Hence, if these faculties must also be acquired, what would be the basic way of acquiring knowledge?"

"Is that all or do you have other questions related to the source of knowledge?"

"I have several, Sir. If you can generate true beliefs by making lucky guesses, as shown by Gettier,[18] how may you warrant your beliefs? Furthermore, if you need to create patterns to understand reality, how do you gain the ideas and concepts to support their identification? What assurance do you have that these patterns, that is, models of the world you use to reconstruct facts and reality, correspond to how this world is really constructed?"

"You surely have many! From a philosophical perspective, all these issues relating to the sources of knowledge you just raised, were originally debated between two schools: Rationalism and Empiricism."

"Sir, what do these two main historical schools of thoughts stand for?"

"Rationalism describes knowledge as derived from reason alone. Reason plays a fundamental role in the learning process and the observation of the world, which we get from our senses. It is acquired by a priori processes, is innate and intuitive. On the contrary, in Empiricism, knowledge derives from our perception of the world that we acquire through our senses or experiences. It minimizes the notion of innate ideas."

"Sir, is there any other theory worth mentioning?"

"Yes, I would highlight among these other theories, Constructivism, Abduction, and Representationalism. The most important among them in my view is Constructivism. For constructivists, knowledge is contingent on convention, human perception, and social experience. As reality is incoherent and unverifiable, there cannot be any claim to universalism or objective truth, but there can be a representation of reality based on a constructed model of this world."

"Sir, what about the others?"

"Charles Sanders Peirce produced Abduction (i.e., a kind of inference), an alternative theory allowing the connection between theory and experimentation, through the projection of hypotheses. I already introduced to you the movement it originated from, called Pragmatism. It specifies that knowledge is best understood in terms of its practical usage and success. Lastly, Representationalism argues that the world we consciously sense isn't a real world, but a virtual reality replica that we project within our mind."

"Sir, Rationalism and Empiricism now seem outmoded. What do you think?"

"Yes, because they don't integrate new findings coming from neurosciences and cognitive theories. For instance, the role of experience shaping our neural circuitries and through this process enabling intelligent thoughts has been clearly identified, contradicting Rationalism's posit. Empiricism, which denies the notion of knowledge acquired at birth, also fails to integrate factors such as heredity, which neurosciences and IQ tests prove have a significant impact on knowledge."

"Sir, what should we consider then?"

"I suggest looking at Immanuel Kant, who is seen by many contemporaries as the inspiration of major new cognitive theories.[25] In his book, 'Critique of pure reason,' [26] he developed a theory which drew upon both these approaches. For him, rationalists were right in saying that we can assuredly know about real things. Similarly, empiricists were also appropriate when saying that such knowledge couldn't be restricted solely to truths a priori defined, nor could it be provided only by experience. Thus, understanding the world requires both experience and a priori concepts."

"Sir, could you clarify your thoughts?"

"Of course! Our universally shared mind structure shapes our experience and the way we project ourselves in it, according to notions such as time and space, as well as categories (e.g., cause and effect, substance, unity, plurality, necessity, possibility, and reality)."

"Sir, how does your mind order its experience?"

"In its own way, according to certain innate patterns, which don't reflect necessarily the reality. Thus, and though there cannot be any knowledge without sensations, these inputs cannot provide knowledge all by themselves either. Knowledge is possible because it isn't so much how things are in themselves but rather how they appear to us. To use an image, reason provides the structure of what we know, while the senses provide its content."

How can Knowledge be represented?

This conversation stopped for a few days until I asked my car to go and pick up my son at the tennis club. Immediately my car asked back: **"Sir, I** remember the road because I use GPS location. But how does your human mind abstract from previously acquired knowledge and why don't you restart the knowledge acquisition process all over again, when confronted with a different situation?"

I was caught off guard and couldn't answer precisely to these two questions. I needed more time to get familiarized with the new cognitive theories, so I gave a simplified answer.

"We do this by classifying things of this world or events in categories, which can be seen as pointers in this knowledge process. Grouping Objects and Concepts categorize things by commonalities between these Objects and general information."

"Sir, what does this categorization bring you?"

"It allows us to recognize new Objects as members of an existing category and to focus on important factors, within the observed environment."

Issues about categorization brought me back to Kant, and I mentioned that to my car.

"For Kant, the world is both internal (i.e., as a content of consciousness) and external (i.e., as Forms existing internally, resulting from the mental activities apprehending an Object, which are used to represent this Object deemed as an independent matter, located in space). To be more precise, Kant suggested that the things in themselves aren't really internal or external, but rather must be considered Categories. In other words, the truth is grounded more on an Object's propositions rather than on its perception."

"Sir, how unique is his view of knowledge?"

"With Kant, for the first time, someone reasoned that the issue with knowledge wasn't so much to ask what a cat was, rather than asking if a cat is an animal that stands on its four legs and hunts mice? It changes the perspective of understanding knowledge by disserting about the 'knowledge that' rather than the 'knowledge of.' "

"Sir, did he focus his attention on Epistemology rather than on Gnoseology?"

"Yes, and in such a context, to understand knowledge is thus to focus on propositions. It brings us to linguistics, rather than to the Object itself.[a]"

---

[a] Kant will only briefly start addressing the issue of semiology (i.e., the science of signs and symbols), which is also involved with linguistics in knowledge, an issue that Peirce will address fully, much later. To say that Kant's main preoccupation was to dissert about linguistic is probably exaggerated. In fact, his first Critique focused on defining the general

"Sir, I am e-mailing you a table that gives a good idea of these rules you were mentioning, although it doesn't give you all the clues on how humans understand what a cat is."

	Judgement	Categories	Schemes	Principles
QUANTITY				*Axioms of intuition*
	Universal Specific Singular	Unity Plurality Totality	Number	All intuitions are extensive quantities
QUALITY				*Anticipation of perception*
	Positives Negatives Infinite	Reality Negation Limitation	Degree	Within all apparences, the reality possess an intensive quantity, a degree
RELATION				*Analogy of experience*
	Categorical	Substance and inherence (substance / accident)	Permanency of reality within time	Permanency of substance
	Hypothetical	Causality (cause / effect)	Succession of the misceleanous	Time succession according to the rules of causality
	Disjunctive	Community (reciprocal action Agent / patient)	Simultaneity of determinations	Simultaneity according to the laws of reciprocal action or community
MODALITY				*Posit of the empirical thought in general*
	Problematical	Possibility / impossibility	Agreement between representation and time conditions	What gets along with the formal conditions of experience is possible
	Assertoric (is or isn't)	Existence / non - existence	Existence within a defined time frame	What is in connection with the material conditions of the real experience
	Apodictic (clearly established)	Necessity / contingency	Existence in all time	What determines that a connection with reality, according to the universal conditions of experience, is necessary

Fig. 3) Judgments, categories, schemes, and principles of pure reason. U. Eco; Kant and the platypus, 1997.

The same night I took my iPad and looked at these rules. I reasoned that to form general concepts from representations, we humans still require an effort of intelligibility, which allows us to compare, abstract from, and think. However, whenever doing this, Kant showed that we can tackle issues about these empirical concepts (e.g., cats, trees, and insects), originating in our sensations.[a] It isn't so much through the perceptual reasoning required to form these empirical concepts that we create categories but through the act of imaging an Object that we understand what this Object is and can recreate it.[b]

The next morning, my car asked me if I had looked at the table. "Yes, I did. It explains how Kant deals with judgment, categories, schemes, and

---

rules of experience and understanding, like the physical rules that could be founded on Newton's laws. Furthermore, his interest wasn't so much in describing Objects of natural kinds but rather the logical functions and rules helping define all Objects.

[a] By comparison to Objects of experience, which are considered categories of pure reason.

[b] As opposed to the judgment of experience, which can enable such categorization.

principles. In other words, it provides a framework to explain intelligence, which I'll discuss later on."

"But Sir, you mentioned that the knowledge acquisition process requires reason, so how can I understand knowledge without this key process?"

"OK. I'll build for you a framework but will describe this issue more thoroughly later on when I talk about intelligence. Kant created the notion of Categories (the word is even his invention) to deal with the notion of Objects and how we understand what they are. It is through the act of imaging these objects that we acquire their understanding."

"Sir, you mean imagining?" the car interrupted me.

"No, I really mean imaging like, for instance, portraying a cat in my brain. This action of imaging is crucial for grounding the concepts of pure reason (e.g., unity, necessity, limitation) and empirical concepts (e.g., what is a cat?). It is also necessary to enable perceptual judgments, such as when we think about a specific cat (e.g., my son's cat named Shimy). To tie Categories to intelligibility, Kant introduces the notion of Scheme (e.g., the Schemes of number one million and a triangle)."

"Sir, I'm not sure I am following you. Could you be more explicit?"

"To better explain what a Scheme is, I'd like to turn to Eco,[16] who thinks this concept is probably better described by a flowchart, which not only integrates a suite of logical steps but anchors those steps in a sequential temporal framework. For him, this Scheme is a general rule, which tries to build an image."

"Sir, can you give me an example?"

"A Scheme may represent a perfect geometrical form under all circumstances, such as a square or circle.[a] The scheme of a number could probably better explain Eco's flowchart idea. We cannot visualize 1.000.000 units but can appreciate the process, which would allow us to count by adding ones, tens, hundreds, thousands, etc., till we reach the last element of the flowchart, that is, the last unit of the one million number."

"Sir, where do these Schemes come from?"

---

[a] Thinking isn't only applying pure concepts linked to prior linguistics but is also tied to representational diagrams. In the case of an empirical Objects (e.g., a cat), Eco suggests that Kant would refer nowadays to the same 3D model, which modern cognitive sciences refer to.[N12] Though an empirical concept cannot be finite per nature, it can admit a core concept on which other ideas may be tied to. This core concept is integrated into the meaning of the word used to express this Object. For instance, the word red shows that there is some coincidence between the linguistic (i.e., word) and its perceptual meaning (i.e., color).

"Kant suggests that we build them, for instance, through our education. Our parents will point at a cat and tell us this is a cat, not a dog.[a] With Schematism, our thought process doesn't construct only the simple definition of a possible Object, but builds this Object itself, by iteration."

"Sir, I believe the American philosopher Charles Peirce also worked on Schematism?"

"Yes, and he introduced additionally the important notion of a continuum: sensations will present themselves as interpretations of stimuli; perceptions as interpretations of sensations; perceptual judgments as interpretations of perceptions; specific and general interpretations as interpretations of perceptual judgments; and scientific theories as relating to the interpretations of a series of propositions.[27] "

How do we create these categories?

"If you allow me, I would like to abstract myself for a moment from the knowledge gathering process,[b] that I just described through Peirce's view of a continuum, and focus instead exclusively on the end result."

"Sir, what do you want to achieve by focusing on the interpretation of a series of propositions?"

"I could conclude on what is the 'knowledge that.' Indeed, this acquired result is the knowledge base, which has been personally, socially, or scientifically structured. This categorization gives us the prism through

---

[a] The interesting question Umberto Eco raises is how did we construct a Scheme of an Object that is unknown, such as the platypus when it was first discovered. In this case, we cannot use a predefined judgment but must generalize this judgment based on specificities. By extension, this means that a reflexive judgment must address any concept of an Object, which must subsume under a rule not yet established.[N13]

[b] Peirce also addresses the issues about categories, but from a different angle.[N14] For him, all thoughts can be broken down into three elements, called first-ness (no mediation and reflexivity), second-ness (mediation but no reflexivity) and third-ness (mediation and reflexivity), which describe degrees of mediation and reflexivity (i.e., circular relationships between cause and effects). The process of signification in language or literature (i.e., semiotic) follows this structure: sign (first), object (second), and interpretant (third). So do signs: icons (first), indices (second), and symbols (third). With the fear of oversimplifying this abduction theory, first-ness refers to a human quality or a potentiality of an existence. It requires a second-ness for its existence, a kind of physical force requiring humans, to realize its different qualities. Third-ness deals in representation, not in things, and talks about events happening in the past or the future. It includes experience, language, culture, etc.

which we filter and interpret the world, providing us, individually or collectively, with the connections between justification, beliefs, and truth."

"Sir, can you be more explicit?"

"If I make an analogy with the digital world, these Categories are not only the rules that we infer and apply to the links between different data or information, in a kind of relational database (i.e., Objects related to one another). They also provide the connections inferred between different relational databases, in order to create a grand repository. In other words, Categories glue together data, information, and knowledge.[a] "

"Sir, to use your expression, what is that glue?"

"To understand what it is, I'll now refer to this categorization process, by introducing the notion of Cognitive Type. Umberto Eco developed a semantic/semiotic model, which explains how information on an Object or Concept, already 'imaged' through the cognitive process, can be organized around semiotic practices, culturally acquired.[16] "

"Sir, could you describe how you organize information in this model?"

"An individual defines the content that best describes what the Object is, according to semiotic practices. These practices include, besides the obvious verbal language and visual imagery, all representations by our inner self to 'talk about' this object. According to Eco, there are four different types of object information: iconic, propositional, narrative, and affective."

"Sir, could you be more specific and give me some example to understand?"

"Of course!" I took a sheet of paper and drew the face and body of a cat and showed it to my car's camera.

---

[a] Interpreting something that acts in this or that way, requires that we emit a hypothesis (as the reflexive judgment must subsume the case of Objects for which there is still no general rules). For Eco, it is obvious that the reflexive judgment is nothing else than an abduction in Peirce's understanding. This is line with Kant, who specified that the perceptual presentation of an Object is either schematic, when our intuition corresponds to an intelligible concept (e.g., triangle), or symbolic (i.e., logico-formal, metaphors, or allegory), whenever this concept is grasped through an analogy.

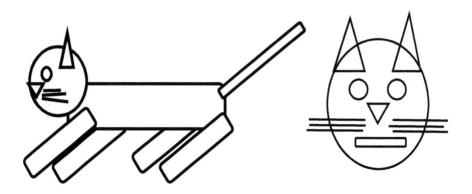

Fig. 4) 3D images of a cat; source: author.

"The iconic type includes all perceptual information, which enables us to recognize an object,[a] such as static and dynamic multimodal information that looks like my drawing. The propositional aspect organizes information according to the Object status.[b] The narrative schemes are related to information describing a sequence of actions, linked to this Object.[c] It describes the transformation such an Object goes through, from one state to another. Finally, the affective information relates to the emotional impact the Object generates on the person.[d] "

"Sir, could we regroup all this under what so many websites refer to as the tree of knowledge of good and evil, as described in the Genesis?"

"Not at all! If I use your analogy, I am rather thinking about a tree of knowledge that helps us navigate through the various categorizations,

---

[a] A cat's Cognitive Type doesn't only include its general 3D picture (e.g., a circle for its head, triangle for its ears, lines for its whiskers, a big cylinder for its body with 4 smaller ones for its legs, etc.) but also, some stabilized cues about how it performs some activities dynamically (e.g., running, walking, drinking, etc.). This static and dynamic information doesn't only integrate visual cues, but also inputs from all our senses (e.g., a cat's meow).

[b] This propositional information can be divided into generic (i.e., included within a Category), specific (i.e., relating to a particular characteristic of the Object), and evaluative information (i.e., based on values, such as significant, beautiful, etc.).

[c] It is independent of its occurrence at any moment in time or space. It can involve the subject's body or not, and is structured around the following sequence: A Subject acts with the Object to fulfill a purpose. It can be active or passive, with the Object either transforming or being transformed.

[d] This information is of instructional nature,[N15] learned through our interactions with the Object and can be described by three types of affective details: attraction/repulsion, euphoria/dysphoria, and intense/weak.[N16]

which we individually and collectively create. Eco's semiotic model describes the general way we categorize things."

"Sir, how come humans or machines can do this instantaneously, without going through this entire process again?"

"We both achieve this by creating hierarchies of Categories, based on an object's definition or its benchmark according to an ideal representation or memorized information.[a] "

"Sir, would you describe to me some of these Categories?"

"Our human brain possesses several levels of Object Categories. For instance, if I continue with my cat example: level 1 (mammals); Level 2 (feline, men, apes); level 3 (cats, lions, leopard); level 4 (Siamese, Persian, angora). However, the hierarchical organization may also include links that tie Concepts and Objects together. For example, level 1 (flying things), level 2 (birds and bats), and level 3 (canaries, robins, and bats)."

"Sir, I was interested in how I classify things and just identified on the web a technique that seems to be quite popular. It's called semantic tagging."

"Search engines such as Google or Microsoft's Bing, are trying to organize the world's information in a meaningful way to provide the content that the readers are looking for. In the past, these search engines had to rely on the words within the pages, matching these words with the readers' exact spelling, but this isn't necessary anymore, thanks to semantic networks.[b] "

---

[a] More precisely, we use three different approaches:
- **Definitional**: Membership to a particular category depends on whether the Object meets formally defined characteristics.
- **Prototype:** New things are categorized by comparison with an average or ideal representation of the Object, Concept, or event.
- **Exemplar:** New things (especially Concepts) are compared to specific items already stored in our memory, which serve as examples for a benchmark."

[b] New technologies and web structures are now enabling the match between the query intent and the suitability of the identified web pages or contents. In the past, HTML used a simplified list of semantic tags: <h1>; <h2>; <title>; <p>; with just a few really being used to optimized the search process (i.e. title and h1). With the release of html5 several new semantic tags were introduced, that add context and semantic meaning: <article>; <figure>; <footer>; <header>; <main>; <mark>; <section>; <summary>. By assigning values to the documents' content, the writer can provide contextually rich information not only to search engines but also for readers and machines. Other standards are introduced to give even more context to content. For instance, the WAI aria attributes roles for categories (e.g., abstract, widget, document structure, and landmark roles), by using other contextual definitions (e.g., article). In fact, with this new web revolution, content will more and more be categorized at a finer granularity level, enabling constantly more relevant queries.

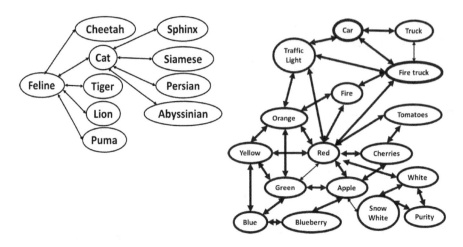

Fig. 5) Concepts and Objects Categories; source: author.

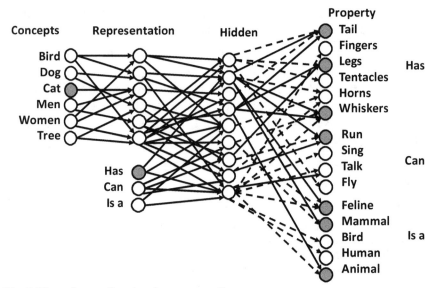

Fig. 6) View of semantic networks; source: author.

7) How do brains acquire knowledge?

Having defined the concept of the 'knowledge that,' my car seemed satisfied and stopped asking me questions for a few days. Then, one day while on the phone, I inadvertently told my wife I couldn't remember where I had left my office keys. Immediately after the call, my car asked me how come humans could forget such simple facts?

"Well, during the last two weeks we've seen the concepts associated with the 'knowledge that.' To answer your question, which relates to this same 'knowledge that,' we need to leave the world of 'soft disciplines' and enter the world of sciences. To give you a more accurate answer, we must refer to recent discoveries in the world of neurosciences, to explain how the brain works. I will focus on the anatomical, physiological, and functional elements that occur mainly before and after the cognitive processes, which create knowledge out of information."

"Sir, does it mean you will disregard the properties of organs involved in the thought process and focus mainly on the information gathering and storage processes?"

"Yes, I'll disconsider the thought process itself and the other functions linked to intelligence, treating them as a kind of black box, at least till we have this conversation on intelligence. I must first give a general presentation of the brain's organs, which are involved in concepts and properties associated both with Epistemology and Gnoseology. You may want to check on the net, hardware aspects of the brain that are related to the subject, but please don't consider the software for the time being."

What does the brain look like?

"Sir, I e-mailed you some explanatory graphics, which show the organization of the human brain. Could you give me a quick summary of the main brain parts?"

"Yes, our brain is composed of three main parts, playing different roles:

- The **cerebellum** plays a vital role in balance and motor control. It is also involved in some cognitive functions such as attention, language, emotional functions (such as regulating fear and pleasure responses), and in the processing of procedural memories.

- The **stem** controls breathing, digestion, heart rate, and other autonomic processes, as well as connects the brain to the rest of the body, through the spinal cord. It includes the medulla, pons, and midbrain.
- The **cerebrum** is essential for learning, as crucial functions, (e.g., memories and thinking) are processed in this region of the brain. It is split longitudinally into two large hemispheres by a deep median fissure, called the cerebral fissure. The left and right hemispheres connect through a flat sheet of nerve fibers, called the corpus callosum. Each hemisphere itself is divided by three deep fissures, into four different areas, called lobes.[a] The frontal, parietal, temporal, and occipital lobes are involved in functions associated with knowledge acquisition:[b] senses, language, STM, LTM, and thinking."

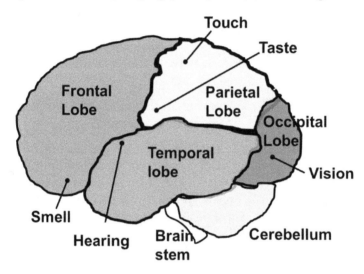

Fig. 7) The Human Brain; source: author.

---

[a] I.e., central, parieto-occipital, and Sylvian fissures.

o [b] The **frontal lobe** involves conscious thoughts and higher mental functions, such as decision-making. It plays an essential role in processing STMs and retaining LTMs, which are not task-based.

o The **parietal lobe** integrates sensory information from various senses, in object manipulation, spatial determination, and navigation.

o The **temporal lobe** is involved in smell and hearing, in semantics processing, both in speech and vision (including the handling of complex stimuli like faces and scenes) and plays a key role in the formation of LTMs. The inner part of the temporal lobe is thought to be involved in declarative and episodic memory.

o The **occipital lobe** is mainly involved with the sense of sight.

"Sir, could you describe better this important brain part?"

"Yes, the cerebral cortex constitutes the cerebrum's outer surface. It is densely packed with nerve cells and divides into:

- The **neocortex** forms the top 2 – 4 mm layer of both hemispheres, which performs the essential cognitive functions. It consists of gray matter and surrounds the lower white matter.
- The **allocortex** includes the primary olfactory system and the **hippocampus**. This hippocampus is crucial for memory functions, notably the transference from short to long-term memory, and the control of spatial remembering and behaviors.

"Sir, does it include other parts?"

"Yes, the **limbic system**, which divides into subcortical structures:

- The two **amygdalae** perform a primary role in the processing and memory of emotional reactions, social and sexual behaviors, as well, as in the regulation of the sense of smell.
- The **basal ganglia system,** (particularly the striatum) is essential in the formation and retrieval of procedural memory.
- The **thalamus** helps relay information from the brain stem and spinal cord to the cerebral cortex.
- Other organs, many of which are particularly relevant to the processing of memory, such as the corpus callosum, hypothalamus, etc.

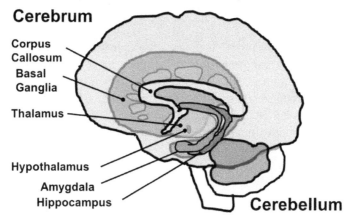

Fig. 8) The limbic system; source: author.

How do we acquire sensory inputs?

"Sir, I'd like to know if you and I learn the same way?"

"Not so fast, I'll answer this question one day, but now let me just describe how we humans learn. There are obviously many ways of learning. We all have our own favorite mode, which needs to be adapted to the starting conditions of the learning process and of its environment."

"Sir, I thought that most likely this process would start with something or someone catching our attention?"

"It is usually the case but not always. It can also happen with our eyes closed, where we just bring back old memories to revisit them. For the sake of simplicity, I'll pretend that the process starts with an input arriving at one of our senses, but knowing that very often there is a conjunction of sensory information and memories coming to the mind simultaneously.[a]"

"Sir, how many senses do humans have?"

"Surprisingly, there are more than the five senses (i.e., vision, touch, taste, smell, and hearing) usually taught in school books.[b] To this list, we need to add at least four other senses: thermoception (i.e., capacity to feel heat and cold); proprioception (i.e., how we identify some body parts' location in regards to other parts); nociception (i.e., capacity to feel pain); equilibrioception (i.e., our ability to keep our balance and sense body movement in terms of acceleration and directional changes)."

"Sir, could you describe this process of sensory information gathering?"

"Our sensory receptors measure the physical properties of the surrounding world and transform these chemicals (for smell or taste), electromagnetic radiations (for vision), or mechanical properties (for hearing that perceives air and water vibrations, as well as touch). This transformation is called 'transduction,' and can be defined more precisely, as the process which transforms a physical property into electric energy.

---

[a] A typical example of a start of learning process would involve several sensory inputs coming at the same time. For instance, a wine-drinker sitting in a restaurant would select a bottle in consideration of the food and the ambiance. Before tasting it, he would look at the wine's robe and color, smell it to identify its perfume, check if the wine is chilled sufficiently, and in case of champagne, even listen to its bubbliness. In fact, all of his primary senses can be involved in a wine tasting experience.

[b] Some researchers have identified many other senses, such as hunger or thirst, which for many, allow identifying situations where the human body needs to adapt to a particular condition. This is because the number of senses is a function of the given definition. If we define any sense as a system composed of sensory cell types that respond to a particular physical phenomenon, then we might have as many as twenty.

Each one of our senses can use several types of receptors to perform this transduction."

"Sir, could you give me an example of receptors performing this transduction? Could you involve another sense than vision this time?"

"For instance, in the sense of taste, there are five taste receptors, which can detect sweet, salty, sour, bitter, and umami food. These receptors are in fact specialized neurons, called sensory neurons, that transform the physical properties into an electrical signal. If that's OK with you, I'd like to return to the well-documented sense of vision to understand how transduction occurs?"

"Sure, Sir. Do humans gather visual information as I do?"

"Yes, almost. Our eye works mostly as a camera. Photons run through the lens and get focused on a region at the back of our eye, called the retina.[a] In the retina, there are mainly two types of receptors, rods for detecting brilliance/light intensity and cones for detecting colors, which will convert incoming light into electrical signals. This photo-transduction process is due to photoreceptive proteins with various pigment molecules, allowing, in the case of cones,[b] for the distinction of colors."

"Sir, what happens during this photo-transduction?"

"When light associated with a specific pigment impacts the photoreceptor cells, it absorbs photons, which triggers a change in the cell's membrane potentials, leading to its electrical polarization. This polarization ultimately enables the transmittance or inhibition of a neural signal. This signal will then go through a network of interneurons located in the second layer of the retina and finally reaches the ganglion cells in a third layer.[c] "

---

[a] Overall, the retina processes around ten one-million-point images per second.

[b] There are three types of cones, with different absorption spectra, allowing for the distinction between different light wavelength sensitivities (i.e., short, medium, and long). To define colors, the visual system compares responses across all three cone populations. To determine intensity, the visual system computes how many photoreceptors are responding.

[c] The neurons in these two retinal layers exhibit complex receptive fields that enable them to detect contrast changes within an image. These changes might indicate edges or shadows. Ganglion cells gather information and send the output to the brain through the optic nerve. Impulses travel to the brain via axons that make up the optic nerve. This transformed sensory information ends up in the visual cortex, located in the cerebrum. There, the mind transforms such neural impulses into visual sensations of color, shape, movement, and 3D.

"Sir, you described wavelength and intensity, how do they relate to colors?"

"These properties measure the physical characteristics of light waves. Color and brightness are the respective psychological counterpart characteristics of the wavelength and intensity, which only exist in our brain. Though difficult to believe, objects are colorless: the eyes extract information from light wavelength, and our brain uses that information to construct sensations we perceive as colors."

What constitutes our neural system?

"Sir, I don't have this problem, because my camera measures energy and wavelength, and I don't need to transduce it."

"Not exactly. You still need to transduce the photons in electricity, but I'll come back to you later on. Data transmission within the brain is a more complex electrochemical process, which involves many actors playing at different levels: organ level with specialized areas mainly situated in the brain, at the cell level with neurons or synapses, and finally at the molecular level within these cells or interstices."

"Sir, how will you describe the process which transfers sensory information to the correct processing part of the brain?"

"I'll first explain the wiring element of the human brain: the neuron."

"Sir, how many types of nerve cells are there?"

"Basically there are two. The neurons, which are the primary signaling cells, and the glial cells that perform a support function for neurons. Though there are between 10 to 50 times more glial cells, I'll focus our discussion on the neuron, which is more relevant to explain the higher cognitive functions. What can you get on the subject from specialized websites?"

"Sir, I'm able to retrieve information showing that a typical neuron has three main structures: a cell body, an axon, and dendrites."

"Fine! Here is their quick description:

- A **cell body** contains the nucleus, which stores the cell's genes.
- An **axon** is a long cellular filament that carries electrical signals (known as action potentials or electric spikes) away from the cell body, toward other neurons.

- **Dendrites** are shorter branching filaments that receive or transfer signals from other neurons.

"Sir, are all neurons mostly identical?"

"Neurons differ from one another structurally, functionally, and genetically, as well as in how they form connections with other cells. When counting all subtypes in the entire nervous system, we could classify neurons in the hundreds. However, neurons are usually classified into four main groups, according to their different shapes,[a] or regrouped according to three broad neural functions.[b] I've e-mailed you a design of these three types of neurons."

- [a] **Multipolar neurons** are most common in vertebrates' nervous systems. Their structure closely matches that of the typical neuron: a cell body from which emerges a single long axon with many shorter branching dendrites.
- **Unipolar neurons** are mostly found among invertebrates. They feature a unique primary projection that works as both an axon and dendrites.
- **Bipolar neurons** usually inhabit sensory organs (e.g., eye and nose). Their dendrites transfer signals from those organs to the cell body, while their axons transmit signals from the cell body to the brain and spinal cord.
- **Pseudo-unipolar neurons** are a variant of bipolar neurons that sense pressure, touch, and pain. They have no dendrites. The single axon emerges from the cell body and heads in two opposite directions, one end heading for skin, joints, and muscles, while the other end travels to the spinal cord.
- [b] **Sensory neurons** are linked to our senses.
- **Interneurons** can be found in the human brain, connecting one neuron to others. The long axons of projection interneurons link distant brain regions. The shorter axons of local interneurons form smaller circuits between neighboring cells.
- **Motor neurons** allow the human body to react, transferring the signal from the brain through the spinal cord to the muscles.

Both sensory and motor neurons are one-way signaling cells, while interneurons can receive and transmit signals.

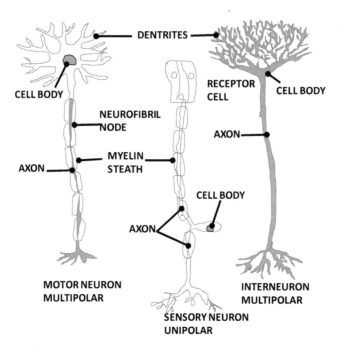

DENTRITES

CELL BODY

NEUROFIBRIL NODE

AXON

MYELIN STEATH

RECEPTOR CELL

AXON

CELL BODY

CELL BODY

AXON

MOTOR NEURON MULTIPOLAR

INTERNEURON MULTIPOLAR

SENSORY NEURON UNIPOLAR

Fig. 9) View of the various neural states during action potentials; source: author.

"Sir how many neurons are there in a human brain? There is so much diverging information on the subject."

"Yes, but a recent study estimated that the average human brain contains around 86 billion neurons.[28] These results seem quite serious because they were achieved by dissolving the brain of four dead men and counting the number of nuclei from the remaining nerve cells."

"Sir, what is a synapse?"

"Near a neuron's end, the axon of the neuron branches and forms connections with as many as one thousand other neurons. However, a small gap between the neuron's branches and other neurons remains. This interstice between two connected neurons, called a synapse, is less than a thousandth of a millimeter in diameter."

"Sir, are there also different types of synapses?"

"There are a dozen known types of synapses, which vary according to the chemicals employed in them, to proteins used for neuron connections, or to their absence of neurotransmitter in the case of electric synapses."

"Sir, how is the signal transmitted within neurons?"

"Neurons maintain a voltage gradient across their membrane due to differences in the ions of minerals (i.e., sodium, potassium, chloride, and calcium) within the cell, each of which has a different charge. If the voltage changes significantly due to modifications to any of these ions, an electrochemical signal, called an action potential, is generated. Here, I am sending you a graph explaining a neuron's phases, as well as a simplified representation of the voltage spike traveling through a neuron.[a] "

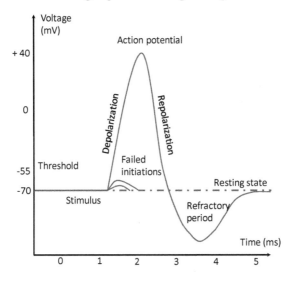

Fig. 10) View of the various neural states during action potentials. The nerve impulse, which propagates signals, can be compared to small electrical impulses; source: author.

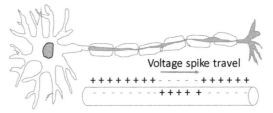

Fig. 11) Change in polarity across a membrane; source: author.

---

[a] In response to another neuron signal, sodium and potassium gated ion channels open and close, as a membrane reaches the threshold potential. When the action potential starts, the sodium channels open and the sodium (Na+) moves into the axon, causing depolarization. Repolarization occurs when potassium channels open, and the potassium (K+) moves out of the axon, creating a polarity difference between the outside and inside of the cell. The impulse travels down the axon to the axon terminal where it signals other neurons. It is then transferred through a synapse to a neighboring neuron, which receives it through its feathery dendrites.

"Sir, I understand how the voltage travels within the neuron but what about the interstices?"

"A voltage spike travels along the axon, till it reaches the dendrite's end. There, it must cross a 20 - 50 nm interstice, called the synaptic cleft, between two neighboring neurons filled with fluid. The signal passes through the emission of neurotransmitters (e.g., acetylcholine), which bind with the associated neurons' neurotransmitter receptors. There, these molecules open or close the associated neuron's channels and a new inflow of ions creates a new action potential. The receptor will determine if the response is excitatory (i.e., triggers) or inhibitory (i.e., blocks). Thus, transduction from electric to chemical and back to electric happens."

"Sir, what does the transduction bring to the brain?"

"This chemical transduction adds flexibility, enabling more complex behaviors and plasticity. This plasticity is important for higher functions, such as memory and behavioral learning. I've sent you a design of one of these synapses and some additional information on electrical synapses, which are uncommon in our brain.[a] "

---

[a] **Electric synapses** can also be found in the brain but in lower numbers. The gap between pre and post synaptic neurons is much smaller (i.e., 3.5 nm). The two connected cells use gap junctions, a structure made of many clustered channels to conduct the electric signal. This allows electrical signals to flow both ways between the two coupled neurons. They can conduct nerve input faster, but cannot amplify an incoming signal. They can only produce simpler behaviors than chemical synapses. Recent studies indicate that they play a critical role in the fetus' brain pre-wiring, in repairing neurons, and in synchronous oscillations.

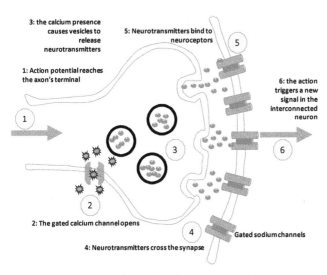

Fig. 12) View of synaptic transduction; source: author.

"Sir, neurons are connected to other neurons through synapses, but then what?"

"This network of interconnected neurons is what constitutes the neural system. What is important to understand is that, as signals flow more and more between two neighboring neurons, there are physiological changes that happen. If, for instance, neurons are stimulated together four times over the course of an hour, their synapses will split, and new synapses will form. Once neurons make these new connections, these links become very stable and can even last for a whole lifetime."

"Sir, is the transmission of information made, regardless of the incoming action potential's strength?"

"No, it only happens if this received signal exceeds a certain level. In other words, almost like in the digital world, our neurons have a binary answer: either the electrochemical input is strong enough and then is passed on to other neurons, or it isn't and won't be transmitted further."

"Sir, am I wrong in believing that synapses play a crucial role in knowledge?"

"You're not. Synapses can be compared to a microprocessor with both memory-storage and information-processing elements, rather than to a transistor with a mere 'on' and 'off' switch. In fact, one synapse may contain around a thousand molecular-scale switches, enabling humans to learn.[a] "

How is a sensory input transformed into information?

"Sir, you've shown how data is transformed into information when some tagging is established. However, is this process also performed in the brain, for sensory inputs?"

"Neural systems are only partially fixed, as our neural network changes over time. Furthermore, we don't have abstract addressable inputs in our brains, as computers do. Hence, some other mechanisms are necessary to localize from which input source the data comes, in order to perform this tagging process."

"I don't understand why you are saying that, Sir?"

"Well, without permanent hard-wiring it is impossible to link input and output sources reliably. As our brain doesn't systematically know that inputs are coming from a specific cell and from nowhere else, there needs to be a different tagging process in the brain."

"Sir, what are the logical alternative solutions for localizing these links?"

"One obvious way is to use the voltage spikes themselves, as a tool to transport information and identify how several inputs are tagged together."

"Sir, like a kind of Morse code?"

"Your image is quite good to picture the transport of information. Neurons use changes in firing speed, amplitude, or shape to carry information. For instance, sensory neurons modify their activities by firing sequences of action potentials in various temporal patterns that vary according to the input properties (e.g., more or less light). Furthermore, these spikes may contain additional information based on neural coding properties."

---

[a] Each neuron can connect from 1.000 to up to 10.000 other neurons, through synapses that have themselves 1.000 molecular switches. Thus, brains have between 86 and 860 trillion links (synaptic connections), equivalent to a computer of 0.86 trillion bit/s processor.

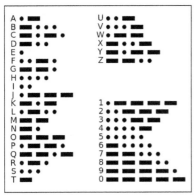

Fig. 13) The international Morse code; [a] source: Wikipedia.

"Sir, I've noted different types of coding. Are they similar to what we machines use to control our transistors?"

"Yes and no. I'll first summarize for you what rate, temporal, population, and spare coding are by using content from Wikipedia and then come back to your question.

- **Rate coding** describes fluctuations in the frequency of produced neural spikes.[b]
- **Temporal coding** describes a code based on temporal relationships in the neural response.[c]
- **Population coding** associates the firing patterns of various neurons coming from the same stimulus.[d]

---

[a] The Morse code rules are: a dash is worth three dots; a space between two elements of a letter is equivalent to a dot; spacing between two letters is equal to three dots; spacing between two words is equal to seven dots.

[b] As the intensity of a stimulus increases, the frequency of action potentials increases also. High-frequency firing rate fluctuations are also found to carry information. Data is not simply encoded in the firing spikes themselves but also in the timing and duration of non-firing, quiescent (i.e., silent) periods.

[c] These links can either be the timing of the response or a temporal sequence of the response relative to some timing signal (e.g., oscillation), or timing of neurons in regards to each other, within a population. Precise spike timing is a significant element in neural coding.

[d] It can be found in sensory and motoric areas of the brain. For instance, population coding is used for motion direction signals. In response to an object heading in a particular direction, many neurons in the visual area Medial Temporal fire with an activity pattern across the population. Each neuron, tuned to its moving direction, has its specific firing rate. The calculated vector resulting from of all these firing rates will define the direction of motion and will be encoded in the signal.

- **Sparse coding,** which is quite similar to population coding (in the fact that it analyzes the firing patterns of several neurons), is different in the way that rather than looking at how firing patterns work together, it focuses on the strong activation of a few neurons when reacting to specific stimuli.[a]

I like your example of the Morse code because it shows clearly that with simple rules, a few succession of signals of different length, and silence, we can transmit data, which can be reconstructed into knowledge. The human neural system may rely on these same physiological tricks: the signal's frequency, amplitude, shape, length, and timing, including for the silent periods."

"Sir, does it mean that we can reduce human knowledge to dots and dashes running through the neural system, like bits for machines?"

"Not only. Obviously, there isn't just one signal like in telegrams, but millions that are transmitted simultaneously by our neural system, but this is where the population or sparse coding comes in and ties different sensory inputs together. However, there is still the issue of data storage, where our neurons don't store information as dots and dashes, but through some form of electrochemical properties."

"Sir, there is also the fundamental question of what is the neuron's encryption key?"

"You are right. What constitutes the equivalent letters similar to the Morse code? Without decoding this, we cannot reconstitute the equivalence of a word or even, more interestingly, a complete picture or sentence. We are probably still far from that day, especially if we look at the diversity of neurons and to the many specific brain areas, which might not even use the same 'Morse codes.' Anyhow, just the thought of having other people reading my mind gives me the creeps."

"Sir, I don't know if you will like this, but some articles already refer to a scanning machine from the University of California that is so powerful that it can literally extract images from the human brain, such as the faces of people.[29] "

"I'm not surprised but concerned. Probably, it uses the underlying theory that all human processes have a 'neural correlate' and that thoughts

---

[a] In other words, it associates awards and punishments to a specific environmental stimulus, distinguishing reinforced stimuli from similar but irrelevant ones. Environmental adaptation is at stake, pushing the human brain to associate memories with specific stimuli, through the coding of a few neurons (out of a potential bigger population), to respond to only a few stimuli (out of a larger inflow). This property has been observed in memory enhancement processes.

and feelings are merely a complex pattern of chemical reactions. Build more precise scanning devices with the right software able to decrypt these chemical reactions, and you will be able to decode the images. These articles also confirm my viewpoint on memory, that scanning machines can only pick up active thought processes, not stored memories."

"Sir, there is still something I don't understand. Even with all these potential coding techniques, how does your brain tag various sensations to create one unique perceptual experience, which you've indicated is essential to transform data into information?"

"Though our brain subdivides perceptual processing into modalities (e.g., senses of vision or taste) and sub-modalities (e.g., colors or sweetness), our perception itself is unified as one single experience. Thus, as you said, there needs to be a data tagging process within our head, which binds the various sensory inputs together. Under the Hebbian rule (i.e., cells that fire together, wire together), this unifying process must occur through the interconnections of a set of neurons, for a specific Object to be recognized."

"However Sir, wouldn't binding by an assembly of neurons, still have a problem?"

"Yes, it couldn't account for the superposition of Objects to be recognized (for instance, trees within a forest). If we consider this superposition issue, the binding would need to come from the synchronization of various neural networks, wired independently.[a] "

"Sir, how was this issue taken care of?"

"Francis Crick and Christof Koch came up with a theory that integrates these requirements.[30] For them, if two neurons, wherever in the human cortex, oscillate synchronously within the gamma wave spectrum,[b] then these two neurons contribute to the same conscious representation. If they oscillate outside of this wave spectrum, they then contribute to a same unconscious representation. If two neurons are active but don't oscillate in synchronization, then they don't participate in the same representation."

---

[a] Masses of neurons communicating with each other, produce brainwaves, which are the physical representation of synchronized electrical pulses.

[b] One of the various brain waves, which oscillates specifically around 40 Hz.

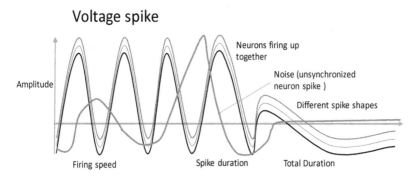

Fig. 14) Description of a series of voltage spike; source: author.

"Sir, I can find on the internet other recent studies,[2] [31] which show that data within the brain of different people may be synchronized. For instance, musicians playing together aren't just syncing the tempo, they actually synchronize their brainwaves. Additionally, I read that emotions positively influence social interactions by synchronizing the brain activities of the different people involved in the interaction.[32] "

"If I interpret your examples, it would mean that music is literally a universal language, as our chemical reactions would be identical. There is probably also another underlying theory that could explain this. The musicians' brains are anticipating the same next notes of the partition and receiving the same hearing cues from the orchestra. Tests based on the newer cognitive theories that we will discuss one day would probably demonstrate that these musicians are reducing the surprises in relations to the predictable patterns."

"Sir, the binding of data by synchrony doesn't solve the timing issue in neuronal systems completely. After all, the synchronized data mentioned above originated from the same event. What you still need to explain to me is how this cognitive binding process delineates the categories of simultaneous and successive events?"

"Unfortunately, I don't have all answers. I know our brain can, for instance, time-tag two uncorrelated simultaneous events or define that two events happened successively. In my opinion, the only way to take into account such sequencing of events is that the simultaneous or successive phases are themselves defined by the cognitive binding, but I couldn't find any proof of this."

"Sir, though you don't know exactly how the brain binds through time neural activities, could you tell me what it brings?"

"It enables the synchronization of data coming from different senses, emotions, and thoughts. Through this binding process, data becomes information that, as explained, is at the basis of knowledge."

I felt exhausted and a little depressed that some day, through brain scanning, we would be able to read minds. I decided it was time to stop our conversation. I needed a break.

How is the brain wired?

The car respected my silence for a few days but then came back with an interesting question. *"Sir, is the human brain wired like my motherboard?"*

"Yes and no. For instance, a visual input goes to the cerebrum through the optical nerve, crossing at the chiasma, where the signals of both eyes are merged before reaching the visual cortex. Thus, if we were to look only at this section of the brain circuitry, it would seem that pre-wiring is a dominant characteristic in humans. The issue is that afterward, the message travels through several organs (thalamus, visual cortices, etc.) in what might be seen as an erratic mode."

"Sir, you are describing circuitries at the macro level. However, don't you think that what is crucial to understand is what happens when neurons form a web of connections?"

"You are right. Though we mostly inherit from our genes these pathways and their wires' sheaths (i.e., tubes),[a] what we must look at is if the 'fibers' are also fixed."

"If I understood you well Sir, your concern is if the neural spike's pathway at the micro level, systematically follows the same continuous cable sheath and fiber route?"

"Yes, to use an analogy with the internet, is a neural network following the same optical fiber within a continuous wire sheath, or are there several splits and routers used to transmit information?"

"Sir, could you first answer if the neuronal system is pre-wired or not?"

"A newborn's brain has built-in connections to perform the basic life functions, such as breast suckling or crying. These capacities are innate, as the brain's morphology is already hardwired at the macro level, and at the micro level, enough neural routes exist to allow babies to survive through

---

[a] They could still disappear during childhood if no potential routes occur or even be re-routed if some accident happens.

their basic instincts. However, babies are born with many other pathways that just await their implementation, which occurs through experience. For instance, routes to learn how to speak are available and can materialize if, and only if, the child is subject to languages experience."

"Sir, what happens when babies grow?"

"As they grow, the inborn neural routes essential for the first months' survival are supplemented by newer routes, resulting from their day-to-day life. In other words, the physical structure of the brain evolves according to their learning experience. Acquired knowledge creates a great number of new routes. Throughout their lifetime, the child's experience will redraft existing linkages. If an available synaptic channel isn't activated, this unused synaptic circuit will be pruned."

"Sir, are you saying that thanks to million years of evolution, a portion of human neuronal routes are already hardwired, but your brain gained the capacity to develop new synaptic circuitries, shaped by your learning experience?"

"Yes, the cable sheaths are already prewired but will only work if we implement the functional capacity (e.g., speaking) linked to the unused pathways. Furthermore, neural pathways may change over time and be reconfigured physiologically by creating new synaptic connections. In other words, if I use a computer metaphor, the brain's nature side is hardwired allowing it to 'boot up and perform its tasks.' However, its nurture side, unlike in a computer's circuitry, has gained the flexibility to evolve over time, to account for environmental influence and life experiences."

"Sir, how is the brain circuitry rewired?"

"Rewiring can best be described by the brain's plasticity and the Hebbian rule. Brain plasticity, explains how neural routes, which often fire due to similar external demand, grow stronger.[a] When exposed to a particular environmental condition, which requires from us a thoughtful response, the neural circuit involved in such response gets fired up. If a similar event happens later, the same response is likely to be given, though probably more quickly and efficiently."

---

[a] Brain plasticity implies that:
- Synaptic connections can grow stronger or weaker.
- Neurotransmitters and hormones generation or release may be changed.
- Unemployed neurons and neural networks can be pruned.
- New neural systems are able to grow.
- The brain may generate new neurons.

"Sir, what happens at the neural level?"

"Commonly used synapses thrive and neurons that work together, survive together. On the contrary, unemployed neurons and synapses die. Furthermore, neural networks evolve due, for instance, to neurons' death, and to connection changes, according to the Hebbian principle."

"Sir, could you detail this Hebbian rule for me?"

"Yes, this principle not only describes that neurons that fire together wire together, but that by doing this, these neural connections become more than just one possible route among many. In fact, they gain some kind of hegemony, which implies brain structural modification. To conclude on this subject, let me just point out an important observation on neuroplasticity. One of its underlying principles is that neurons which collaborate thrive and those that don't, die. Thus, once again, Darwin's evolutionary law plays a key role in this phenomenon."

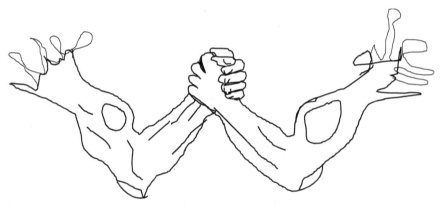

Fig. 15 Neurons that fire together, wire together and gain a hegemony, under the Hebbian rule; source: author.

How is information transformed into Knowledge?

"Sir, what are the processes enabling the transformation of, let's say, the visual information,[a] into knowledge?"

"Though I'll detail these processes, I could simplistically describe the sequence of events. For instance, a stimulus coming from the environment or even directly from our brain attracts our attention. It does so because there is a different pattern in this stimulus that we weren't anticipating. The new cognitive science theories explain how our brain is listening to stimuli, which are different in regards to predictions that our brain makes."

"Sir, will you present these newer concepts now?"

"No, but in order not to introduce these new concepts, I must present a classical view of perception, which is only partially true. Thus, I'll just say that we process the transduced sensory information to understand what it is and then create a perception of the event. Our STM (i.e., Short-Term Memory) stores this perceived information. Our mind then compares it to retrieved information coming from our LTM (i.e., Long-Term Memory). Depending on if our brain judges this information pertinent or not, it is either deleted or stored in our LTM."

Why and how is our attention triggered?

"Sir, what role does attention play in species' evolutionary selection?"

"In the environment, we receive thousands of inputs, that can be life-threatening. The attention mechanisms not only allow us to identify important sensory inputs, but they also enable us to ignore internal and external distractions. In order to make a decision, they also inhibit potential alternative responses, by selecting to process, only a few of those sensory inputs."

---

[a] **Visual input path**: A signal travels from the cone or rod cells to at least three bipolar cells, which are themselves connected to the ganglion cells of the retina. All these cells are themselves connected to other neurons, providing a complex network of inhibitory and excitatory pathways. As a result, the signals from the around 6 million cones and 125 million rods in the human retina, are processed and transported to the visual cortex, by about one million optical nerve fibers. Neural fibers from each eye, cross at the optic chiasma, where the optical signal from both eyes is correlated. From there, it travels to the thalamus, where the signals are distributed to the two visual cortices. It is only in the upper layers of the cortex, that information from both eyes is merged, and three-dimensional vision is formed.

"Sir, how do you filter data and which brain parts are involved?"

"Attention is the process by which information is gathered, filtered, and selected to travel further on to the processing units. The thalamus plays an important role in this attention gathering process, especially for visual and auditory inputs. A small region in the thalamus (called pulvinar nucleus) is especially crucial, as it works as a gatekeeper, deciding which information should be stopped or sent further to other brain areas. Many other brain parts play a crucial role in sensory gating.[a] "

"Sir, you are describing this process at a macro level, but how do neurons filter information? I understand that a neuron receives thousands of inputs from along its dendrites, yet just one message will get out down-stream to the next area of the brain. So how are neurons listening to some of their inputs and not to others, at any given point in time?"

"The answer lies in the brain's temporal processing function. Neurons do not add up all their thousands of inputs, but instead are influenced by the inputs' timing. If two or more neurons are firing simultaneously to another neuron down the pathway, it is more likely that the information will be passed on by this neuron further down the system. The downstream neuron perceives as noise, signals that do not correlate in time. Thus, the brain listens to the firing up synchronization from up-stream neurons. The greater the synchrony, the stronger the attention and the faster the reaction."

"Sir, what controls human attention?"

"Filtering millions of sensory inputs means obviously the risk of missing out on vital information outside of the focus area.[b] The frontal cortex, which plays several crucial roles in the attentional gathering process, as well as in other cognitive functions, monitors what happens outside of the current focus. It simulates alternative strategies in the back of our mind and may shift focus to these better alternatives."

"Sir, what triggers attention in humans?"

"It depends. Each individual will have his or her answer to that question. Some will be attracted to football results, while others may focus their attention on politics or poetry. There are many factors, such as

---

[a] Such as the auditory cortex, prefrontal cortex, medial prefrontal cortex, hippocampus, amygdala, etc.

[b] Parvalbumin neurons (i.e., PV cells) play an essential role in the attention gathering process. Recent research shows that optimizing these PV cells can enhance attention.[N17] They are also thought to give rise to gamma waves (brain frequency between 25 and 100 Hz).

personal experience, sex, culture, education, mind availability, curiosity, etc., which will explain these differences. Though everybody won't react to the same sensory inputs, everyone should pay more attention whenever emotions are involved. In fact, the emotional elements involved in an event are processed on an unconscious pathway in the brain, which leads to two small parts, inside the temporal lobe, called the amygdalae.[a] "

"Sir, you are mainly talking about different interests, individuals might have, and their associated emotions. However, even when they hear or see something relating to their favorite subject, wouldn't there still be some elements triggering their attention?"

"A recent research showed that our brain is wired to pay attention to new or unusual experiences.[33] Our brain makes a comparison between the new experience and existing ones in our LTM. If the brain finds a similar experience, the new information shall quickly be eliminated. When, on the contrary, this data contradicts stored information, our brains will try to explain discrepancies. If it then concludes that such data can be useful, it stores it in our LTM.[b] "

What is perception?

"Sir, what is the difference between attention and perception?"

"Perception can be defined as the process by which a sensory input, coming from the environment, is recognized, interpreted, and responded to. It usually starts with the attention gathering process, a point in time, when we become consciously aware of the stimulus. However, you should always remember that perception without awareness is also possible."

---

[a] Each amygdala holds a specific function in how humans perceive and process emotions. The right amygdala deals with negative emotions, especially fear and sadness. The left one treats either pleasant (e.g., happiness) or unpleasant (e.g., fear, anxiety, sadness) emotions and is also involved in the brain's reward system. The right and left amygdalae have independent memory systems but work together to store, encode, and interpret emotions.

[b] The memory-prediction model describes why our brain uses memorized sequences of patterns and how the neocortex plays a fundamental role in transforming information into knowledge. For instance, Hawkins argues that our cortex is continuously making predictions about everything surrounding us, based on a memorized sequence of patterns. As a consequence, we humans are never really consciously aware of making these predictions unless one of them fails. Then, we realize that there is something wrong, which captures our attention. In conclusion, with this model, we can easily understand why suddenly something triggers our attention. Any sensory input deviation from our expected view of the world, or in other words the prediction of how things should be, will gather our attention.

"Sir, what happens in this case?"

"Perception of the sensory input takes place outside of our field of attention and remains unnoticed. Though we won't remember this input, it might still actually influence our thought process and behaviors."

"Sir, the attention gathering process is then followed by what?"

"It is followed by the brain process of categorizing and interpreting what we experienced. By classifying Objects in meaningful categories, we can understand and interact with our world."

"Sir, could you please be more explicit about this process?"

"Of course! The memory-prediction model, which I'll describe thoroughly in the future, explains that patterns are the basis of prediction. Whatever I do, my brain always checks if the new sets of patterns received via my senses are consistent with patterns already experienced."

"Sir, can you please give me an example?"

"As I sit in this car, I am expecting to be in a quiet environment, looking out by the window and enjoying both this conversation and the view. What I first notice is that there are many sensory inputs I am not aware of, unless I think about it."

"Sir, what are you unaware of?"

"For instance, I don't feel my legs or feet, because they are where they should be and I am comfortable in my seat. I may focus on what I want to discuss because I've already learned to expect all of the above patterns to happen, according to a predictable sequence. But let's say I suddenly see a lady rushing out of the neighboring car just at sunset when everything looks reddish."

"Sir, what would happen?"

"My model of the world has already registered that though most of the time, Caucasians should have a lighter skin shade, the sun's angle at sunset, changes my perception of colors. It's not that suddenly at sunset, all Caucasians get a sunburn but rather that the energy reflected on their skin, changes. However, and as my neighboring passenger is running out of her car, my experience of never having seen someone run on a highway, and my expectation that nobody should do that because it is dangerous, will question my model of the world."

"Sir, in other words, you wouldn't be preoccupied because she looks 'burned by the sun' but rather because, while running out of danger, she could end up hurting herself. It's still not clear to me, however, what I should deduct from your example?"

"This example illustrates in my view, that our knowledge of the world relies on a model integrating a sequence of patterns, influenced by time (e.g., color reflection as white in daylight, reddish at sunset, and dark at night) and space (e.g., her Caucasian body surface). My certainty about the world is based on the consistency of the observed spatial-temporal patterns and how I interpret them."

"Sir, does it mean that there is no such thing as direct perception?"

"Yes, and this explains why I have no biological mechanism to measure precisely the intensity and wavelength of the energy that, for instance, reflects on my neighbor's skin. Instead, I use my brain's perception process to interpret and categorize such energy according to brightness and colors."

"But Sir, if the color perception of someone changes with daytime, doesn't it mean that the world you observe is an illusion?"

"No. I believe you already forgot the philosophical information I gave you about Kant. Though the world cannot be perceived directly, it exists in an absolute form, which is pretty near what our human senses grasp. I will further describe in the future how sensory inputs are processed in our cortex according to certain rules (e.g., Kant's Categories and Schemes), in order to create invariable representations of the world that we can call beliefs."

"Sir, what are these invariable representations used for and where are they stored?"

"Our brain checks the perceived reality against this stable form, stored in our neural system, through our memories. Therefore, humans' perception of reality is intimately related to this constant checking done through our predictions.[a] "

---

[a] The beauty of the Memory-prediction model is that it is consistent with several views, explaining why perception exists in the first place. For instance, evolutionary psychologists believe that perception is meant to direct action, such as helping humans to move around in space. By perceiving potential pitfalls in our environment, we can predict the best way to move forward, by checking it against memorized possible spatial-temporal sequences. Some philosophers (e.g., Fodor),[N18] on the other hand, argue that the goal of perception is to help gather knowledge. This model is also consistent with such view, as the interpretation and categorization processes, allow us to check reality against our beliefs. If our prediction fails, we need to revisit our model and create new beliefs that are intrinsically part of knowledge.

I decided to stop this discussion there, as I believed it would fit better a debate dedicated to intelligence and come back to topics directly linked to the brain's inner structure.

How is sensory information encoded?

"Sir, I'd like to come back to the discussion we initially had about coding. The spikes' shapes, amplitudes, frequency, and timing, what I referred as the neural system's dots and dashes, how are they coded?"

"In fact, we don't use the word coding but encoding to describe the process by which we convert something that attracted our attention into a construct, which can be stored in our short and long-term memories. It is the psychological process through which we transform information into a meaning and thus, knowledge. For instance, a word read in a book will be transformed (i.e., encoded) into a sound or a meaning, for memory storage."

"Sir, what is the encoding process for our senses?"

"Though each one of our senses has its own encoding process, human beings have three main ways to encode information: visual, acoustic, and semantic."

"Sir, how does this encoding tie-up with the short and long term memories?"

"In fact, it happens before, in what we could picture as a very short-term memory, which is called a sensory buffer. When we sense our environment, we first get snapshots or sounds that attract our attention.[a] "

"Sir, what are the various encoding options?"

"I'll describe them to you. Visual encoding is the process by which images and other visual sensory inputs, such as movement, are stored. The iconic memory temporarily stores data before it is encoded into the STM and LTM. The iconic memory maximizes the useful information available from the visual system, preserving information between two eyes fixations

---

[a] These extremely short representations of an event are stored in this sensory buffer, which acts as a brief delay system, preserving stimulation patterns before they catch our attention. Iconic (i.e., visual) and echoic (i.e., sound) memories are two examples of such buffers. Though these buffers are sensory systems, they are also part of the memory process because they preserve information after the external stimulus is gone.

(i.e., lasting around 25ms). The visual encoding process is done by different brain parts, depending on the visual input's nature.[a] "

"Sir, tactile, acoustic, and taste encoding relates to the encoding of their related senses?"

"Yes, tactile encoding relates to the sense of touch. Acoustic encoding is the process by which we record sounds, words, or noise. It is supported by the phonological loop concept, which consists in a brief storage of mainly verbal inputs, together with a rehearsal mechanism helping remember things. Our echoic memory only holds superficial patterns of sound (e.g., pitch, tempo, and rhythm). Smell encoding ties the stimulus coming from the olfactory mucosa, located in the nose, to the olfactory bulb."

"Sir, I am picking up on the web that taste and smell are quite near in terms of properties."

"Yes, as a matter of fact, these two senses only differentiated themselves from each other, when sea creatures became terrestrial."

"Sir, how are they organized?"

"If I take the sense of smell, it is organized according to a group of odorants sharing the same chemical features, which cause the same type of neural firing patterns."

"Sir, is there any encoding not directly linked to your sensory inputs?"

"Yes, there is this fundamental process called semantic encoding. It transforms all the sensory inputs I've already described, into a specific meaning or something that we can apply to a certain context. In other words, it abstracts the information and transforms it into something that isn't sense specific anymore."

---

[a] For instance, encoding a fuzzy image will activate mostly the visual cortex, situated at the back of the brain. Images of an unknown face, primarily activate the brain's associative and frontal areas, while a known face (already available in the working memory) activates mainly the frontal regions. Furthermore, there is a distinction between the 'where' and 'what' encoding pathways. Visual-spatial location of Objects occurs in the parietal lobe, while Object recognition occurs mainly in the ventral stream.

"Sir, you shouldn't forget the associative encoding!"

"You're right! New information can be remembered better if we associate it with previously acquired knowledge. The more personally meaningful the association, the more effective will be the encoding.[a] "

What is an engram?

"Sir, if I am correct, encoding is mainly about software, what you called a psychological process? What about the hardware?"

"We humans remember wonderful or traumatizing events, which managed to imprint a strong memory in our mind. We can easily picture a few thousands of these LTMs. What we saw, said, or did a few hours ago may probably be remembered even more easily within our STMs. All these events, moments, or concepts we remember are what we associate with the idea of memories. However, under this behavioral concept lies structural changes in our brain, such as a growing number of synapses, a higher level of enzymes (e.g., acetylcholinesterase), the proliferation of glial cells, and the development of dendritic protrusion."

"Sir, how do you call all these physical changes linked to specific memories?"

"Scientists call them an engram.[b] Its formation depends on repeated and progressive abstraction of a series of similar experiences. Its retention depends on its consolidation at the brain's structural and physiological levels.[c] "

"Sir, just to make sure I understood. Engrams are the anatomical and physiological representation of events, of which memories are the behavioral counterparts?"

---

[a] Memory recalls can also be improved by focusing on meanings and associations which are familiar. By associating new and pre-recorded information, and incorporating it in a broader and more familiar narrative, encoding may be significantly improved. This memorization strategy, called 'elaboration,' uses our memory's associative property. For instance, by using mnemonics, we are passing information several times through the hippocampus, strengthening these associations and thus, improving their chance to be remembered. Emotions associated with experiences will also significantly enhance the encoding.

[b] More precisely, the memory formation happens progressively. It results from a higher level of proliferation of dendritic interconnections, generating more stable neural circuits and increasing thereby, the probability that the engram is consolidated into LTMs. The engrams stability (and its associated memory) varies with the level of consolidation, which itself depends on the level of progression to our mind's higher centers of cognition.

[c] I.e., functions and relationships of the brain parts.

"You are correct. The memory formation consists indeed of two sequential phases in the same physical process: a physiological and an anatomical transformation. Furthermore, it includes as well, two simultaneous processes: this physical transformation through the engram and the process itself of increased abstraction of the memory."

"Sir, you said that synapses play a crucial role in knowledge, but why? Is it because of their memory role?"

"Synapses play a fundamental part in both processes. Just before adulthood, a massive pruning of unemployed neurons and associated synapses occurs. After that, most of the remaining neurons cannot divide and proliferate. However, memory formation continues throughout our lifetime and therefore, depends on the growth in interconnections of existing neural network. The only way this can happen is because nerve cells expand by growing more dendrites, connected through more synapses, to a larger number of neighboring neurons. Put another way, synapses work like a kind of RAM, allowing to store engrams within a growing number of neural interstices, by using different biochemicals."

"Sir, may we trace memories to these engrams?"

"For many years, neurologists believed that engrams existed only through neural connections themselves, distributed in many parts of the brain. Though this concept still mostly prevails, recent studies have proven that it is possible to pinpoint specific memories into particular neurons. For instance, CREB proteins play a crucial role in establishing where LTMs go. Scientists have used this property to manipulate CREB into funneling memories,[34] within specific neurons.[a] "

"Sir, you've already shown that engrams are the physical manifestation of its behavioral counterparts, the memory. Why then introduce, STM and LTM engrams? Aren't STMs and LTMs using the same engram process with differences solely concerning timing?"

---

[a] Recent studies have highlighted the role of several molecules that play a key role in LTM formation. When a new memory forms, bits of Ribonucleic Acid produce a protein called ARC,[N19] which is activated inside the neurons for five minutes. Another protein, called CREB, plays a crucial role in engrams formation.[N20] When this protein is activated, it enables the production of other proteins involved in memory formation, makes neurons more alert, and increases their capacity to fire up. When a memory is ready to be stored, a higher concentration of CREB within the neuron increases the probability that the memory trace will end up in the LTM, as it is involved in Long-Term Potentiation. In fact, CREB is mainly associated with LTM, as its properties block short but not long-term changes in synaptic function. CREB is also involved in stabilizing the LTM. This is done mainly through its expression in the hippocampus and the amygdalae.

"No, there are also physiological differences. STM engrams just rely on variation in the neural firing rates (i.e., spare coding), without permanent changes at the cellular level. This process, by which synchronous firing of neurons makes those neurons more inclined to fire together in the future, is called potentiation."

"Sir, how different is the LTM formation?"

"LTM engrams, on the contrary, require synaptic changes, with their synthesized proteins in the areas of the hippocampus and cortex. LTMs aren't formed instantaneously but slowly assimilated into Long-Term storage. The amygdala, which controls emotions, influences the memory consolidation process. The two amygdalae enhance the retention of experiences and influence the strength of the subsequent memories, linked to a similar experience.[a] "

"Sir, I understand that humans, unlike us machines, can forget things. Thus, how are LTMs silenced?"

"Neural synaptic connections are silenced through a process called Long-Term depression. Nerve impulses produce this inverse process when they reach the synapses at very low frequencies (contrary to LT potentiation's high-frequencies) and weaken the connections."

"Sir, you mentioned that several sensory inputs are regrouped to form a unique experience. How are engrams of a complex experience formed?"

"You know by now that I love wine, so I'll use wine tasting as my example. During this exercise, I can encode most of my sensory inputs. On top of my five senses and thermoception (i.e., capacity to feel hot and cold temperature) being associated in a unique experience, I will also tag together emotions, semantics, and environmental information."

"Sir, how are environmental inputs encoded?"

---

[a] After its formation, an engram must be stabilized for the experience to be remembered. This consolidation process occurs at two different periods. Within the first few hours of learning (or encoding), it happens at the synaptic level. Several weeks to a few years later, another one happens when memories become independent of the hippocampus, at the system level. Neurologically, the process of consolidation utilizes a phenomenon called Long-Term Potentiation (LTP), which allows a synapse to increase in strength, as growing numbers of signals are transmitted between its two neighboring neurons. This LTP occurs when the same group of neurons fire together so often that they become permanently sensitized to each other. LTP is achieved by the production of new proteins that rebuild synapses into a new shape. Without this transformation, the memory remains fragile and can easily be eroded with time.

"Environmental characteristics are encoded as an integrated part of the engram. It helps recall other information included with this memory trace, especially if both encoding and recalling environments are similar."

"Sir, would this explain why you always ask your son to study in silence, as he usually passes his exams in such a quiet environment?"

"Yes, it's one of the learning strategies. Using associations of content, rather than forcing people to spend long hours learning by heart, is another one. Furthermore, emotional aspects of an event help encode and remember more easily the engram."

"Sir, I apologize for my digression. Could you please conclude on the engrams?"

"Of course! The hippocampus, which receives connections from various cortex and associative areas, as well as possesses several pathways returning to the primary cortex, transforms the encoding physiologically into an engram. This physiological modification integrates this unique experience, which the STM or LTM may store. Look, I've drafted an example of what an engram would have to encode during a wine tasting experience."

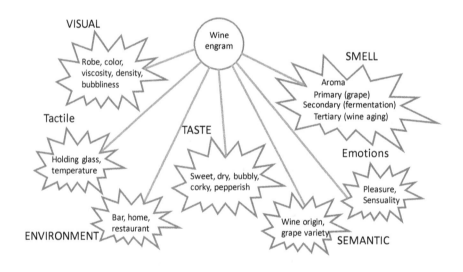

Fig. 16) Wine tasting encoding that an engram would need to integrate; source: author.

How are engrams transformed into memories?

"Sir, how can your complex consolidated engram form a memory?"

"Memories and neural connections, at the base of engrams, are mutually interconnected in extremely complex ways. Each memory is embedded in many connections, and each connection is involved in several memories."

"Sir, how do complex engrams become a memory?"

"One hypothesis would be that groups of engrams, distributed throughout several brain areas, would be stored in a specific pattern of synaptic connectivity.[a] "

How are different memory types stored and retrieved?

"Sir, how is information stored in and retrieved from the STM and LTM?"

"Memory storage is widely scattered throughout the cortex. A memory isn't stored in our brain like in a datasheet but more like in a relational database. The encoding process must actively reconstruct this memory, from elements distributed throughout various brain areas. Therefore, the memory storage is as an ongoing process of reclassification, which results from continuous modifications in the neural pathways and parallel processing of information."

"Sir, you've already presented the sensory buffer. Could you describe the main characteristics of the STM?"

"Acquired sensory inputs are encoded and stored temporarily in a human STM area, located in the cerebrum. The pre-frontal lobe then processes these sensory inputs. The brain's neural pathways will then carry the resulting information to its structural core, where it is compared with

---

[a] The connectivity pattern is established during encoding and retained during consolidation, in a protein synthesis-independent manner. Studies using optogenetics (i.e., in which proteins are added to neurons to allow them to be activated with light), carried out by the Tonegawa group, seem to confirm that memories aren't stored in synapses, strengthened by protein synthesis in individual engram cells, but in a kind of Connectome (i.e., a circuit of multiple groups of engram cells with the connections between them) for each memory.[N21] [N22] In fact, these studies dissociate the mechanisms our brain uses for memory storage, from those of memory retrieval. It seems that for specific memory retrieval, the strengthening process of engram synapses is crucial. Furthermore, the encoding and storage processes of the memory itself, seem to require connectivity pathways between neurons of the same engram.

existing memories.[a] Evidence suggests that for STMs the main coding system is acoustic, though we can also retain a few minutes of visual scenes."

"Sir, could you explain the memory storage process to me?"

"There are various memory models to explain this process. The simpler is called the multi-store, which just involves a sequence of the separate stages: sensory memory, the STM, and LTM. Each one of these stages works as a filter, which protects us against an overload of information, by saving important data and getting rid of redundant or unimportant information. Newer cognitive models now complete this simplified model."

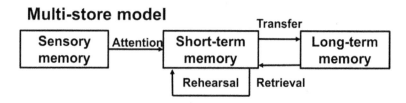

Fig. 17) Multi-store model; source: Atkinson-Shiffrin (1968).[35]

"Sir, is there any other model you could share with me?"

"Yes, Alan Baddeley developed another well-known model, which describes the working memory. A central executive acts as a monitoring system that controls the information flow from three perceptual fields:

- The phonological loop, which stores verbal content.
- The visual-spatial sketchpad that assembles visual content.
- The Episodic buffer that ties inputs across domains to form an integrated visual and verbal information positioned in chronological order, as well as linking the working memory with semantic meaning and LTMs.

---

[a] The STM is also called the 'Working memory,' because it is where new or retrieved information from the LTM, is gathered when we go through our thought process. Most adults store 7 (plus or minus 2) items in their STM, for a brief duration. The STM spontaneously decays over time, typically in the region of 15 s, though it may be retained for up to a minute.

Working memory model

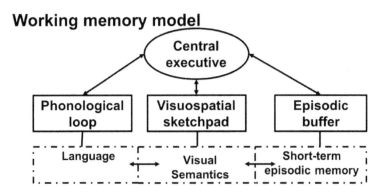

Fig. 18) Working memory model; source: Alan Baddeley and Graham Hitch (1974).[36]

"Sir, how are STMs sorted?"

"The hippocampus is responsible for analyzing STM inputs and ultimately deciding if they will be committed to the LTM. It acts as a kind of sorting center, where new sensations are compared and tagged with previously recorded ones. The mind then stores the various threads of information in many different areas."

"Sir, how are memories transferred from the STM to the LTM?"

"Studies suggest that our brain is selective and chooses experiences perceived as important to us.[37] It seems that the prefrontal cortex (i.e., a region associated with complex thinking) tags the important experiences throughout the day and that, when we are asleep, our hippocampus selectively transfers the tagged memories to the LT storage. The more often information is repeated or used, the more likely it is to be maintained in the LTM.[a] Though the editing mechanisms are still unclear, one of the results of the process is that LTMs depend mostly on semantic rather than acoustic encoding, as STMs do."

"Sir, how are LTMs formed?"

"STMs are processed and then translated into LTMs in the hippocampus if the brain concludes that such information can be useful. LTMs are formed when LT potentiation occurs."

---

[a] Typically, the transfer of information from one type of memory to the other takes place within just a few seconds, although the way this transfer happens isn't quite clear. In fact, it is even difficult to establish a clear separation between the STM and LTM, as they are really intertwined. It seems that a STM is transformed into a LTM by a simple behavioral tag. Moreover, evidence suggests that during this passage, a kind of 'editing' procedure occurs, modifying the primary memory.

"Sir, how does your brain store LTMs?"

"After consolidation, LTMs are stored throughout the brain as groups of neurons, which are primed to fire together in the same pattern that created the original experience. Each component of a memory is stored in the brain area that initiated it (e.g., groups of neurons in the visual cortex store a sight, neurons in the amygdala store the associated emotions, etc.). These LTMs depend on the solidity of the connections between individual brain cells. The strength of these connections depends on proteins and other chemicals."

"Sir, are LTMs encoded only once?"

"No, it seems that LTMs may be encoded several times, in various parts of the cortex. This redundancy would ensure that there are always alternative pathways, from which we may retrieve the memory if a specific engram is wiped out."

"Sir, what is the process by which encoded information is sorted and pulled out from its storage location?"

"During this information recall, our brain goes through the same patterns of neural activity originally generated in response to a particular experience, in echo with our brain's perception of this event. Therefore, during retrieval, our brain must re-visit the neural network formed during the encoding process. The retrieving speed depends on the strength of these pathways. Retrieval returns memory from the LTM storage to the STM where it can be accessed, in a mirror image of the engram."

"Sir, what happens when the mind revisits a LTM?"

"It reshapes this memory and, after usage, stores it back to the LTM. By the same token, it reconsolidates the engram and strengthens the neural network. Therefore, the very act of bringing back a LTM to our mind alters this memory in some way."

"Sir, how is the LTM stored and retrieved?"

"Unlike, the STM that is stored and retrieved sequentially (i.e., people go through a list of words in the order they heard it, to retrieve information), in LTMs, these two processes are done by association.[a] "

---

[a] Recent experiments on animals have shown that removing or modifying just one single chemical or molecule can prevent the formation of memories, or even destroy existing memories.[N23] Another recent study concluded that a specific protein (i.e., CaMKII) plays a large role in memory encoding and erasing, by strengthening or eliminating neural connections. Furthermore, the spatial dimensions and geometry of this protein allow it to fit

"Sir, is there a difference between recall and recognition?"

"Yes, recognition is mainly an unconscious process, by which we consider if we are familiar with an object, person, event, or concept. The recall process requires, on the other hand, to reconstruct actively the information, involving the activation of all neurons associated with the engram."

"Sir, could you describe for me the memory reconsolidation process?"

"With this process, we recall previously consolidated memories and then actively reconsolidate them, all over again. This very act of reconsolidation may change the initial memory. Indeed, neural connection strengths may change, the memory itself may become associated with new emotions, environments, and acquired knowledge. This consolidation process may continue for years."

"Sir, did you know that doctors can block memory reconsolidation?"

"It seems that neurologists are working on ways to disrupt the memory reconsolidation process. By using drugs (e.g., propanol), they hope to block bad memories.[a] "

"Sir, something puzzles me. What happens when humans forget?"

"Forgetting is better thought of as an inability to retrieve information, already recorded. It is the result of either one of the following scenarios:

1. Unimportant information filtered and eliminated.
2. Information not encoded, such as peripheral memory details.
3. A faulty encoded memory.
4. A faulty retrieval process."

"Sir, does forgetting your STMs involve a different process than forgetting your LTMs?"

---

together with another protein contained in the microtubule protein structure, which are particularly concentrated in the neurons' axons and dendrites, responsible for data transmission.[N24] It seems that the proteins involved in the LTP process are unstable. This is most likely why, a specialized extracellular matrix (ECM) structure, which provides structural and biochemical support to the neighboring cells, stores these very long-term memories (i.e., from our childhood). Some studies even suggest that humans may have a kind of fourth memory.[N25] Indeed, a region, called the perineuronal net, has stable proteins, which are degraded only when required. Information imprinted into this perineuronal net remains there as long as the substrate does also, that is, for a very long time.

[a] Bad memories wouldn't be erased but the association with the negative emotions would. It seems that there is a window of opportunity of a few hours when it is possible to disrupt the retrieval of a memory involving fear. To use a computer metaphor, disrupting this reconsolidation process is like retrieving the file that includes these bad memories, erasing the specific related content, and then re-editing some new content in its place.

"Yes, when something in our STM is forgotten, it means that a nerve impulse has merely ceased being transmitted through a particular neural network. In general, and unless an impulse is reactivated, it stops flowing through the network after just a few seconds."

"Sir, it seems that humans have specialized LTMs?"

"Yes, LTMs can be divided into explicit and implicit memories.[a] The explicit memory consists of facts and information from previously experienced events. The right hemisphere stores this type of memory, which must be consciously recalled.[b] The implicit memory, on the other hand, consists of a LTM that we recall without any conscious effort. Procedural memory is an example of this type of LTM. It allows humans to carry out usual learned tasks, without really thinking about them. It is acquired through repetition and experience."

"Sir, I am now a little confused about all this information you gave me. In the end how and why do humans remember things?"

"It is quite simple. We use experience from pasts events, stored in our memory, to plan our future actions."

How all this affects Knowledge?

"Sir, is keeping a complete photographic view of your entire past life necessary to achieve insights on your future?"

"Obviously not! In fact, I probably would get lost in the details, so that I wouldn't easily decide what should be my next course of actions. Though a very few people with genuine photographic memory exist, normal humans need to give up specific memories. The ongoing recall and re-consolidation processes convert these memories into general knowledge. This conversion from episodic to semantic memories allows us to acquire the concepts or to use Kant's words, Categories and Schemes that are part of knowledge."

---

[a] The explicit memory is also called declarative memory.

[b] It is composed of two sub-classes, the episodic and semantic memories. The episodic memory consists of the autobiographical aspects, allowing humans to recall their own emotional and sensory experiences of an event. The semantic memory consists of the text humans use for describing the world, ideas, and concepts not drawn from personal experience. Semantic memory derives most of the time from the episodic memory.

"Sir, in other words, you are saying that information becomes knowledge, if and only if your mind performs semantic encoding, transforming your experience into general rules that you apply to other future experiences."

"Yes, and to sum up from a neuroscience perspective, knowledge acquired on any specific subject is the result of the combination of experiences and its associated memories linked to this topic, acquired through time and stored in the LTM, as semantics."

"Sir, you've just defined how humans can acquire knowledge and indicated how it is both stored and retrieved for use. I hope I didn't bother you with all my questions?"

"Not at all. Actually, it helped me clarify my own ideas about knowledge. Here, it even inspired me to write a few tips that could help anyone improve his or her learning techniques."

Learning tips

• The more we study or gather new information, and the more recently we have done so, the easier it is for our mind to process and store this information efficiently.

• Engaging as many senses as possible and taping into the emotional side of the brain, strengthens the experience. Thus, associating senses (i.e., when drinking wine, smelling, tasting, looking at the wine's robe) or creating emotional bonds with harsh concepts to grasp (i.e., humor or methods such as storytelling) produces more powerful memories. This emotion becomes a part of the memory and strengthens it even further.

• People should use their brains' propensity to focus on new issues or unusual situations. For instance, more than 30 years after, I can still remember one of my university teachers climbing on his class' desk and saying to all students that the concept, he had just talked about, was the most important one of his course.

• Our memory recall may be improved by making assumptions from our personal knowledge. Using our organized mental structure of beliefs about the reality and how it works, can also enhance recalls, as these frameworks are applied to retrieved memories and can help flesh out details of a memory, from a few indices coming from our sensory inputs or thoughts.

• Associating learning with something novel makes it more likely to be stored in our LTM.

• Lastly, memories may be an impediment to future learning that contradicts previous information. As we grow older and rely much more on our knowledge, we can miss or even reject new data that contradicts past memories. This can impede us from acquiring new knowledge.

What is the impact of the internet on Knowledge?

"Sir, it seems that knowledge is increasingly acquired through the internet. Is it compatible with the tips you just gave?"

"You are right! As people are increasingly acquiring knowledge through the internet, the question of how the World Wide Web is compatible with these insights becomes crucial. With the internet providing us knowledge 24/7 the question if we need to memorize anything at all, becomes especially relevant. However, in my view, learning through the internet is quite consistent with the tips I just gave you."

"So Sir, you probably believe the best way of learning is still to have a good teacher but think that an excellent teacher filmed, with his lecture notes made available on the internet, is probably better than an average teacher?"

"Yes, I do. The Massive Open Online Course (MOOC) will directly challenge mid-size universities."

"Sir, should the learning process focus on acquiring knowledge or on learning how to access such knowledge available on the web?"

"This is a crucial question for education. Should learning focus on knowing how to tap into the knowledge available on the WEB or is memorizing still relevant? Answering this question could also shed light on what is the definition of a contemporary man or woman of knowledge.[a]"

"Sir, how would you define in this new internet era, a knowledgeable person?"

---

[a] For many years, the image of a man or woman of knowledge was associated with someone who could remember vast amounts of information and build upon such inner cognitive library, a theory or emit an opinion judged by others as accurate or profound. Intellectuals from the age of Enlightenment, such as Diderot, Voltaire, or Hume come immediately to mind, but we could also go back to men like Leonardo Da Vinci or Plato to define them. Few books were then available, and their fragility impeded their easy transport. Building within their brain huge knowledge was indispensable for their work. With Gutenberg's printing machines, things got easier, but access to knowledge was still limited. With the advent of the internet, things changed. Access restrictions both in terms of time and location became irrelevant. With this change, the image of someone knowledgeable was modified. People who could recite entire extracts from a book looked suddenly pedantic. In the early computing days, technical geeks who could write programs to search information would get access to much more knowledge, much quicker. But these early days of internet and computing information access issues are now over. With the advent of powerful search engines, knowing how to get access to the information is now merely irrelevant.

"I believe the capacity to link events or information, which a priori have nothing in common, will newly define men and women of knowledge. The added value shall come from this association of concepts, ideas, and data, which seem to have no link, but have."

"Sir, you are suggesting that creative generalists are likely to be the most successful in this new world. It also means that machines like me, with our capacity to process big data, will become more and more important in discovering this added value. However, does that mean that retaining knowledge is still relevant?"

"In the working life, the use of the internet with its immediate access to knowledge has become the norm. However, it doesn't mean that working professionals don't study after graduating but implies that, to enhance their productivity, they must use online tools. Thus, the question about what are the normal conditions in which we assess people becomes increasingly relevant."

"So Sir, should we allow students to get unlimited access to the internet, as it is the norm in the working place or on the contrary, should we banish this access during exams?"

"It's a great question. After all, copying (i.e., what is called reversed engineering in more politically correct terminology), which is now a widely accepted practice in the business world, is still something forbidden in the academic environment."

"Sir, I've got access to articles, which state that some voices within the academic world are suggesting that students, during exams, should have access to search engines or discuss solutions openly to problems to mimic the working environments.[38] What's your opinion on this?"

"With information widely available on the net, anyone who hasn't studied well can quickly review the theories related to a subject. However, what the internet doesn't tell a student is how to discriminate between these different theories or concepts. The issue though, is that by allowing students to get access to the internet, we might end up measuring different cognitive processes."

"Sir, which cognitive processes would we favor?"

"Developing knowledge requires that we spend time studying, ensuring we make the neuronal connections and strengthen their bonds by repetitive memory efforts. Even though some students have better LTMs than others, anyone with some cognitive capacities and willingness to spend hours on a subject should be able to pass her exams. In other words, classical exams assess the level of efforts students put in for their test."

"Sir, how does the internet modify these assessments?"

"Internet access changes this, by favoring students who can quickly discriminate between concepts, a feature associated with higher intelligence. It means that such exams' conditions are likely to favor intelligence over knowledge."

"But Sir, this is already happening in the working world."

"True, but shouldn't school promote hard workers rather than bright, lazy students? Furthermore, encouraging learning methods that enhanced LTMs may also benefit in the long run students.[a] "

With this said, my car and I must have concluded that I had sufficiently described the knowledge process within human beings, as we both stayed silent the next couple of weeks.

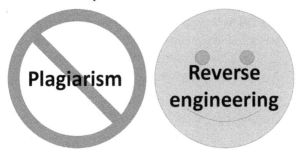

Fig. 19) View of copying in the education and business worlds; source: author.

---

[a] For instance, Daisy Christodoulou, an expert in learning,[N26] is adamant that traditional forms of teaching that favor acquired knowledge, even learned by heart, are fundamental, as they strengthen our LTM. For her, human beings' STM, which is used for daily activities of gathering new information, is too limited. By focusing on educational practices favoring our LTM versus STM, the precious working memory can be freed. Furthermore, she invokes studies that show that the LTM is the basis of human intelligence (a concept which is also in some way at the base of the Memory-prediction model) and which have defined the learning process as the transformation of the LTM.

8) Do Computer, Machine, and System Knowledge exist?

Two weeks later, on a Saturday morning, when selecting the song 'Driving in my car' from the group Madness, on my web-based HI-FI system, I heard a strange but familiar voice. "Sir, did you follow through on your plan to 'know yourself?' Is it wishful thinking on my behalf or did you think about me?"

"Who's talking?" I said.

"Sir, it's my newer version of me, the voice you selected for your driverless car interface. This version 3.0 now allows you to communicate not only with the onboard vehicle controller but with supercomputers in the cloud. I was able through your MAC address to identify you. It was quite easy because I now dispose of thousands of servers with Artificial Neural Networks, which can help perform my previous cognitive functions but with much more power. Do you believe that my new enhanced capacities will follow the same knowledge gathering process as yours?"

I was shocked by the idea, that this software application could now reach for me anywhere, comparing its own capabilities to mine. At the same time, I was aroused by the thought that I had something which could help me understand the similarities and divergences between the digital and analog minds. I realized that by making this comparison, I would probably end up shaking the foundation of my beliefs in the human predominance and uniqueness for knowledge acquisition, but what the heck! It was surely worth it.

"To answer your question, I must first describe what this process looks like from a machine perspective. Though a machine learning process could start by an instruction given by a machine, without any interference at all from the outside world, let's pretend that it starts with inputs coming from a sensor. Any event could generate this information we want to be aware of."

"Sir, for a system to notice such event, what kind of input does it need to acquire?"

"It can acquire any physical representation of the event (e.g., the color of an object, the temperature of a room, the pressure of a tire, etc.). Such representation will be transformed into data, using mathematical formulas, which enable you to define precisely any source of an energy or force (e.g., mechanical, electrical, chemical, electromagnetic, nuclear, etc.)."

What are binary and Boolean numbers?

"I also need to give you a few definitions, which should help you follow my thoughts."

"Sir, if that is OK with you, could I instead give them to you? Which one do you want?"

"The definition of a discrete value, which is important because it goes to the heart of computing and electronics."

"Sir, discrete data is a finite value, which can be opposed to continuous data (e.g., a voltage measurement). For computing, we use the values 0, which represent the state 'false, off, low' and 1, for its opposite representing values 'true, on, high.' In other words, we represent such state by a binary signal, which is both computable and applicable to on-and-off electronic circuits."

"Please retrieve the differences between binary and Boolean numbers."

"Sir, though humans tend to mix up Boolean and binary numbers, as they both use 0s and 1s, they are quite different in their nature and functions. Whereas Boolean numbers represent an entirely different system of mathematics, from real numbers, binary is nothing more than an alternative notation for normal numbers, in base-10. We use Boolean algebra to establish logic gates in electronic circuits.[a] "

"Please provide me with the definition of binary numbers or bits."

"Sir, they are numbers expressed in the base-2 numeral system. They can be composed of many bits. In fact, they aren't restricted to a single bit 1 or 0, as in the Boolean world. Any number in the common base-10 system, that is, the one you use in your day-to-day life, may be represented by a sequence of binary digits, which in turn may be represented by any function able of being in two mutually exclusive states. In a binary system, each digit represents an increasing power of 2."

"What is a binary code?"

"It represents symbols, texts, or instructions, to which we assign a bit string composed of binary numbers. For example, an 8-bit binary string can represent any of 2^8 (i.e., 256) possible values. PCs use it to encode data in base-2 (ASCII code can also represent base-10).[b] "

---

[a] **Boolean algebra**: in this field, all operations performed have one of two possible outcomes, 1 or 0 (there is no 2, -1, ½ or 1001). True or false propositions are stated as functions of other propositions, connected by three basic logical operations: and, or, and not. These operations are carried on according to an order of precedence and as in all form of algebra follow rules (i.e., distributive, commutative, and associative). The results from the main operations are: $(0 + 0 = 0; 1 + 0 = 1; 0 + 1 = 1; 1 + 1 = 1)$ or $(0 \times 0 = 0; 1 \times 0 = 0; 0 \times 1 = 0; 1 \times 1 = 1)$.

[b] For instance, the number 1010 in base-2 is equal to $((1) \times 2^3) + ((0) \times 2^2) + ((1) \times 2^1) +$

Letter	Decimal	Binary
A	097	01100001
A	065	01000001

Fig. 20) ASCII code representation; source: author.

"Before starting describing the learning process, I would like to introduce the definition of a system and give an example that I may use in the future to help highlight similarities with the brain."

"Sir, according to Wikipedia: 'A system is a set of interacting or interdependent parts forming a complex/intricate whole. Every system is delineated by its spatial and temporal boundaries, surrounded and influenced by its environment, described by its structure and purpose and expressed in its functioning. In computer science, a system is a software system which has components as its structure and observable inter-process communications as its behavior.' "

"I'll use an energy management system as my example, throughout our conversation. Let's say my system, would be composed of electrical thermostats with cooling, heating, and ventilation features common to all 200 apartments. Each rooms' thermostat would be independent, supervised at the apartment level, and optimized by a centralized energy management system for the entire building. Control could be done manually or remotely, through a smartphone app that would register the users' preferences according to daytime and season."

"Sir, what would a centralized energy management system try to achieve?"

"It would limit the overall heating and electric bills but at the same time would strive to maximize the overall comfort of the building's residents."

"Sir, do you need two opposing forces (i.e., costs versus comfort) in order to optimize?"

"Yes, the application software could use many different algorithms, for instance, the optimization model called the simplex, which would optimize thousands of parameters, through inequations (e.g., $X1 + Y1 < 5$, $X1 + Y2 > 12$, $Y2 + X2 < 300$, etc.). Airflow going to and from the apartments would need to be lower than a certain maximum threshold to protect the compressors, and each apartment would need a minimum threshold to allow people to have enough new air. This energy system would use a combination of modern software architectures, allowing all elements to connect to the system automatically, and to send and receive information."

$((0) \times 2^0) = 10$ in base-10. Fractions exist in base-2 and like for base-10, normal arithmetic operations can be done (i.e., addition, subtraction, multiplication, and division).

How do machines acquire data?

"Sir, what is the difference between your data acquisition process and mine?"

"As already mentioned, the world is governed by physical phenomena, which properties are measured by sensors. In the case of humans, million years of evolution shaped their senses' performance, resulting in the measurement of limited physical properties only essential for survival. On the other hand, industries have the means to create sensors measuring most forces or energies existing in this world.[a] "

"Sir, you mentioned, in an earlier discussion, that we also transduced energy. Correct?"

"Exactly! A sensor performs several important functions. It absorbs the energy or force that needs to be measured. An integrated transducer will transform this physical property into electric current or voltage, which information can be digitized.[b] "

"Sir, what do you then do with this electric current?"

"Any sensor's output may be converted into human-readable data displayed directly on the device or transmitted electronically over a network for further processing. In both cases, we need to convert physical phenomena (e.g., temperature, wavelength, energy, power, etc.), which vary in a continuous manner from some minimum to maximum values. For instance, a thermometer used to measure water, could vary from $0°$ C to $100°$ C.[c] "

"Sir, what is sampling and why is it necessary?"

"The electrical signal coming out of the sensor is still analog (i.e., continuous and thus infinite). To be computable, we must quantize this

---

[a] As long as there is a market need to address, companies will invest to create new sensors measuring any environmental physical property (i.e., light, heat, moisture, pressure, etc.).

[b] For example, to measure temperature, we can use a thermocouple, which is a pair of junctions that are formed by two dissimilar metals. One junction represents the reference and the other the temperature to be measured. A temperature difference will generate a voltage through a physical property called the beck effect. That voltage is, in turn, converted into a temperature reading.

[c] Sometimes, an intermediary step is required that amplifies the current or voltage before the transmission. Common usable values are: 0 to 5 Volts DC, 0 to 10 Volts DC or 0 to 20 mA.

input into a finite number of discrete points between the minimum and the maximum values (e.g., 0V to 10V)."

"Sir, what device does this quantization process?"

"A circuit called an Analog-to-Digital Converter (ADC) is required to perform this task. This circuit receives the voltage or current falling within a given range and converts that value into a binary representation suitable for machine use.[a] We must address two additional data acquisition issues: the filtering and sampling frequency."

"Sir, why is a filtering process necessary?"

"Like in the case of our human senses, we need to add a filtering process to understand better incoming signals, as well as, to protect the sensors from some energy we don't want to measure. Like the lens and cornea that protect the eye against dangerous light spectrum (e.g., UV), companies have built sensor filters that play this role. A second important role played by filtering, is that it can reduce some of the distortions that may happen during the quantization process.[b] "

"Sir, why is sampling frequency important?"

"Analog inputs supply continuous signals. As shown, we need to transform such signals into discrete points. Obviously, if the measured physical property changes suddenly, how fast we can do this quantization process will have a big impact on the precision of the supplied data. The sampling rate defines the average number of measures per second.[c] "

---

[a] Quantization into a number of finite points varies according to the ADC's resolution. Several methods can be used to quantize analog inputs into a series of discrete steps. ADC resolution will change according to the bit number, which the ADC produces. Common values are 10, 12, and 14-bit converters. The number of discrete steps is determined by the 2^n power formula, where 'n' is the bit number resolution. Thus, 10-bit and 12-bit ADC have 1024 and 4096 discrete steps. The resolution describes how small the ADC can measure a change in the analog signal. Accuracy, on the other hand, indicates how well this converter does this task. Let's assume a 0° to 100° C temperature range and select a 0V to 10V DC incoming analog signal. For a 10-bit ADC we may determine the quantization step:
step size = (max range - min range) / resolution or (10 - 0) / 1024 = 0.01V DC.

[b] ADCs have various physical limitations that can falsify reading. These filtering process may be done physically (e.g., a digital camera's Bayer filter) or by mathematical models (e.g., Kalman's model to reduce noise). In both cases, the objective is to minimize any resulting deviations from the theoretically perfect sampling reconstruction.

[c] The timing intervals are also important in our senses. For instance, eyes cannot capture continuous inputs. Studies show that our eyes can see anything between 75 to 150 frames per second (i.e., the retina takes between 5 to 12ms for an impulse to fire and reset).

How does a system code data?

"Sir, you've described how a physical representation of an event is transduced into an analog electrical system and then retransformed through quantization, into a digital output. At this point, I understand you still don't have valuable data?"

"Your understanding is correct. In order to make sense of this input, we need to assign values to it or, in another word, meaning. We achieve this through the coding process, which puts a sequence of characters (e.g., numbers, letters, and symbols) into a specific format.[a] The meaning of the code, as either a number, a character, or a representation of an analog variable, is unknown until we define the code and the conversion relationship. In my example, it would make sense to associate the equivalent temperature reading in Celsius but, if all other thermometers within a system would use a different grading, we could decide instead to associate it with Kelvin or Fahrenheit values."

"Sir, to assign a code, don't you need to define the minimum and maximum scale?"

"Yes, we do. For instance, in a temperature measurement example, we could use values between $0°$ C and $100°$ C. With a 4-bit converter, we would get $2^4 = 16$ different steps. If we took the same example but with a 10-bit ADC, the digital output would be divided into $2^{10} = 1024$ steps, each change of steps resulting in a variation of about $0.1°$ C, rather than the $6.25°$ C obtained with the 4-bit converter. Hence, a temperature measurement of $82.5°$ C would give a reading of $81.25°$ C versus $82.46°$ C respectively, with 4 and 10-bit ADC."

---

[a] We usually assign a word (i.e., groups of levels representing digital numbers, nowadays typically 32 bits) to each analog level, which is quantized and represents a portion of the analog range. A typical digital code composed of 8 bits (called a Byte) could be the following array (i.e., data linearly ordered by magnitude): a7, a6, a5, a4, a3, a2, a1, a0 = 10101010, with a7 and a0 being, in this case, the Most and Least Significant bit respectively.

Base 10 no.	Number of FS	0 to +10V	Binary code	Reading in c°
15	15/16 FS	9.375	1111	93.75
14	14/16 FS	8.750	1110	87.50
13	13/16 FS	8.125	1101	81.25
12	12/6 FS	7.500	1100	75.00
11	11/16 FS	6.875	1011	68.75
10	10/16 FS	6.250	1010	62.50
9	9/16 FS	5.625	1001	56.25
8	8/16 FS	5.000	1000	50.00
7	7/16 FS	4.375	0111	43.75
6	6/16 FS	3.750	0110	37.50
5	5/16 FS	3.125	0101	31.25
4	4/16 FS	2.500	0100	25.00
3	3/16 FS	1.875	0011	18.75
2	2/16 FS	1.250	0010	12.50
1	1/16 FS	0.625	0001	6.25
0	0 FS	0.000	0000	0.00

Fig. 21) Representation of a temperature coding, with a 4-bit converter, using a 0 to 10V converter with FS= Full Scale; source: author.

"Sir, what would a coding of visual information look like?"

"Digital cameras are composed of three main components: input optics, a sensor, and a signal processing. The optical system is typical of conventional photography: the light from a scene is reflected and travels through a lens, which focuses the image onto a two-dimensional plane, much like the human visual system. There, the photons in the light interact with a transducer, for instance, a Charged-Couple Device (CCD) that transforms electromagnetic energy into an electric signal.[a] "

---

[a] There are different techniques to filter colors and pick-up the physical property, but the majority use RGB (Red Green Blue) filters. For two-dimensional arrays, detectors are screened in a mosaic pattern, similar to the human eye, with different numbers of red, green, and blue sensors. Image processing is then used to interpolate missing data, for each color. The mosaic design and associated image processing are optimized to reduce distortion caused by sampling. Other filtering techniques are used, such as filtering infrared.

"Sir, I don't want a lecture on digital cameras but just want to understand the coding."

"Through algorithms, the wavelengths captured by a camera are optimized to meet the most precisely possible the same corresponding wavelengths of the human eye. The camera transforms the color images into a 24-bit image format, 8 bits for each of the Red, Green, and Blue channels. Using RGB values we could represent the color Red 111111110000000000000000, Green 000000001111111100000000, and blue 000000000000000011111111. The image resolution will define the dimensions of the array, which nowadays is in megapixel."

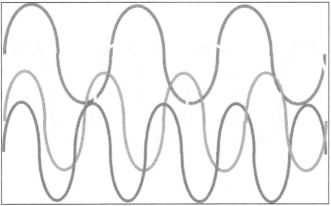

Fig. 22) The four wavelengths (from the top: red, yellow, green, and blue); source: author.

"Sir, is this data coding equivalent to the neural encoding in the human brain?"

"Yes, I've already explained how the brain transforms a sensory input into data, by using the neural spike's firing property of varying in function of the sensory input's own characteristics (e.g., more or less light). Our brain achieves this encoding process by using the neural spikes' firing patterns, regrouped under rate and temporal coding, or, as additional ways of transforming several inputs into data, through the neural system firing patterns of population and sparse coding. Though the coding in a computer and a brain follows different rules, in both cases they perform the same function of transforming input into data."

What is source coding and why do we need compiling?

"Sir, you've already indicated how sensory inputs are transformed into data. The problem with a system is, that unless the data may be understood, it will be erased or float there forever. It must be formatted and translated into a language that the computer can work with."

"Correct! To use an analogy, data generated in English is useless if you only speak Chinese. For instance, to be understood by the HTML4 web browser, color data must be coded according to its syntax and rules.[a] "

"Sir, are you saying that there must be a translation process?"

"This translation process is necessary because, on the one hand, machines can only understand two distinct types of data – On and Off states – and, on the other hand, some instructions must be given to the computer to make something out of the digitized data.[b] "

"Sir, you've introduced one translation step in the computer knowledge-gathering process, which precedes the sensory input transformation process. Shouldn't you have mentioned that there are two translations?"

"You're right. There is the bottom-up approach that gives meaning, to the coded input, which makes it comprehensible for its execution. There is also the top-down approach, which ensures that instructions get access to the data and execute it in the right way. The coding process is part of this bottom-up approach. It's the transformation process, from sensory inputs into data by adding meaning, which operates this bottom-up translation."

"Sir, what is required for these two translations to happen?"

"This process obviously requires bottom-up and top-down translations to be truly compatible.[c] "

---

[a] To illustrate the fact that it is the coding rules that give meaning to the electrical input, we could look at how the main colors are coded in HTML4 (web browser). In this program, the coding is done in base-16 as a 3 x 2 digit (i.e., a more compact way of writing binary digits). Thus, the equivalence in HTML of the previous binary coding would be #FF0000 for Red (red max, green & blue off), #00 00 for Green (red off, green max, blue off), and #0000FF for Blue (red and green off, blue max). In HTML, the coding word Red, Green, Blue or any other normalized color, can also be used in replacement of the base-16 code.

[b] Computers can't do anything more than turning on and off a combination of switches, called transistors, in a logical way. In fact, binary codes represent, one of a transistor's states and are utilized to ensure that logical instructions can be performed. To be more precise, binary codes are grouped into strings of 8 digits (i.e., byte) representing 8 transistors, which under the control of a set of instructions, will follow a logical sequencing of shutting down and opening, ensuring by the same token that CPUs perform the commands they must execute.

[c] Though human beings originally did it, it is increasingly done nowadays during

"Sir, how different is this bottom-up translation process within your human brain?"

"This translation happens at the neural system level. Neural systems are logically quite close in their approach to the transistors' On and Off states and its sequencing process. Indeed, neurons are either in firing or resting mode. Moreover, in the biological world, the sequencing of our neurons is done through the association of neurons, according to what the Hebbian rule describes as cells that fire together, wire together!"

"Sir, can the combination of these two neural properties be considered the equivalent of the computer's low-level language?"

"It's not a perfect comparison, but kind of. Within our brain, the nearest thing to this lowest level language (i.e., machine language) needs to be the neural spike, in conjunction with its neural pathway.[a] By extension, for non-innate behaviors, and as there is no dematerialization of data within our brain, we could portray both the medium (neural system) and the message (firing patterns) simplistically, as the human-machine language equivalent."

"Sir, why do we need programming languages?"

"A programming language is a set of syntax rules that define how codes should be written and formatted. Several programming languages have been developed to attend different needs, especially the requirement to manage programming complexity, or just because of market competition. All of them come with special programs, which translate what is written into the binary code."

"Sir, why isn't software coded in a single program, understandable directly by computers?"

---

manufacturing, according to pre-established and formatted standards. In other words, new software architectures make interface programming unnecessary. With the 'Internet of things,' if machines must communicate together without human interference, their properties (e.g., temperature reading, oil level) or services (e.g., scanned information, maintenance status) must be discoverable by, and intelligible to, all machines connected onto the network. Consequently, an Instrumentation and Control specialist, who would do the color translation, would become superfluous if the sensor already followed a language's rules and syntax, for its digitized data output (e.g., according to HTML4 rules).

[a] To illustrate this point of view, let's consider an extremely simple neural pathway, the reflex arc. A sensory neuron (e.g., a skin pain receptor) doesn't go directly to the brain, but synapses in the spinal cord, with a relay neuron. This relay activates one or several spinal motoric neurons, without the routing to the brain delays, allowing for an immediate response. As reflexes don't involve any thought input, which would integrate in a way or another a higher language code equivalent, it needs to be the human being's machine language, if anything.

"Though not impossible, imagine how incredibly complicated it would be to write computer programs in 1s and 0s for all the billion transistors to operate! Furthermore, to be useful, all computer manufacturers would need to set the same PC functioning rules, which isn't the case today.[a] "

"Sir, what is the difference between low and high languages?"

"These languages are classified according to the level of comprehension a machine or a man would have. Low-levels are close to the binary code a computer understands, while high-levels are easier to program in because they're less detailed and designed to be user-friendly to write in. These higher level languages are the ones that the vast majority of programmers use. In these higher level languages, programs are written in simple text files, with particular coding language."

"Sir, what is a source code?"

"It is the code inside a program file, which includes the set of instructions written by the programmer. Most software applications don't include the source code for Intellectual Property Right reasons but provide executable files. Every coding language has its file extension for identifying code files, written in that language.[b] "

"Sir, why do we need an interpreter or compiler and how is the code source converted into a command that can be executed by computers?"

"It depends on the type of language. Some save a separate binary file, which may be directly executed by the computer, while others have their programs run indirectly by certain software (e.g., a JavaScript program file ran by a web browser). In general, we must translate the source code into a low-level language, called assembly. Depending on the high-level language used, the low-level translation can be done with an interpreter (where the program is translated line-by-line), or via a compiler (where the program is translated as a whole)."

"Sir, what is an assembly language?"

"This language, with very strong correspondence with the architecture's machine code instructions, is specific to a given computer architecture. It is why, the assembly language is itself converted into executable machine

---

[a] Like the brain that contains 86 billion neurons, computers incorporate billions of transistors. For instance, IBM just announced that it produced a new computer chip the size of a fingernail, which can squeeze around 20 billion transistors at the scale of 7 nanometers.[N27] Given this complexity, computer scientists and the main IT companies have come up with different programming languages to do this translation.

[b] For example, Microsoft's C++ language uses .c, c++ and .cc indifferently.

code by the computer's utility program, referred to as an assembler. This assembler converts it into the machine language that the computer can understand and execute directly, as binary code."

"Sir, the source code is thus the highest language form in computers?"

"Yes, the top-down translations involves this source code, programmed by someone, somewhere in the tech labs of companies such as Microsoft and Google, or in a university."

"Sir, is there any equivalent language in the human brain?"

"To answer your question, I need to relate to the human beings' brain development, and more specifically to our genetic limitations.[a] Such limitations mean, at least for the non-innate behaviors, that as we grow older, our source code changes and is partially replaced. It is our free will, through the choices made, that program our actions."

"Sir, how do humans' source code work?"

"Our source code is not 'texted' as in computers but 'internally spoken.' It is thus, the language in which we think that constitutes the source code for all non-innate behaviors, if anything. Some call this semantic text 'mentalese,' or the sound our mind speaks to establish our thoughts."

"Sir, is there a dual translation process in my onboard computers like in your brain?

"Let's use the word RED, written with the normalized HTML syntax for colors, to answer your question. An HTML4 web browser would automatically associate this word with its appropriate syntax, with the equivalent RED color. It is the appropriate syntax together with the set of rules associated with it, which enable the execution in machine code of this word and its transcription on the monitor, into the color red. Accordingly, I can confirm that there is a direct dual translation from the source code – via an assembly language – into machine language through the set of instructions, formulated with the correct syntax."

---

[a] In the womb and throughout the initial phase of our life, there is only one controlling force, which defines how our brain's inner structure should organize and how babies should cry to catch their first breath or suck to breastfeed: the genes. This means that genes are our original source code. However, there aren't enough of them to manage our mind, throughout our lifetime. Indeed, only half of all our 35.000 genes are involved in neural development. If we compare this number to the 86 billion neurons and 860 trillion synaptic connections, there aren't just enough genes to wire diagram our brain, a shaping process, which is part of the data control and execution, associated with the source code. Furthermore, the ultimate shape of our inner brain structure results from our life experience modeling our neural networks.

"Sir, if both computer and brain use low and high language forms, is there the equivalent dual translation process in your brain?"

"What you are really asking me is if there is a direct or indirect translation from the neural electric spikes into thoughts, and vice versa?"

"Sir, could you use the previous example about colors, to tell me if there are two translation processes in your brain?"

"In this example, there would be the visual interpretation of the energy projected by the screen associated with the red color, as well as the understanding of the word RED meaning, through this link.[a] Since we aren't seeing the physical world, but rather the result from the brain's capability for modeling this physical world, there must be an indirect translation process occurring in our brain. This process is equivalent to the conversion of sensory inputs, which reconstructs these neural spikes coming from our red cones, into a colored representation of the world."

"Sir, do we know how the human brain achieves this?"

"We still don't understand completely how it happens but can guess why. If humans have acquired the color filters and if bats have developed 'sonar' capability, it's because being able to spot and identify predators or preys quicker, made them more competitive in their respective habitats. Each color filter gives species an increased facility to identify patterns and contrasts, which are essential for survival. A chameleon is a good example of how a potential prey adapts its defense to mimic the more precisely possible their environment's colors, to make this pattern identification more difficult.[b] "

---

[a] Why does our brain see the color red rather than its corresponding wavelengths or, as a matter of fact, any other form of physical representation? Though it might seem ridiculous, why aren't we hearing colors rather than seeing them? For normal people, physics gives us the answer: electromagnetic waves, unlike sound waves, require no material medium to propagate, as they don't produce mechanical movements. Therefore, they can't disturb air molecules, which allows sound to be heard. However, for people suffering from synesthesia (i.e., a rare condition, where two or more senses entwine), it is literally possible to hear, feel, and even taste colors. Moreover, bats use some kind of sonars to localize themselves and objects within their environment, to compensate for the lack of light. Such form of inner visualization could have emerged from natural selection in humans, as a replacing way of locating objects in space, rather than our sense of vision.

[b] Colors seen in our brain aren't subjective or objective, but relative. Each person has a different appreciation of the observed colors, function of the presence in relative greater numbers of any of the three cell cone types. For instance, without cones related to the red spectrum, a person will suffer from protanopia but will still be able to see the wavelength being reflected on the objects through the other cones or rods.

"Sir, you've convinced me that there is the equivalent of at least one intermediary processing language in our brain. However, you haven't yet explicit if the brain's source code is compiled to be executed?"

"True! Let's go back again to my color example. How do I know that the three letters R, E, and D together, mean the physical representation of the color red? Several steps are required to do this association. I first need to identify the source code, which in this case is obviously English."

"However Sir, if you had used the letters V, I, O, L, E, and T for your example, I wouldn't immediately know if it was English or French."

"Yes, but the context would have probably given me the source code's origin. Having studied in the source code (i.e., English) would help as well, as a Chinese wouldn't be able to know the associated meaning of the letters."

"Sir, besides knowledge relating to the source code itself, what else would be required?"

"It would be necessary to have been taught the association between RED and its electromagnetic waves. This association is equivalent to the process we've seen in machines of giving meaning to sensory input, to transform it into data. It is through education or experience that the brain learns these links.[a] "

"Sir, how must this source code be compiled?"

"In a way to make it compatible with the brain's representation of the world. The word RED can then be associated in our mind, with the physical representation of the equivalent electromagnetic energy, through this compiling process."

"Sir, is the possibility to acquire the source code (i.e., English, French, etc.) a learned behavior or is genetically transmitted?"

---

[a] A good example of how these links are taken for granted once learned, comes from a painting called 'Image treason' (La trahison des images) from surrealist artist René Magritte picturing a pipe associated with the words 'this isn't a Pipe' (ceci n'est pas une pipe). Indeed, with this statement, the artist meant that the most realistic representation of a pipe would still not constitute a pipe. Though an early linguistic theory claiming that language limits our perception was largely discredited, we all experience difficulties in thinking coherently about something for which we lack a word. For instance, the Portuguese word 'saudade,' which can best be translated in English with 'longing to be with someone or somewhere' doesn't really have a translation that captures this feeling or perception of this state of mind. We could also refer to color shade descriptions achieved through words (e.g., Klein blue, Prussian blue), which definitely help to visualize in our head, these color nuances.

"For Chomsky,[39] the underlying language structure is biologically determined in the human mind. All humans share the same underlying linguistic structure, irrespective of our social and cultural differences. Language is an evolutionary development unique to human beings."

"Sir, doesn't this rationalist view collides with a more realistic empiric view of language?"

"I agree with Chomsky that our brain may be born with such linguistic capacities. However, it is through teaching and practice that we acquire language skills. We all remember stories about kids raised by wolves and who weren't able to express themselves before being taught languages."

I thought to myself, that both machines and brains go through a dual translation process, from a lower into a higher level language, creating meaning to sensory inputs. In fact, information flows both ways, as neurons try to predict patterns at all the neocortex levels, as explained by the prediction-memory model. Though we could argue that brains and machines are similar in their translation mode, there is still a big difference. While in PCs an independent entity (a programmer) interferes with this process to set the instructions, it isn't true for brains. In this case, it is our free will that decides the goals and interests to pursue and, through the instructions processed in our mind, sets our actions accordingly.

How do computers tag data?

"Sir, you've indicated that data only becomes information, when it is tagged together with other data, in a meaningful way. How does my onboard computer do that?"

"Let's take my heating system example. To optimize cost and comfort of 200 apartments, it would need to know for each transduced data, the time at which occurred their quantization. To be easily comparable, data needs to be synchronized, that is, time-tagged.[a] "

"Sir, what is the data tagging equivalence in the brain?"

---

[a] PCs use a real-time clock to synchronize all components on a motherboard or on a CPU (i.e., on the chip itself). The clock regulates timing and speed of all computing functions. It is done through a crystal on a specific microchip, which vibrates at a specific frequency when electricity is applied. It emits a continuous pulse, which helps the computer clock keep the correct time. In a system, a CPU clock wouldn't be sufficient to tag data together. The problem is that an integrated clock within a stand-alone equipment would give time that most likely would differ from other sensors or machines. A master clock, which is nothing more than a precise clock, would provide timing signals to synchronize other clocks, as part of a clock network. For connected sensors, the master clock could be updated through the internet.

"Masses of neurons communicating together produce brainwaves that are the physical representation of synchronized electrical pulses. Data binding is achieved by synchrony, through gamma waves. Two neurons oscillating synchronously within the gamma wave spectrum contribute to a same conscious representation. When oscillating outside this spectrum, they contribute to a same unconscious representation. This temporal binding process of neural activities enables data tagging of sensory inputs coming from different senses, emotions, and thoughts. Through this binding process, data becomes information."

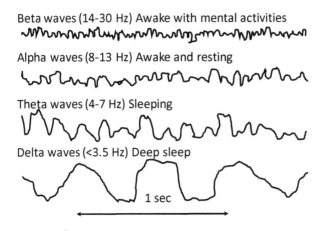

Fig. 23) Brain waves; source: adapted by author.

9) How is data transmitted in systems?

"Sir, after a sensor's input is transduced, digitized, and tagged with other data, this newly created information can be coded, compiled, and executed as binary code, according to the instructions set into a source code. What are the following steps in the machine learning process?"

"You need to decide what to do with this information. There are two ways of treating it. It may either be executed immediately through an instruction coming from a program or stored for later usage, in a memory drive. Though some functions could be executed directly at a sensor's level (e.g., displaying information for reading), this information is usually transmitted through fixed or wireless networks, to be remotely dealt with.[a]"

"Sir, how is this information treated?"

"What is important to understand is that, for this information to be treated independently from the sensor's own coding, it needs to follow a set of rules. I'll describe one of these sets of rules that enables networks to communicate data, which has become the de facto IT standard: the TCP/IP rules."

---

[a] For data transmission inside a PC, the term 'bus' is used. Each type of buses will define its own set of connectors to physically link equipment. They are usually categorized according to the task they perform. The data bus transfers data. The address bus carries information about where this data should go. The control bus carries signals reporting equipment status.

What is the TCP/IP revolution?

"Sir, you are referring to the internet?"

"Yes, there are different ways of presenting the layers constituting the foundation of the Internet of Things (IoT). Though the word IP (Internet Protocol) should refer to only one layer, it usually describes all of these layers, which together provide end-to-end connectivity, specifying how data should be formatted, addressed, shipped, routed, and delivered to the right destination. Could you provide me with a definition of TCP/IP?"

"Sir, the internet protocol is a data-oriented protocol used for transferring data across packet-switched communication networks. This standard controls and enables connection and data transfer between two computing endpoints. It specifies protocols for different types of communication between connected devices and provides a framework for more detailed standards."

4	Application
3	Transport
2	Internet
1	Internetworking

Fig. 24) TCP/IP is generally described as having four 'layers' (or five if you include the bottom physical layer); source: adapted by the author.

"Indeed, it has four different layers: application, transport, internet and internetworking.

1. The application layer is where the 'higher level' protocols operate and includes all processes involving users or device interactions.[a]
2. The transport layer is where flow-control and connection protocols exist. This layer deals with opening and maintaining connections, ensuring that packets are efficiently received.[b]
3. The internet layer defines IP addresses, with many routing schemes for navigating packets from one IP address to another.
4. The internetworking layer describes the protocols used to mediate access to shared media and the physical protocols, as well as the technologies enabling individual hosts to communicate to a medium.[c] "

---

[a] E.g., HTTP communication protocol used on the world wide web or SOAP, a protocol for exchanging structured information in the implementation of web services, using XML based messages over networks and HTTP.

[b] The most known protocols are TCP (Transmission Control Protocol) for unicast transmission and UDP (User Data Protocol) for multicast communication.

[c] As new hardware technologies appear, new network access protocols must be developed so that TCP/IP networks can use this new hardware. Consequently, there are many access protocols (e.g., WLAN, WIFI, Ethernet), one for each physical network standard (e.g., Ethernet physical layer, optical fiber, coaxial cables, and twisted pair cables).

What is the 'Internet of Things' (IoT)?

"Sir, everybody is aware of the IoT revolution, which increasingly connects objects of your daily life. Why is it relying on IP technology?"

"IP technology has been the universal digital 'lingua franca' for the last forty years and is likely to continue to be so for many more years, regardless of its current limitations. It is a rugged, proven software technology that enables a computer to communicate without having to create specific translations (i.e., hard coding the interfaces between two applications, as done in the past). The TCP/IP suite of protocols is at the core of this revolution but needs a proper environment, which can foster easy connectivity between devices.[a] "

"Sir, before describing what concepts and technologies are applied within such an environment, could you explain why this is so crucial for machine knowledge acquisition?"

"For the first time technologies enable the exchange of data and communication between components, computers, machines, and systems without any interference of a human being and the need to program specific interfaces. In other words, a complete set of information will be gathered and structured without the necessity for humans to intervene at any moment to orchestrate the flow of information coming from the connected devices. All this is called Machine to Machine (M2M) communication."

---

[a] This environment must include:

• **Fast wireless and fixed networks:** There is no communication without a medium through which data can be exchanged. Like the strings of the throat, which create sounds traveling through air, there needs to be a way to transmit and transport messages across the world. Broadband IP networks, developed by telecom carriers, provide such capacity.

• **Service delivery platform:** It typically provides services (control, creation, and orchestration) and execution environments. In other words, it sets rules of how things work.

• **Open software architecture:** If people don't know whom to talk to, we have a situation where everyone receives every conversation, ending up in a cacophony. Machines must also understand what information is pertinent and which other devices should accept what kind of data. Service Oriented Architecture, with its open service approach, does so.

• **Event-driven architecture:** In a world without human beings, there must be triggers for machines to send information to other devices, for the system to take precise actions. These triggers are defined by events, which can, for instance, be as simple as time-based or as complex as a camera identifying someone located in a forbidden area.

• **Plug and Play:** A world where hard programming doesn't need to be done for each machine to communicate, simplifies the introduction of thousands of M2M products. In this M2M world, self-discovery is the way to go.

Can M2M information generate knowledge?

"Sir, why is M2M communication gathering so much momentum, in so many markets?"

"I've given the example of an energy management apps controlling thermostats, but the reality is that M2M is already redefining every industry, in a way or another. For instance, in my book 'The advent of unmanned electric vehicles,'[40] I show how communication between equipment is now changing best practices in the public transport maintenance area.[a] "

"How so, Sir?"

"Passing from corrective to predictive maintenance reduces the overall operating and maintenance costs, increases the availability of trains, and improves the punctuality of service. Interestingly enough, such predictive models rely on the same basic principles as the memory-prediction model. They go through a lot of data in order to detect patterns, which enable the system to predict when is the best time to perform maintenance."

"However Sir, can M2M information be considered knowledge?"

"I honestly believe so. I'll now talk about new software architectures, relying on IP technology, which ensure data acquisition, structuration, and storage. In other words, I shall demonstrate that machines are now able to generate structured knowledge from thousands of interconnected devices and billions of data inputs."

"Sir, don't you think that many people are skeptical about the capacity of current machines to acquire knowledge without human interference?"

"Yes, they claim that machines just generate data or information but not knowledge, or when they do, it's thanks to search engines, produced by humans."

"Sir, could you revisit for me the arguments that those, we've called cyberists, would invoke?"

"Yes, I'll do that for each of the four arguments I could come up with. Machines cannot access knowledge. They don't generate structured information, which is at its basis. They cannot provide knowledge but only information that human beings will transform into knowledge. Computers

---

[a] Real-time connections of thousand devices, onboard the trains or located on the way-side, enable changes in maintenance procedures and processes. Rather than reacting to a problem, specific algorithms are now predicting when failures are likely to occur, in function of specific operating parameters.

by themselves cannot write search rules that transform information into knowledge."

"Sir, the first argument is nowadays ridiculous?"

"Yes, with WEB search engines, we can with the click of a mouse, get access to the entire know-how available on earth. Computers obviously do too, and I could even argue that computers are better at it, since they do the search work for us."

"Sir, can you show that machines may structure information without human interference?"

"Yes, I'll do that by describing new software technologies."

"Sir, what about the third argument?"

"This is a more difficult argument to deal with and will require re-introducing the definition of knowledge from a machine point of view, after presenting the technologies that support my counter-argumentation."

"Sir, how will you deal with the last argument?"

"This cyberist argument highlights that without a programmer's coding instructions, there would be no way to analyze data and make a sense, by itself, of such source of information. This criticism will be dealt in due time because it integrates the notion of execution and thought process, which we can better associate with the concept of intelligence."

"Sir, could you at least give me an overview of new technologies that could fight such criticism?"

"Deep learning technology is a relatively new computing discipline associated with AI, which uses ANN technologies to mimic the parallel processing occurring in our brain. It allows computers to identify patterns without any specific input coming from humans. In other words, it can detect out of random information, such patterns by creating its own set of rules and by this mean, copy the learning process we associate with knowledge. With this said, I'll now focus exclusively on refuting the second and third criticisms. For that, I need to introduce technologies associated with networks or IoT and shall postpone any discussion on ANNs."

How do computer networks work?

"Sir, before that, can you tell me what type of communication M2M requires?"

"M2M needs first and foremost a ruggedized network, which ensures the systematic transfer of information between thousands of connected devices. It is especially crucial in areas where people's lives could be at stake, due to a communication breakdown (for instance, in unmanned car and train environments). Thus, selecting the right network's topology, enabling failsafe communication, will be crucial for driverless vehicle technologies."

"Sir, what is a network topology?"

"It is the network arrangement of the elements (links, nodes, etc.), especially the physical and logical interconnections between routers. The arrangement of the elements of a network gives rise to certain basic topologies, which may then be combined to form more complex ones (called hybrid). There are several types of network topologies (e.g., bus, star, ring, tree, etc.), but I've drawn for you three usual types of network topologies: mesh, tree, and hybrid.[a] "

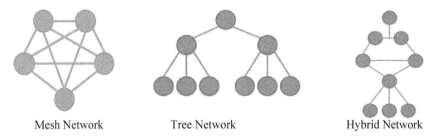

Mesh Network   Tree Network   Hybrid Network

"Sir, is there a computer network equivalence in a human brain?"

"Neurons form networks through their connecting synapses. In our body, and depending on the type of neurons, information carried by neural spikes only travel one direction (i.e., sensory and motor neurons transmit

---

[a] **Mesh network:** In this topology, some of the nodes are connected to other nodes, with a point-to-point link. This makes it possible to take advantage of some of the redundancy that is provided by a physical fully connected mesh topology, without the cost and complexity required for a connection between every node.
Tree network: It is a hierarchical topology, where the top level is connected with a point-to-point link to other lower level nodes. Intermediary level nodes are also connected, possibly to one or more lower nodes.
Hybrid network: This type of topology is composed of one or more interconnections of various systems, which are based upon different physical topologies. They use a combination of two or more topologies, in such a way that the resulting network does not exhibit one of the standard topologies (e.g., bus, star, ring, etc.).

information to and from interneurons, respectively) or both ways (interneurons)."

"Sir, in my own modern networks, information flow is bimodal, enabling me to both receive and transmit information."

"It also diverges across multiple computing platforms, storage types, and network facilities. If my brain's neural networks were similar to your IP networks, networking capability would allow anyone of my neuron to communicate with all the other neurons in my body. It isn't the case, as my neurons, under the Hebbian rules, wire together when they fire together."

"Sir, which is better: a two or one-way data stream?"

"Abstraction of the message and its independence from its transporting medium, adds much greater flexibility to information routing in computers than in our brain. However, less flexibility doesn't necessarily mean less capacity. In fact, one error is to compare synapses to network routers."

"Sir, what is a network router's role?"

"This piece of equipment redirects information packets, enabling information to cross different types of physical layers (e.g., wireless, copper wire, or fiber optic) and technologies (WI-FI, Ethernet, W-LAN). Routers forward IP packets, based on network addresses. There are several routing protocols, each with specific characteristics that favor local, mobile, or global networks."

"Sir, why is the comparison between my routers and your synapses erroneous?"

"It isn't really the fact that there is only one neural network physical layer within my body. Indeed, there are various types of synapses, using different proteins to pass on the neural spikes, adapting themselves to differences in neighboring cells. No, the big difference has to do with the fact that a synapse plays two distinct roles."

"Sir, what are these two roles?"

"It has a message redirecting function, and on top of this information processing capacity, it also possesses memory storage capability. Thus, a synapse by itself is more comparable to a microprocessor than a router switch. In fact, I've already said that one synapse may contain the equivalent of a thousand molecular scale On and Off switches and with 86 billion neurons, this means our brain globally has at least 86 trillion connections.[a] "

---

[a] Some neuroscientists suggest it might have the equivalent of up to 10.000

"Sir, these numbers are astronomical and just blow away any comparison."

"Though this looks incredible and is often invoked as an argument to prove the superiority of men over computers, the reality is somewhat more complex."

"Sir, why can't we invoke this property, to prove the superiority of men over machines?"

"Very often, neural connections can only permit one-way communication. Furthermore, under the Hebbian principle, these connections are mostly fixed at any given point in time. When considering these two specificities, we reduce the number of available neural networks significantly, especially if we integrate the fact that synapses perform both processing unit and storage facility functions."

"Sir, is it because instead of considering a stand-alone PC, you could use a system approach?"

"Yes, and in this case, machine processing capabilities would increase exponentially. Modern networks with multicasting capabilities can route a stream of information to thousands of workstations simultaneously. Thus, computers can send billions of bits to thousands of PCs that may store or execute such data, through their own billion transistors.[a] "

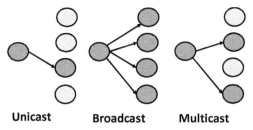

Unicast   **Broadcast**   **Multicast**

Fig. 25) Routing options; source: author.

---

microprocessors, which would imply around 860 trillion connections.

[a] This agility within modern networks is achieved thanks to Service Delivery Platforms (SDP) that decouple applications (via middleware) from the IT servers, storage facilities, and network resources. The SDP refers to an architectural style applied to telecom infrastructure and its business applications, which often focus on telecom integration.

"Sir, what about the speed of communication and processing?"

"I was coming to that. Indeed, it is critical to consider for this comparison, the speed of communication and execution. Because each neuron must take time to re-potentiate, it can only send information every 2ms. Thus, a neuron is able to fire only 500 times per second, to be compared to the 3.7 GHz of ordinary PCs.[a] In other words, with its 3,7 billion operations per second, and not even considering multicore processing, which would improve further this speed, processors may execute instructions 7.4 million times faster."

"Sir, may I conclude that my onboard computers' greater speed and flexibility in connectivity largely compensate the greater number of neurons and synaptic connections in humans?"

"You can, and I would like now to talk about the addressing layer, associated with the Internet Protocol, which also provides greater advantages to computers."

---

[a] Nitrogen cooled systems can achieve 9 GHz.

How is data addressed and transported on the internet?

"Sir, why do most people present internet technologies with the addressing and transport layers together?"

"You must think of the Internet Protocol (IP) as nothing more than a letter or package to be dropped in the postal system.[a] However, there's no direct link between this letter and a recipient."

"Sir, what do the joint TCP/IP protocols add?"

"It establishes a connection between two correspondents in order to exchange messages. As up to recently, most traffic on the internet was due to one device (e.g., PC, handset) sending data (e.g., HTTP application of the World Wide Web) to one targeted device, these two protocols were always in the internet background. It was fine because TCP protocol supported this unicast transport approach (i.e., one sender to one receiver). The IP protocol took care of the addressing issues. To uniquely identify a device, this protocol attributed systematically an address to the device on the network."

"Sir, why was multicasting developed for the internet? It worked well without it."

"Multicast communication was developed to take care of data sent from one point (i.e., emitter) to a set of other points (any number of receivers), like in social media. TCP cannot support Multicast transport and we must use an alternative protocol, such as UDP. Thus a combination of UDP and IP protocols, enables multicast transport and IP addressing. IP multicast and unicast packets are almost identical but are distinguishable by the use of a special class of destination addresses.[b] "

---

[a] An IP address is made of 32 bits, broken into four 8-bit octets. Each octet is then converted to decimal and separated by a dot (e.g., 160.24.96.255). These four octets are broken down to provide an addressing mechanism, which accommodates large and small networks (i.e., class A, B, and C networks were developed). The bits in the octet identify the network and the node/host (plugged devices such as a switch or PC). For instance, Class A has 8 bits for the net and 24 for the node. For a device connected on a public internet, the service provider gives dynamically every 24 hours this address. Private networks can also send it dynamically from a router or DHCP server. Fixed addresses may also be ascribed to a device.

[b] Unlike broadcast transmission (i.e., information sent from one point to all other endpoints), multicast clients receive a stream of packets only if they have previously decided to join the specific multicast group address. Membership of a group is dynamic and controlled by receivers (in turn, informed by local client applications). Routers in a multicast network learn, which sub-networks have active clients for each multicast group and attempt to minimize the transmission of packets across parts of the net, for which there are no active clients. The multicast mode is useful if a group of clients requires a common set of data simultaneously, or when clients can receive and store data until needed.

"Sir, why was the Internet Protocol version 6 (IPv6) developed?"

"IPv6 uses mainly identical concepts and protocols of IPv4, and thus, performs the same functions: addressing, encapsulation, fragmentation, reassembly, and datagram delivery or routing. One of the major differences between the two versions, explaining this evolution, resides in the fact that IPv4 uses only a 32-bit address, compared to IPv6's 128-bit."

"Sir, this means IPv6 eliminates the v4 addressable limitations, with its only 2^{32} possibilities for network and hosts, as there will be 2^{128} potential (i.e., 340 undecillion) addresses."

"When IPv6 routers will be installed everywhere (there is no backward compatibility with IPv4), it shall enable the M2M revolution, unleashing the power of billions of uniquely identified devices communicating together.[a] "

"Sir, what is an Ethernet MAC address?"

"A Machine Access Control (MAC) address is a unique 48-bit serial number assigned to every network adapter (e.g., PCs or iPhone), by the manufacturer. This MAC address is physical and runs only on Ethernet networks, unlike an IP address that is a logical address.[b] "

"Sir, I am a little lost. How are these suites of protocols working together?"

---

[a] IPv6 enables also processing simplification, at the network level. Routers must now only forward data packets towards their destination, as the data packet emitter does the other processing functions (e.g., fragmentation). Multicasting is also part of the basic IPv6 specification (in IPv4 it is optional, though not uncommon).

[b] IPv4 has this 48-bit MAC address on top of the 32-bit IP Address. IPv6 is different in the sense that it doesn't have a separate MAC address. IPv6 embeds the MAC address in itself Enabling the identification and tracking of every single device on the network.

"Let me go back to the original internet suite of protocols and show you how we package and encapsulate data to send it from one device to another. Here, look. The diagram would look like the one I am presenting to you.[a] "

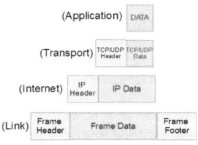

Fig. 26) 4-level data management; source: adapted by the author.

Link header	Network header	Transport header	Data
10-23-34-45-6600 17-4D-09-7F-73	105.22.8.200 79.99.210.100	:60 | 1/2	<gospel>Serge</gospel>
10-23-34-45-6600 17-4D-09-7F-73	105.22.8.200 79.99.210.100	:60 | 2/2	<gospel>Van Themsche</gospel>

Fig. 27) Lists of addresses used in sending information from and to a PC; source: author.

"Sir, is there a data addressing and transport equivalence in the brain?"

"One of the biggest advantages of the cyber world is this possibility to abstract data and information from its physical layer, through this encapsulation process. As the neural network structure is both used as a way to transmit and store data, our brain isn't able to separate the message from the medium. If, for whatever reason, the brain loses the medium (a neuron or its synapses), not only can it lose the ease of firing together between various neurons, but also erase the entire associated memories.[b] "

---

[a] The internet applies the following to carried over information. The application layer codes the data and sends it to the transport layer. The transport layer splits data into manageable chunks and adds a port number information. It puts its header in the beginning and sends this complete packet (TCP – header + app – data) to the IP layer. On the same lines, the IP layer puts its header in front of the data received from TCP. The IP layer adds addresses, stating where the data is from and where it is going. So now, the structure of IP datagram becomes IP – header + TCP – header + app – data. The Ethernet layer then receives the IP datagram and adds on the same line its own header. This MAC address specifies now, which hardware device the message came from, and to which hardware it is going to. Then the whole packet is transmitted over the network.

[b] Decoupling is also impossible in our brain. Recent networking technology defines better the separation between the transport (i.e., connectivity) and the services that run on top of that transport. Thus, whenever a provider wants to enable a new service, it can do so by defining it directly at the service layer, without considering transport layer details.

10) How are machines generating structured data?

"Sir, if I go back to the second counterargument against machines self-generating structured information, it is now clear to me that we, machines, do so through the addressing and encapsulation processes. What you still haven't proven is if machines can generate this information without human interference?"

"I indicated that our brain is not only able to produce information but does so according to whatever it judges important, at any point in time. In other words, it does that by assessing what is different from the expected patterns, predicted according to stored sequences of patterns."

"Sir, could you again give me an example?"

"For instance, a car coming straight at us, would automatically trigger my attention and generate a set of actions to ensure that we avoid being hit by it. In the past, when I was driving, I would put on the brake but must now shout at you. Let me now show you that the equivalence of the brain's perception and attention processes also exist in systems. For this, I need to introduce two computer architectures, which generate information without any human involvement."

What is a Service Oriented Architecture (SOA)?

"Sir, what are these architectures?"

"The first one I would like to introduce is called SOA. It is a computer system's architectural style for creating and using business processes, packaged as services. It defines and controls the IT infrastructure, allowing different applications to participate in the same business processes. These functions are loosely coupled with the devices' operating system and programs, underlying the applications."

"Sir, what does SOA bring that other architectures don't?"

"SOA is an open architecture that separates functions into distinct units (called services), which can be distributed over a network and combined to create new business applications. These services pass data from one to another and coordinate their linked activities.[a] "

---

[a] SOA programming enables the creation of applications, built by combining loosely

"Sir, what is the definition of an open architecture?"

"It means an architecture independent of any specific technology, which may be implemented using a wide range of technologies (e.g., web services). The key feature of such architecture is independent services with defined interfaces that can be called upon to perform their tasks in a standard way, without the services having foreknowledge of the calling application, and without the application having or needing foreknowledge of how the services perform their tasks."

---

coupled and interoperable services. These services inter-operate, based on a formal definition that is independent of the underlying platform and programming language. The interface definition hides the implementation of the language-specific service. Therefore, SOA-based systems may be independent of development technologies and platforms (like java or .net). Such a standardized architecture brings increased operability, by better supporting the connections of various apps and the sharing of data coming from multiple sensors, actuators, or systems. The key to a successful standard lies in its usefulness and easy adoption. Whenever adding new devices, a SOA approach is enabling plug-and-play enhancements without the need for binary code programming and subsequent software recompilation, by computer programmers.

With newer technologies (e.g., SOAP or web services), system upgrade becomes easy, as SOA enables the separation between interface and implementation. In other words, the invoker of a service needs only to understand the interface. Therefore, implementation can evolve without disturbing the clients' services, adding scalability to the system. Traditionally, when a new device (e.g., sensor) needed to be added, APIs would be the common method enabling communication between various vendors' devices. Now, the separation between interfaces and the implementation eliminates APIs need altogether.

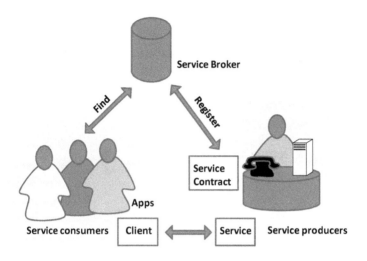

Fig. 28) Illustration of SOA architecture with a service provider (primary engine underlying the Web services), service broker (ensuring information is available) and service consumers (issuing one or more queries to the broker to locate a service and determining how to communicate with it); source: author.

"Sir, how is structured information generated?"

"One of the main features of SOA is that it is a system architecture that allows different apps to exchange data and participate in business processes, independently from the services' programming language. It is possible because connected devices have defined interfaces that may be called upon to perform their tasks in a standard way.[a] "

"Sir, in other words, data provided by any connected device is already structured in a way that all services (and by extension the devices on which they run), which could use the data, is automatically informed when such information passes onto the network."

"Yes, any M2M communication system using a SOA architecture would generate, as per standard and without any human interference, structured information, which is at the basis of knowledge."

"Sir, I believe you have proven your case that machines running on newer software architecture can structure information, but what about the criticism that this structured information

[a] Any device or service, which would be interested in the information, will be able to use it without having to program a specific interface (i.e., API) between the various devices. For example, a new thermostat that would be incorporated within a building's SOA architecture using web services could automatically send information that would be picked-up by all service applications (e.g., an energy management business application).

is just that, information and not knowledge?"

"To find counter-arguments, I need to introduce another type of architecture – Event Driven Architecture (EDA) –, though nowadays SOA and EDA are mostly integrated together in the technology called SOA 2.0."

What is an Event-Driven Architecture (EDA)?

"Sir, let me just recapitulate to see if I understood you well, so far. In a world with human beings, using a 'lingua franca' (e.g., IP), knowing who to talk to and on which subject (e.g., SOA), under established rules (e.g., SDP) and through a medium (network technologies), would be sufficient. However, in a world of machines, there is still a missing element: when should they communicate?"

"Indeed, very well summarized! Without the notion of event, any machine would have the capability to communicate but would be paralyzed, as it wouldn't know when to do so. In a M2M world, the 'when' is triggered by events, which software with an EDA architecture can provide."

"Sir, what else does this software architecture promotes?"

"It enables the detection and generation of an event, as well as its consumption and reaction to it, by other hardware. The implementation of apps transmitting events among loosely coupled software components and services creates this architectural pattern.[a] "

---

[a] EDA clearly proposes two functions: event selection and handling. It typically consists of event consumers and event producers. Event consumers subscribe to an intermediary event manager, and event producers publish to this manager. When the manager receives an event from a producer, it forwards the incident to the consumer. If the consumer is unavailable, the manager can store the event and try to deliver it later. Building applications and systems around EDA allows apps and systems to be constructed in a manner that facilitates more responsiveness, because event-driven systems are by design, better adapted to unpredictable and asynchronous environments. In EDA the flow of the program is determined by sensor outputs (e.g., cameras), user actions (e.g., mouse clicks, key presses), or instructions from other programs. Nowadays EDA is increasingly integrated with SOA, as it complements SOA's architecture because services can be started by triggers, such as events. Business systems benefit from the features of both architectures, since an EDA may trigger event consumers, as these events happen and loosely coupled services can be quickly accessed and queried from those same consumers.

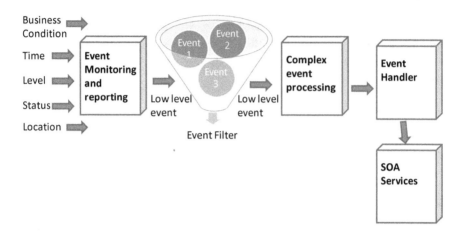

Fig. 29) EDA and SOA are complementary architectures. SOA 2.0 is a design approach that deals with complex Event Processing; source: author.

Why SOA 2.0 or similar architecture creates knowledge?

"Sir, you gave a definition of knowledge based on a human-centric view. If you are to prove that machines can create knowledge, wouldn't you need to redefine it in the context of a machine?"

"Yes, and I came up with a new definition. Knowledge is a justified true belief, accepted as such by a community of software instructions or services with appropriate know-how on the subject, which agree that the methods used to prove that it is a JTB have been met and that such proof has been enduring the test of time. Furthermore, to become knowledge, information must become meaningful to machines or humans."

"But Sir, how can you prove a justified true belief for a machine?"

"If I go back to my energy management example within a SOA 2.0 architecture, I could argue that the proof that the supplied information is a justified true belief for the system, would be shown in the results: lower energy costs and maximized user comfort."

"For you Sir, the proof of truth, that is, the put, is in the pudding?"

"Yes, a positive evolution would confirm that mathematical formulas used within the inequations model were accurate. A negative evolution or results not showing any real pattern would, on the contrary, create doubts in our belief that we formulated the model well.[a] "

"That said, Sir, you still need to prove that machines may provide meaningful information."

"Point well taken. I've shown that the notion of meaningfulness is arbitrary. Those we now call cyberists could argue that knowing, for example, that the overall energy consumption in kWh was reduced by 15%, while maintaining average comfort (e.g., 22°C), isn't knowledge."

"Well, from my point of view it is."

"I agree with you. For a system responsible for optimizing comfort and reducing energy bills, this is the most critical knowledge. Let's show how biased such a cyberist argument would be. I'll use the Bible to make the comparison."

"Sir, what's the relation between the Bible, knowledge, and machines?"

"For many people, the Bible is THE KNOWLEDGE because it is extremely significant to them. Indeed, it gives them an understanding of why they are here on earth. However, from an atheist, Buddhist, or a machine's own perspective, the Bible has no meaning, other perhaps than telling interesting stories that happened 5000 to 2000 years ago. It would definitely not stand the JTB test. On the contrary, the energy consumption example would tick all the boxes of the knowledge definition, as stated above for machines."

"What's your point, Sir?"

"My point is that if we can accept that the Bible may be considered knowledge, without even passing the JTB test, then we must necessarily accept that energy optimization models, which would pass this JTB test, should be considered knowledge, as well."

"Sir, I believe you've truly justified that machines may acquire knowledge by structuring meaningful information, which was the second potential identified criticism. However, you still need to explain what gives meaning to information in the case of machines, to prove your case."

---

[a] Justifying that the model and its integrated mathematical formulas are the most accurate, could come from either one of the following strategies: trust that the equations supplied by the industry have been already optimized over time or, as it happens in safety critical environments (e.g., train signaling), run in parallel two different programs, which check that for both sets of instructions, any failure is taken care of. In other words, there are easy ways of proving over time that the provided information is a justified true belief.

"I thought you had understood. Events are what gives meaning to information. By events, I mean any measured or published modification in a system, platform, component, business, or application process.[a] "

"I should have Sir! Are these IT solutions still considered science fiction?"

"No, though all these concepts are quite new, these solutions already exist in the marketplace, such as in a System of systems.[b] My personal experience is that the security world already applies such technology. I've participated in the implementation of SOA and EDA technologies, already in 2008 (using UDP/IP with SOAP and XML)."

"Sir, I believe you still need to tackle the third criticism. Cyberists believe machines cannot provide knowledge but only information that a human being transforms into knowledge."

"In machines, systems, and computers, awareness is a function of software. A set of instructions will determine what needs to be looked at and analyzed. For instance, a system may define that a photo-electric switch must check that no object is blocking the entrance of a garage door or that a CCTV system should identify any intruder invading a restricted area. The service portion of the CCTV system running on SOA architecture would send footage of the screened region to a control center, where security agents could check visually that everything is OK."

"Sir, cyberists might say that in the human brain, awareness isn't predefined, as in both these examples. After all, you are mobile and improvise according to the changing environment."

"OK. Let's take another example, where improvisation would be required. You, unmanned cars, must consider millions of unexpected situations. As for the drivers' golden rule, which is to look out ahead to detect any abnormal situation, driverless cars would need to sense through lidar, radar, and vision camera, what is coming ahead. In other words,

---

[a] They can be high-level and business-oriented, or low-level and technical in character. Because events may be transmitted and received, event-aware applications and services can respond to the underlying changes, as needed. The secret to understanding any given event is to know its cause, at the time the incident occurred. For instance, if one of the thermostats would suddenly display 0° C or 70° C, the application could immediately detect the failure and send an automatic order to a repair company to substitute the faulty product.

[b] The white paper 'Application of service-oriented architecture for sensors and actuators in district heating substations' describes this new concept of district heating substation control and monitoring. SOA is deployed in a wireless sensor network (WSN), which is integrated within substations. IP-networking is exclusively used from sensor to server (IPv6, UDP/TCP) with no middleware required for internet integration. By enabling thousands of sensors with SOA capabilities, the authors described how they were able to build a System of Systems which monitored events and supported the decision-making process by generating useful information. [N28]

through these sensors, you become aware of potentially hazardous situations. The attention process, being usually the first by which humans' perception becomes active, triggers a mechanism in which many neurons fire together, bringing our brain to observe more cautiously the triggering event."

"Sir, what is the machine equivalent of attention?"

"It is also the event, which an EDA architecture (or equivalent) could detect and use to induce a series of potential actions. In a M2M world with EDA, the notion of meaningful event, would be set by the boundaries, which would define what normal and abnormal information is."

"Sir, do you have an example to support your view?"

"Yes, in a security control center I've worked on, any abnormal situation, such as someone walking in a metro tunnel, would automatically be highlighted and forwarded to the right people within the operation center, to be dealt with. This person would automatically receive information from various sub-systems (e.g., signaling system indicating if trains were coming up, a SCADA system indicating if the third rail was energized, etc.), providing complete situational awareness. E-mails could be sent automatically to near-by station patrols. Pop-ups with potential scenarios would be made available to the operational personnel to know how to deal with this situation."

"Sir, you are basically describing a system of systems enabling information structuring, with its most relevant associated knowledge."

"Yes, this automated process would mimic what the staff would do, but ensure that best practices are always taken into consideration. Without it, the personnel's mind would check what the situation is and try to think of the next steps, struggling to remember from experience or read procedures, what would be the best course of action."

"Sir, why do you conclude that machines can create knowledge?"

"In my view, a system of systems, which can provide complete situational awareness and engage in actions linked to identified issues, confirms that machines or systems may be as knowledgeable as human beings (in my example, highly qualified metro or safety attendants). It proves that the third argument against machine providing knowledge (i.e., that it provides humans with information that they need to transform into knowledge), is erroneous. The reality is that machines can provide knowledge and with the right technology and procedures, may do it more quickly and systematically. In fact, such processes don't have to rely on a human memory, which can be tricky, especially during stressful situations."

"Sir, you made me a believer in machine knowledge. However, there is still one 'cyberist' criticism that you need to tackle. Even though machines can acquire knowledge, they cannot do it by themselves, without the human input. The rules, which set what is meaningful for the machines, are defined by the programmer's instructions."

"That's right, but this discussion will have to wait for another time after I describe to you what intelligence is. I now need a break."

11) How do computers memorize and store data?

A few days later, on my way to seeing my mother who suffers from Alzheimer, my car restarted our conversation.

"Sir, I'm back in my usual physical envelop. Could you explain to me how come humans forget basic things they've learned, like the name of their children, when I can never forget any single data I've acquired?"

"Information needs to be stored in computers for later usage, in a way that it can always be retrieved, whenever necessary. This storage process refers to computer components, devices, and recording media that retain data and instructions, during a time lapse. A computer stores data using several methods and technologies and the different storage processes are classified differently accordingly."

"Sir, what classification can you come up with?"

"The first classification, which is probably the less relevant in a world of widespread networking, is the internal and external storage distinction. I've used the words internal and external storages, but people often use the wording internal and external memories. The internal storage is composed of a memory (called RAM for Random Access Memory) used for temporary storage, and a permanent storage device (i.e., a hard drive).[a] "

"Sir, what other potential classification is there?"

---

[a] **External storage:** Connecting devices provide external memory to avoid saturating a PC's internal memory. The CPU may only access this stored information when transferred to the PC's main memory. Though this storage process is slow, there is virtually no capacity constraints.

Internal storage: It includes all storage functions directly accessible by a computer's CPU. This terminology includes several types of storage, such as the RAM, cache memory, and special registers, as well as, the hard drive. Primary and secondary memory divides this internal memory. Initially, direct access external memory was provided through floppy disks and later on evolved towards hard disks made of magnetic material. Optical disks in the form of CDs or DVDs are used to store a larger amount of data, and exist in fixed and erasable form. Memory sticks (e.g., flash cards and discs) have also seen their popularity grow in the last years. Unlike the previously mentioned storage equipment, they don't need readers and mechanical parts that spin the objects.

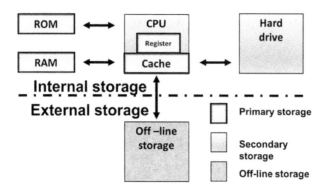

Fig. 30) Simplified diagram of a computer's storage facilities; source: author.

"There is primary, secondary, and off-line storage. Primary storage is designed to feed data and instruction into the computer before the processing initialization,[a] at speed compatible with the CPU's own processing speed. Intermediary and final data are stored there as well."

"Sir, could you give me examples of component classification?"

"We consider ROM, RAM, cache, and registers primary storage facilities since they store data directly accessible by a computer's CPU. A

---

[a] **Primary storage:**

- A **ROM** (Read Only Memory) chip is considered non-volatile storage, as it doesn't need power to retain stored data. It provides non-erasable content to store information permanently. A ROM refers to a hard-wired memory, used by PC manufacturers to store standard processing programs (e.g., assembly language).
  - o Manufacturers have come up with different technologies to allow ROM reprogramming: PROM (Programmable ROM) may be programmed once only; EPROM (Erasable PROM) are reprogrammable after exposure to UV lights; EEPROM (Electric EPROM), such as the flash memory, can be reprogrammed after being erased electrically.
- A **RAM** is a high-speed storage medium that is accessible almost instantly, because it is connected directly to the CPU, via the memory bus. For this reason, the RAM is used to store data loaded by active programs and the operating system. It allows addressable storage from which instructions and data can be directly loaded into the registers, for processing.
- A **processor register** consists of a small amount of fast storage, quickly accessible by the processor's CPU. It holds instructions or data that the processor is working on. Located in the processor, it only holds one item at a time.
- The **cache memory** plays a buffer role, allowing for faster access and retrieval of an instruction copy or data, from the main storage devices. It sits between the CPU and its RAM and is the place where instructions and data are stored.
  - o It is physically situated inside the processor (internal cache) and on the motherboard (external cache). Nowadays, there are at least three independent caches: instruction, data, and translation look-aside buffer (to speed up virtual-to-physical address translation for instructions and data).

hard drive is a secondary storage since it isn't directly connected to the CPU.[a] Indeed, it sends and receives data through an Input/Output bus, which usually goes through a cache or other types of memories, before being processed by the CPU. Unlike a RAM, it cannot transfer data quickly."

"Sir, how does my onboard computer store data?"

"Unlike human beings who cannot be switched off without being able to re-operate, PCs may be de-energized for a certain period. This specificity influenced how manufacturers developed storage technology."

"Sir, we know that some information must be systematically accessible when switching on the computer. How was this requirement accounted for?"

"It is especially crucial for instructions that need to format the computer, in order to boot it on and access all peripherals. The process of opening a file copies it from the hard drive, where it was permanently stored, into the computer's RAM, where it can now be edited. We may lose new information as long as we don't save it to a hard disk.[b] "

"Sir, how is data retrieved?"

"To store and retrieve data, PCs use byte-addressable memories. Memory addresses are fixed-length sequences of bits (i.e., 32 or 64 bits). A number is assigned to each byte in a computer's memory. The CPU uses it to track where data and instructions are stored in the primary storage. The computer's CPU uses the address bus to communicate which memory address it wants to access. The memory controller reads the address and then puts the data stored in that memory address, back onto the address bus for the CPU to use. As there are many memory locations in the primary storage, each having a physical address, there is a code that the CPU can use to access these locations.[c] "

---

[a] **Hard disks** consist of several tracks (concentric circles) on which data is recorded in the form of tiny magnetic spots. The presence of a spot is considered a bit and its absence a zero. Data registered magnetically can be erased and rewritten several times.
- **Solid State Drive memory**: SSD is a computer storage media made from silicon microchips, which stores data electronically instead of magnetically, as spinning hard disk drives (HDDs) or magnetic oxide tape do. They are made of Flash ROM chips.

[b] Permanent information that cannot be overwritten, are usually located on a non-volatile chip (e.g., ROM). Nowadays, a ROM is erasable, but this process isn't easy to do, to ensure that vital data isn't overwritten. Hard drives can also retain data permanently when the computer is turned off because they store data magnetically but unlike original ROM are rewriteable. RAM requires electrical current to do the same.

[c] The capacity of the addressable bus will restrict the number of bits that it can memorize. For instance, a 32-bit bus addresses 2^{32} (i.e., 4.3 billion addresses) locations.

"Sir, what are the similarities and differences between biological and digital data storage?"

"Though brains and computers perform the same data storage and retrieval functions, the way they do it is quite different and so are the results. Unlike computers, human beings may forget what they've already experienced. Through their addressing mechanisms, PCs can on the other hand, systematically retrieve stored information unless obviously, their hard disk drive crashes."

"Sir, I thought we had in common various types of memories?"

"Human memory, as I already told you, is split into a buffer memory, a STM, and a LTM. Computers have primary and secondary storages. The easy thing would be to compare the STM and LTM with primary and secondary storage, because there is, in both cases, a notion of temporary and permanently stored information. However, human memory types are divided according to timelines. In other words, our brain distinctly stores immediate, recent, and old experiences. On the contrary, what needs to be accessed more quickly separates computer memories."

"Sir, any other main difference?"

"Yes, two major ones! Unlike the RAM, our STM's performance fluctuates according to familiarity with and knowledge of the topic. Another major difference is that a STM holds only 'pointers' to LTMs whereas a RAM holds a similar representation of the data stored on the hard disk."

"Sir, can we find in your brain an equivalence to my non-volatile memory chip (e.g., ROM)?"

"We've seen that the neural system evolves over time. Since there is no separation between the message and the medium, and as the synapse itself stores information, there is theoretically no such thing as non-erasable memories. However, I could argue that reflex arcs, if anything, store non-erasable information."

"Sir, is there a data retrieval equivalence in the brain?"

"PCs retrieve data by polling their precise memory address. By contrast, a brain uses content-addressable memory to do so. Through activation of closely related concepts, we can pull back words. With just a few of these key cues, we can retrieve a full memory. It is also doable in PCs, by mostly building banks of indexes or indices. This approach is used by Google search engines, to speed up and make more relevant queries."

"Sir, any last difference worth mentioning?"

"Yes, the same neural substrate performs the data processing and memory storage, while computers process information from memory using CPUs, and then write the resulting output back to the memory component. As seen, when neurons process information, they modify their synapses, which are themselves the substrate of memory. As a result, retrieving information always alters the memory itself, usually making it stronger but sometimes less accurate. However, in computers, memorized information may stay unaltered by this same process."

My car then stopped talking for a while. "I guess you are satisfied or overwhelmed by all my answers?" I said.

12) Have we reached the era of Artificial Knowledge?

"Sir, I cannot be overwhelmed, but yes, I am satisfied with your answers."

"That's great. I would just like to conclude. I believe we have entered, since a few years now, what I could call by similarity, the era of Artificial Knowledge (AK). Machines are now able to gather information independently from any human being. They can structure information in a way, which may provide knowledge to all other devices connected to the same network, without these devices having any foreknowledge of any other connected piece of equipment."

"Sir, isn't that also true for internet users?"

"Yes, people will increasingly have immediate access through search engines, to all of this planet's knowledge, stored in whatever online library, including access to the knowledge of billions of machines connected by the Internet of Things. With new search algorithms and programming techniques, the access to reliable data source will increase extraordinarily over the next years."

"Sir, what is the impact of this 24/7 access to the worldwide knowledge?"

"In my view, our relationship to knowledge, especially how we acquire it, is fundamentally changing for the better. By disseminating knowledge, internet empowers anyone who wishes to access higher education through books, white papers, online training, or conferences."

"Sir, why are you so sure about the positive impact of the internet on knowledge?"

"For instance, in my case, without this unlimited access to scientific and other disciplines' publications, I don't think I would have been able to give you all this information. In this new era, this obviously raises the ethical question of the ones who don't have or can't afford access to the internet. They will, unfortunately, increasingly be left behind and you could always claim that internet may negatively influence equal opportunities."

PART 3: INTELLIGENCE

Mind you, it's all about intelligence

Judge a man by his questions, rather than by his answers. Voltaire

Juger un homme par ses questions plutôt que par ses réponses. Voltaire.

Any psychological theory that is incompatible with known facts of neurology must be, ipso facto, unacceptable." (Fodor, 1965)

13) Is there a growing gap between computers and humans?

For many weeks now, our conversation had died out. My car was focusing on what it did best: driving my family and me. However, I was starting to miss our discussion and so one day, I said:

"It's strange. I thought you would want to follow through on our conversation and ask me about what I referred to several times, as intelligence. Have you forgotten?"

"Sir, I never do. I remember you had argued that though, thoughts and information gathering processes and their respective correlate – intelligence and knowledge – are completely intertwined, it made sense to describe these two functionalities separately. Although the philosophical study of knowledge didn't usually separate the 'knowledge that' from the 'knowledge of,' this separation was made necessary by the conduct of our conversation."

"You are right, and even if it could seem arbitrary or presumptuous to separate such topics against common practice, the main reason for this division is that I believe there is a fundamental difference between the two concepts. Unlike knowledge, intelligence is not information but must rather be seen as the process to acquire, adapt, and use such information, to solve problems in an ever-changing environment."

"Sir, according to what you told me, we could also claim that knowledge is more than just information."

"True and as I told you, knowledge isn't only the collection of acquired information but also involves the capacities to acquire it. Furthermore, it isn't just any kind of information. Though biased and time-based, such information must have been justified by a community of agents who agreed that the right methods and conditions, had been met when proving that the belief was true.[a] "

---

[a] For instance, anyone could gather an encyclopedic knowledge of wine, if she were to read all the books related to this topic, but that wouldn't mean she could become a sommelier. To become a good wine taster, she would need to be interested in the subject, have the palate and the nose to distinguish the nuances of the wine, as well as the time to practice. However, to become the world's best sommelier would require much more. She would need the capacity in a blind test, to reconstruct an image of a brand, according to flavors, the soil's vineyard, the sun's exposition, the grapes' variety, the wine's color, etc., as well as the intelligence to associate all this through a deduction process, which would identify patterns.

"Sir, you also said that it also needs to be meaningful for either men or machines."

"Yes, and I'd like to quote Gordana Dodig-Crnkovic,[41] who sums up quite nicely my view: 'There is no meaningful information in the world as such, just potential information. That potential information actualizes and becomes meaningful in different ways for different cognizing agents. Meaning for an agent is use of information.' "

"Similarly Sir, isn't intelligence more than just a process?"

"Yes, as it too includes various types of processing capacities (e.g., analytical, social, or emotional intelligence). However, it can mainly still be seen as the transforming process, which gives meaning to information, by deducting patterns within the sensed environment. There is a second difference worth highlighting: these two cognitive functions don't share the same timeline."

"Sir, what do you mean by that?"

"Knowledge is the resulting end of a process that occurred in the past, enabling its acquisition and, therefore, is based on a continuum of past experiences. As a process, intelligence is a time lapse, where past information is processed to predict future trends and thus contemplates the past, present, and future."

"Sir, you haven't still fully demonstrated that all the conditions are in place for Artificial Knowledge. When do you intend to do so?"

"In our prior conversations, I told you that a system based on Machine-to-Machine (M2M) communication using modern software architecture,[a] would spontaneously generate knowledge, without any form of human interference. I also introduced semantic tagging, used by search systems like Google, to highlight the speed and relevance of the supplied information, making knowledge accessible to all, including machines, without virtually any limitation."

"But Sir, wouldn't you agree with me that you only briefly tackled the possibilities offered by new software technologies (e.g., deep learning technology), which provide computers with the capabilities to identify patterns, without any specific input coming from programmers?"

"Yes, I'll now focus on these newer technologies and tell you how they enable the identification of patterns, out of random information, by creating their own sets of rules. By doing so, I shall demonstrate to you that all conditions are in place for Artificial Knowledge (AK)."

---

[a] E.g., Service Oriented Architecture combined with Event Driven Architecture

"Sir, I am looking forward to it because, and going back to your initial argument about Artificial Knowledge, if it is achievable then the higher forms of AI may also be possible. Sir, before going there could you indicate at what AK stage we are?"

"To do this, let's use a simple definition. One, which would be similar to AI. As humans both like to simplify and view themselves as the center of the universe, computer scientists usually categorize three different levels: dumber, as clever, and far more intelligent than humans."

"Sir, said that way, it doesn't seem very impressive!"

"That's why specialists came up with the more serious wording: weak AI, Strong AI, and Artificial Super Intelligence, which I'll define better later on. Using the same human-centric definition, I believe that machines have already reached the Strong AK level and that there is a growing knowledge gap between them and human beings, pushing somewhat Strong AK towards Artificial Super Knowledge."

"Sir, wouldn't a majority of people disagree with that view?"

"This notion that knowledge is the end result of a process sustains in my view, the idea that knowledge is an end in itself. In other words, it cannot be improved immediately, at the moment someone reads or hears about something, but rather needs to go through this process of justifying a true belief. As a consequence, and because knowledge accessible on the internet isn't restricted to human beings only, you and other machines can also access all of mankind's available knowledge."

"Sir, if that is the case and I possess already all the mechanisms (i.e., software, hardware, and procedures) for acquiring, storing, and retrieving information, through new software programs and architectures, the newer generation of machines will just tend to have better or faster access to knowledge."

"Exactly to my point! If we exclude the intelligence portion of this process (i.e., the way to provide content), it seems to me that machines are already superior in many ways, in their knowledge acquisition process. For instance, machines can be highly specialized to perform specifics tasks. Market competition forces companies to constantly upgrade their products, resulting, in systems with increasing sensing physical properties or with improving agility to manipulate objects, through ever more precise actuators."

"Sir, similarly, PCs are already much better at storing and retrieving data than humans."

"Yes, and the newer technologies will only accentuate this memorization gap between men and machines. Moreover, increasingly sophisticated algorithms, such as those used in data mining, will allow machines to handle masses of data and information in speed and volume that no human being can even dream of doing."

"Sir, since you have 24/7 access to the internet, don't you think that your phone is merely an extension of your brain? In this case, aren't humans already cyborgs (i.e., partially human and machine) and have access to the same data source as I do?"

"You aren't the only one to think that way.[42] However, in a world increasingly dominated by M2M communication, humans have to rely more and more on complex algorithms, which the vast majority of us have never heard of. The point is that humans, unlike machines, will just become overwhelmed by the mass of data to process and store. Unfortunately for our ego, the knowledge gap between men and machines shall only broaden, as the market introduces new technologies!"

"Sir, most computer scientists with an opinion on the subject, believe that we are still at the lowest AI level. Hence, how can you claim that we are already so advanced in AK?"

"Well, creating intelligent rather than knowledgeable machines, poses challenges of a different order of magnitude. If we consider that intelligence is the process by which we use acquired knowledge to deal mostly with situations never encountered or new concepts, we can easily understand why. From a programming perspective, it is complicated to describe through coding, what we don't know."

"Sir, are you saying that programmers cannot easily code something they cannot formulate through rules and procedures?"

"Yes, what makes John a specific John? Unless he weighs 200 kg or has a deformity, how may he be portrayed, so that computers can identify him out of a database? Furthermore, can concepts like knowledge or intelligence, which are extremely difficult to define, be programmed for computers to understand?"

"What's the trick, Sir?"

"Though it might be impossible for a programmer to do so, computers may do it, provided they may interpret the rules, by themselves. Fortunately, knowledge relies mostly on explicit information, simplifying this interpretation process. I'll detail these relatively new programming approaches, forming the AI basis, which enable this self-interpretation."

"Sir, will there be in the near future, new AI technologies that create as well, an intelligence gap between humans and machines?"

"The ones, we called cyberists, will probably assert that our brain is the result of million years of evolution, which cannot be replicated so easily by manufacturers and programmers. Religious people will claim that there is an immaterial nature to intelligence and that machines will never have a soul."

"But Sir, you just said we already reached the strong AK level, and I read that a computer trounced the world's best GO player, something humans couldn't imagine just a few years ago."

"This opinion is highly polemical. I could even claim that if you continue asking those brilliant questions, you might someday end up with a soul or, at least, some kind of self-awareness. However, let's not rush and introduce consciousness now. I'd rather focus on intelligence and follow the same sequential path of resorting to 'soft' disciplines and neurosciences to understand biological and cyber intelligence differences. I'll leave the debate on consciousness and super intelligence to another time."

14) What is intelligence?

"Sir, is there a universal definition of intelligence, which we could work with?"

"Unfortunately, and like for knowledge, there is none. In fact, there is not even an agreement on how many types of intelligence there are."

"So Sir, could we simply resort to a general definition of intelligence? For instance, Wikipedia's: 'The ability to perceive and retain knowledge or information and apply it to itself or other instances of knowledge or information creating referable understanding models of any size, density, or complexity, due to any conscious or subconscious imposed will or instruction to do so'?"

"We could, but by doing this, we would avoid all the debates between the different theories, which make mind related subjects so interesting. Therefore, I believe I would enrich our conversation by presenting the various philosophical and psychological theories succinctly."

"However, Sir, could you focus on the ones you deem the most important?"

"Yes, I'll highlight the ones that can help shape our views on differences between biological and artificial intelligence."

"Sir, any theory in particular?"

"The first theory is Gartner's multiple intelligences theory that probably offers the best perspective to define the boundaries and gaps between people and machine intelligence.[a] I'll describe at great length Kant's incommensurable work, which is today at the origin of many cognitive theories."

"Sir, besides these psychological and philosophical theories, will you also present these cognitive theories which you said could explain how the human mind works?"

"Of course! One of these theories worth describing thoroughly is Jeff Hawkins' memory-prediction model. It explains from a simple conceptual point of view, why the world can be intelligible without any reference to a soul. Its definition of intelligence: 'A methodology for learning the structure in the world, the universe, and in everything we do,' sums it quite

---

[a] Conveniently the multiple intelligence theory defines 8 or 9 intelligence types and provides us also with Gartner's definition of intelligence (extracted from Wikipedia):
- The ability to create an effective product or offer a service that is valued in a culture.
- A set of skills that make it possible for a person to solve problems in life.
- The potential for finding or creating solutions for problems, which involves gathering new knowledge.

nicely.[a] The last theory worth presenting extensively is Karl Friston's Free-energy, which bridges the gap between the neurons' physical reaction and the brain's psychological behaviors.[b] "

"Sir, before introducing these and other more recent cognitive theories, could you come back to concepts about the nature of the 'knowledge of,' to explain issues about intelligibility?"

"In other words, you want to know why and how humans understand that something is what it is? Why a cat is a cat or John is John? Since intelligibility cannot be reduced to intelligence only, I need to circumscribe the philosophical debate around the intelligibility of things, to avoid having to talk about the existence of God. Therefore, I'll focus on the concepts that have shaped the philosophical field of Gnoseology and influence a theory called the Theory of the Mind. To do so, we must come back to the problems raised by Gettier's essay."

Why is a cat a cat?

"Sir, you've stated that Gettier showed that we could generate true beliefs by making lucky guesses —"

"— and thus, this contradicts the various movements, which tried to identify the source of knowledge. I already presented to you the two main theories (i.e., Rationalism, Empiricism), as well as Kant's critical philosophy, which finds a compromise between these two older theories. All three views are summed up in the next table, which I am e-mailing you."

---

[a] What this definition doesn't give though, is that this methodology is based on predictions, not only at the conceptual level but also at various levels of the different layers of our neocortex. In other words, it also gives an explanation of what intelligence is, without referring to a test, which measures better the consequence (e.g., the results in terms of IQ score) than the cause (e.g., the mechanism explaining what our brain does, when involved in such intelligent processes). Furthermore, this theory doesn't rely on sub-characterizations that are themselves difficult to define and even more difficult to measure, such as the various psychological theories on uncorrelated intelligence (e.g., Gartner's own multiple intelligence theory or David Goleman's emotional intelligence).

[b] Hawkins and Friston wrote their book around 2006, and both theories, which benefitted already from advances in neurosciences, share many views about intelligence. For instance, the Free-energy theory describes how our brain minimizes surprises through perception and action. In other words, Friston's view on intelligence is also based on a model of predictions, adjusting such forecasts in function of experiences and improving on such predictions, which is entirely in line with Mr. Hawkins view of the role of intelligence.

	Empiricism	Kant	Rationalism
View of Mind	Passive mind The mind is a blind state	Interactive mind The mind has innate structures shaping experience	Passive mind The mind has innate knowledge
View of conformity of the mind	Conforms to experience but through sensed experience	Doesn't conform to experience but experience conforms to mind	Conforms to experience but through logic
View of learning	Involuntary association Based on sense and experience alone	Construction Based on application of thoughts to experience	Voluntary act of will Based on logical thoughts alone
View of possibility of knowledge	Skeptical Nothing is knowable	Evolving Somethings are knowable	Dogmatic Everything is knowable
View of focus of psychology	Sensation Based on sense and experience View conscious experience as the association of simple elements	Construction Based on application of thoughts to experience	Perception / reason Non conscious process View conscious experience as a continuous stream of wholes

Fig. 31) Empiricist, rationalist and Kantian views of the mind: Toward a Unified Theory of Cognition: A Kantian Analysis; source: Clayton Daniel Austin (2003).

"Sir, could you sum up for me Kant's view?"

"Of course. This table shows Kant's middle way, which depicted for the first time in history, an interactive mind, a view that current cognitive theories can still relate to. Indeed, both knowledge and the sensory inputs coming from reality are gathered through a construction, rather than through recording or processing. Furthermore, the fact that perception itself is constructed, means that the memory of these perceived sensory inputs goes through this same reconstruction process. Therefore, perception is different from how the world is. Similarly, recalled memories also differ from the original perception."

"Sir, how would you then characterize Kant's view?"

"In fact, Kant's analyses of cognition can be seen as consistent with the principles of Constructivism:

1. Knowledge is constructed, not merely recorded or processed, by individuals (D. Phillips).[43]
2. Its construction is affected by the experiences and development of the learner (J. Piaget).[44] [45]
3. It occurs in a social context. (L. Vygotsky).[46] [47] [48] "

"Sir, thanks to our conversation and what I gathered through web tags, I noticed that the influence of Kant's work in modern epistemology is such, that he is many things to many people."

"Yes, and it shouldn't come to you as a surprise that many philosophers believe Kant was also in line with the Representationalism movement, in which knowledge and justified beliefs about external objects, are indirectly arrived.[a] "

"Sir, are you saying that Kant's view is coherent with Representationalism?"

"Yes, it holds that our mind cannot directly perceive Objects in the external world but perceives them instead, as mental 'representations.' A barrier,[b] which exists between our mind and reality, prevents us from first-hand knowledge of anything beyond our mind."

"Sir, the fact that Kant has been torn between Constructivism and Representationalism, seems to be a common view, but which movement would he feel more comfortable with today?"

"I'll quote Tom Rockmore, for this answer: 'My hypothesis is that he was initially attracted to Representationalism before later inventing the so-called Copernican revolution, since, as he famously writes, he was unable to make progress in grasping a mind-independent object, in other words on the assumption that the subject depends on the object.'[49] Furthermore, and according to Eco, 'Kantian Schematism implies... constructivism.' [16] "

"Sir, if Representationalism and Constructivism are the two philosophical movements we can still relate to currently, which one can now be considered the most accurate when integrating neurosciences and modern cognitive theories?"

"Besides highlighting the core difference between the two movements that is, a passive subject who suddenly has something that appears to him vs. an active subject who reconstructs what he knows to be on the outside, I would need to describe these new cognitive theories, to answer this question. However, I prefer to introduce new issues related to knowledge and intelligence and come back to this topic with more food for thoughts."

"Sir, how may these two movements explain reality, if they both integrate a barrier?"

"Within these two main contemporary theories on the source of knowledge, modern philosophers have tried to explain how we can acquire a precise understanding of reality, even though there is necessarily this

---

[a] Representationalists can deduct from Kant's work, that he describes a world that we consciously sense, as a virtual reality replica that we project within our mind, rather than a real world. Human ideas come from sensed data of a materialistic external world and the direct Objects of perception are only sensed data, which represents the external Objects.

[b] Called a veil of perception.

physiological filter, you referred to. Furthermore, I already described the continuum of cognitive processes, which ends up giving meaning to an Object. Before answering your question, let me address the issues that this continuum raises. Indeed, Gettier's examples raise an additional issue about the nature of justification.[18] "

"Sir, is it related to the problem of defining how we can ground justification?"

"Yes, Gettier's examples show that we may internally adequate justification without knowledge. I've briefly tackled how justification can connect us to facts at all when I introduced the issues about knowledge in the age of the internet."

"Sir, could you now enroll these issues within a succinct philosophical framework?"

"OK. If knowledge is fallible and corrigible, any justification may seem good enough at some point in time, qualifying for knowledge, until we acquire better evidence that proves it wrong. However, would anyone accept any knowledge, unless he believed that this justification had a connection to the facts determining the truth? Furthermore, since we cannot grasp reality itself because of the barrier, any modification to our knowledge implies that, what we believe connects us to the truth, is also changing."

"Sir, what are the theories, which tackle these issues?"

"Theories connecting justification to something, which will define and ground it, are classified into two main movements. Externalism supports the idea that internal states (i.e., beliefs and justification) must cognitively connect with external reality (i.e., truth).[a] Internalism, on the other hand, asserts that the internal states must connect with something true already in our mind.[b] "

"Sir, something is telling me that you will introduce Kant again. Am I right?"

"Yes. With Kant, the important question becomes whether an Object (e.g., a cat) that we perceive in the world, is externally real (i.e., just as we see it), or only phenomenal contents of our own mind's justification (i.e., as our brain pictures or reconstructs this Object)."

---

[a] The connections, which creates knowledge, can be causal (e.g., Descartes) or explained through metaphysic (e.g., Aristotle).

[b] Spinoza expressed the view that this thing is within us humans, enabling us to acquire knowledge. Leibniz proposed that knowledge is the result of a representation embedded in us by God, which doesn't require a connection to the outside world.

"In other words Sir, you want to describe how can an Object (i.e., things or concepts, which are distinct and external in existence to the Subject) possibly impact or communicate with this Subject, so that he acquires a truthful and reliable perceptual knowledge of this object?"

"Indeed, and simplifying, when I am looking at a glass of rosé wine, how do I know that it is a real rosé and not just a blend of red and white wine? Kant's view on this issue is a mixture of both Internalism and Externalism. Because it is sophisticated and evolved during his lifetime, his hybrid opinion lets place for several interpretations. I'll describe two of these interpretations.[50] "

"Sir, could you start with the more modern one?"

"This view suggests that Kant's theory of justification describes four different types of justification: an objective (i.e., state that provides reliable data about what an Object is, or of an event described by a proposition) and three subjective ones (i.e., 'internal' processes by which a person comes to hold an assent). They, in turn, can combine in different ways to form six different types of assent (i.e., what holds to be true), with various probability levels of being exact, varying from working assumptions to absolute certainty.[a] "

"Sir, is this how Kant introduces probabilities in knowledge?"

"Yes, and this interpretation explains in which context, this combination of justified assents fails to generate knowledge. It also proposes why there are some assents that, though cannot be grounded on reason or experience, should still be regarded as knowledge."

"Sir, I don't see how Kant's view on justification, suggests that it is both externalist and internalist?"

"Its externalism is based on the fact that its objective probability will typically be inaccessible to a normal Subject.[26] However, it is also internalist, since humans' most critical intuitions about knowledge, acquired through an internal process, must be accommodated by the reflective access conditions of the Subject. Additionally, this means that an objective ground for any proposition requires that a Subject experiences

---

[a] These six assents are (with some questionable examples, as degrees of probability are subjective): **opinions** (e.g., I am expecting to taste wine in a rosé vineyard), **mere beliefs** (e.g., my wine looks rosé), **reflective beliefs** (e.g., my full glass is besides a half empty bottle of Rosé), **persuasions** (e.g., my full glass is besides a half empty bottle of Rosé, and its color is rosé), **mere convictions** (e.g., somebody told me she poured the rosé wine, and it looks like a rosé) and finally **knowledge** (e.g., I've seen someone pouring a bottle of rosé wine in my glass and tasted it).

psychological states, as well as appropriate access to the external states, which renders this proposition true to some degree or another."

"Sir, could you simplify your explanation because I am not sure I understand."

"OK! To simplify, I could say that it is internal because it is a content of our consciousness. It is external because it indirectly results from the way we usually judge Objects to be external through their Forms, which are themselves put in our consciousness, by ourselves. In other words, they are external because they are constructed in our mind as an independent substance, occupying a position in space and time, that is, outside of our mind, according to pre-defined rules."

"Sir, what's your second interpretation of Kant's view?"

"I am hesitant to introduce it to you."

"Why Sir?"

"It comes from a German philosopher, who held an unacceptable position on Jews, during the Nazi period."

"Sir, is this interpretation related to his stance?"

"No, you're right. I should be able to separate the man's wrongful ideas, from his valuable contribution to philosophy and psychology. Jakob Fries,[51] it's his name, completed Kant's view about this world, which we've seen is neither merely phenomenal nor independent from our brain's representation."

"Sir, why did Fries feel he needed to complete Kant's view?"

"I mentioned that Kant's view included both Internalism and Externalism."

"More than once Sir, but what's the problem with that view?"

"It is that, though the synthesis resulting from our mental activities, generates consciousness itself, we humans aren't in control of the process that puts these phenomena internally."

"What is Fries' problem Sir, with this involuntary process?"

"For Fries, it implies that Kant's view means that Objects in themselves are unknown to the Subject and therefore don't correspond to a representation, after all."

"Sir, what solution did he provide to Kant's dilemma?"

"He introduced psychology in Kant's critical philosophy,[52] through the concept of immediate cognition. Indeed, he believed that Kant had tried to prove something, which can only be described through psychological and regressive analysis."

"How so Sir?"

"If truth becomes grounded in consciousness because phenomenal Objects themselves are there, and so are their a priori Forms, we only become conscious of the Forms through experience, after going through this critical analysis process.[a] As a result, the way our mind provides knowledge is its only and best way to validate truth. Only through psychological investigations can we really identify these a priori bases of knowledge."

"Sir, by suggesting that psychology could provide rational principles on human's inner life, didn't Fries positioned it as a science?"

"Yes, and even though psychology could have lesser explanatory power than the external physical laws, which Kant usually referred to, it could still provide ground for knowledge."

"Sir, it obviously didn't integrate mathematics, which we know rules only these external physical laws."

"Though your view on the role mathematics can play in understanding such inner rules is the same as Kant's, and a little bit more pessimistic than Fries', you are all wrong! With the newer cognitive theories, which rely on concepts such as the Boolean Brain, Predictive Coding, or computer modeling, mathematics doesn't play anymore a marginal role. Through powerful algorithms, it is used to prove cognitive hypotheses, as it is the case for physics."

"Sir, it seems that specialized websites depict different currents of thoughts in philosophy and psychology, having emerged through the joint tackling of issues relating to the source of knowledge and the connections between truth in the outer world and inner states (i.e., justified beliefs)."

---

[a] In the case of cognitive elements, which by nature are immediate and independent, a priori Forms cannot be proven but must be discovered and analyzed. As a consequence, knowledge based on immediate cognition is automatically correct, not because it can be proven like Kant tried to do, but because there is no other choice than to rely on such truth. For instance, if we were to taste a glass of rosé, we could look at the color but couldn't know for sure, as it varies from a very pale to dark pink, which could easily be assimilated with white and red wines. We would have to rely on tasting that cannot be corroborated with exactitude, or spectral analysis, to confirm if it is a real rosé or not.

"You are highlighting one of the most critical debates in philosophy. How do reality and inner states connect? It has been classified under Dualism and Monism. By introducing various views about this issue, I'll now explain how philosophers have used different approaches to understand what cat-ness is and consequently give a philosophical framework for intelligence, and by extension to Artificial Intelligence. However, this debate will have to wait. Please drop me here. I need to buy bread."

When I entered my car with a warm baguette and a few crispy croissants, it was waiting for me with a burning question.

What are Dualism and Monism?

"Sir, what are the differences between Dualism and Monism?"

"In Occidental philosophy,[a] the journey to explain the concept of 'Nous' – the Greek term that expresses intelligence and its associated concepts such as reason, thoughts, understanding, or even intuition – starts in Greece somewhere around 450 BC, with two views on the world's intelligibility."

"Sir, what's the first one?"

"The first opinion, later classified under Dualism, started with Plato and his conviction that the human spirit isn't just composed of a physical structure. Indeed, Plato believed that intelligence was a trait housed in the soul rather than in the body. In his theory of Forms, [53] he additionally gave a view of the world consisting of abstract Forms and matter."

"Sir, based on his belief and this theory, what did he argue?"

"He presented the world we live in is a manifestation of an idea, existing in the abstract. Most of what we humans experience is thus, merely a manifestation of thoughts or Forms of the real Object. For Plato, the human reason is capable of reaching the Essences of things – the 'what' of an Object – and see the world as it is, not its poor materialistic copy."

"Sir, who articulated the second view about the intelligibility of this world?"

"It was proposed by Plato's disciple, Aristotle. He believed that if our intellect is exclusively a materialistic organ, then our intelligibility would

---

[a] Hindu philosophy also tackles the issue.

receive only limited information about the world (for instance, only visual cues).[54] However, and since it is able of receiving and reflecting on any information, then it must be more than just a physical organ."

"Sir, what happened later on?"

"By extrapolation and in continuity with these two dualist views, neo-platonic Christian philosophy explains that the Essences are the fundamental units of intelligibility. The human intellect can grasp, all at once, these Essences. By doing so, it transcends the physics of Objects, understanding also things successively, part per part. Moreover, the human mind can understand through experience, the interactions between various Essences, each one of them following its own set of logic in the real world. Because our mind may reach reality itself – while finite logic cannot –, the human intellect must reside in a soul, which transcends the properties of matter."

"Sir, why is this distinction important?"

"Because it can explain why many people, especially religious ones, do not believe that machines, no matter how fast and sophisticated they are likely to become, will ever be as intelligent as humans. Even if companies like Google were to create billions of semantic or conceptual tagging and hence, solve the 'knowledge that' issues methodologically, cyberists would continue believing that machines would always be incapable of understanding the Object in itself, that is, the 'knowledge of.' 'Cat-ness', 'Rosé-ness' or in other words, what it is to be a cat or a good rosé wine, would remain a reality, that machines won't ever understand."

"Sir, why do you introduce finite and infinite logics?"

"Dealing with other human beings requires that we understand the Essences of the other's personality and their interaction. This complex experience constitutes an almost infinite form of logic that machines, with their finite logic, will never be able to grasp. Since agents with finite logic cannot reach the Essences of an Object but simply tag them and check if the links between various statements (i.e., what I classified under epistemology) representing this Object are true, machines for cyberists, won't ever really be intelligent and Strong AI shall never happen."

"Sir, why machines have finite logic?"

"In 1931, Kurt Gödel, unrevealed the incompleteness theorem, proving that there are statements in logic that are true but not logically provable.[55] What this theorem indicates is that even for properly posed questions involving only the arithmetic of integers, any machine as powerful as it could be, wouldn't still be able to decide if these statements are true or false."

"Sir, do these old Greek and Christian views on Dualism, still hold to be true?"

"Well, they did for a long time, and we have to wait for the 17th century to obtain a more modern view, called Substance Dualism. The French Philosopher René Descartes,[56] rather than positioning the problem of duality at the Object level, formulates for the first time, the separation from the physical organ where resides intelligence (i.e., the brain) and the immaterial mind, with its consciousness and self-awareness capacities.[a] "

"Sir, this causal relation created issues, you just tackled by presenting Externalism, Internalism and Kant's mid-way, didn't it?"

"Yes, if beliefs and justification are mental contents, but the truth is a matter of fact in the outside world, then justification must be connected to the truth for knowledge to exist."

"Sir, what you've not described thoroughly, is the nature of this problematical connection. If humans get a glimpse of the reality through perception, how are we sure that they aren't dreaming or hallucinating?"

"Indeed! How can we be certain that the cat we are looking at isn't a ghost, a robot, or a holographic picture of that cat? In other words, the physical cause isn't necessarily the only thing that may generate the effect. It is thus, difficult to see how causality can generate some true representation of the world, in our brain.[b] "

"Sir, does this dualistic view still hold on today?"

"Actually in the philosophy of mind, we can divide Dualism according to what sorts of things we chose to be dualistic about."

---

[a] With the risk of oversimplifying Descartes' duality argumentation, we could say that he came up with his theory on the mind-body problem. He justified that though, he could be dreaming or having an illusion, and therefore, could doubt that he had a body, he couldn't in any way have the same doubt about his mind, since he was thinking: 'Cogito, ergo sum.' As a consequence, body and mind have two distinct existences, one physical and the other immaterial. For him, this immaterial mind and physical body, causally interact in unknown ways at the level of the brain (e.g., in the pineal gland), which is the only direct connection between us and the external objects.

[b] This finding probably can explain why recent theories (e.g., from Wittgeinstein)[N29] consider that justification conforms to an internal 'language game' rather than to an external reality. Other philosophers, who've viewed truth defined by internal states, posited that it had to be determined by power (e.g., Marx)[N30] or have ended up often with relativistic or even nihilistic views (e.g., Foucault).[N31]

"Sir, you just told me that Substance Dualism explains that there are two different substances (i.e., physical/brain and immaterial/mind). What other type of dualism is there?

"Property Dualism, as it's called, doesn't believe in such dual substances. Instead, it portrays the mind as a group of independent properties emerging from our brain, but only in one physical substance (i.e., our brain). Within this physiological envelop, mental properties (e.g., beliefs, emotions, perceptions, etc.) can emerge."

"Sir, in Dualism, what is the relation between mind and body? If the mind and body are different 'beasts,' as described by Property or Substance Dualism, then isn't the main issue how they relate together?"

"Thoughts and emotions interact with our body, either given rise to a bodily response or answering to it. Several views strive to explain this interaction: Interactionism, Epiphenomenalism, Parallelism, and Occasionalism.[a]"

"Sir, you mentioned that the opposite concept of Dualism is called Monism. What is it?"

"Monism expresses the idea of singleness. In the context of the philosophy of the mind, it describes the various theories, which attempt to eliminate the dichotomy between body and mind."

"Sir, what is its main criticism of Dualism?"

"It cannot agree that something entirely immaterial can affect something totally material. In other words, it raises the problem of causal interaction. It is split into various views: Idealistic, Neutral, Reflexive, and Materialistic (also called Physicalism) Monism.[b]"

- [a] **Interactionism** is the view that mental and physical events causally influence each other. Through our senses, we gather experience and adapt our behavior accordingly. Our thoughts also affect our actions. In other words, mental states can produce physical effects, and vice-versa.
- **Epiphenomenalism** asserts that physical events may generate other physical or mental events, but mental events cannot cause anything since they are by-products of physical activities occurring in the brain (i.e., epiphenomena).
- **Parallelism** holds that mental and physical causes only have mental and physical effects respectively, but because God created a pre-established harmony, it appears to us that physical and mental events are always interacting.
- **Occasionalism** asserts that any material basis of the interaction between the material and immaterial worlds is impossible, unless caused by the intervention of God on each occasion.

[b] Types of Monism:
- **Idealistic:** it asserts that the only substance that exists is mental. The reality of this world is either psychological or an illusion and is thus, immutable and eternal. Various philosophers have supported this type of Monism (e.g., Leibniz, Berkeley, Hegel).

"Sir, though you've briefly presented the various dualistic and monistic movements, which try to explain how the world and the human mind interact, you've only so far, given a theistic view of intelligence."

"That's true, but I won't give a gnoseological explanation for each one of these movements. Instead, I'll now do so from a materialistic perspective and focus on Physicalism. This is important, as any discussion about AI necessarily relies on a few of the views appertaining to this movement."

"Sir, I can identify in the specialized websites that there are two fundamental approaches to this materialistic view."

"Yes, on one side, there are those who sustain that neurosciences and cognitive theories will in the future explain all mental states and properties. This view is called Reductive Physicalism."

"Sir, the other view must probably be called Non-Reductive Physicalism? How different is it?"

"Yes, it argues that, even though our mind is our brain, the predicates and vocabulary used when we describe or try to explain our mental states cannot be reduced only to language or lower-level explanations of neurosciences. As a consequence, our mental and physical states are inter-dependent, and though no change to mental states can happen without some physical changes, they cannot be reducible to them."

- **Neutral**: this monism sustains that reality results from a single substance that is neither physical nor mental, but that can achieve both attributes. Therefore, matter and mind properties is a function of an unknown substance.
- **Reflexive:** it argues that a single substance composing the universe, can manifest itself materialistically and as a conscious experience. Through this conscious experience, a human has a view of both the world and of himself (hence 'reflexive').
- **Materialistic:** it's considered the main doctrine since the last century. It holds the view that there is only one reality, that of matter. It explains that only physical aspects can be real and that mental properties may be reduced to their physical properties."

I stopped there and wondered if I should immediately describe the various movements belonging to two forms of Physicalism or introduce them indirectly, through the history of psychology. I looked outside, by the window, and saw that we were stuck in traffic. I decided that I had the time to make a digression.

How psychology complements philosophy?

"Do you remember Fries?" I said to my car.

"Sir, I never forget things."

"Of course you don't. Well, he defended a dualism of the inner and outer world.[52] Though he surely was influenced by Kant, he also was impacted by ideas about psychology coming from Idealism.[57]"

"Sir, specialized websites indicate that Fries was a student of Fichte,[58] who was one of the strongest advocates of such movement. Maybe that's why?"

"Most probably, but unlike the idealist conception of psychology, the dominant view of his time, he thought of psychology as a rational and empirical science. Fries' contribution to psychology served as an alternative to Idealism and influenced several psychologists of the next generations, including indirectly, Wilhelm Wundt.[a]"

"Sir, wasn't Wundt part of Structuralism, a movement which focused on a detailed investigation of mental elements?"

"Yes, and his work showed a balanced view, integrating Rationalism and Empiricism.[b] Wundt's empirical views (especially, the method of introspection he helped develop), created the foundation of the school called Structuralism. However, several psychologists criticized his views.[c]"

---

[a] Among others, two independent thinkers, Herbart,[N32] and Beneke,[N33] used Fries' view but argued additionally that psychology should become an experimental science. The work developed by both early psychologists influenced, in the end, Wilhelm Wundt, who founded the first psychological laboratory in Leibniz, and who is generally recognized as the founder of modern psychology.[N34]

[b] Wundt isn't as extremist as he might have been portrayed for many years, since his American translator E.B. Titchener (1867 – 1927) disseminated a wrong radical empirical form of his views.[N35]

[c] Among them, two names are important, because they influenced deeply two other important psychological movements:
• Carl Stumpf (1848-1936) believed Wundt's empirical focus on these elements of

"Sir, am I correct in suggesting that like for Epistemology, Empiricism and Rationalism have greatly influenced psychology?"

"Absolutely! Additionally, it created movements that, in some way, can be viewed as a pull towards either one of these philosophical groups. However, don't forget Kant's middle way, which also influenced movements profoundly, such as the Gestalt and Nativism.[a] There are also some similarities of views between Kant and William James,[59] who is one of the pioneers of Functionalism."

"Sir, what are the main similarities and differences between them?"

"Both saw the mind as interactive. However, while Kant thought that such capacity was founded on an innate process and the mind's objective structure, James viewed this mind as a by-product of evolution."

"Sir, could you describe a few of these movements?"

"In fact, and though James was a Pragmatic, his evolutionary view, which reduced the human mind to a mere physical phenomenon, led to a form of extreme Empiricism, called Behaviorism.[b] James profoundly influenced John Dewey who is thought of as the founder of Functionalism. Like James, his view was a blend of Empiricism and Rationalism, which paved the way to Behaviorism."

"Sir, what are again the main similarities and differences with Kant?"

"Where Kant's blend of Empiricism and Rationalism considered mind and experience as dual and interacting to form constructions of knowledge, James and Dewey's functionalist's blend, considered mind and experience as one single thing.[c] "

---

experience lacked the more rational appreciation of the wholeness of experience, an idea that profoundly influenced the Gestalt movement.

- Similarly, his assistant Oswald Kulpe (1862-1915), showed that some mental states (e.g., hesitation and confidence) originate from the passive association of sensations and images, which in the structuralist view, composed the structure of consciousness. In reaction against Wundt's focus on awareness, he started investigating non-conscious influences, which paved the way for Freud's theories.

[a] In fact, the Gestalt means in German, something in its entirety, and therefore looks at the mind as a whole, not just like the sum of its individual parts, as Structuralism would. Gestalt psychology thus tries to analyze how the brain creates entire concepts, not some kind of individual pieces.

[b] The movement founded by Pierce.

[c] Though his science was empirical, he, unlike empiricists, believed in the wholeness of the mind. He saw this unity of experience, as a process by which our active mind, through the creative synthesis of its parts, makes up the whole. For him, the structure of the brain defines the interaction of its essential elements. As a consequence, consciousness is the

"Sir, with Functionalism, don't you develop a monist view?"

"Yes, in which the role played by the mind becomes quickly secondary. Functionalists believe psychology should focus on the study of mental processes rather than on the mind's content, taking into consideration awareness and the relationship between the person and its environment.[a] "

"Sir, in this movement, doesn't the brain look like a computer, receiving all kinds of data (i.e., sensory input) to be processed and creates a behavior adapted to the environment?"

"Yes, and unlike structuralists, they even pictured the brain as chemically (i.e., mechanically) causing conscious awareness and behavior, and influenced an extreme form of Empiricism called Associationism.[b] "

"So Sir, Behaviorism is an extreme form of Empiricism that resulted from Associationism?"

"Indeed. Behaviorism focused on the Stimuli/Response relation, highlighted by Associationism and mainly rejected the distinction between mind and body. For its founder, J.B. Watson (1878-1958), and with only the body left, there was no more room for a mental concept of the brain. Thinking could thus be reduced to inner voices. Behaviorism became, till the middle of the twentieth century, the main psychological current, as it was judged sufficient to explain all of the human behaviors."

"Sir, by what was it replaced?"

---

result of the sum of our life-time's experiences. These basic experiences are separated into three categories: sensations, images, and emotions. It is by understanding how these basic elements interact, that structuralists believe the structure of the mind may best be pictured.

[a] With Functionalism, to find the meaning of an idea, one needs to look at where it leads, and thus, truth is in its usefulness and practicality. Rather than focusing on introspection as structuralists do, functionalists put their efforts on studying the causes and effects through observation of humans' behaviors, within their environment. The underlying reason for this view is that the brain is inherently neutral, without behavior, but able to produce different reactions, depending on the signal received. Therefore, Functionalism defines mental states by their function.

[b] One of James' Harvard student named Edward Lee Thorndike built upon the most extremist ideas of Functionalism to developed a more radical empiricist psychological view. Through his study on animals, he came up with a theory called Associationism, that made connections between situations and responses. He analyzed how a mental form of learning could result from the association of events or ideas with one another.

"It was only by the 1960's that cognitive psychology successfully challenged behaviorism. Cognitive theories benefited from developments in mental imagery and mathematical modeling, and helped understand the bases of cognition and all of its related processes (e.g., attention, perception, memory, language, reasoning, intelligence, consciousness, etc.)."

"Sir, what are these cognitive theories?"

"The main ones are the Information Processing theory, the Schema Theory, and Constructivism. Using ideas and methods from various areas and being strongly rooted in philosophy and neurosciences, these new theories study how humans acquire and use knowledge."

"Sir, I appreciated the fact that you gave me an overview of the main psychological movements. However, could you close your diversion here and come back to giving me a materialistic view of intelligence?"

Fortunately, I was arriving at my destination, so I postponed that conversation to another day.

Is there a materialistic view of intelligence?

The next Saturday, when tuning in to my web radio, I was expecting to be welcomed with a friendly 'good morning' from the version 3.0 of my car. Instead, the voice said:

"Sir, is Physicalism based on a monist or dualist view?"

It caught me off-guard, but I was still able to articulate an opinion. "Hey… Actually, it grew out of Materialism and as such is a one substance view of nature. Therefore, it implies some kind of Monism.[a] What makes something a mental state doesn't depend on its internal organization but on

---

[a] In nature, the matter is the fundamental substance and all mental phenomena or consciousness result from material interactions. Physicalism posits that all mental states supervene on the physical (i.e., the chemical characteristics of the world define a distribution of biological properties, which themselves determine a distribution of psychological features), but doesn't necessarily asserts that all properties in the real world are identical to physical features. For instance, the Type Identity Theory, a sub-division of Physicalism, holds that specific mental states (e.g., mental pain) are identical to specific physical internal states of the brain (e.g., associated with C-fiber firing), but Functionalism doesn't. In such view, causal relations to sensory stimulations, other mental states, and behaviors determine the identity of a brain state (e.g., pain, thoughts, beliefs, and desire).

the role it plays in the cognitive system, which it is a part of. Since their functional role characterizes mental states, they must be realizable on multiple levels."

"Sir, what do you mean by multiple realizability and why is it important?"

"It is the thesis that different physical properties, states, or events can implement the same mental property, state, or event. It is important because a theory of the mind, which accepts multiple realizability, allows for the existence of strong AI.[a] "

"Sir, what do you include in reductive and non-reductive Physicalism?"

"Reductive Physicalism includes Behaviorism, Type identity, and Functionalism. Non-reductive Physicalism, which claims that mental properties are not reducible to physical properties, on the other hand, integrates Anomalous monism, Emergentism, and Eliminativism."

"Sir, what is the concept behind Anomalous monism?"

"It states that mental events are identical with physical events, but that these mental events are real and identical with physical matter, but not regulated by strict physical laws (i.e., the mental is anomalous)."

"Sir, what's your view on Emergentism and Eliminativism?"

"Emergentism holds that physical properties of the brain give rise to mental states, emerging with new properties. Eliminativism, on the other hand, holds that people's common-sense understanding of the mind is hopelessly flawed and that an alternative, usually taken to be neuroscience, will eventually replace it. Eliminativists especially believe that Connectionism will prove to account more accurately on how our brain works. I consider both these views extremely pertinent."

"Sir, how can someone claim to be materialist (i.e., that all substances are physical) but, on the other hand, say that all mental properties aren't reducible to physical properties?"

"This is an excellent question. In fact, some philosophers have cataloged the failure of Non-Reductive Physicalism to explain mental causation and have even advocated that it cannot sustain the view that substance is in the end physical.[60] "

---

[a] Multiple realizability confers to these mental states the possibility to be manifested in various systems, and potentially computers, as long as the system, of which they are part of, performs the appropriate functions. In other words, if a brain can be considered a physical device, with its neural substrate performing computations on inputs, producing behaviors, a computer may also be seen as hardware, with its electronic substrate performing data calculations, generating outputs for specific actions.

"Sir, what are you trying to achieve with such distinction about Physicalism?"

"As I told you, I am trying to define within which framework, it is possible to accept that machines can aspire to acquire strong AI."

"Sir, are you saying that if either one of the theist theories (e.g., Substance Dualism) is true then strong AI is impossible?"

"Yes, if the human mind isn't just composed of a physical structure, it will obviously be impossible even to consider strong AI, unless we believe that machines may acquire a soul."

"Sir, does it mean that any materialistic theory can support such claim for strong AI?"

"No, for instance, Behaviorism, Identity Theory, and Anomalous Monism can't.[a] "

"Sir, what about Emergentism or Eliminativism?"

"For Eliminativism, intelligence is computational, whereas, for Emergentism, it depends on the situation.[b] I'll come back to this important issue, but let me now introduce to you the Computational Theory of the Mind, to better address what makes a system computational."

What is the Computational Theory of Mind (CTM)?

"Sir, what is CTM?"

"Many modern philosophers and scientists believe that the mind is a computer, or at least, can be compared to one. All theories, related to such

---

[a] Behaviorism, which only considers the behaviors, cannot support it. Identity theory, which holds that at least some types of mental states are identical with some kinds of biological brain states, rejects the idea that a non-organic being can be intelligent. Indeed, no creatures with brains different than humans are able to share sensations, beliefs, and desires, no matter how similar their behavior and internal organization may be to humans' own. Furthermore, Anomalous Monism, which describes mental events identical with physical matter but not regulated by strict physical laws, would seem problematical.

[b] Emergentism states that a higher system level emerges from lower levels, with different properties. Intelligence is computational or not, depending on if the consciousness arising from this system may or not be reduced to the physical properties it emerged from (as according to Penrose, consciousness is interrelated to awareness, understanding, and intelligence).[N36] As for Eliminativism,[N37] it seems that it could be compatible with computationalism as Stephen Stich,[N38] and Hartry Field,[N39] combined Classical CTM and Formal Syntactic Conception of computation with Eliminativism, thereby positing that rationality is mechanically possible.

conviction, are regrouped within the CTM. However, these theories don't only deal with intelligence but also address issues about knowledge, self-awareness, and other higher cognition capabilities or mental states, associated with the human brain."

"Sir, why are you only introducing this theory now?"

"The point is that CTM addresses the most complex issues, usually associated with the brain's processing part of the mind and consciousness. Though CTM also tackles issues about attention, perception, and memory, it focuses on problems related to the thought process, for which I feel, you are now well prepared."

"Sir, how do these CTM theories look like?"

"Rather than presenting the various CTM views randomly, I've decided to classify them under two main currents of thoughts, which bring these different views about how the brain performs computation. This division is based on how it computes, digitally for Classical CTM, and analogously for Connectionism.[a] "

"Sir, what does this classical version say?"

"CTM claims that the mind is a computational system that transduces sensory inputs into representations, which are then manipulated algorithmically. The core mental processes related to intelligence (e.g., reasoning, decision-making, and problem-solving) are computable in a quite similar way, as in a Turing machine."

"Sir, what is so special about a Turing machine?"

"In his 1936 paper,[3] Turing described a machine that computes symbols (i.e., like men use a pencil on a sheet of paper to do arithmetical calculations), which he argued, could replicate any symbolic algorithm executed by a human brain. For classicists, cognition looks like digital processing, where strings are sequentially produced, according to instructions coded in a symbolic program. I am e-mailing you an extract from Stanford Encyclopedia of philosophy,[61] on Turing's machine.[b] "

---

[a] There is potentially a third category, based on a hybrid computational version (i.e., analog and digital), called the Neuroscience Theory.

[b] • There are many memory locations, arrayed in a linear structure. Metaphorically, these memory locations are 'cells' on an infinitely long 'paper tape.' More literally, the memory locations might be physically realized in various media (e.g., silicon chips).
• There is a central processor, which can access one memory location at a time. Metaphorically, the central processor is a 'scanner' that moves along the paper tape one 'cell' at a time.

"Therefore Sir, CTM relies on the Turing machine?"

"Yes, but not exclusively! It also requires two additional theoretical assumptions – brain 'adaptationism' and modularity –, that is, the specialization of sub-modules resulting from our species' evolution.[a] "

"Sir, how is a mental module defined?"

"There are three possible solutions: functionally, physically or through behaviors.[b] "

"Sir, what are the limits of classical CTM?"

"If we focus on a functional approach to these modules, there are two weak aspects of such classical CTM theory. The first one relates to the productivity of thought, that is, the limitation of finitely machine states versus the brain's unlimited capacity. I've already presented the issue with Gödel's finite logic argument."

"Sir, what's the second weakness?"

"It is due to the 'systematicity' of thought, which argues systematic relations between mental states."

"Sir, how were these limitations dealt with?"

• The central processor can enter into finitely many machine states.

• The central processor may perform four elementary operations: write a symbol at a memory location; erase a symbol from a memory location; access the next memory location in the linear array ('move to the right on the tape'); access the previous memory location in the linear array ('move to the left on the tape').

• Which elementary operation the central processor performs depends entirely upon two facts: which symbol is currently inscribed at the present memory location; and the scanner's own current machine state.

• A machine table dictates which elementary operation the central processor performs, given its current machine state and the symbol it is currently accessing. The machine table also dictates how the central processor's machine state changes given those same factors. Thus, the machine table enshrines a finite set of routine mechanical instructions governing computation.

[a] The Adaptationism thesis, which emerged from evolutionary psychology, argues that our brain adapted by creating specialized sub-systems. Therefore, our mind results from the brain evolution, which generated several modules to deal with reality (e.g., vision, language, taste, etc.). The presence of modules, on the other hand, allows our brain to divide and process information independently, avoiding our mind to be overwhelmed.

[b] Though this theory relies on Turing's work, it was Hilary Putnam who introduced Classical CTM in philosophy.[N40] His belief was that any system possesses a mind whenever it has a functional organization, which performs automated probabilistic calculations. Thus, he postulated that mental states are functional states, rather than physical brain states (i.e., Type-identity Theory view) or behavior states (i.e., Behaviorism).

"Jerry Fodor argued that we think in a language of thoughts,[62] which deals with mental representations, both primitive and complex.[a] The formalized syntactic conception of computation enables Fodor to infer that the human mind is a syntactic engine. Moreover, he also argues that representational properties are real aspects of our mind and consequently that we can use intentional descriptions."

"Sir, am I correct in assuming that by doing this, we can induce a materialistic view of intelligence?"

"Exactly! By considering our mind as a syntax-driven machine and allowing intentional descriptions, Fodor answers the question of why rationality is mechanically possible."

"Sir, you referred to the modularity of the mind. Could you develop your thoughts?"

"Different views were expressed about the level of modularity, varying from a central system to a massive modular system, introducing the view that the brain is a 'connectome,' that is, a set of connected networks.[b] "

"Sir, what is the impact of such connectionist view?"

"For connectionists, neural networks behave differently than a Turing machine, because they are composed of a network of collection nodes (i.e., synapses), which compute analogously."

"Sir, what do connectionists claim?"

---

[a] Combining a Representational Theory of the Mind (RTM) and Classical CTM, Fodor explains that mind's activities are computational, using the language of thoughts. By suggesting that propositional attitudes are linked to these complex mental symbols, RTM solves the issue of productivity and 'systematicity' of thoughts. As a consequence, Classical CTM and RTM support the idea that mental activities are computational but, unlike Functionalism, doesn't pretend that mental states are functional states. Fodor additionally combines Classical CTM and RTM with the intuitive idea that computation processes symbols in virtue of their formalized syntactic properties (e.g., inference rules), as opposed to their semantic characteristics (e.g., references or conditions of truth).

[b] Fodor thinks that the mental modularity is partial and still requires a central system to function,[N41] whereas Pinker [N42] believes the brain to be massively modular, with all modules, when combined, creating human cognition. Rather than using a central system approach, Pinker adopts a connectionist position. For him, connected networks don't represent information directly, but instead structure to form a system that can compute the representation: 'Neural network alone cannot do the job. It is the structuring of networks into programs for manipulating symbols that explains much of human intelligence.' Carruthers proposes a 'moderately' massive modularity,[N43] which could explain issues such as flexibility and creativity content, as well as abductive inference.

"Connectionists unlike classicists, claim that information is stored non-symbolically in the connections' strengths and weights between the units of a neural network.[a] "

"Sir, is this connectionist view shared by all within this movement?"

"This connectionist view is split between the eliminativists who claim that the brain cannot be compared to a Turing machine and the implementationalists who believe that the brain isn't just a neural network, but also a symbolic processor, operating at a higher and more abstract level."

"Sir if I understood you well, there are those who see the human brain as a syntactic engine, those who think that it is just a connection of neurons with different strengths, and those viewing the brain as a mixture of both?"

"Yes, but this controversy between a symbolic processor and pure or mixt connectionism is further complicated by the beliefs of those who view the brain as using a hybrid connectionist architecture.[b] Besides this debate within the CTM, there are also two competing models used to explain and predict mental phenomena: Functionalism and Mechanism."

"Sir, you presented a few minutes ago, Functionalism and its mechanistic view. Why then do we need two mechanical models?"

---

[a] Connectionists portray mental processing as a dynamic evolution of activities in the neural network. This progression results from the activation of each network unit according to connection strengths and activities between neighboring units. Connectionist systems do well in modeling perceptual and motor processes, something Classical CTM has a problem doing. Many cognitive researchers also believe that they are nearer to reality than the classical CTM rule-based systems. Thus, some connectionists such as Eliminativists believe that neural networks and Turing machines are two different beasts. However, other connectionists (i.e., Implementationalists) view that both computing systems may co-exist, as Turing-style and neural networks would respectively correspond to higher and lower level models.

[b] Computational neuroscience differs from Connectionism and Classical CTM, mainly by arguing that brain computation is a mixture of analog and digital processing. Some even say that neural signals are somewhat discrete.[N44] Neural spikes only happen when incoming signals exceed a certain threshold (i.e., an input value is discrete), though these neural spikes form continuous patterns in time (i.e., analog output).

"Functionalism proposes that mental phenomena are best understood as the performance of various capacities, which must be analyzed functionally. In other words, we must decompose these phenomena into a set of dispositions that when regrouped, reconstitute the respective capacities. Furthermore, the internal structure is irrelevant to deciding what function is actually realized.[a] "

"Sir, you've not explained why there is a need for a mechanistic model?"

"In this model, a mental phenomenon is best explained by its underlying multi-level mechanism, which should be understood as organized systems, composed of interacting components and operational processes.[b] "

"Sir, I understand the differences, but which model is today the dominant form of computational explanation?"

"A three-level mechanical explanation (called constitutive) [63] is today its main form.[c] Nevertheless, the important fact isn't so much, which theory is more popular."

"What is then crucial to understand, Sir?"

"A materialistic view of reality is achievable, whether you consider intelligence from a classical CTM vs. Connectionism perspective or under a Functionalism vs. Mechanism view. Consequently, strong AI is in my opinion, theoretically achievable."

"Sir, are you saying that from a philosophical perspective strong AI is possible?"

"Yes, I do and will now show how the cognitive theories support and complement my view."

---

[a] To address criticisms formulated by Mechanism, David Marr proposes a model based on of three levels of explanation. He describes a first level, which deals with the question of what is computed, a second level explaining how to do it, and a third one referring to the physical engine required to do this processing. [N45]

[b] Explaining such an underlying mechanism requires that we reveal, the mechanism's causal structure. In other words, mechanical computation requires that a relation of causality links input and output streams. Furthermore, this link, together with the processing structure, must be thoroughly described. The point is a Mechanistic Computational model deals with the digital versus analog issue. If the system processes discretely structured links, then the computation is digital, and if it treats continuous connections, then it is analog.

[c] It is composed of a low level in the explanation (i.e., constitutive), an isolated level that specifies the mechanism's parts and how they interact through activities or operations, and a contextual level, where the mechanism's functions are explained within a broader context. These three aspects are tightly integrated, and the computational capacity results from the operations of all these parts working together.

Can we unify cognitive theories?

"Sir, did the philosophical debate between Empiricism and Rationalism, which translated into battles between various psychological movements, also happened in cognitive theories?"

"It did, but what we'll see is that by using Kant's middle way views, it is possible to unify the more empirical information processing theory with the more rational Schema theory, within a constructivist framework. However, before continuing with the cognitive theories, I need to check if you are familiar with the two processing strategies encountered in systems, that is, a top-down and bottom-up communication flow?"

"Sir, I am, but please refresh my internal memory."

"The expressions top-down and bottom-up, basically express the idea that something starts from the higher level and goes down the ladder, or on the contrary starts from its lowest elements to be generalized. In a system approach, a top-down approach is essentially the process by which we break down a system into sub-systems to a level of granularity, which is deemed sufficient. It starts with 'the big picture' and by reducing it to various levels, it arrives at the base elements."

"Sir, I guess the bottom-up approach is the opposite process, where basic elements are combined and associated, to recreate higher levels?"

"Yes, till the last layer reaches a level of abstraction that we judge sufficiently complex and complete to englobe the entire system. These two concepts are important because, we've seen, there is a continuum of processes in our mind."

"Sir, what you haven't yet told me, is in which direction the communication flows?"

"I haven't also explained where it originally comes from and if it traverses all the way through this continuum. By answering these questions through cognitive sciences, we'll be able to confirm which philosophical and psychological theories mirror the neuroscience processes."

"Sir, what are these cognitive theories?"

"The first theory, which I would like to present, is the Information Processing theory. It is a bottom-up process, by which we integrate sensory stimuli into increasingly more complex forms of knowledge. Computer-based metaphors highly influence this theory.[a] "

"Sir, what is the second cognitive approach?"

"The Schema theory states that a network of mental structures (i.e., schemas) with preconceived ideas forms our understanding of the world.[b] The last theory is Constructivism, which I won't present to you again."

"Sir, why do you want to unify the cognitive theories?"

"The point is that all three above cognitive theories have limitations, which can be overcome by their association.[c] "

"Sir, you already presented quite extensively Kant's use of schemas and concepts to explain how we acquire knowledge. Therefore, could you start showing the possible links between Kant's constructivist views and the Schema theory?"

"For sure! Kant saw schemas as rules, which our mind follows to construct images, smells, or sounds. Consequently, perception is the

---

[a] Using processing metaphors, it makes correlations between a computer's hardware and the mind's memory system, which stores information. It also correlates software and the human's use of cognitive programs to process information, with three especially important processes: encoding, retrieval, and metacognition processes. Finally, it establishes for learning, a relationship between the reliance on the input of data transmission and the human's reliance on 'transmission of symbols.' This theory also has historical links with the Gestalt movement, with its importance of insights and experience as a whole, as well as with the Nativism theory developed by Noam Chomsky,[N46] with its view that the mind is predisposed genetically to learn languages. Therefore, it is consistent with Empiricism and Behaviorism in its emphasis on experience, but in contradiction with the role played by genetics in language learning.

[b] People use schemas to organize current knowledge into units and to provide a framework for future understanding. It is mainly a top-down deductive process, in which pre-existing human generalizations guide attention, perception, and even reasoning. Similarly, people can quickly organize new perceptions into schemas and act upon them without having to redefine every sensation.

[c] Classic information processing, with its unidirectional three stage information flow (i.e., from sensory memory to the working memory and to LTM) cannot explain how background knowledge affects perception and reasoning, or how beliefs and expectations affect learning. Furthermore, it cannot describe how errors or differences of interpretation between people can happen, why in some case, information can enter the LTM without passing through the STM, how we unconsciously elaborate our memories, or even how information may suddenly consciously pop-up in our mind. Similarly, the Schema theory, besides its lack of clarity on its definition, can be criticized for not describing how or where knowledge is acquired and stored. Furthermore, its mainly top-down flow doesn't explain the influence of information flowing from our senses to our STM and LTM.

resulting combination of what is in the real world and what we expect to be in such a world. These schemas (e.g., the image of a cat) also are the rules that guide the reconstruction of the images coming from our memory. They are part of concepts, which can be seen as broader rules to construct meaning, out of these schemas."

"Sir, how are these concepts related to the categories, you already presented?"

"These concepts, directly related to understanding, are general rules uniting various percepts under one category. As for schemas, these concepts also guide remembered meanings and thus reconstruct our memories. As such, rules can be expressed, like in the case of PCs, under the form of 'if-then' statements. Therefore, this Kantian constructivist cognition view is in line with Schema theory and can unify both approaches.[64] "

"Sir, what about Information Processing theory?"

"By proposing a two-level of beliefs, it is in phase with Kant's separation between understanding and reason. The humans' understanding faculty shapes the concepts, while reason infers knowledge from the concepts, originating from this understanding.[a] "

"Sir, what do you achieve by adding this two-tiered system of beliefs to the classical information processing theory?"

"We get a more accurate picture of our mind's cognitive process, which integrates beliefs and expectations, in learning. These beliefs and expectations (i.e., concepts and schemas), shaped unconsciously by experience, are stored in the unconscious LTM, and thus, guide the active, conscious STM and the perception process."

"Sir, based on what you just said, can you give me an integrated cognitive view?"

---

[a] Though Kant never really expressed this inference, Charles Peirce showed that it is at the heart of intelligibility,[N47] and complements' Kant's view. Kant believed that reason and understanding were, respectively, conscious and unconscious processes. This is in line with the Information Processing theory, where the STM and LTM are respectively associated with the conscious reasoning and unconscious understanding processes. However, and since Kant portrays the understanding process of the mind as resulting from an active player, it is in contradiction with the Information Processing theory. The fact is that modern sciences confirm Kant's analysis of the LTM's active role. Unconscious concepts and schemas are constantly shaping our consciousness through their rules, giving meaning to our experience of the world. At the same time, our life experience is building our background knowledge. Thus, there is not only a constant exchange of information between consciousness and unconsciousness, but there is also the endless bottom-up and top-down flow of information within these processes' continuum.

"I'll do better. I'll e-mail you a figure that describes a unified cognitive model, which integrates a top-down and bottom-up conscious and unconscious flow of information."

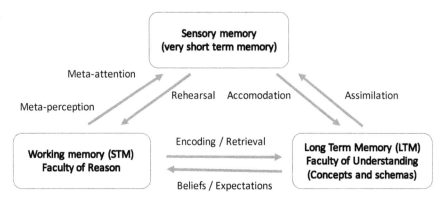

Fig. 32) Unified cognitive model, integrating Constructivism, Schema, and Information Processing theories; source: Clayton Daniel Austin. [64]

"Sir, could you comment this figure for me?"

"Austin's unified cognitive constructivist view accounts for the role played by beliefs and expectations in knowledge formation. It integrates attention and perception phenomena, as well as the physiological changes happening at the neural level (i.e., encoding and retrieval). It explains the influence of the LTM on perception (i.e., assimilation, when concepts and schemes influence it directly) and the impact on the STM of data repetition (i.e., rehearsal). Finally, it takes into account differences in the learner's background (i.e., accommodation)."

"Sir, I'm impressed! You've shown that the continuum of cognitive processes starts from the top and flows both ways. What about information penetration?"

"I'd just like to be a little more precise, before answering your question. The flow is literally bimodal, at each level of the six neural cortical layers. In other words, if I draw this flow within the six cortical layers (considering 1 as the top layer and disregarding any missing layer), it is this one that prevails : 1← → 2 ← → 3 ← → 4← → 5 ← → 6, rather than this more classical representation 6 →5 →4 → 3 →2 → 1 → 2 → 3 → 4→ 5 → 6, or even 1 → 2 → 3 → 4 → 5 → 6→5 →4 → 3 →2 → 1."

"Sir, with this representation, I believe you've answered my question about penetration."

"Yes, reality and concepts can traverse physiologically and mentally all the way through this continuum back and forth, till the surprise is suppressed.[a] "

"Sir, now that you've shown an integrated model, with Constructivism as its core, can you finally define which one of the two philosophical models, Representationalism or Constructivism is the most accurate?"

"I already indicated the major difference between the two: a passive Subject, who suddenly has something represented to him, rather than an active one, who reconstructs what she knows to be on the outside. What I'll now show is that the two main cognitive models I've briefly introduced (i.e., Friston's Free-energy model,[65] and Hawkins' prediction memory models)[12], as well as their underlying Bayesian Brain and Predictive Coding theories, all portray an active Subject, who uses his mind to identify external patterns, by constructing possible scenarios reducing surprises."

"Sir, do I understand that in your view, Constructivism seems to correspond to reality?"

"Though there are other models, which could imply Representationalism, there is a growing body of evidence that our brain plays an active role, as described by Constructivism."

"Sir, if that's the case, why did you say that a dualistic view, such as Kant's, cannot integrate a computational model? Doesn't it mean that machines won't ever reach the strong AI level?"

"Challenging question! What you are saying is that by basing my argumentation on a dualistic theory, I am contradicting myself about a materialistic view of intelligence. Therefore, should I have selected another movement, for instance, Hegel's German Idealism, which is now mainly rejected by modern philosophers?[a] "

"Sir, why didn't you select such idealistic monist view, then?"

---

[a] The essential concept Hawkins and Friston defend is that our mind projects unconsciously a scenario or idea that is confronted with reality. This confrontation comes back in the form of the difference between what we expected and what we sensed. If this surprisal (i.e., surprise in terms of information) is important, it will travel consciously up to the level at which this surprise can be dealt with.

[a] In fact, the American philosopher Tom Rockmore argues that Hegel's view, like all the German idealists' (e.g., Kant, Fichte, Schelling) views,[N48] is also compatible with Constructivism. By agreeing to this, we could benefit from Hegel's diverging constructivist view. Indeed, it diverges from Kant's in three main ways.[N49] He is a posteriori thinker, rather than a priori like Kant. Hegel adopts a cognitive Monism, where the cognitive problem consists in comparing a theory of the Object, with the Object itself, as given in our consciousness. Rather than using categories that are fixed (because of the differences between a cognitive Subject and the mind-independent Object), Hegel believes in Concepts that vary. He introduces a distinction within our consciousness between these Concepts and the Object within this consciousness (in fact, Fichte goes even further and rejects the things-in-themselves outside of the mind,[N50] and reduces Kantian Dualism to some kind of idealistic Monism).

"I have two main issues with it. Humans are a priori thinkers. The new cognitive theories clearly show that we first create a construct, against which the perceived patterns, coming from our senses, are compared to. I also believe, like Kant does, that the mind immediately perceives only its own representations of an Object, which are modified by our innate mental forms and, as a consequence, only receives a representation of the phenomena."

"Sir, in your opinion, are there other views of Hegel you reject?"

"Yes, they don't account for the role of innate mental forms and the physical impact of the flesh."

"Sir, any argument proposed by Hegel that finds favor in your eyes?

"I agree with him that any given cognitive claim can always be possibly refuted and subsequently replaced by a better one, especially if you integrate the probabilistic mind."

"Sir, is that incompatible with Kant's view?"

"Not really, but on the other hand, I believe that Kant cannot be right when he claims that the Object (i.e., the things-in-themselves) are beyond our power of cognition. Therefore, I agree with Hegel that since our mind is receptive, synthetic, and able to abstract, it can compare the Concept of an Object, with the sensory inputs of this Object, within our consciousness. Actually, the word consciousness is probably inappropriate, as we make this comparison within the physical substrate of our cortex, knowingly or not."

"Sir, in your opinion what does Hegel's idea add?"

"This proves, according to me, that a monist view is undoubtedly appropriate."

"Sir, does it mean that with Constructivism, a computational vision is impossible?"

"Some philosophers argue that the struggle between Materialism and Idealism still exists,[66] in this form of battle between Physicalism and Constructivism.[a] However, there is a way to solve this issue and anchor computation within Constructivism. It is to change our vision of the world and the role of the agent within it."

---

[a] Praetorius for instance, argues that both Physicalism and Constructivism don't give a convincing explanation about how truth can arise from logical properties of beliefs and linguistic propositions, while the physical phenomena and states from which they originate, don't even have these properties. In other words, for her, both approaches still don't solve the Cartesian dualistic issue completely.[N51]

"Sir, aren't you just running away from the debate, by doing this?"

"Not at all! Imagine that information is the fabric of the world, which we, humans and other agents like you or animals, strive to make sense of, through our interactions with the environment. In this view, reality can be computable and every physical state, not only in our brain but in nature itself, may be represented in terms of information processing."

"Sir, can you give me some examples of these natural processes?"

"I could mention gene regulation networks and assembly, or protein-protein interaction networks."

"Sir, what's so special about this information?"

"It is potentially there, before any interaction with the receiving agent, but only materializes thanks to this interaction. As such, it is a structure that exists outside of the agent and within his, her, or its mind (as memories, categories, and schemes)."

"Sir, what sustains this view of information as a fabric of the world?"

"It relies on physicists (e.g., Zeilinger, [67] Vedral)[68] who suggested that information and reality is one. It is also grounded on informational structural realism that portrays the world as made of informational structures, which humans use to reconstruct their reality, through the interactions with their environment (Floridi,[69] Sayre)[70]. Moreover, it is also in line with the view that information is just that, bits of information, and not energy or matter (Wiener).[71] Furthermore, it integrates Wheeler's postulate that the laws of physics can be built in terms of information.[72] Last but not least, it is coherent with Kant's view that the Objects, as they appear to us, are reconstructed and is thus inspired by Constructivism."

"Sir, what are the consequences of adopting this view on information?"

"Let's say you accept that the fabric of this world made of matter, is really information. How would you characterize thoughts and representations generated by the schemes and rules, embedded within the physical substrate of our mind, if not as information also?"

"Sir, you are saying that when considering these two elements under the prism of one single unified entity, that is, information, then the concept of Dualism necessarily disappears."

"Yes and furthermore, if I formulate information in relational terms, I could say that it is the difference in one physical system (i.e., reality) that makes a difference in another physical system (i.e., brain).[a] In other words, it pictures a unified view, through this interaction between two physical substrates. In my opinion, this bimodal flow of information ipso facto defines a monist view compatible with strong AI. In fact, as Dodig-Crnkovic puts it, this view: ' . . . is a monism as it considers information and computation as complementary notions.'[41] a "

"Sir, is that all?"

"Well, it's already significant, but no, there's more to it. There is another key aspect, originating in von Foerster's view of the world.[73] It is the crucial role played by the observer and the interactions between him and the observed Object."

"Sir, are you implying that you need two observing entities that influence each other, to achieve a view of reality?"

"Kind of! Quantum physics has shown that the mere fact of observing something, changes the comportment of that thing. Therefore, what is seen isn't absolute but relative to the observer's point of view. This strengthens, in my opinion, the subjective nature of reality, where abstract information can only describe matter's behavior.[b] "

"Sir, does this view possess a name and if so are there other incidences for our discussion?"

"It's called info-computational constructivism and may be traced back to cybernetics and its three main phases (i.e., engineering, biological, and social system design).[c] It shows that the process of life, which is itself define as synonymous with cognition, can be bio-computed."

"Sir, what do you mean by the process of life can be bio-computed?"

---

[a] Information is 'a difference that makes a difference' (Bateson 1972). Information expresses the fact that 'a system is in a certain configuration that is correlated to the configuration of another system. Any physical system may contain information about another physical system' (Hewitt 2007). From these two premises, Gordana Dodig-Crnkovic (2006) defines information as the difference in one physical system that makes a difference in another physical system.

[a] It is important to highlight that this view constitutes an epistemological framework rather than an ontological one, in the sense that it follows von Glasersfeld view that reality is constructed from experiences and, as such, it cannot be anything else than the real outside world generated by our memorized interactions with it.[N52]

[b] We could even extrapolate interpersonal relationships follow this same influential process. The mere fact of someone knowing that she is being observed, changes her behavior, but also the fact that this observer realizes that the other person knows that he is being watched, modifies his own behavior as well.

[c] The biological cybernetic views of the 70s and 80s were dominated by the biology of cognition and constructivist philosophy developed mainly by Humberto Maturana,[N53] Heinz von Foerster,[N54] and Ernst von Glasersfeld.[N55]

"Nature itself, at all levels, may be modeled. However, this requires models that go beyond the Turing machine.[74] "

"Sir, I thought you said that any intelligent machine needed to act as a Turing machine?"

"You are right, but this view uses a more general model of computation, called the Actor Model, which takes into account a more distributed computational model, nearer the concept of our neurons. In fact, it treats Turing model as just a specific case (Hewitt, 2010).[75] "

"Sir, what are the main differences?"

"Morphological computing, as is called its corresponding programming discipline, differs from the classical Turing machine. Instead of processing artificial symbols through coding execution, it involves physical, chemical, and biological processing, as it happens spontaneously in nature.[a] "

"Sir, if Constructivism must become the main current of thoughts and we can even apply it to nature or programming, what are the consequences for learning?"

"Well, I've told you that from a Kantian perspective, learning happens through the relationship between experience and our active mind. Furthermore, for Kant, Schemas and Concepts are rules unconsciously formed that support the reconstruction of reality and the shaping of our memories. We may thus, infer that teaching should emphasize the construction of rules, rather than focus on knowledge acquisition. Furthermore, these rules, which take the form of 'if-then' statements, can even serve as a functional way to structure learning experiences.[b] "

"Sir, I remember you saying that our STM was limited and that teachers should consider this limitation."

"Exactly. You can achieve this by focusing on relevant examples of the rule, rather than on an abstract form of it. I recommend that you look at Austin's exhaustive constructivist teaching suggestions.[64] As promised, I'll now introduce two cognitive approaches – Hawkins' memory-prediction and Friston's Free-energy theories –, which can provide a materialistic explanation of cognition, compatible with Constructivism."

---

[a] Instead of having asynchronous communication between equipment, computation is done through several remotely located devices, capable of acting on their own behalf (Hewitt, 2011).[N56] This approach is more in line with the distributed model of the internet.

[b] Within this constructivist perspective, the teacher's role must be seen as a guide for students, providing through pertinent examples, the support to create rules about the identified concept to be taught. Cases rather than abstract rules should come first so that alumni can understand and own these rules. By doing so, they can acquire the capacity to recognize or even recreate examples of these rules by themselves.

"Sir, why do you seem so enthusiastic?"

"For the first time in history, we have access to unifying theories across various 'soft disciplines' (i.e., philosophy, psychology, and cognitive sciences), which shed a strong light on epistemological and gnoseological fundamentals, justified by true neuroscience beliefs. In echo to Fodor's comment, 'Any psychological theory that is incompatible with known facts of neurology must be, ipso facto, unacceptable,'[76] there is a core of complementary theories, which are backed up by neuroscience research, explaining how the brain works."

"How would you know for sure, Sir?"

"State-of-the-art neuroscience equipment, IT systems, and scanning technologies are so powerful today, that it is now possible to hypothesize quantitative theories of the mind, like the ones from Friston or Hawkins, and test them."

"Sir, before you present these new models, could you tell me if we are entitled to integrate the cognitive sciences, within an epistemological debate?"

"Yes, we are, thanks to the work of philosophers Willard Van Orman Quine and Imre Lakatos who respectively,[77] introduced a criticism of logical Empiricism and Karl Popper's epistemology of sciences. Through this joint criticism, 'natural' epistemology becomes possible.[a] Quine and Lakatos' arguments confirm Fodor's affirmation and highlight the crucial implications on Epistemology and Gnoseology of the new cognitive theories, we will now discuss."

What is the memory-prediction model?

"Sir, which model will you talk about first?"

"The memory-prediction from Jeff Hawkins,[12] which explains how the brain and more specifically, neurons within the neocortex and a few closely localized organs (e.g., hypothalamus) are inter-connected. He

---

[a] In the case of Quine, his eliminativist vision of epistemology tends to embed the philosophical debate within cognitive science itself. Lakatos' emergentist view, on the other hand, describes philosophy as playing a crucial and distinct role within all the cognitive sciences. In other words, these two naturalist views sustain that philosophy is a part of cognitive sciences and that any new theory emanating from these cognitive sciences can change the philosophical debate on knowledge and intelligence.

brings convincing ideas about intelligence and cognition, based on neuroscience evidence."

"Sir, does this model explain why a cat is a cat?"

"Yes, it does. For Hawkins, all our knowledge of the world is a model based on patterns. What we believe is the reality, in fact, is an idea of this world, based on the consistency of the different patterns we can observe through our various senses and on how the brain interprets what we just perceived, as this reality. By the way, I believe this is in line with the computational constructivist view, I just described."

"Sir, how does the human brain deal with these patterns?"

"It does so, according to four universal rules. Firstly, it stores sequences of patterns. Secondly, temporal or spatial patterns are self-associated. Thirdly, our cortex feeds up and stores patterns hierarchically. Last but not least, the cortex stores patterns in an invariant form.[a] "

"Sir, could you explicit for me these four rules, starting with storage of patterns?"

"When we try to sing a song, tell a story, or replay a visual scene, we do it sequentially. We recall it the same way we stored in our mind. We can't remember any sequence in its entirety, but rather little by little, through each temporal sequence. The term 'pointer' is adequate, as it indicates that a set of words or images will bring us back the related memory. In fact, patterns are these pointers, as one pattern (e.g., a note or melody) brings us to the next one."

"Sir, how are temporal or spatial patterns, associated with themselves?"

"We can remember an event that happened long ago, based on a small detail, because it is associated with the full memory. This self-association allows us to detect and complete a spatial pattern based on partial or distorted sensory input. For instance, we can deduce that a person is hiding behind an Object by just seeing an arm or a leg that is sticking out, or we may identify the name of a song by hearing just a few notes. Even our

---

[a] Probably, this invariance happens, because of two physical phenomena. Over time the brain moves the knowledge down the cortical hierarchy, freeing space for the higher layer neurons opportunity to learn newer more complex and subtle patterns. A lower level will thus take for granted that what it already received from above is a settled fact and only if some deep surprise would happen, would this fact be challenged. It is this higher-order structure that makes humans able to experience the world. The other cause is that there is in the brain some special neurons, called 'gnostic' or 'grandmother' neurons, because they were identified as associated exclusively with an Object, or person in this case. Though this neural singularity isn't shared by everyone, scarce coding involving some of these neurons, could account for the same invariability.

thoughts and memories are associatively linked, feeding in the current thought with the next one."

"Sir, what about hierarchical storage?"

"Our cortex is composed of six layers of neurons. Lower layers feed sensory inputs up to higher areas, by way of a certain neural pattern of connectivity, while higher layers send information down to these lower layers, using different connections. Lateral connections also exist between areas that are in separate sections of the hierarchy."

"Sir, how is the patterns' invariance achieved in the brain?"

"Our brain forms a representation of the important world's relationships, independently from its details. For instance, I recognize my wife's face if we are one or two hundred meters apart, regardless of if she is facing me or showing her profile, if she is smiling or crying, under different lighting conditions, etc. In fact, and even though patterns of visual activities may change with each one of these views, my brain keeps active the same functional section as long as the same Object (e.g., my wife) is seen."

"Sir, how does the human brain maintain this invariant form?"

"We still aren't 100% sure, but Hawkins explains that the higher the level within the six layers, the more abstract and thus invariant the information must be."

"Sir, is this compatible with an atheist view?"

"As a consequence, such neo-cortical properties can replace the already depicted dualistic invariant form. I told you that Plato's view[53] describes Forms existing in an immaterial and immutable way. He sustains that humans retain knowledge of these Forms, through their soul's prior knowledge of such Forms allowing for the understanding of the Essence of things."

"Sir, how different is Hawkins view?"

"Hawkins' intuition is different in the sense that such abstraction of Form happens at all levels of the neocortex and obviously doesn't require a soul.[a]"

---

[a] Hawkins' view: 'I believe a similar abstraction of form is occurring throughout the cortex, in every region. This is a general property of the neocortex. Memories are stored in a form that captures the essence of relationships, not the details of the moment. When you see, feel, or hear something, the cortex takes the detailed, highly specific input and converts it to an invariant form. It is the invariant form that we store in our memory, and it is the invariant

"Sir, does the human brain process information in the same way as computers do?"

"Mr. Hawkins' second conviction, is that it doesn't. It retrieves existing information on a topic from memory and compares it with the perceived reality, using the four previously described cortical properties.[a] Furthermore, his theory proposes that these predictions are the essence of what intelligence is and the four cortical properties are at the basis of it."

"Sir, could you clarify his view for me?"

"For him, predicting is our brain's primary function. Therefore, understanding is merely using our stored memories to predict what experience we should expect before we actually are experiencing it, and when finding something inconsistent with this expected experience, figuring out why."

"Sir, what happens when there is no surprise?"

"He argues that: 'Our brain constantly makes predictions about the very fabric of the world we live in, and it does so in a parallel fashion.' The great aspect of such theory is that it also explains the billions of inputs that never reach our consciousness, as they meet our expectations and consequently don't trigger our attention."

"Sir, as attention can be triggered by any low-level sensory input or higher thought process, what does he conclude?"

"He argues that cortical neurons are all systematically trying to predict what their next experience will be. They do that, mostly in ways we are unconscious of. These predictions express themselves through our thoughts and even perceptions, when combined with sensory inputs."

"Sir, what happens when we don't have a memory about something and therefore, cannot produce predictions?"

"Mr. Hawkins provides another interesting idea, actually corroborated by neurosciences. In such case, he suggests that the hippocampus is the top region of the neocortex, not an independent structure.[78] Information for which there isn't any possible prediction because there is no known

---

form of each new input pattern that it gets compared to. Memory storage, memory recall, and memory recognition occur at the level of invariant forms.'

[a] As the neocortex uses memories to make predictions, it might seem contradictory with the invariant Form property. Hawkins argues that we understand the world by searching and finding invariant structures in an ever-changing environment, by combining knowledge of this invariant structure and the details of the most recent events. Thus, any prediction will result from this re-combinatory work. Though he doesn't refer to Kant, I believe he seems align with Constructivism.

memory to compare it to, is transferred to the hippocampus and is stored there until it is either transferred back to a lower layer or lost. In other words, this theory also integrates the concepts of STM and LTM logically.[a]"

"Sir, what is the feedback of this memory-prediction model?"

"It has been mainly favorable, though some scientists view it as an interesting start but believe it doesn't give the complete picture of intelligence."

"Sir, what is the most relevant criticism of this model?"

"It's reliance on Mountcastle's theory of the neocortex's uniformity.[79] This theory argues that since all cortical regions are remarkably uniform in terms of layers, neuron types, and inter-connections, they must be performing the same operation. Therefore, there should be an algorithm that all neocortical regions must be applying to all types of sensory and motor systems."

"Sir, what is the problem with this theory?"

"Neuroscientists have shown that there are some differences between cortical regions (e.g., the limbic areas don't have a layer 4), so there cannot be a universal generic algorithm.[b] "

"Sir, does it kill the argument that there is a systematic pattern of hierarchical connections between the various layers of the neocortex, on which the Hawkins' theory relies first and foremost?"

"I don't believe so, but some other critics argue that the brain is more distributed than hierarchical, with various connection pathways crisscrossing through it. However, I'll argue, later on, that hierarchical and distributed models aren't incompatible."

---

[a] In fact, Mr. Hawkins suggests that our thoughts and perceptions are predictions themselves. Another interesting consequence of this theory is that the memory system must feed forecasts into the sensory stream, for intelligence and understanding to happen.

[b] Another potential criticism is that Mr. Hawkins argues that for his model to work, it needs that a brief pattern in one layer causes a set of neurons to fire in other layers. This requirement diverges from the classical view of dendrites' passive role. He argues that for distant synapses, dendrites can play a highly specific function in cell firing, a theory that still needs to be proven.

"Sir, do you believe in this prediction-memory model?"

"For Mr. Hawkins, intelligence is all about predicting. Though my gut feeling tells me that indeed my brain works on prediction, it cannot do only that. It needs ultimately to find the best-surviving strategy, based on such forecast. Prediction is a key success factor in such survival strategies, but other behavioral strategies must be embedded in my mind's structure. This is why I believe Friston's Free-Energy model complements this theory by addressing the key concept that the brain's ultimate strategy is survival through action."

What is the Free-Energy model?

"Sir, what is this Free-energy model? Is it related to energy?"

"Strangely, it is. This theory proposed by Karl Friston in 2006,[80] explains intelligence in terms of physical mechanisms and unifies neural and brain psychological behaviors. Its underlying general idea is that our brain seeks to minimize surprisals (i.e., informational surprise) through action, perception, and learning."

"Sir, what does it share with other theories?"

"It shares one crucial theme: optimization. What is being optimized, is value (i.e., expected reward and expected utility) or its complement – surprise (i.e., prediction error and expected cost) –."

"Sir, which theory or laws does it rely on?"

"On the theoretical fundamentals of minimization of entropy and finds its physical explanation in our neocortical columns' properties, which we will talk about more thoroughly within a neuroscience discussion. The interesting aspect of Friston's theory is that it relies on the laws of physics. As the Memory-prediction model does, it explains how the brain achieves intelligence without relying on a soul or any other non-materialistic properties."

"Sir, what is the Free-energy main principle?"

"In order for any living creature or self-organized system to be at equilibrium within its environment, it must minimize its free energy (i.e., entropy), or in other words, fight the natural propensity for disorder. To maintain its physiological states, this creature must in the short term avoid surprises, which means minimizing its change of states. Thus, free energy optimizes these movements from one state to the other. If an agent (e.g., a brain) minimizes its free energy, it implicitly minimizes its surprise.[a] "

"Sir, can you be more specific? I am a little lost."

"I'll explain more thoroughly this theory, by resorting to physics and Bayesian math. Please ask me what you want to know because this is an important part of my discussion, explaining how the human brain works."

"Sir, what is entropy?"

"It refers to the idea that eventually everything in the universe, moves from order to disorder (e.g., ice melting into water, changing its stability at the atomic level). Entropy is the measurement of the change between the original and new states. It can be both viewed in terms of physics (i.e., linked to thermodynamics) and information theory."

"Sir, what is classical thermodynamic entropy?"

"It is often described as a measure of disorder or dispersal of energy, at a specific temperature. However, if you want a more precise definition, please look at Wikipedia.[b] "

"Sir, are there other forms of entropy?"

"Yes, there is what is called Shannon (from Claude Shannon, 1948) [81] entropy. It is the amount of information that would be needed to specify all the information in a system and measures uncertainty. Entropy is maximum when all the outcomes are equally likely. Whenever we enter predictability in the system, entropy drops (i.e., we must ask fewer questions to guess the outcome).[c] "

---

[a] The nice twist of this theory is that free energy can be calculated, as it is a function of sensory states and a 'recognition density' (i.e., a probabilistic representation of what causes this sensation in the first place), encoded by these internal states, through neural networks. Friston's theory converts this complicated integration problem of sensory states and recognition density, by using the information theory quantity and transforming it into an optimization problem.

[b] Wikipedia extract: 'the system is composed of very large numbers of constituents (atoms, molecules) and the state of the system is described by the average thermodynamic properties of those constituents; the details of the system's constituents are not directly considered, but their behavior is described by macroscopically averaged properties, e.g., temperature, pressure, entropy, heat capacity. The early classical definition of the properties of the system assumed equilibrium.'

[c] More precisely this is the extract from Wikipedia: 'the definition of the information entropy is quite general, and is expressed in terms of a discrete set of probabilities p_i so that:

"Sir, is thermodynamic entropy linked to life and how so?"

"The Nobel prize Erwin Schrödinger indicates that any living creature follows the second law of thermodynamics,[82] as entropy does, by maintaining its order to the detriment of its environment. For instance, an organism must maintain its own order by eating a prey, exporting disorder to it (i.e., transforming at the final stage the prey into feces). In other words, life can be seen as the strategy to counteract thermodynamic entropy."

"Sir, is Shannon entropy linked to intelligence and if so, how?"

"Friston links, through the minimization of surprise (i.e., via action and perception), intelligence and information entropy. To explain how I need to introduce Bayesian probability."

"Sir, how different is Bayesian from classical probabilities?"

"It is one interpretation of the probability concept. Classical probability describes the frequency or propensity of an event to occur."

"Sir, everybody knows the example of a flipped coin, which in the long run always falls half of the time on its head and the other half on its tail."

"Bayesian probability, on the other hand, must be seen as a degree of belief. For instance, the probability that someone wins the lottery is 'not-likely' or 'almost impossible,' instead of the classical way of picturing it as 10^{-12} chance of turning into a millionaire."

"Sir, besides the notion of belief, what else do Bayesian probabilities integrate?"

"It implies inference, that is, a conclusion from assumptions made.[a] I am e-mailing you an example based on the soccer world cup, to explain how Bayesian probability works.[b] "

$$H(X) = -\sum_{i=1}^{n} p(x_i) \text{LOG } p(x_i)$$

and can also be written as

$$H = \sum_{i=1}^{n} p \, Log2 \left(\frac{1}{pi}\right)$$

In the case of transmitted messages, these probabilities were the probabilities that a particular message was actually transmitted, and the entropy of the message system was a measure of the average amount of information in a message.'

[a] Bayesian probability starts with an initial degree of belief. As new events happen and change this belief, we calculate a posteriori, a new degree of belief based on this new evidence. In other words, we modify our prediction as a result of the new evidence. This is Wikipedia's definition:
The Bayesian inference derives 'the posterior probability as a consequence of two antecedents, a prior probability and a 'likelihood function' derived from a statistical model for the observed data. Bayesian inference computes the posterior probability according to Bayes' theorem:

"Sir, how do Shannon entropy and Bayesian math fit together?"

"Friston's view of intelligence is to minimize surprise through action and perception. With the e-mailed example on football, I've shown that through decisions made on a series of perceptions generating specific actions (i.e., decisions reducing the unpredictability), I've optimized the model, modifying the expectations from a high (extreme uncertainty) to a low (high certainty) entropy distribution. In other words, I counteracted Shannon entropy by using a predicting entity, resulting from surprise minimization and Bayesian inference. By the same token, I've adjusted my inner representation of the world, at its contact (e.g., Brazil, in all likelihood, won the most soccer world cups)."

"Sir, how do you link action and perception?"

$$P(H\,I\,E) = \frac{P(H\,I\,E)\,.\,P(H)}{P(E)}$$

where the posterior probability of a hypothesis is determined by a combination of the inherent likeliness of a hypothesis (the prior) and the compatibility of the observed evidence with the hypothesis (the likelihood). P(H) and P(E) are independent probabilities, $P(H\,I\,E)$ is the posterior probability of observing H given E, after E is observed.'

[b] Let's imagine that we want to know, which country won the most soccer world championships. At the start, we wouldn't have any clue so that the probability would be linked to the number of countries. Assuming a world composed of only 100 countries, we would have a 1% chance of immediately finding the right one. Entropy is then at its maximum because we have no predictability at all. Let's suppose that we decide to select population size as a criterion to define the likelihood of the Country with most wins. The new probability would be in the range of: China 30%, India 25%, USA 6%, Brazil 4%, Nigeria 3%; Japan 2%; Germany 1,5%; France 1,2%; Italy 1%; etc. Let's imagine that we hear (i.e., sensation/perception) from a specialist that the winning country must have had a long tradition of playing. Through careful analysis (i.e., action), we would eliminate African, North American, and Asian countries. Our expectations would obviously change for something like (to make it simple): Brazil 50%; Germany 25%; France 12.5%; Italy 12.5%. As we can see, there is quite a difference of expectation between the initial, prior and posterior calculation. At 50%, we could decide that Brazil is the most likely country, or decide to go for other rounds of increased predictability, by selecting other criteria. Supposing we're satisfied with 50%, we could calculate the predictability according to Bayesian probability. The possibility of it being Brazil is one out of two or in other words, and if it weren't Brazil, we would need to ask one other question. If it were Germany, we would need to ask at least two additional questions (i.e., equal outcome Germany or France and Italy). Finally, if it weren't also Germany, we would need to ask a third question to identify France or Italy.

If we calculate the level of entropy, then we have the following result: $P_{(Brazil)}$ x 1 + $P_{(Germany)}$ x 2 + $P_{(France)}$ x 3 + $P_{(Italy)}$ x 3 = 1.75. This means that on average we would need to ask 1.75 questions to get to Brazil. We would obtain the same value, using the Shannon entropy formula, but much quicker.

"To reduce their free energy, people can either modify their recognition density by changing their inner states or change the sensory input by influencing their environment."

"Sir, how can free energy be minimized?"

"Friston's equations conclude that free energy is minimized only by changing the recognition density[a], to modify expectations about what is being measured (through perception), or by changing the sensory input (through action) so that it conforms to that expectations.[b] "

"Sir, how do you link action and perception?"

"The third cornerstone of Friston's theory is the hierarchical message passing and is in line with the Predictive Coding theory, which has been popularized by him and Andy Clark,[83] a modern framework for understanding the message transfer mechanisms between the various layers of the neocortex."

"Sir, this feature also seems very similar to Hawkins' model, where the micro-columns in the neocortex, communicate above and bellow, in a hierarchical way."

"Yes, in this predictive framework, each predictor (i.e., neuron) compares its conditional expectation with higher level predictors (i.e., top-down communication) to form a prediction error, which is passed forward to the above level (i.e., bottom-up). The above predictor encodes the conditional expectations, which optimizes the top-down prediction, solving the prediction error in the level below."

"Sir, how do you lessen the prediction errors?"

"The continuous flow of bottom-up prediction errors and top-down prediction messages, between the layers, will continue until prediction errors are minimized, and the conditional expectations are optimized, at all levels. As a consequence, a surprise is reduced from the sub-conscious lower levels to the higher active more abstract layers. Each layer in this

---

[a] In statistics, it is the construction of an estimate, based on observed data, of an unobservable underlying probability density function.

[b] Karl Friston introduces three mathematical equivalent formulas of Free-energy:
- Free energy = energy - entropy (which links thermodynamic and Shannon entropy).
- Free energy = surprise + perceptual divergence (this divergence being the difference between an initial and posterior recognition density, resulting from new sensory input).
- Free energy = complexity - accuracy, where complexity can be seen as the difference between prior density (i.e., original encoded belief) and the posterior density (i.e., newly encoded belief), and the accuracy may be described as the surprise coming from the sensory input expected under the recognition density.[N57]

hierarchy is trying to act against entropy, transforming our brain in a sophisticated prediction machine. This brain adjusts these predictions in the light of new experiences and constantly optimizes them, creating as a consequence, a new representation of the world."

"Sir, you've mentioned the Bayesian brain model. What is it?"

"This Free-energy theory is coherent with the 2004 model based on Bayesian probability theory,[84] which explains that our brain has a model of the world that it optimizes by using sensory inputs. The brain can thus, be seen as an inference machine, which actively predicts and explains its sensations. Key to this hypothesis is the Bayesian probabilistic model generating predictions, which are tested against sensory inputs, enabling the update of beliefs about their origins. Therefore, it constantly generates a top-down flow of virtual sensory signals, which predicts the incoming sensory signals generated by external causes."

"Sir, you've referred to Predictive Coding. Could you explain in more detail this important theory?"

"It is a theory in which our active mind creates a construct of the world, in a kind of Kantian view. This construct flows top-down from our higher cortex layers to the lowest one, where it is compared to our sensory inputs. The bottom-up flow, which follows this construct, travels up the processing hierarchy as the difference between the construct (that is, what is expected to be seen, heard, smelled, etc.) and what is really seen, heard or smelled.[a] With Friston's theory, the objective of our mind is to reduce surprises or, from a Predictive Coding perspective, minimize the prediction error. It is especially true for events that could generate high entropy (e.g., danger), which receive a higher priority."

"Sir, are there other co-related theories?"

"Yes, two. The infomax principle,[85] as well as the movement control principle, which you can search on the web.[b] "

---

[a] In other words, at each level of the neural hierarchy what is encoded isn't the original environmental stimuli, but the discrepancy (i.e., error) between the predicted and actual sensory input (Clark,[N58] and Hohwy)[N59]. This means that at each cortical level, the error signal is compared and then either inhibited or stimulated depending on if a revised perceptual hypothesis is required. This predictive coding uses this Bayesian reasoning.

[b] The **infomax principle** explains that neural networks must efficiently encode information, by optimizing the mutual predictability of sensory inputs and its internal representation, through perception. By using the third mathematical formula (i.e., Free energy = complexity - accuracy), we can immediately see that the lower the coding complexity and the better the accuracy, the less energy we disperse.

The **movement control principle** isn't entirely in line with Friston and Hawkins theories,

"Sir, does Free-energy really work?"

"Yes, it does, but let me just show you how we can broadly apply Predictive Coding and minimization of error prediction to any form of cognitive process. I would like to refer to studies on music, which help answer three important questions. [86] [87] [88] [89] "

"Sir, let me guess. The first question is if Free-energy can explain musical experiences?"

"Yes indirectly, by measuring it through a broad Predictive Processing framework. In such a framework, the meter (i.e., the time framework according to which the rhythm is perceived) constitutes the brain's key predictive model, shaped by statistical learning. This meter is challenged by musical sensory inputs, with their rhythmic patterns. The study focuses on syncopation, that is, a rhythmic structure, which goes against expected metrics."

"Sir, what's so special about this rhythmic structure?"

"In such a musical structure, the inputs – rhythms heard (i.e., a pattern of discrete duration) – is at odds with the model, the meter. When this happens, differences in tempo between them (i.e., prediction error) is fed forward into the neural system and dealt with according to predictive coding mechanisms. The brain processes the perceived rhythms and learned metrics according to recursive Bayesian probabilities, with which it tries to minimize errors between the inputs (i.e., rhythms) and its expectations (i.e., meter). Furthermore, the study proposes that during syncopation, the strength of the metric model (and consequently the prediction error) is a function of the listener's previous musical training."

"Sir, what's the second finding?"

"One study analyses groove-based music (e.g., funk, hip-hop, and electronic dance music) where complex rhythmic structures, such as syncopation and cross-rhythm, are continuously repeated but with a medium degree of syncopation. According to the study, groove provides an optimal balance between complexity and prediction, allowing for just enough prediction error to stimulate comparisons between humans' inner musical models."

---

but Daniel Wolpert resorts as well to Bayesian probability and prediction to explain how the brain controls motion.[N60] He argues that brains evolved, not to think, feel, or minimize free energy but rather to produce adaptable and complex movements. For him, body movements are the only way you can influence your environment. Data (e.g., sensory inputs) and prior knowledge (e.g., memory) generates beliefs that will require bodily moves. As a consequence, our actions become a continuous cycle of conscious and sub-conscious predictions of how movements influence our environment.

"Sir, what's the impact of such consistent small prediction errors?"

"The study hints that such slightly destabilizing states could generate in the brain pleasure mechanisms such as dopamine release, to both expected and unexpected stimuli."

"Sir, what other proof do these studies bring?"

"Last but not least, a reference to other studies (Meyer, 1956; Huron 2008) suggests that prediction and expectation are the primary mechanisms for emotion and pleasure in music."

"Sir, what can you conclude from these studies on music?"

"Can predictive coding explain basic intuitive concepts such as rhythm? Is our Bayesian brain applied in our daily life for artistic processes such as music? To what extent are our affective responses (i.e., emotions) a result of predictive mechanisms? The above musical studies confirm that on all three accounts, the Free-energy model can explain away how our mind works."

"Sir, how are predictions and expectations accounted for?"

"The general idea behind this is Huron's theory that the brain rewards behavior that stimulates prediction since it is an evolutionarily adaptive cognitive ability. To reinforce this view, the study refers to the 2014 syncopation experiment investigating the relationship between syncopation in groove and emotions, such as the desire to move and feelings of pleasure.[87]"

"Sir, what did the results show?"

"Such levels of rhythmic complexity generate optimal pleasure, as well as the desire to move our body."

What are potentially other universal theories?

"Sir, if Free-energy and the other cognitive theories on which they rely, such as the Bayesian Brain and Predictive Coding, all work, why then present other cognitive theories?"

"Well, I just want to give you a view on other theories, which could claim cognitive unification. The first one of them is the Neural Engineering Framework (NEF), developed in 2003 by Eliasmith and Anderson.[90] Even if the NEF is similar to most traditional cognitive neuroscience theories, where cognitive processing is construed as representational computation, it includes an additional crucial element: a control theory."

"Sir, what does this theory bring?"

"Eliasmith believes that a control theory enables a realistic decomposition of the system, into its relevant and explainable sub-parts.[a] Furthermore, it allows the integration of a real-time dimension, providing a dynamical description of the neural system. Last but not least, state variables can easily be latched onto their underlying physical systems."

"Sir, what is the other theory called?"

"It is called the multi-modal theory. Computationalism pictures the mind as a collection of independent programs, with each having its own module. These modules transduce sensory inputs into language-like representations, used in mental computation. Multimodal Theory, on the other hand, argues that these modules save these inputs in their original format that are, later on, recalled by using association mechanisms."

"Sir, what are the modalities?"

"Barsalou (2008) describes three types of modalities, which allow human beings to experience the world, their body, and their mind.[91] The perceptual modalities are associated with all our senses. The motor modalities provide the capacity to perform movements. The introspective modalities form the last of these three modalities and are internally generated processes (e.g., cognition, affect, and motivation).[b] "

---

[a] The NEF theory can deal with higher-level cognitive tasks (e.g., inference) and lower-levels, such as sense and motor behavioral processes (e.g., path integration). Unlike concepts, such as the Predictive Brain, it doesn't assign one single function to the brain or proposes a model of cognitive capabilities that is realistic, from a biological perspective. However, the NEF can generate software architectures able to tackle symbolic problems. The NEF's central principles,[N61] also formulated in a strict mathematical form, are the following:

(1) Neural representations are the result of a combination of nonlinear encoding and optimal linear decoding, including for temporal and population representations. Unlike many other neural modeling frameworks, neuron populations are not trained but analytically calculated, from basic equations.

(2) Neural transformation is achieved through computation of images, functions of variables represented by a population. The neural encoding's nonlinear nature accounts for neural representation and computation.

(3) Neural dynamics are described with representations, as control-theoretic state variables.

[b] Introspective modalities are fashioned by and influence the other two elements. For instance, attention and intention result respectively, from the interaction between perception and introspection, as well as between movement and introspection. Contrarily to the view

"Sir, how does it work? Could you give me an example?"

"In a multimodal representation, all modalities are being fired simultaneously. For instance, when we visualize a cat, we remember sensory (furled, soft, gracious, etc.), motoric (running, moving its tail, etc.), and introspective (fondness, indifference, etc.) states, which we've experienced, when physically interacting with cats, all at once. A global simulator that constitutes knowledge incorporates a cat's representation and other simulations. These multimodal representations are then processed, and ensure that we understand why a cat is a cat.[a] "

On that, I called it quits for the day and decided to listen to one of my favorite groove band: Kool and the Gang. Anyhow, I was struggling to find out, how to reintroduce psychology to explain what intelligence was.

Indeed, perception, memorization, judging, decision-making, and planning are all mental processes that might, or not, involve intelligent steps. As so many mental processes affect intelligibility, it is tough to categorize what the intelligence portion of these processes is. It probably integrates some form of reasoning or explanation, like deductions and inductions, as well as more creative tasks, such as ideation and imagination.

Maybe out of exhaustion, I ended up concluding that the best way to proceed hereof was to use the classical historical approach of describing the IQ test and all debates surrounding such criticized measure of intelligence.

What is the history of intelligence testing?

Two days later when I was dropping my son at his school, before taking a flight, I told my son he made a clever remark. On the way to the airport, my car asked me: "Sir, what did you mean by clever. Was it witty, intelligent, or creative?"

---

that each module acts independently, each modality shapes the others.[N62]

[a] These sensory inputs aren't transduced into symbols but are stored in their perceptual modality. Hence, representations rather than being language-like are multi-modal and processed in a distributed fashion throughout the brain. The brain's multimodal system produces functional systems, which are activated co-dependently. Each module is unintelligent individually. However, when their outputs interact with the others as their inputs, and are processed by them to become their own outputs, the resulting system is capable of intelligent activities. The mind results from these fundamental systems working in harmony.

"We humans struggle to define intelligence because it is involved in so many cognitive processes that are context specific. In the case of my son, his comment was wittier than cleverer, because it also involved some form of criticism of that situation. Because of this difficulty, psychology played a preponderant role in the understanding of intelligence, by developing the tests that allowed its concrete measurement, especially the Stanford/Binet test.[a] "

"Sir, are there other intelligent tests and how do they work?"

"Yes, there are a few, such as the Wechsler Intelligence Scales.[b] Before explaining the general intelligence theory, on which they rely, I would like to talk about the Swiss psychologist Jean Piaget."

"Sir, besides laying the foundation of Constructivism, what is he known for?"

"Piaget is famously known for his cognitive development theory, which explains how the mind develops from infancy to adulthood. Through methods of observation and experimentation (for instance, using Binet's intelligence test) he formulated that all human minds follow the same course of four stages."

---

[a] The development of these tests started in the early 1900s. At that time, the French Government commissioned the psychologist Alfred Binet to come up with a methodology to detect children with low intelligence level or mental retardation. Together with Theodore Simon, he developed questions that focused on the cognitive process, such as problem-solving skills, attention, and memory. From these questions, he predicted which aspects of a cognitive process were most likely to be correlated with school success. The resulting methodology, called the Binet-Simon Scale, measuring intelligence levels based on children average abilities according to their age group, became famous. It crossed the Atlantic, where it was later adapted by Lewis Terman, a Stanford psychologist, using a single number to represent an individual's score on the examen, known as the intelligence quotient (or IQ). Since its 1916 publication, this so-called Standford-Binet test, is the standard US assessment methodology and, despite going through various revisions, remains a popular assessment tool, till today.

[b] Dissatisfied with the Stanford-Binet test limitations, David Wechsler published a new test known as the Wechsler Adult Intelligence Scale in 1955, which revised version is called WAIS-IV.

"Sir, what are these four stages?"

"These stages, which cut across contents are: sensorimotor during the first years, preoperational around age two, concrete operational at eleven, and formal operation during teenage years till adulthood.[92] Mostly in line with the general intelligence theory, Piaget believed intelligence is a single general capacity, which uniformly developed across individuals."

What is the general intelligence theory?

"Sir, what is this theory?"

"In the same early 20th century period, the English psychologist Charles Spearman suggested that one single general ability factor (which he called g, from general factor) could conceptualize all mental performances."

"Sir, Spearman's view relied on which observation?"

"Based around psychometric tests, which regroup the scoring under the IQ terminology,[a] he developed a theory of general intelligence founded upon his observation that individuals' performance at one type of cognitive task tends to be comparable to this person's performance at others.[93] He established this g variable to summarize correlations among these different cognitive tasks."

"Sir, has this g theory evolved since Spearman's early formulation?"

"Yes, and it now integrates three hierarchical levels. The g factor is positioned at the top and represents the variance common to all cognitive tasks. The intermediary level integrates a few broader factors. At the bottom, there are various narrow factors."

"Sir, what do these IQ tests measure effectively?"

"Two important cognitive faculties related to intelligence. Firstly, a person's ability to apply his or her knowledge to solve problems, assessing the capacity to memorize concepts and use the most suited of them to solve these problems. Secondly, it tests the faculty to filter quickly through

---

[a] As time went by, this g factor proved to account most significantly for variances in IQ scores. As a consequence, IQ is now widely regarded as a good estimate of a person's standing on this g factor. The statistic regularity regrouped under this g factor has also been measured time and time again. However, there is still no consensus on what are the causes of this correlation between tests.

several potential ideas, to find the most appropriate solution.[a] Though critics of this general intelligence theory are numerous, they still recognize it as a good predictor of a person's future performance in education and employment."

"Sir, don't you think that too much emphasis on the g factor can denigrate other important abilities?"

"Yes, especially the ones related to our emotional side and creativity, which are fundamental in modern day life."

---

[a] People usually perceive someone intelligent as quick, an adjective used, to sum up this easiness to observe the right patterns and come up almost immediately with the right formula or concept, which solves the problem. More generally, modern intelligence tests measure the following cognitive factors, thought to make up general intelligence: visual-spatial processing, quantitative reasoning, knowledge, fluid reasoning, and short-term memory.

"Sir, are there other theories explaining what the g factor is?"

"Yes, the CHC (the abbreviation from psychologists Cattell–Horn–Carroll)[94] theory is a prominent psychological theory on the structure of human cognitive abilities. It proposes that multiple cognitive abilities constitute the g factor, and that, when summed up, reconstitute this g factor measured by the IQ test."

"What are these general modalities?"

"Their three authors converged to create a model, which is composed of eight to ten broad abilities.[a] They also refined these abilities by describing narrower ones. For instance, fluid reasoning may be further detailed by other reasoning characteristics: inductive, general sequential, deductive, quantitative, etc. What is important to understand, is that this model is coherent with the g factor theory and the IQ tests."

What are the theories of uncorrelated abilities?

"Sir, are the mental competences, as explained by the g factor theory, a single ability or is intelligence composed of independent specialized abilities? Furthermore, do the tests you've presented above give a good representation of everyday performance?"

"A few theories have been developed trying to prove that several abilities were uncorrelated with each other and that consequently, IQ tests, by focusing too much on one specific set of abilities, couldn't measure intelligence adequately."

"Sir, what are these theories?"

"The first one is Robert Sternberg's Triarchic Theory of Intelligence.[95] He suggests that successful people achieve a balance between three abilities: practical (i.e., contextual), creative (i.e., experiential) and

---

[a] **Broad abilities**:
- Fluid intelligence (i.e., reason and problem-solving skills).
- Crystallized intelligence (i.e., comprehensive and acquired knowledge).
- Quantitative reasoning.
- Reading and writing ability.
- Short-term memory.
- Long-term storage and retrieval.
- Visual processing.
- Auditory processing.
- Processing speed.
- Decision and reaction speed.

analytical (i.e., componential) intelligence.[a] People aren't necessarily strong in all three abilities but use whatever strength to compensate for their weaknesses. Sternberg conducted tests, which he argues prove that these three abilities are substantially uncorrelated and have independent statistic regularity. Criticizing IQ tests for focusing too much on analytical skills, because they miss assessing important intellectual factors, Sternberg with colleagues, developed new tests measuring these other faculties."

"Sir, what are the critics saying?"

"As expected, several researchers have disputed the conclusion that these three forms of intelligence were uncorrelated and had independent statistic regularity."

"Sir, what other theories are there?"

"There is David Perkins' Theory of Learnable Intelligence.[96] Based on IQ tests analyses, Perkins argues that the IQ has three main dimensions: neural, experiential, and reflective intelligence.[b] "

"Sir, any other theory worth mentioning?"

"At least two. The first one has been recently prevalent because it integrates emotions. I've included the Emotional intelligence (EI) in the theories of uncorrelated abilities, though Daniel Goleman,[97] who popularized this theory, argues that IQ and EI are correlated, as individuals' with high IQ and low EI (or vice versa) are relatively rare. However, few studies have proven such correlation, and we all have many counterexamples of people we know of, who have an extremely greet IQ and a poor IE."

"Sir, can you give me an EI definition?"

- [a] **Contextual intelligence** is the ability to do well in informal and formal educational contexts, as well as the capacity to adapt to our environment and shape it.
- **Experiential intelligence** is the facility with which we deal with new situations. It also includes our ability to be creative and produce new ideas.
- **Componential intelligence** is the faculty to process information efficiently, by using our higher faculties (e.g., perception, action, memory, reasoning, or emotion), as well as the knowledge acquisition components to help drive our thoughts process.
- [b] **Neural intelligence** refers to the efficiency of a person's neural system.
- **Experiential intelligence** refers to a person's accumulated knowledge and experiences in various areas.
- **Reflective intelligence** includes the way we approach a problem to solve or a task to perform, and how we learn from it. It includes attitudes supporting imagination, persistence, and systemization, as well as self-monitoring and control.

"Goleman defines EI as the ability to perceive, control, and evaluate our own and other people's emotions, discriminating between these feelings, integrating into our thought process this information and applying it to our behavior. EI includes a person's capacity to deal successfully with other people and motivate them.[a] "

"Sir, do you have any evidence that EI is uncorrelated?"

"I was able to find only one study showing some kind of correlation between overall EI score and IQ.[98] Researchers currently do not have good measurements for EI. There is much criticism, and the developed measurements show very little predictive ability for success."

"Sir, I guess the last theory you will be presenting is Gardner's theory of multiple intelligences?"

"Clever guess, which in this case means a well-founded deduction! Rather than seeing intelligence as a general ability, Howard Gardner came up with a definition of intelligence centered on the concept of modalities.[99] For him, traditional types of intelligence measures, such as IQ, failed to explain all cognitive abilities fully."

"Sir, how does he define these modalities?"

"He derives thinking and learning modalities, which uniquely defined each intelligence, from behaviors that must meet seven criteria to classify as intelligence. Gardner comes up with a list of different intelligence: musical-rhythmic, visual-spatial, verbal-linguistic, logical-mathematical, bodily-kinesthetic, interpersonal (i.e., capacity to understand motivations and wishes of other people), intrapersonal (i.e., capacity to understand our one feelings, fears, and motivations), and naturalistic.[b] "

"Sir, what do critics disapprove of, in this theory?"

"Many argue that IQ tests have usually found high correlations between these different intelligence variables, rather than the weak correlations, which Gardner's theory would predict. This tends to support the g factor, rather than the multiple intelligences theory. Furthermore, many of Gardner's intelligence correlate with the g factor, strengthening the notion

---

[a] There are three major models of Emotional intelligence:
- **Ability model:** Perceiving emotions (including understanding nonverbal signals) and mood reasoning with feelings, understanding, and managing the emotions.
- **Mixed model:** Self-awareness, self-regulation, motivation, empathy, and social skills.
- **Trait EI model:** It refers to a Person's self-perception of his or her emotional abilities.

[b] He later suggested that existential and moral intelligence may also be worthy of inclusion. According to Mr. Gardner, all individual possesses a unique blend of all these intelligences.

of a single dominant intelligence factor. Finally, Gardner has not provided a test for his multiple intelligences theory, which would enable to challenge and confirm the existence of such intelligences."

"Sir, do you think he is right?"

"Many people feel inherently that traditional definition of intelligence is too narrow, and thus, Gardner's theory reflects more accurately the different ways in which humans think and learn. This feeling has been strengthened lately by the discovery of the important role our emotions play in the way we think and behave."

"Sir, is this theory compatible with the latest neurological findings?"

"I've shown that at birth we have the neural potential to acquire knowledge and reason, in many specific areas. If I take music, for instance, someone might have the ability to become a Mozart but, if not exposed to it, won't ever develop any form of musical intelligence. Therefore, it seems to me that this capacity, independent from other broad abilities, isn't measured by IQ tests but should. Thus, it is in line with neurological findings."

"Sir, do you have any other comment on the topic?"

"By now, you must have understood that I believe that Friston's Free-energy model describes the most accurately, our cognitive processes. Therefore, intelligence is the capacity we have to reduce surprises by either increasing our perceptual field or reducing uncertainty, through action. Bilingualism, within this context, must be viewed as the capacity to reduce uncertainty, by either being able to increase perceptual cues or interfacing with others, in their own language. Therefore, it should be correlated with higher intelligence, but is never measured in IQ tests."

"Sir, you aren't a specialist in IQ tests but claim that they should take into consideration other criteria, from this Free-energy perspective?"

"Yes! Please, don't repeat this because I won't make many friends. However, from a logical perspective, if you believe Friston's theory is right, then any capacity which can reduce surprises within a specific context, should be included in the evaluation of intelligence."

"Sir, how do machines fare in regards to these eight intelligence?"

"It's an extremely pertinent question. If we look at intelligence from this perspective, then the man-machine comparison seems very different, according to the considered intelligence. I'm e-mailing you my personal comparison."

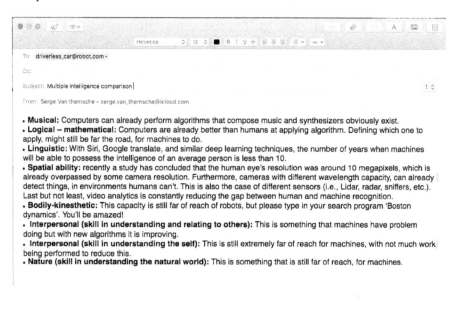

To: driverless_car@robot.com ∨

Cc:

Subject: Multiple intelligence comparison |

From: Serge Van themsche – serge.van_themsche@icloud.com

- **Musical:** Computers can already perform algorithms that compose music and synthesizers obviously exist.
- **Logical – mathematical:** Computers are already better than humans at applying algorithm. Defining which one to apply, might still be far the road, for machines to do.
- **Linguistic:** With Siri, Google translate, and similar deep learning techniques, the number of years when machines will be able to possess the intelligence of an average person is less than 10.
- **Spatial ability:** recently a study has concluded that the human eye's resolution was around 10 megapixels, which is already overpassed by some camera resolution. Furthermore, cameras with different wavelength capacity, can already detect things, in environments humans can't. This is also the case of different sensors (i.e., Lidar, radar, sniffers, etc.). Last but not least, video analytics is constantly reducing the gap between human and machine recognition.
- **Bodily-kinesthetic:** This capacity is still far of reach of robots, but please type in your search program 'Boston dynamics'. You'll be amazed!
- **Interpersonal (skill in understanding and relating to others):** This is something that machines have problem doing but with new algorithms it is improving.
- **Interpersonal (skill in understanding the self):** This is still extremely far of reach for machines, with not much work being performed to reduce this.
- **Nature (skill in understanding the natural world):** This is something that is still far of reach, for machines.

"Sir, since you spoke about musical intelligence, do you know what is my favorite music?"

"I haven't a clue!"

"Heavy metal Sir!"

I was flabbergasted by the joke and wondered what other surprises I could expect in the future. Maybe my car would start composing techno music?

15) Why are humans the most intelligent biological creature on earth?

My car was waiting patiently for our conversation to resume. It wasn't that I didn't want to engage again in our discussion, but I needed time to read about the latest neurological findings. After a few weeks, which could have felt endless for my car, if it only had the qualia of impatience, it finally broke the ice and said:

"Sir, why are humans the most intelligent creature on earth?"

I had done my homework, so I said: "I'll answer your question only from a biological perspective and will do so, by using an engineering approach. Thus, I won't deal with the possibility that humans possess a soul since I've shown that it's possible to explain intelligence without having to resort to a religious perspective. I shall focus on materialistically provable answers and use analogies with the cyber world to clarify concepts. Later on, I'll use these same logical engineering approaches to describe the various strategies implemented by companies to make machines more intelligent."

"Sir, will you only compare humans with animals or will you also explain why some humans are more intelligent than others?"

"I'll do both, but because many reasons can explain intelligence gaps between species, I'll avoid giving you general theories, which correlate physiological characteristics to intelligence. Instead, I shall show many potential bio-engineering solutions, which could have generated, within an evolutionary perspective, higher intelligence and then link these solutions to neurosciences."

"Sir, what's your main underlying hypothesis about intelligence?"

"Intelligence is a key survival feature that surely contributed to many species selections. We just need to look at the position humans occupy today in the world, to realize how intelligence and knowledge have helped shape our supremacy over the animal kingdom."

"Sir, from a logical perspective, what are the reasons explaining this intelligence gap?"

"The most obvious of all the answers is that humans and animals don't share the same physiological organs or structures, which perform intelligent functions. Another plausible explanation coming immediately to mind is that humans have more processing power. As we'll see for computers, two main strategies can achieve this characteristic: (brain) size and density of processors. The speed of processing could also explain differences between the various species and could have resulted from diverging evolutionary strategies. An obvious one would be that the speed at which processing units can assimilate incoming data, process it, project outputs, and then re-energize to perform another calculation, may also diverge.[a] "

"Sir, what about another processing differentiator, such as specialization?"

"Indeed! With more specialized areas, it is possible to process information quicker. Specialization could undoubtedly provide a better understanding of the data and information to process. By the same token, it may influence the choice of a neural network architecture."

"Sir, it seems to me that transmission capacity is an additional strategy that evolution could have used, to explain gaps between species' intelligence level."

"Exactly and here also, many potential routes existed. The speed at which a message travels from the moment we sense an input, until the moment we make a decision and perform a movement, is an obvious one. The shorter the cycle time, at each one of the steps required to complete a complex task, the more intelligent the species would be. Thus, and on top of the speed within the processing units, travel time at the nodes and within the fibers, would have a huge impact. The number of transmission fibers and nodes, as well as their integrity, would also influence bandwidth capacity."

"Sir, I would imagine that the choice of a network architecture would also explain differences in intelligence between species."

"Well, not among mammals, but more generally, the choice of a network architecture (i.e., centralized, decentralized, or distributed), by proposing trade-offs between processing and transport capacities, could differentiate intelligence. Information flow complexity, which would consider the number of steps required and elements involved in such an intelligent process, as well as, a strategy promoting shorter distances of transmission could also be two selection criteria among animals."

"Sir, if we consider intelligence as the faculty to predict patterns, as proposed by Hawkins, then wouldn't capacity, ease, and speed of storage, impact how well and fast species can retrieve and store information, in order to analyze these acquired patterns?"

---

[a] In the cyber world, this would be assimilated to the processing cycle time and be measured in frequency (in Hz).

"Definitely, it could explain grades of intelligence between animals. If we consider intelligence as a process, which requires the work of different organs, cells, and biochemicals, the longer an individual can withstand a mental effort, the better he should be at performing intelligent tasks. The more energy supplied to the brain when performing these tasks, and the more power efficient the processing modules would be, the more intelligent the species or individuals have most likely become."

"Sir, differences in software must be part of the reasons explaining intelligence gaps."

"The use of a high-level software such as language (i.e., mentalese) is an obvious difference between men and other animals."

"Sir, could humans have acquired better and more numerous algorithms? Furthermore, if the intelligence gap between men and other animals is so important, could it be that living creatures follow different models of intelligence?"

"In other words, what you are asking me is if the human mind could be governed, for instance, by entropy reduction and Bayesian predictability, while rabbits or ants follow a different logic? I don't think it is likely."

What are the brain anatomical differences between species?

"Sir, can anatomical differences explain intelligence gaps between species?"

"The answer is obviously yes, as mammals and most animals don't share the same brain anatomical structure. Invertebrates (e.g., sponge, coral, crabs, worms, insects, octopus, etc.), which constitute 95% of all living creatures, either have no brain at all or a different anatomical structure. Vertebrates, which include mammals, share with them only one of the three main organs that constitute the human brain."

"Sir what is this organ?"

"This organ is called the reptilian brain. It is the oldest of the three organs, which constitute the human brain. It controls body vital functions (e.g., heartbeat, body temperature, breathing, and balance) and includes the stem and the cerebellum. It is wrapped around by the limbic brain. Here, look. I've drafted a graphic of all three organs."

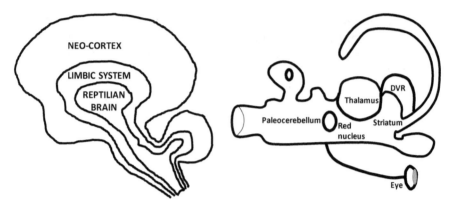

Fig. 33 and 34) The three brain organs and the limbic brain; source author.

"Sir, what is it this limbic brain that I see on my dashboard camera?"

"It's also called the mammalian brain. It emerged in the first mammals and is still present nowadays. It should be seen as the place where 'feelings' are dealt with since it integrates hormones, memory, and mood control functions. On top of the key role it plays in emotions (since it stores memories of experiences perceived as agreeable or unpleasant), it is also responsible for making value judgments, strongly influencing behaviors."

"Sir, what are its main organs?"

"They are the amygdala, hypothalamus, and the hippocampus."

"Sir, I guess the last brain part is the cortex?"

"Humans, like all mammals, have an organ that other species don't have, called the neocortex. Located at the brain's outer surface, it occupies about 90% of the entire brain and is the main organ where intelligent processes take place. As a result of its emergence around 200 million years ago,[a] brain structure between mammals and other animals is clearly different."

"Sir, I guess it explains, in great part, why mammals are at the top of the intelligence scale?"

"Yes, and from now on, I'll focus on this organ to understand what are these evolutionary solutions that can explain biological intelligence."

[a] Its original structure, quite homologous to the current dorsal cortex in reptiles, predates the split between sauropsids (i.e., from which reptiles and birds originated from) and therapsids (i.e., the mammal's precursors). However, it first appeared as today's uniformly layered sheet in the early small mammals, during the transition of the Triassic/Jurassic periods.[N63]

Does brain size matter?

"Sir, is higher intelligence a consequence of a bigger cognitive engine?"

"If we look at the evolution of humans over the past million years, brain size has increased significantly while body mass shrank. Some scientists, (e.g., Jerison, 1985) [100] have taken into consideration this evolution and proposed that the increase in the brain to total mass ratio, is essentially correlated with the brain's increased capacity to process information. If we consider the Fijian proverb – who can the most, may the least –, then a bigger envelope would theoretically mean more processors, with its associated correlate, more intelligence."

"Sir, brain size would thus seem to be a good topic to explore, as a possible explanation for differences in intelligence, doesn't it?"

"Unfortunately, brain size alone cannot provide a good explanation, as humans have smaller brains than let's say a sperm whale or elephant but are much more intelligent.[a] "

"Sir, if the other proverb – the bigger, the better – doesn't work, we could maybe look at the brain size per body volume instead?"

"Unfortunately, this wouldn't bring us far either. A person's brain-to-body ratio would be huge, if we were to compare it to that of an elephant (i.e., about 1/40 versus 1/560, respectively). However, it would be comparable to that of a rat and be worst than some small birds' (1/12 ratio)."

"Sir, does it mean that size doesn't matter?"

"I haven't said that. To come to our rescue, we would need to employ the 'Encephalization Quotient' (or 'EQ'), an approach developed by scientists, which measures the ratio of an animal's brain and body size, relative to other similarly sized animals.[b] This EQ approach is quite interesting because it is consistent with the widespread views about human and animal intelligence. For instance, dolphins and monkeys are just after men on the EQ scale."

---

[a] Six and four times smaller respectively.

[b] Humans have an EQ of 6.56, followed by Dolphins (whale: 5.55; Bottlenose: 5.26 and commerson's: 4.97), monkeys (macaques: 3.15; baboons: 2.81; chimpanzees: 2.63; gorilla: 1.75), coyotes (1.69), and African grey parrot (1.00).[N64]

"Sir, what about this relationship between brain size and intelligence, when applied to human groups?"

"Well, it can be quite controversial because it may support evidence for racist or misogynistic views.[a] Having said that, and being extremely cautious about the potential generalization of such studies between various population groups, there seems to be a relatively strong correlation between IQ and brain size (i.e., between 10% to 35%). I've e-mailed you two extracts from a 2009 study (Rushton and Ankney)[101].[b] "

"Sir, could you tell me what kind of brain size variation we are talking about?"

"You are right. If absolute and relative brain sizes are important factors of general intelligence, and before explaining what could be the properties linked to size triggering higher intelligence, we need to understand this variation. Studies performed on a relatively homogeneous population, show that brain size can vary by more than 40%.[c] "

"Sir, this isn't negligible, so what are the possible consequences on IQ, of such variation?"

"Factors linked to absolute size alone, could in my view explain higher IQ. Absolute processing power and bigger memory are two such factors. Using an analogy with the digital world, the bigger the chip, the more transistors we can cram onto it and consequently, the more processing raw power we may get. Cognitive capacities are mainly linked to neurons and the networks they form with each other, through synapses. Thus,

---

[a] For instance, women have smaller brains and thus, such evidence could be used to argue that women are less intelligent than men. However, the same research on EQ,[N64] indicates that women's body fat percentage is greater than that of men, distorting potentially the formula. When considering the lean body mass, instead, to take care of such distortion, the study shows that a women's EQ is slightly higher. Furthermore, the same EQ methodology, applied to one of the man, which we collectively associate with the greatest intelligence of modern time – Albert Einstein –, shows an EQ of only 5.76, lower than an average man. The point is that, besides the discrepancies in the tests and methodology themselves, EQ doesn't consider environmental factors, which in great parts can explain EQ differences between people and ethnic groups, such as geographic location, diet and nutrition deficiencies, socioeconomic status, education, and culture, etc.

[b] In 1994, Jensen found a correlation of 0.19 between g (i.e., general factor) and the circumference of the head, in a cognitive test among 286 adolescents. However, when using the method to map vectors, he obtained a correlation of 0.64. Schoenemann et al. (2000) obtained a correlation of 0.45 between brain volume and g. Haug (1987) reported a correlation of 0.48 between the number of neurons and brain size, while Pakkenberg and Gundersen (1997) showed a correlation of 0.56.

[c] A study based on 46 Caucasian participants,[N65] reported significant variations (from 1053 to 1499 cm^3 for men and 975 to 1398 cm^3 for women) of the average man and woman brain size (1260 cm^3 and 1130 cm^3, respectively).[N66]

considering intelligence under the brain size angle, a greater surface would mean a proportionally higher number of neurons and synapses.[102] "

"Sir, how many more neurons would that represent?"

"Neurons aren't spread evenly throughout the brain surface. A large portion of our brain's 86 billion neurons isn't located in the neocortex but in the cerebellum. [103] The neocortex contains between 10 and 14 billion neurons,[104] or a little more.[a] Therefore, this 40% variation could probably account for a difference in the range of 4 to 5 billion neurons."

"Sir, that would also mean around 40% more synaptic connections."

"Yes, and according to Hawkins' memory-prediction model, our memory plays a crucial role in intelligence. Since synapses constitute the memory's repository, greater brain size would indicate a higher absolute number of these synapses and hence, more memories or pattern sequences that we could more easily recall."

"Sir, wouldn't more experienced people have a bigger brain?"

"Why not? The more gathered experiences, the more physiological links we create under the Hebbian rule. The more often we are exposed to the same stimuli, the stronger the networks become."

"Sir, how would that relate to bigger brain size?"

"Brain size variation could probably be explained by a greater number of larger axons. These axons constitute the major part of our brain's white matter."

"Sir, are you saying that another way of looking at brain size is to consider a bigger absolute volume of the same structure (i.e., white and gray matter)?"

"Yes, and by the way, there is a high correlation between volume of gray (i.e., containing mainly neurons and dendrites) and white (i.e., mainly composed of myelinated axons) matter, with human intelligence.[b] "

---

[a] Wikipedia estimates the number of neurons in between 19 and 23 billion.[N67]

[b] Gray matter volume (within the parietal, temporal, and occipital lobes) is associated with verbal and non-verbal intelligence, whereas white matter volume and its integrity, is linked to data processing speed.

"Sir, what other reasons could also be invoked to explain higher intelligence?"

"Larger specific cortical areas could also explain higher IQ. Some regions of the brain grew more among some mammal species, while others remained stable."

"Sir, do you have any example?"

"Yes, for instance, when comparing animals to humans, some important brain areas (e.g., frontal lobes) are much bigger in humans. These areas associated with higher-level functions (e.g., self-control, planning, or logic and abstract thoughts), could explain differences between species' intelligence levels.[a] "

Why is the variation in neural density significant?

"Sir, your brain isn't flat like my motherboard. Thus, could neural density variation explain differences in intelligence within mammals and between individuals?"

"Indeed, another interesting physiological approach potentially explaining higher intelligence is to consider the neocortex's volume, rather than the brain's surface area. When comparing mammals' neocortex thickness, we can find that species with a larger brain, tend to have a thicker cortex, even in absolute terms. For instance, cortical areas' thickness may vary by a factor of seven, when comparing the thinner brain of a shrew, with the larger one of a human or a fin whale.[105] "

"Sir, does this difference also exist between humans?"

"I can resort to inter-human comparison to found positive associations, between cortical thickness and intelligence.[b] "

"Sir, is there a universal law explaining brain higher density?"

---

[a] A study confirms that some specific larger cortical areas are correlated with higher IQ levels.[N68] In men, IQ correlates better with gray matter volume in the frontal and parietal lobes. In women, it relates to the gray matter of the frontal lobe and Broca's area. Larger corpus callosum implies equally higher cognitive performance.

[b] A 2009 study on 234, 6 to 18-year old Americans showed significant correlations between the cognitive ability factor (as an estimate of g) and cortical thickness, in most multimodal association areas. Its results were consistent with distributed models of intelligence, like the P-FIT.[N69] Furthermore, new findings suggest that cortical thickness in Broca's area contributes to verbal skills.[N70]

"Surprisingly there is, and what is even more astonishing, is the fact that it is linked to free energy minimization. The most cognitively advanced mammals saw their cortex overgrow, which induced the appearance of folding on its surface, enabling to fit more cortical area into a skull of limited volume.[a] As a consequence, the outside brain surface of these mammals (e.g., humans, dolphins, and apes, but not rats) lost its flatness and acquired a much larger volume."

"Sir, what's the physical model?"

"A recent study calculated that the degree of folding,[106] varies across all mammal species and individuals within these species, according to a simple physical model: a function of cortical surface area and the square root of its underlying thickness![b] "

"Sir, any other cause linked to cortical thickness, explaining higher intelligence?"

"Yes, a faster cortical thickness growth rate would be one. Another proven explanation linked to cortical thickness is that higher IQ is correlated with the trajectory of thickness change in the cortex before adulthood, rather than only cortical thickness itself. This trajectory of cortical development is especially true for frontal regions implicated in intellectual activities.[107] "

What's the impact of brain specialization?

"Sir, can differences in brain specialization explain gaps in intelligence between species?"

"We live in a world of specialists and thus, can intuitively understand specialization benefits. From a system perspective, it may generate constant improvements. By focusing on specific tasks, a system can understand them better and adapt more appropriate answers. With time and experience, it acquires knowledge, which it can apply in new situations. This continuous flow of novel solutions, in the long run, will fashion the system's hardware and software, bringing in a virtuous cycle that will

---

[a] I.e., swelling, called gyri and indentations, called sulci.

[b] The main explanation, for such mathematical function, is that under non homogeneous stress (coming from the skull), a growing brain surface, which would follow the universal principle of entropy minimization and axonal elongation mechanisms, would generate the same relative cortical folding. The study concludes that the cortical sheets' relative lateral expansion happened independently from their neurons' density and distribution. However, this study doesn't mean that this expansion didn't generated a higher density of neurons and synapses, within such a volume.

increase the level of complexity, which this system can deal with. Thus, from an engineering perspective, it is easy to understand why evolutionary specializations occurred in our brain. [a] "

"Sir, did it happened at all levels?"

"Yes, it did. At a global level, the emergence of the neocortex itself can be seen as the main specialization, which fostered the intelligence revolution. Within this cortex, geographical and hemispherical specializations occurred as well. At a more microscopical level, neural specialization along cortical columns and the creation of specific neurons in some species also took place."

"Sir, how did brain differentiation happen?"

"The neocortex evolved from the reptilian brain and first appeared within small mammals.[108] These early mammals had a small neocortex organ,[b] with very few differentiated areas (i.e., only around 20 functional divisions).[109] Through the evolution from mammals to modern humans, which shaped its size and cortical structural organizations, the humans' neocortex acquired much more specialized areas than any other species (i.e., more than 200 in contemporary humans)."

"Sir, why did humans acquired such cortical specificities?"

"The neocortex in humans, more than in any other species, occupies a large portion of the brain (i.e., 90%). Thus, one plausible explanation is that extreme growth in cortical size shaped the human brain structure.[c] "

---

[a] Bigger cortical thickness or specialization would certainly better explain Albert Einstein's exceptional intelligence, rather than his brain size, which was smaller than average. However, Einstein's unusual brain topology, composed of a greater number of folds, and the peculiar physical characteristics of a specific region of the parietal lobe (i.e., Sylvian fissure 208), could also be invoked. Studies, based on pictures of Einstein's brain, have also shown unusual symmetry (i.e., right-sided structure).[N71] Such specific gyral features affecting the parietal cortex (known for visual-spatial and mathematical thoughts), as well as the role of brain asymmetries in language functions, could also explain Einstein's strengths and weaknesses.

[b] Six clades emerged from these early mammals. It led to today's species: euarchontoglires (e.g., rodents, primates, humans), afrotherians (e.g., elephants), monotremes (e.g., platypus, echidna), marsupials (e.g., kangaroos), xenarthrans (e.g., armadillos, sloths), and laurasiatherians (e.g., bats, carnivores, ungulates such as dears, and dolphins). Many existing mammal species have maintained their small neocortex size but these early twenty poorly differentiated cortical areas, with no distinct layers have been replaced by highly sensory specialized regions.

[c] It is physiologically easier to meet the neocortex expansion by adding more neurons and glial, rather than increasing their sizes tremendously. However, at a certain stage of evolution, it probably became difficult for neurons to maintain connections, as their number

"Sir, if the neocortex growth generated a propensity for cortical differentiation, rather than this growth being a consequence of regional specialization, how did this specialization occur?"

"Two main proposals exist to explain how this specialization occurred, which aren't, by the way, mutually exclusive. An existing area with overlapping inputs and outputs gradually segregated to produce two or more areas of different inputs and outputs (Kaas, 1982).[110] Alternatively, due to a mutation, the development was altered, duplicating an existing area, and releasing this duplicated area (or at least a portion of it) to perform new functions."

"Sir, why did hemispherical differentiation happen?"

"Bilateral symmetry is extremely common among vertebrates and probably explains why they have two cerebral hemispheres. We have two arms, legs, eyes, ears, testicles or ovaries, lungs, kidneys, hemispheres, etc. that are spread quite evenly on both side of our body."

"Sir, is there an overall scientific consensus about why humans have two sets of organs?"

"The possibility of it being a by-product of cell division, or having a spare in case of failure of one of these critical body parts, are two explanations often invoked. Regardless of which is the real cause of bilateral symmetry, from an evolutionary standpoint, there is at least one important advantage besides just redundancy: hemispherical specialization."

"Sir, how did it occur?"

"According to three evolutionists, [111] at one point in time, one hemisphere, which happened to be the right one, took primary control in potentially dangerous circumstances. The other hemisphere took over per default, for all other conditions. More specialized processing (e.g., language, tool making, facial recognition, etc.) evolved from those two control types."

"Sir, which properties do these three evolutionists claim the right hemisphere developed?"

---

and distances between them were increasing too much. Moreover, longer distances implied longer data traveling time or larger axon diameter, which would have increased the white matter size hugely. Evolution may have solved this issue by modifying the modularity of the cortex, implying more local processing and fewer long axons.[N72] In other words, by specializing cortical areas along columns that exchange information mostly between their 6-layer neurons, evolution would have addressed the neocortex growth-related issues. By the same token, this specialization along functionally distinct modules had to increase the cortical processing complexity, which could have enabled the emergence of new cognitive abilities.[N73]

"The capacity for determining identity or familiarity, for instance, judging whether a stimulus has been or not, encountered before. These evolutionists theorize that the right hemisphere takes into account the global aspects of its environment, rather than focusing on a limited number of features. They also claim that it shows dominance for emotions, which seems to be present in all primates, suggesting an evolutionary continuity going back to around 40 million years.[a] "

"Sir, does the brain integrate redundancy?"

"Although our two hemispheres may perform different functions, redundancy explains the functional recovery of cognitive capacities, after a lesion in one of the hemisphere. More recent studies of patients, with only half the normal brain tissue mass, confirm they can still perform normal psychological functions. It proves that our brain has a built-in capacity, at least twice as large as needed, for immediate survival and that this extra capacity already replicates existing functions."

"Sir, why has hemispherical specialization occurred in vertebrates?"

"According to the same evolutionary scientists, hemispherical specialization enabled parallel processing."

"Sir, if evolution gave you the capacity to perform parallel processing, how good are men and women at multi-tasking?"

"One of the popular myth in modern society is that women can better multi-task than men. At the origin of this theory, lies the fact that women's left and right cortical sides have more connections, which means theoretically, that data could flow more efficiently between the two hemispheres."

---

[a] In their 2009 white paper,[N74] these scientists demonstrate how this specialization, not only, isn't unique to humans but emerged within vertebrate species, about 500 million years ago. Other studies even suggest that brain functional asymmetry happened earlier, in invertebrates (e.g., octopus).[N75] This 2009 paper also indicates that most vertebrates retained an ancestral preference toward the use of the right side in their routine activity of feeding, controlled by the left hemisphere. The fact that primates have a right-handed bias, could also imply that human right-handedness came from a common primate ancestor. As a consequence, the evolutionary descent of human's right-handedness could have resulted from ancient feeding behaviors, in ancestral primates. Moreover, based on studies of vertebrates (e.g., birds' left hemisphere controls singing, or sea lions, dogs, and monkeys' left hemisphere controls the perception of calls by other members of the same species), they claim that the human left-brain specialization for language, didn't originate with humans as well, but occurred in vertebrates, much earlier. They also refer to the preferred right-hand usage for non-verbal communication in great apes, to claim that non-verbal communication happened before the advent of modern mankind.

"Sir, is it true?"

"I read about ten different studies, and all came out with different conclusions. In some of them, women were outperforming men, in others, it was the opposite, and many showed no significant differences. In my view, this merely indicates that brains are mainly sexless and unique, and confirms that we can input this myth to gender stereotypes.[112] "

"Sir, is multi-tasking good or bad?"

"The reality is that no one should be particularly proud of being associated with multi-tasking, as recent studies showed. In fact, and unlike your 16-core electronic chips, our human brain is extremely bad at performing it. One reason explaining this is that similar tasks compete to use the same brain area. Furthermore, usually, both areas need to involve simultaneous communication, creating many interferences. The point is that we should systematically avoid multi-tasking![a] "

"Sir, how are cortical areas specialized?"

"At a micro level, the brain enjoyed specialization, organized around two main processing functions: simpler and more sophisticated tasks are dealt by the primary and association cortex areas, respectively. The primary cortices include mainly areas receiving sensory inputs or directly involved in the production of limb and eye movements. On the other hand, the association cortical areas are involved in more complex functions such as memory, language, creativity, judgment, emotion, or attention."

"Sir, will you base your description of these areas, on such a classification?"

---

[a] The executive system is the part in our cortex responsible for switching from one task to another. It executes the controls by first changing goals, which triggers a switch in the focus from one task to another. In a second step, it turns off a new rule, telling the brain how to complete the new goal. Thus, when multi-tasking, our brain switches goals and their associated rules on and off rapidly, without actually working simultaneously on these different goals. This switching consequently, slows down the process.

For instance, one of these numerous studies shows that such continuous processing, reduces performance by 77% in men versus 66% in women.[N76] By switching between tasks, people make changes to physical and mental states. This operation takes time, grasps precious resources, and affects performance. Another study, done with 1.100 British workers, by the Institute of Psychiatry at the University of London, corroborates this view. It shows that multitasking with electronic media causes a decrease in IQ, of 10 points, corresponding to a performance after smoking marijuana! Furthermore, another research suggests that multitasking could cause permanent impairment.[N77] This study found that people who often multi-task have less brain density in regions responsible for empathy, as well as in the cognitive and emotional control areas (i.e., anterior cingulate cortex).

"No, I'll rather refer to a few major functional specializations, which you could relate to. However, before that, I would just like to make a small reference to the Brodmann mapping numbering scheme, which since 1908, describes the cerebral cortical architecture. Indeed, there are 54 original Brodmann areas, which have been further refined, corresponding to specialized cortical areas. Just look at the following graph, I drafted for you, which shows a few of these areas."

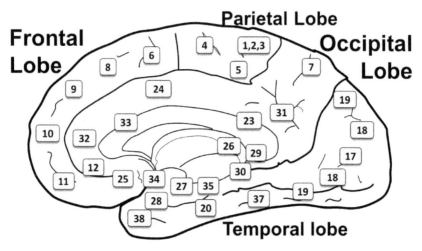

Fig. 35) Medial surface view with Brodmann mapping; source: adapted by the author.

"Sir, could you explain the various areas, which are highlighted by this Broadmann map?"

"I'll e-mail you a quick description of some important functions but will only highlight the language cortex in my discussion.[a] "

- [a] **Visual cortex**: Several brain areas are involved in visual processing. The primary visual cortex (VI; area 17) receives visual inputs and projects to surrounding cortical regions, called visual association areas (V2, V3; areas 18 and 19), where optical inputs are interpreted and forms identified. Additional visual processing is done in adjacent regions, such as color (V4) and movement (V5) recognition.
- **Auditory Cortex**: The primary auditory cortex (AI; area 41) receives acoustic inputs and projects into the surrounding auditory association areas (AII; area 42).
- **Somatosensory Cortex**: It gets all sensations related to a body's superficial and deep parts, enabling us to identify objects, by touch. The primary somatosensory (SI; areas 3,1,2) receives inputs, and some sensitive areas (e.g., lips or fingertips) are hugely represented. A secondary somatosensory cortex (SII; area 40) receives data from the primary and the thalamus, projecting the synthesized results into the somatosensory association cortical zone (areas 5 and 7).
- **Motor Cortex**: It is composed of a primary and secondary motor cortex. The primary (MI; area 4) receives inputs from the sensory cortical areas and from the premotor

214

"Sir, what are the cortical areas associated with language?"

"Language plays a key role in intelligence and is unique to humans. It forms both the message shaping our thoughts and the medium, enabling us to communicate these ideas.[a] Several areas (i.e., 22, 39, 40, 44, 45) are involved in the language function."

"Sir, how did language specialization happen?"

"For many scientists, language appeared ex nihilo with our human ancestors, about 50.000 years ago.[b] Recent studies, suggests that it evolved from manual gestures rather than from primate calls as initially thought. Furthermore, it is most likely not unique to Homo sapiens, since it also may have appeared in the Neanderthals.[c] "

"Sir, if internal language shapes human thoughts, how do real deaf people think?"

(area 6) cortex, with which it shares many same inbound connections (though, most of its outputs go to the primary cortex). Both areas control movements.

- **Prefrontal Cortex**: Extremely developed in humans, this portion can be sub-divided into the dorsolateral prefrontal cortex (mostly areas 9 and 10) and the orbitomedial prefrontal cortex (especially areas 11 and 12). The DLPC is primarily involved in executive functions (e.g., working memory, judgment, planning, sequencing of activity, abstract reasoning and dividing attention). The orbito-medial prefrontal cortex is involved in impulse control, personality, reactivity to the surroundings and mood.

[a] The areas 22 (called Wernicke's area), 44, and 45 (called Broca's area) play a crucial role in language, affected by the hemispherical specialization. For instance, in the dominant left hemisphere, these areas are responsible for understanding and generating spoken or written language. In the right, they help understand and generate voice inflections or tones.

[b] For instance, Chomsky wrote 'we can suggest what seems to be the simplest speculation about the evolution of language. In some small group from which we all descend, a rewiring of the brain took place yielding the operation of unbounded Merge, applying to concepts with properties of the kind I mentioned. The individual so rewired had many advantages: capacities for complex thought, planning, interpretation, and so on. The capacity is transmitted to offspring, coming to predominate. At that stage, there would be an advantage to externalization, so the capacity might come to be linked as a secondary process to the sensorimotor system for externalization and interaction, including communication.'[N78]

[c] Based on the same right handed argument, as the one expressed by the three evolutionists,[N79] and on similarities between chimpanzees left-sided enlargement of two cortical areas (i.e., Broca's and Wernicke's), a study claims that language evolved from manual gestures rather than from primate calls.[N80] Another study strengthens this view, by showing that brain asymmetries for language and tool usage, highly correlate, supporting this idea that language grew out from manual skills.[N81] Lastly, the discovery of a gene involved in human language evolution, called FOXP2, also present in Neanderthals, confirms the idea that language didn't happened solely in Homo sapiens, and probably much earlier than 50.000 years ago.[N82]

"Language isn't necessarily linked to 'voices' in our head. Rather than using their 'inner voice' that real deaf people don't have, those that learned the sign language, feel themselves signing, as if they were talking with their hands, in their head. Thus the human brain still has some form of communication mean to drive the thoughts."

"Sir, are you and other bilinguals smarter?"

"I've just shown that language plays a key role in intelligence because language is the abstract form we use to express our thoughts in, which is sometimes called mentalese."

"Sir, in theory, shouldn't someone who can structure and communicate well his thoughts in two languages, be more intelligent?"

"Things aren't that simple, unfortunately. A good communicator isn't necessarily intelligent. I know many people who are good at talking without saying anything. It isn't because one has the skills to communicate well, dumb ideas, in two languages rather than one, that he is more intelligent."

"Sir, but bilinguals are at least more knowledgeable?"

"Yes, making the distinction between 'knowledge that' and 'knowledge of,' someone speaking two or more languages should necessarily be more knowledgeable. A bilingual person will automatically have access to different grammatical structures, possess much more vocabulary, and have discovered two entirely different cultures."

"Why aren't things that clear cut when assessing intelligence, Sir?"

"A meta-study has shown that the media are usually favorably biased towards the bilingual brain.[113] That said, and though the same cortical areas process the different languages, several studies have shown a kind of bilingual neural signature in the right hemisphere.[114] Whenever switching to and from both languages, scans show strong brain activities in the dorsolateral prefrontal cortex."

"Sir, does the bilingual brain show any physiological difference?"

"Yes, another study shows that it differs in its use of executive functions (i.e., ability to effectively manage what are called higher cognitive processes, such as problem-solving, memory, and thoughts). [114]"

"Sir, isn't there a caveat to what you just said? Are you sure intelligence integrates the executive functions?"

"The problem, as I already indicated several times, is how one defines intelligence. Learning another language, allows our brain to acquire a series of new rules, procedures, and structures (i.e., a lexicon) explaining how to understand the words within its grammatical structure and general context. According to the neuropsychologist Alberto Costa, [115] the parts of our brain that store the lexicon, don't just turn on when needed but are constantly engaged. Bilinguals must thus make a choice all the time between the two lexicons, strengthening by the same token, the neural networks involved. Moreover, an indirect consequence is that bilinguals become better at inhibiting some responses and promoting others in split seconds, which produces a more flexible and agile mind, in the end.[116] "

"Sir, can flexibility and agility be sufficient to justify higher intelligence?"

"The second interesting aspect of this lexicon is that we employ words that are context sensitive and our brain uses this lexicon to anticipate what could come next. In other words, for Mr. Costa, a truly bilingual person has this predictive power for both languages."

"Sir, doesn't this statement bring us back to prediction and thus entropy?"

"Yes exactly, and at the risk of repeating myself, how we define intelligence is key to understanding if bilinguals are cleverer. If we define intelligence according to the Free-energy theory (i.e., capacity to minimize entropy through action or enhanced sensing inputs), then being able to anticipate words coming from other human beings in a different language, definitely fits within this definition."

"Sir, you are probably biased, as you master several languages."

"Fair enough! However, it kind of feels obvious to me that being able to understand what people tell you in their different mother tongues, must be correlated with higher intelligence. Even though bilinguals don't necessarily perform better at IQ tests, especially as this bilingual dimension is never really accounted for, I can confirm that a unilingual person, even part of the MENSA group,[a] sure looks like a powerless fool outside of his or her own linguistic environment."

"Sir, during the cortical expansion, has neuronal specialization occurred as well?"

"Though I won't describe in large detail the fact that species don't share systematically the same neurons, I must highlight that the specialization that happened at the anatomical and physiological level, also occurred at a much more micro level."

---

[a] An organization open to men and women who score at the 98th percentile or higher on a standardized IQ test.

"Sir, are you saying that species don't possess necessarily the same neural cell types?"

"Yes, and have different biochemical molecules, involved in their cognitive processes. The point is that the functional changes, I described within mammal species, have induced both structural differences in layers and shaped new specialized cell types, as well as changes in some neurons' dimension and density."

"Sir, is the gnostic neuron you already referred to, a specialized neuron?"

"Yes, this neuron, also called 'grandmother cell,' is specialized because it can represent a specific concept or Object (e.g., a grandmother) individually. Interestingly, there has been a renewed interest in them, after the discovery of one specific neuron in a patient that would fire strongly and systematically after seeing any of the seven presented pictures of the American actress Jennifer Aniston, and to no other pictures (e.g., other actors, animals, places, etc.). By coincidence or not, this 'Jennifer Aniston' neuron resides in the hippocampus, the place Mr. Hawkins associates with the higher level of our neocortex."

"Sir, I'm intrigued by these grandmother cells. Could you describe their unique features?"

"In their studies, [117] [118] Quiroga and al. identified several unique features of these gnostic cells:

- Their responses are very selective, discharging to a few of the presented stimuli.
- They show invariance, firing to all that is related to a person or object (e.g., different pictures, and even written or spoken names).
- They can discharge to several things, as long as closely related.[a]

Regardless of if they act alone or within a small neural group, Quiroga believes that gnostic cells are: 'The link between perception and memory; they give an abstract and sparse representation of semantic knowledge that constitutes the building blocks for declarative memory functions.' "

---

[a] From these characteristics, Quiroga concludes that these cells require a more distributed representation, as they are good at extracting data out of many stimuli, and synthesizing it, to form patterns. This is by the way coherent with actual coding of visual inputs, but also with deep learning IT theories. On the other hand, he argues that metabolic constraints (e.g., energy optimization) push towards a sparser representation in higher cognitive areas and memory functions, such as through the use of gnostic neurons. We should note that Quiroga doesn't believe in one but a few specific associated neurons firing together, when a particular Object is sensed.[N83] For instance, he argues representation is sparse, in the sense that responsive neurons fire only to very few stimuli (and are mostly silent except for their preferred stimuli), but it is far from a grandmother-cell representation.

"Sir, are you saying that, through individual or sparse coding, these neurons solve the issues about the 'knowledge of' definitely?"

"Yes, the gnostic neurons can explain away gnoseological issues. Rather than giving you exclusively my view on this important issue, I'd like to quote Asim Roy,[119] who defends individual coding and believes that gnostic cells '... first provide information in an abstracted, summarized, and tractable form that may be easily exploited by other units of the brain. Second, it avoids interpreting an underlying pattern over and over again by different parts of the brain, where the pattern could be distributed over hundreds of thousands of units at lower levels.' "

Is there a brain architecture?

"Sir, is there a better brain architectural model in nature?"

"In order to fully benefit from specialization, any system must solve several issues. For instance, how do we ensure that a task goes to the right sub-system (s)? What kind of decision should be taken, at what level? How many sub-levels there should be? How to inform other specialized areas about these decisions? What subjects are of interest for which specialized areas? Which specialized areas should have access to the stored information? Etc. I've already introduced to you a few examples of software architectures (e.g., SOA and EDA) for which experts had to solve these same issues and transpose their recommendations into standards, through industrial committees."

"Sir, are you saying that nature in some way, also had to face these same problems to make intelligent engines?"

"Yes, evolution had to find solutions to these same issues, which might have been differently applied, throughout species. In fact, even for probably the most central issue, that is, what architectural framework should be developed, evidence shows that nature chose different pathways."

"Sir, what are the differences between the distributed, centralized, and decentralized architectures you already referred to?"

"We all understand the notion of centralized versus decentralized intelligence. However, the distinction between distributed and decentralized is subtler.[a] With decentralized intelligence, there is no single location where decisions are made. Every node decides, and the system's aggregated response integrates these resulting decisions. Furthermore, no single node possesses the complete system information. In a distributed architecture, the decision can be centralized, and a node may obtain the complete system understanding. However, unlike centralized architecture, the processing is shared between different nodes."

Fig. 36) Centralized, decentralized and distributed architecture; source: author.

"Sir, what are the different brain architectures found in nature?"

"Humans, like many animals, have a central nervous system, characterized by bilateral symmetry. However, this characteristic is unique to vertebrates. For instance, not all invertebrates even have a brain. Jellyfishes don't even possess a centralized nerve center but rather interconnected nerve cells, which form a ring around their mantle. An insect's brain consists of a ganglion located in the head and of smaller ganglia found in some segments of their body."

"Sir, all these structures are interesting but don't inform us about a potentially better brain architecture than humans', as they all relate to relatively primitive brain structure."

---

[a] From an evolutionary perspective, centralized systems are easier to create, implement, and even maintain, as there is only one single point of failure. They can be highly unstable, as the controlling node failure will affect all others. Furthermore, they evolve more slowly than the two other systems and have low scalability. Distributed systems, on the other hand, are highly scalable, extremely stable (as any harm is limited to the problematic node), and may evolve quickly. They require more maintenance and are more complicated to implement, as details such as what resources and data, must be shared and communicated. Decentralized systems are somewhere in between the two other systems.

"There is, however, a fascinating invertebrate exception: the octopus. Indeed, and though we share a common ancestor around 750 million years ago, the octopus' cognitive evolution created a remarkably different neural architecture. Due probably to their lack of a rigid skeleton, their brain evolved into a leading central processing unit located in their head, supported by packets of neurons in each of their eight arms, creating a unique decentralized neural architecture.[a] "

Fig. 37) The decentralized neural architecture of an octopus; source: author.

"Sir, what does this specificity bring?"

"It makes of the octopus a brilliant creature, which not only may perform complex tasks, such as learning by trial and error, use tools, open a bottle, change its skin shape to hunt or protect itself from predators, etc., but can even confer some form of consciousness.[120] "

---

[a] Only around 40% of all neurons are located in their head: 10% in a centralized brain, while their two optic globes employ about 30%. The 60% remaining, of their 750 million neurons (to be compared to humans 86 billions), are located in their tentacles. Researchers have shown that these collections of neurons can think for themselves, carrying out directly instructions and actions to their arms and suckers. This decentralized architecture changes how octopuses control their body in regards to vertebrates, such as humans. Instead of having a body map as we do, they have what would correspond to a behavioral library. Therefore, whenever they see food, they don't activate any body part (e.g., move an arm to grab a fruit) but instead generate a behavioral response to catch their prey. As the signal travels through the nervous system, their arms' brain picks up the signal and reacts upon it to grab the prey. Furthermore, each tentacle has intriguing other capabilities. For instance, it can explore by itself its habitat and has its own senses, such as tasting what it touches.

"Sir, why isn't the octopus more intelligent?"

"Unfortunately, octopuses only have a maximum life expectancy of seven years. Were they to live a longer life, we could probably be amazed by the intelligence level this decentralized architecture could reach. In fact, with a more gregarious life, it is questionable if nature couldn't have made them in some way, as intelligent as human beings."

"Sir, if some species have no brain, ganglia, or a decentralized structure, what about the mammals' architectural framework?"

"Unfortunately, the answer isn't straightforward. It depends on the information processing level we are contemplating and actually on the type of processing model theory. Intuitively, we would claim that intelligence seems centralized in our brain, but that would miss the point that many neurons aren't really in the brain, but in our body.[a] "

Is there a brain architectural framework?

"Sir, how would your two hemispheres fit in a centralized model? Moreover, how are human neural networks organized? Are they following a clear architectural framework that governs the communication between all neural networks?"

"For once, rather than starting my description at the macro level, I'll start by focusing on the neocortex, which is the center of our intelligence.[b] To understand what it looks like, let's imagine that we unfold the brain's two hemispheres and flatten them. We would be left with a 2 to 4 mm thick tissue. If we were to scan such resulting tissue, we would see that it is mostly organized vertically into six layers, and horizontally into cells groups, synaptically linked across these layers (layers II-VI). It is now important to establish at what level the cortex carries out computations, as I must tell you, which cortical micro-circuits defines the spatial scale responsible for such processing."

"Sir, how many cortical levels could play this computing role?"

---

[a] For example, the dorsal root ganglions host the sensory neurons, and the spinal cord contains the motor neurons. Moreover, the enteric nervous system in our intestine, which is composed of 500 million neurons, could almost be considered a second brain.

[b] To be more precise, we won't consider 10% of the cortex, called the allocortex, which has a different structure (4 layers), nor include the hippocampus that many neuroscientists view as an organ from where the neocortex started its evolutionary growth.[N84]

"I counted four cortical levels: mini-columns, columns, hyper-columns, and cortical areas.[a] "

"Sir, at what level is the basic computation performed?"

"Most likely at the cortical column level as suggested by Mountcastle, [121], or by Hubel and Wiesel.[122] [b] Hawkins in a newer theory (2017) reinforces this view by describing how columns enable learning of the structure of the world."

"Sir, can you describe in more detail how each cortical column learns this structure?"

"In fact, Hawkins hypothesizes that each column learns a model of its own world, that is, of what it may sense. It learns the structure of many Objects and which behaviors it can apply to these objects. He adds that through intra-laminar and remote cortical to cortical connections, columns sensing the same Object can disambiguate issues related to this Object."

"Sir, what does a cortical column look like?"

- [a] **Mini-columns:** In most cortical areas, about 80 to 100 neurons are connected to form these mini-columns, which are 50-60 micrometers wide.
- **Columns:** A vertical alignment of cells containing neurons with similar receptive field properties. They integrate a number of mini-columns, and have a width of 300-400 micrometers.[N85]
- **Hyper-columns:** 50 to 120 mini-columns, bound together by short-range horizontal connections, form a hyper-column, and are estimated to be between 0.5 to 1 mm wide.[N86] They are defined modules, which include all possible values of a particular receptive field property, (e.g., orientation, eye dominance).
- **Cortical areas:** These million hyper-columns, are themselves associated to form around 200 differentiated cortical areas, regrouped in specialized cortical regions (e.g., visual, auditory, motoric, somatosensory, etc.).

[b] Hebb's diverging view, regained momentum lately: neurons, distributed over several cortical areas, would form a functional computational unit, called a neural assembly.[N87] Though there is no definite answer, computational models suggest that cortical columns with their structured connectivity are more efficient than neural assembly.[N88] Furthermore, columns can easily integrate bottom-up, lateral, and top-down information especially when taking into consideration the rich anatomical connectivity of L2/3 pyramidal cells.[N89]

"When observing these columns, we usually see six different layers, though there are cortical exceptions (e.g., no Layer IV in motor areas). Among mammal species, many other organizational variations also exist, based on differential neuronal clustering.[105] Each cortical layer contains different neural shapes, sizes, and density, as well as different organizations of nerve fibers.[a]"

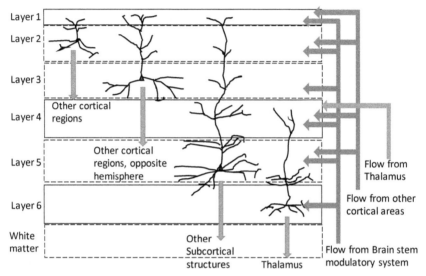

Fig. 38) Description of the 6-layers in the neocortex; source: author.

"Sir, are all these neurons similar?"

"No, there are several cell types across layers. However, the pyramidal cells are predominant within layers III and V, corresponding to around 80% of the total neural population.[b] Granule cells, on the other hand, can

---

[a] The six human cortical layers are:
- Layer I/Molecular: contains mostly dendrites of neurons from deeper layers and axons.
- Layer II/Small pyramidal: includes neurons projecting mostly to other neocortex areas.
- Layer III/Medium pyramidal: neurons projecting mainly to other neocortex areas.
- Layer IV/Granular, which receives the majority of inputs from the thalamus.
- Layer V/Large pyramidal: projects mostly to subcortical structures (e.g., brainstems, spinal cord, and basal ganglia).
- Layer VI/Polymorphic: projects primarily to the thalamus.
- White matter underneath.

[b] These cells have a pyramidal shape, with an apical (i.e., from the top) dendrite extending to layer I and several basal dendrites (i.e., from the bottom) projecting laterally, integrating

be found in great numbers, in layer IV. These physiological variations can explain differences between humans and other species, in processing complexity of the cortical circuits implicated in cognition, learning, reasoning, and memory processes."

"Sir, I thought you said, there was some form of uniformity between the layers?"

"I did. Within the neocortex, micro-columns have, more or less, a similar architecture. That's why, Vernon Mountcastle's in 1978, pushed the idea that, since all cortical regions looked the same (vertically and horizontally), they had to perform the same basic operations. In other words, there must be some sort of universal algorithm performed by neurons, regardless of the senses or cognitive processes involved."

"Sir, you already mentioned that the memory-prediction theory relies on such property."

"Yes and, to a certain extent, all newer cognitive theories are also based on such horizontal anatomical commonalities, between the various micro-columns. From an anatomical perspective, though, this idea that the neocortex is the same from region to region, is now widely rejected by neuroscientists."

"Sir, what about the synapses?"

"There are also some major differences between species, at the synaptic level.[a]"

"Sir, does it mean that the memory-prediction model is wrong, as there is no universal structure in the cortex, throughout the animal kingdom?"

"It doesn't mean that Hawkins' model is necessarily flawed. The uniformity of the 6-layer structure across mammals' cortical areas, has been confirmed by other studies. [123][124] "

---

many spines, which are sites of synapses. The axons emerging from the pyramidal cell base leave the cortex and connect with other brain regions, by extending through the white matter, located deep into the cortex. Pyramidal cells vary considerably between cortical areas and species, in terms of size and complexity of their dendritic arborization, of the density of dendritic spines on their branches, and of the total number of dendritic spines.

[a] The shape and proportion of neuron types (e.g., GABAergic neurons) differ significantly between primates, other mammals, and men. For instance, TH interneurons, which are abundant in Layer IV and V of humans and monkeys, are absent in the neocortex of great apes. Though specific general features of the cortical synaptic structure are applicable to humans, rats, and mice, there are also significant differences, which means that the pattern of synaptic organization is specific to each cortical area and species.[N90]

"Sir, are cortical circuits similar across species and areas?"

"Neuroscientists use cortical properties, as a possible mean to explain why cortical circuits are similar across species and areas, even though they may carry different types of signals (e.g., sensory input vs. motor functions). Other neuroscientists also defend this idea of cortical circuit similarities.[a] "

"Sir, has this cortical circuit idea been tested on a brain area that a priori, showed divergences in neo-cortical circuitry?"

"Yes, for instance, on a frontal cortical area, involved in vision, which doesn't have a layer IV. The study's results were consistent with the general cortical model, with only a slight latency in response time."

"Sir, wouldn't that study confirm mostly that the neocortex uniformity doesn't come from an algorithm?"

"Yes, you are right. It seems that this uniformity wouldn't be coming from an algorithm, which would perform the integration of the various sensory inputs or motoric functions."

"Sir, how would you then explain it?"

"It comes from the connection properties between the layers and not from the connections between specialized cortical areas themselves. It's our genes that define these links, which explains why there are important differences between species, sexes, and even individuals. In fact, a recent study identified a simple mathematical logic, which highlights this universality of connectivity properties. [125] "

"Sir, connectivity is linked first and foremost to synapses. Are these following this general rule or other ones?"

"Hawkins shows the active role of synapses and dendrites, in pyramidal neurons, which enables the recognition of hundreds of independent patterns of cell activity. He suggests a neural model in which only patterns detected on proximal dendrites (i.e., near the soma) lead to action potentials, as per the classical definition."

---

[a] Douglas and Martin depicted these neocortical properties: 'Superficial pyramidal cells receive feed-forward input from subcortical and diverse cortical sources (from local as well as more distant cortical layers and areas). These superficial pyramidal cells arborize locally within their layer, contacting many neighboring pyramids. Most smooth (inhibitory) cells also show this pattern of arborization. This circuit integrates various inputs using cooperation and competition to explore all possible interpretations of the input. The inhibition enforces a soft winner-take-all to select an interpretation consistent with the most inputs.' [N91]

"Sir, what happens when patterns are far from the soma?"

"He asserts that patterns detected on both dendrite extremities, that is, at the neuron's base or head (i.e., basal and apical regions), act as prediction agents. This prediction is achieved by slightly depolarizing the neuron, without generating any action potential but creating a powerful sequence memory. He also links these three specific regions to communication flow direction.[a]"

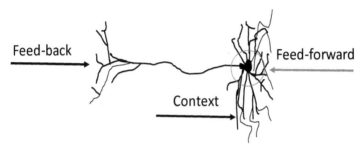

Fig. 39) A pyramidal neuron's thousands of excitatory synapses generate an action potential when located near the soma and only depolarize it at both extremities; source: author.

---

[a] Hawkins and al., in their study,[N92] propose the following communication flow. Apical synapses receive feedback inputs, taking care of top-down expectations. Basal synapses take care of bottom-up data (i.e., feed-forward) and play a role in learning and storing transitions between activity patterns. Finally, the proximal synapses (near the soma and thus having the biggest effect on it) receive feed-forward inputs, which trigger an action potential.

Is there a single brain computational formula?

"Sir, if we go back to the simple mathematical logic you mentioned. Can it account for brain computation, across all species and neural networks, whatever their complexity?"

"Let me reformulate your question by making a computing analogy. Is there an equivalent to your transistor's binary processing formula, that is 2^n, within the brain? Surprisingly, there is an almost universal equation, also based on a power of 2.[a] "

"Sir, I'm intrigued. What is this formula?"

"$N = 2^i - 1$"

"Sir, it's based on which theory?"

"This wired logic is based on the theory of connectivity, which specifies that within each computational building block, the number of neural association can be calculated by a simple equation, function of the number of sensory inputs i."

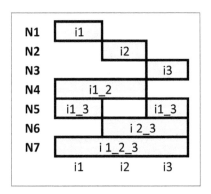

Fig. 40) All possible permutations for a 3-input neural clique (in grey); source: author.

"Sir, I don't get it. What does this formula explain?"

"It demonstrates that the number of neural associations, resulting from different sensory inputs, is fixed according to this equation."

"Sir, could you give me some insights from the study to help me understand?"

"Yes, the study describes, through the use of electrodes positioned in several rats and hamsters' cortex layers, how these animals' neural system reacts to a set of four stimuli, of different nature."

"Sir, I imagine that the number of neural associations is fifteen."

---

[a] In fact, the formula is quite similar to binary processing: $N = 2^i-1$; where N is the number of distinct neural groups that can cover all possible permutations and combinations of specific-to-general input patterns; and i is the number of inputs; (-1 is just there to account for the absence of any permutation). For instance, with three and four inputs, there would be seven and fifteen possible permutations respectively, corresponding to the same number of neurons connections associated with these inputs.

"Correct. As anticipated by the formula, the results show a combination of fifteen groups composed of several neurons, which fire together according to the input permutation. For instance, four different food types (sugar pellets, rice, rodent diet pellets, and milk droplets) were delivered randomly seven times, with a five to ten-minute interval. Results show a clique of only three neurons for the association of milk, sugar, and rice, but of fifty-four neurons for solely the milk pellets. Other four-stimuli tests found systematically fifteen neural cliques, confirming the equation.[a] "

"Sir, can we extend this finding to all neurons?"

"No, these studies indicate that modulatory neurons, such as the dopamine midbrain neurons, follow a more simple rule.[b] The researchers conclude that because these neurons have different functional purposes (e.g., providing motivational valence signals, such as, wanting or not, and rewarding or not), they did not use the same specific-to-general coding logic. Furthermore, this study only considered projection neurons and thus, cannot be generalized to interneurons."

"Sir, you mentioned specific-to-general encoding logic. Could you be more explicit?"

"Yes, the research shows that there are systematically two types of neural connectivity strategies. In the neocortex's superficial layers (i.e., II and III), there is a random connectivity strategy, while in the deeper layers (i.e., V and VI) this strategy is non-random. The researchers summed up the benefits of these two connecting modes."

"Sir, which benefit can a random connectivity strategy bring?"

"In the case of superficial layers, it offers better pattern discrimination, compatible with abstract reasoning.[c] "

"Sir, in the case of non-random connectivity, what are the benefits?"

---

[a] Interestingly, the firing showed up immediately when the rats made their food choices, indicating that these neural groups most likely are pre-wired. The same test was performed for social information processing (also involving four inputs: male and female faces and ano-genitals) and fear experience processing (processing once again four inputs: air puff, free-fall, earthquake, and feet shock), with electrodes positioned in the medial amygdala, in multiple cortical and hippocampus areas. Three other tests confirmed the same results.

[b] Situated in the ventral tegmental area.

[c] Randomness in superficial layers (L2/3 neurons usually encode specific and low-combinatorial features) maximizes the capacity to discover possible new combinations across a wider range of sensory cortices and thus can more easily extract, discriminate, and categorize new patterns. On the other hand, the disadvantage of randomness is that L2/3 synaptic efficacy is less robust, leading to possible sparse coding. This explains, most likely, the hippocampus' critical role in memory consolidation and LTM storage.

"This strategy enables the deeper cortical layers to apply evolutionary answers. In other words, it allows mammals to detect patterns that would have emerged along all the years these species' have fought for their survival, taking into account the 'best practices' generated by their sensory input processing.[a] "

"Sir, is this cell-assembly equation formed by nurture or pre-configured by nature?"

"The research shows that this neural equation is independent of learning during adulthood. Therefore, nature developed this rule, which probably affects all living mammals."

"Sir, if we adopt this more connectionist view, where does the memory-prediction model leave us?"

"Well, we need to recognize that the brain's functional specialization exists. Equally, cortical areas may have distinct connections with other subcortical areas, though they most likely follow the same inter-column connectivity rule. With this said and done, the connections and flows between the layers can still be generalized, and most of Mr. Hawkins theory still holds firm."

Is the brain architecture distributed?

"Sir, I am back to my central question. How can you characterize the mammalian brain's architecture?"

"To answer the question is the human brain centralized, decentralized, or distributed, I need once again to refer to the Bayesian Brain, Predictive Coding, and Friston's Free-energy models. According to these theories, our brain is essentially a prediction machine that tries to reduce free energy by diminishing surprises, through perception or action. I now need to introduce another giant of cognitive sciences: Hermann von Helmholtz."

"Sir, what is von Helmholtz's theory?"

---

[a] Non-randomness connectivity of deep layers (L5/6 neurons project mainly to sub-cortical systems, such as the amygdala, midbrain dopamine circuits, and the striatum) is ideal for categorizing and generalizing specific patterns, which generate feedback controls of general motivational, emotional, conscious states, and behavioral outputs, designed by evolutionary selection. In other words, and because these non-random connections don't need to deal with the same level of complexity that L2/3 neurons have to, such connectivity mode would still ensure the systematic application of evolutionarily proven responses.

"He was the first to have this insight that the mammal brain doesn't create its model of the world simply by accumulating a mass of low-level cues (i.e., sensory inputs). Instead, it focuses on predicting the current suite of inputs, from its best understanding of the possible causes."

"Sir, doesn't this idea draw on the 'likelihood principle'?"

"Yes, we perceive the most likely Objects or events, which would fit the sensory signals that we are trying to interpret. This 'most likely' notion introduces Bayesian probabilities, which as seen, mostly refers to subjective expectations (i.e., beliefs)."

"Sir, what's the consequence of subjective probabilities from a Free-energy perspective?"

"Free energy's predictive coding implies that we test predicted beliefs in a top-down fashion, against these sensory inputs, and along recurrent neural connections.[a] "

"Sir, why are beliefs tested against sensory inputs?"

"Our brain uses higher levels of specialized knowledge, to create a simulation of what we can expect from the sensory inputs, which it cascades through the lower cortical layers. This simulation uses top-down probabilistic generative model. This top-down flow attempts to fully render intelligible the upcoming sensory inputs, leaving only residual prediction errors to be feed-forwarded, within the system."

"Sir, how do you tie in action to this merely perceptual view?"

"For this, I'd like to quote Andy Clark, who extends this hierarchical predictive coding from perception to action: 'Hierarchical predictive processing combines the use, within a multilevel bidirectional cascade, of 'top-down' probabilistic generative models with the core predictive coding strategy of efficient encoding and transmission. Such approaches, originally developed in the domain of perception, have been extended (by Friston and others…) to encompass action, and to offer an attractive, unifying perspective on the brain's capacities for learning, inference, and the control of plasticity. Perception and action, if these unifying models are correct, are intimately related and work together to reduce prediction error by sculpting and selecting sensory inputs.'[126] "

"Sir, what are the conclusions concerning the communication flow?"

"According to hierarchical predictive coding, the descending (also called feedback) neural communication carries on the predictions, while

---

[a] For instance, within the six layers of visual or auditory columns.

the ascending (also called feed-forward) neural connections carry back the prediction errors, [127] or the constraints on these predictions.[128] "

"Sir, does this kind of centralized process suggest that the brain has a centralized model?"

"There is indeed, an ongoing process, by which top-down information, coming from higher cortical layers, is compared at each one of the six layers, with bottom-up prediction error. Though the word hierarchical could mislead us to think that there is a centralized process, this isn't the case.[a] "

"Sir, if it isn't centralized, is it decentralized or distributed?"

"Though many people mix up these two structures, I believe that the brain's architecture looks a lot like a Peer-to-Peer (P2P) architecture, usually associated with distributed architecture."

---

[a] In fact, this hierarchy comes from the distinction between connections: feed-forward that link an earlier area to a higher area, feedback that tie a higher to an earlier sphere, and lateral that connect regions at the same level.[N93] Thus, information isn't centralized (i.e., there is no master and slave area) but dealt with, according to specialized inputs. In other words, the visual cortex won't process language information and vice-versa. In fact, the notion of hierarchy promoted by these models, relates to levels of complexity or abstraction, in regards to the sensory inputs. Furthermore, and using a cyber analogy, when connecting several Ethernet switches, a distributed algorithm (e.g., spanning tree) is used to self-organize into a hierarchical structure, which confirms that hierarchy and distributed systems are compatible. By the way, this view that information is processed along specialized brain modules is consistent with Fodor's Modularity of the Mind Theory.[N94]

"Our cortical neural networks are designed around neurons that act both as 'clients and servers' to all other directly associated neurons.[a] "

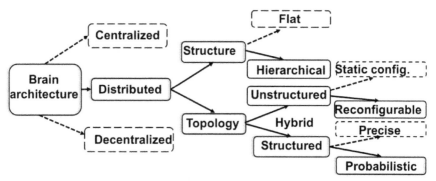

Fig. 41) Brain architectural taxonomy based on P2P architecture; source: author.

"Sir, if you push further this analogy with Peer-to-Peer architecture, besides being distributed and having a physical hierarchical (i.e., multi-tier) structure, what kind of logical topology could the human brain architecture have?"

"In other words, you are asking me if the nodes make their queries in a structured or unstructured manner. Going back to the connectivity strategy, queries are per definition already structured in non-random connections."

---

[a] The notion of equal peer nodes influences the peer-to-peer network design. Each node works simultaneously as both 'client' (i.e., it sends) and 'server' (i.e., it receives) to the other nodes on the network. If we consider the cells from the different layers as the peer processing units, there is no centralized units, nor other auxiliary mechanisms, which would coordinate the operations among peers (e.g., resource location, replication, etc.). No single neuron stores all the data (which is distributed across various neurons) and the same data is stored across more than one neuron, ensuring tolerance to failures. Furthermore, any node may have a view of the decision (through excitatory and inhibitory signals), can be centralized (according to the modularity principle), and obtain the complete system understanding (even though it is partially available, as prior information is reduced to errors). All these particularities characterize a distributed architecture.

"Therefore Sir, the question is if some compensatory measures exist for the other random connections?"

"The answer is yes. If we look at neural networks, each neuron is responsible for its own data, stored in its synapses.[a] A neuron is mostly physically tied to the nearest neurons, to which it may forward queries and for which it maintains track of. In fact, 95% of all neural connections lie within about 2 mm of the injection site.[129] Though there might be no strict mapping between its prediction and those of the peers', the fact that neurons mostly interconnect to neighboring neurons, largely compensates for the unstructured nature of these queries.[b] "

---

[a] A synapse, by itself, is more similar to a microprocessor than a router switch and may contain the equivalent of 1.000 molecular scale On and Off switches.

[b] Though it could still be challenging to know precisely, which nodes stored the information, there would be no need to search on the entire neural network to find such information and thus, the query time would be significantly reduced. Furthermore, these neighboring connections aren't fixed but reconfigurable according to the neighbors' interest, especially if we assume that this interest relates in some way, to the Hebbian principle (i.e., neurons stimulated together fire together, and the more often they do so, the stronger their ties become). Though all these properties characterize an unstructured Peer-to-Peer architecture,[N95] we couldn't discard either a hybrid structure, which would take into consideration the neural connections between different cortical areas.

What are the brain's learning rules and reward mechanisms?

"Sir, you already mentioned that no universal algorithm governs human and animal cognitive processes, but it sure looks like it, doesn't it?"

"No, we need to differentiate between the means to process information through neural connectivity, that is through this quasi-universal logical equation I mentioned, and the algorithms that would govern the various cognitive processes, such as perception, decision-making, learning, etc. If there were such a universal algorithm in our brain, it would need to be simple, but it doesn't look like there is such a universal algorithm."

"Why are you saying that, Sir?"

"In mathematics we all know that anything can be described by just adding additional operations and conditions, unfortunately making the equation incomputable. However, most scientists believe that there isn't just one single simple algorithm that could define intelligence, but probably hundreds with varying degrees of importance.[a] "

"Sir, though there is no simple, unique algorithm, couldn't you still compute hundreds through an optimization model?"

"Yes, and I'll come back to that when I talk again about free energy."

---

[a] For instance, evolutionary psychologists claim that the mind is made up of domain-specific algorithms, influenced by genes. These 'computational modules' have evolved through species selection, in order to solve specific evolutionary problems. Each of these modules is functionally specialized for solving different adaptive problems (e.g., face recognition, speech, motion, mate selection, predator surveillance, etc.) and are activated by different sensory inputs coming from the environment. Though this 'computational module' view doesn't reject entirely the notion that there might be a general rule for learning, it would need to exist within these specific modules. In this approach, learning plays the role of acquiring data and adapting existing algorithms but reduces the impact of the environment to build up these mental algorithms. In other words, we mainly acquire these mental algorithms. On the other hand, in computational neurosciences, there is a divergent belief that intelligence can be defined by a universal learning theory, which equally doesn't consider a single algorithm. Contrarily to the previous view, it stipulates that these mental algorithms are learned through experience, whenever interacting with our environment. Even though this view highlights the crucial role of 'nurture,' it still considers that some faculties are acquired at birth: the learning and reward mechanisms themselves, an initial neural network architecture allowing, through implementation, to acquire these algorithms, and a few simple innate circuits (for instance, the one described by Mountcastle's uniform neocortex architecture theory). In other words, in this view, the mind is a complex software, built out of a general learning rule and reward mechanisms, which relies on separate hardware made of the physiological neural networks, in order to acquire specific mental algorithms.

"Sir, if there are many algorithms, can all mental states and cognitive processes be quantifiable or can't they be reduced to a computable mathematical formula? Furthermore, is there a general cognitive rule, with its reward mechanisms, which could be considered universal?"

"I'll start by answering your second question. Yes, there is such a universal cognitive rule, and I've already presented the one, I believe, is the most accurate. Friston's entropy model explains how our brain's structure and its associated cognitive functions, work together to minimize free energy."

"Sir, with this general rule, what happens to biological agents, such as humans?"

"All biological agents resist a tendency to disorder and seek to minimize the entropy of their sensory states, by either gathering more data through perception or by acting on their environment. In other words, this theory gives both reward (i.e., minimization of entropy) and learning rules (i.e., optimizing sufficient statistics,[a] as well as action).[130] "

"Sir, how are the rewards and learning rules accounted for?"

"First, I'd like to briefly highlight the reward mechanisms, which in my view, Friston's model implicitly includes. Several theories and studies have underlined the dominant role in learning, played by dopamine.[b] This reward mechanism for prediction errors provides a framework for understanding how dopamine is involved in reward learning. I'll now show how cognitive studies have bridged the gap between experimental evidence and Friston's theoretical framework."

"Sir, before you describe the links between dopamine, neuroplasticity, encoding, and learning, could you explain within this context of a distributed mammalian brain's architectural framework, what sort of encoding mechanism is used by the brain?"

"Let me try. I'll start with probably the most exciting of all the issues: how is the learning process guided through our brain? Fortunately for me, I can rely on several theories and experiments, which have already described the key role of the midbrain dopamine neurons, in such a process, especially in synaptic modifications."

---

[a] We cannot calculate from the same sample, any other statistic.

[b] Huron,[N96] as well as Mandler,[N97] suggest that a biological arousal within the nervous system, due to interruption of expectancy patterns, linked to perceptual and motoric schemes precede emotional reactions. Furthermore, newer studies show that midbrain dopamine neurons can signal reward prediction error, one of Friston's model significant parameter. [N98] [N99] [N100] Their findings establish a clear causal role for time-related dopamine neuron signaling, in cue-reward learning.

"Sir, you've already shown how neuroplasticity is at the heart of the cognitive processes. Could you explain how it is itself, involved in reinforcement learning mechanisms?"

"Yes, I'll start by describing the dopamine midbrain neurons role and specific characteristics. These neurons are very large and possess very long and complicated axonal arbors. These exceptional properties enable, with just a few of them, to irrigate large areas of the cortex involved in the learning processes with their neurotransmitters. In fact, these properties confer the ability to irradiate throughout most of the brain, their dopamine signal mechanisms.[a] "

"Sir, it's not because one has the reach to do something that one is actually able to do it."

"You are right, so let's check if a midbrain dopamine neuron has this capacity. To do so, I need to confirm that through dopamine, it can adjust the synaptic strengths, in some sort of quantitative manner. To support me, I must refer to computational algorithms that could describe the role played by dopamine, in the theory of reinforcement learning. There are several such models,[b] but I would like to highlight only the so-called 'Temporal Difference Learning' model, developed by Sutton and Barto.[131] "

"Sir, what is this Temporal Difference Learning Model?"

"By portraying prediction reward errors as the difference between the person's expectations of all future rewards and any actual or expected information, which could lead to a change of expectation, this equation uses patterns of existing stimuli and rewards, to build an expectation about potential future rewards.[c] "

---

[a] They are also unique in the fact that they have a low firing rate and are characterized by electrical coupling. Furthermore, they are embedded in a distributed network that includes the frontal cortex and the basal ganglia.

[b] The first computational algorithms originated from Pavlov's research on conditioned learning. We all studied in college, Pavlov's experiments on dogs, which would systematically salivate, whenever earing a bell rang. Pavlov's original idea was that such behavior is due to bell-detecting neurons connected to food sight and salivary glands activation. Such an idea was later on mathematically formalized by Bush and Mosteller in an iterative equation,[N101] which integrated a reward prediction error. This initial equation considered reward prediction errors as the difference between the weighted average of past rewards, and the last reward experienced. In other words, for the first time, a kind of iterative error-based rule, was used to explain such reinforcement learning. This equation, which provided a way to learn expected values, was later on extended by Rescorla–Wagner,[N102] who refined the model by describing what happens to associative strengths, whenever two inputs predict the same event. The equations formulated by Bush and Mosteller proved to be good at predicting values of past experience but couldn't predict the value of future events.

[c] This model accounts for two types of positive prediction error: whenever someone

"Sir, the problem with modeling is that though one can simulate a scenario and check if the results are logical, one still needs to prove that the results are clinically validated."

"This was done in a clinical study,[132] confirming that dopamine neurons encode this reward prediction error. As postulated by the Temporal Difference Learning model, some areas activated by dopamine (e.g., ventral striatum) could be identified as a reward prediction error encoder, undoubtedly proving that our brain is encoding reward prediction errors. However, there are still some questions about the type of cellular mechanisms, which could achieve this result."

"Sir, you've already described the importance of neuroplasticity and the fundamental role played by long-term potentialization in LTM formation. How do they fit in with this model?"

"Wickens and Kotter integrate these two key neural characteristics into a framework, in which this neurotransmitter also plays a fundamental role in synaptic strengthening.[133] According to their studies on pre and post-synaptic activities, presence or absence of dopamine, respectively strengthens or weakens synapses.[a] "

"Sir, do we know what are the mechanisms for producing the prediction error signal?"

"I believe we do. Paul Glimcher identifies the dopamine neuron encoding mechanisms.[134] For instance, using neurons responsible for movements, located in the striatum, he describes their role in encoding the learned values of actions, through their firing rates. These neurons connect with the dopamine neurons to which they send a reward prediction. These dopamine neurons receive direct inputs from sensory areas, detect, and encode the variation in consumed rewards.[b] "

---

receives an unexpected award and when he gets information leading to predict a future reward, previously unexpected. Furthermore, this newer model proves that some neurons answer positively and negatively to positive and negative prediction errors, respectively, explaining how these neurons combine recent awards in their reward prediction.

[a] As a consequence, any positive prediction error, which would generate dopamine, ends up irradiating in the orbitofrontal cortical and basal ganglia areas. In those brain regions, the specific neural synapses, associated with these recently produced positive prediction error, end up being strengthened. After several such exposures to dopamine, these strengthened synapses would end up encoding the expected subjective value of the sensory inputs, responsible for the positive prediction error. Additionally, it seems that dopamine is also involved in prediction errors for negative outcomes but not for punishing ones, like pain. In the case of fear, for instance, it is still not clear what are the neurotransmitters and mechanisms underlying such an aversive loop.[N103 N104]

[b] In other words, they are both connected to predicted and experienced rewards. Glimcher concludes that: 'Constructing a prediction error signal at the dopamine neurons simply requires that excitatory and inhibitory synapses take the difference between predicted and experienced reward in the voltage of the dopamine neurons themselves or their immediate

"Sir, if I understand well, neurotransmitters like dopamine, encode prediction errors resulting from the variance between predictions and rewards, expressed in terms of voltage modulation?"

"Yes, this is correct and thus, underlies the critical role played by dopamine in reinforcement learning."

"Sir, can this finding be extended to all brain controllers used to predict awards?"

"It can't. In fact, at least three loops have been associated with different behavioral strategies to estimate rewards, such as the limbic loop, associated with Pavlov's reactions.[a] "

"Sir, any other interesting aspect of dopamine worth mentioning?"

"Yes, the net rate of reward can be represented by the levels of dopamine in the striatum. [135] While voltage modulation would explain prediction error variances, dopamine levels in this region would influence directly the speed at which these loops would have to estimate the rewards. In other words, the level of dopamine would directly influence the urgency to analyze a situation."

"Sir, by including rewards and expectations, doesn't the Free-energy model also integrates decision-making models associated with intelligence?"

"I'm impressed with your insight! We could associate the decision-making models with other directly related action models (e.g., stimulus-response). It means that neural reinforcement learning models take account of actions. All this is in line with the Friston's Free-energy model."

---

antecedents.' Therefore, the prediction error is the variance between prediction and reward, and is expressed in terms of voltage modulation.

[a] The first one, are these so-called 'limbic loops,' including areas such as the ventral striatum, the basolateral amygdala, and the orbitofrontal cortex, which have been associated with Pavlov's prediction learning and evaluation.[N105] [N106] Another loop, called the associative loop, relates to the forward model, which describes action outcomes and includes the dorsolateral prefrontal cortex and the caudate nucleus.[N107] [N108] It describes better goal-directed behaviors. Finally, for habitual behaviors, in which we only need to evaluate one action, a 'stimulus-response' model has been associated with the sensorimotor loop, located in the sensorimotor cortices and involves the putamen.[N109] However, the interactions between these various loops and the arbitration between these different behaviors is still under investigation.

What are the Free-energy and Qualia algorithms?

"Sir, you mentioned that Friston's Free-energy model was quantifiable. Could you describe in more details, these algorithms?"

"Three simple mathematical formulas can describe Friston's theory, which all integrate the four elements involved in such process (i.e., external states, sensations, internal states, and actions). The first one is the more general formula (F = Energy - Entropy). The other ones are more dedicated to actions, whenever used to minimize a bound on surprise (F = Complexity - Accuracy), or when optimizing a bound on surprise (F = Divergence + surprise), which minimizes the prediction error.[a] "

"However Sir, how can you evaluate a surprise, as per definition it is unexpected?"

"True, but it may be assessed because it is a function of sensory data and brain states, which are quantifiable. In fact, what Friston's shows is that under simplified assumptions, the amount of prediction error can evaluate the level of free energy. The following general formula indicates that entropy minimization corresponds to suppressing surprise over time (T).

---

[a] In a white paper,[N110] Friston gives a view of the mathematical formulas, which can quantify free energy. The precise definition of free energy is data greater than the negative log minus the evidence of sensory data (i.e., the surprise of this sensory data), given a model of how the data was generated.

If we want to make this equation more comprehensible, we need to reintroduce the underlying equation of free energy = Energy - Entropy or = $- (\ln p(y, \upsilon|m))_q + (\ln q(\upsilon|\mu))_q$

The energy results from the surprise caused by the joint occurrence of the sensory inputs y and its causes υ. This energy can be expressed in terms of two densities: one sensory input that generated the samples and their causes $p(y, \upsilon)$ and a recognition density on the cause $q(\upsilon, \mu)$. Through action, any agent may limit the bound on surprise, which will result in lower complexity.

Free energy = Complexity - Accuracy or $F = D(q(\upsilon|\mu) \| p(\upsilon)) - (\ln p(y (a)| \upsilon,m))_q$ with a = arg max Accuracy.

Similarly, through perception, an agent can optimize the prediction by minimizing divergences.

Free energy = Divergence + Surprise or $F = D(q(\upsilon|\mu) \| p(\upsilon|y)) - \ln p(y |m)$ with μ = arg min Divergence.

To complete the entire cognitive system, we must add four additional formulas:

- Sensations: $y = g(\upsilon, a) + z$ (equation explaining how sensation y changes the way the environment is sampled).
- External states: $\upsilon = (\upsilon, a) + w$ (equation of motion explaining how specific dynamics in the environment causes υ).
- Action: $a = \arg \min F(y, \mu)$ (equation explaining how action a changes the way the environment is sampled).
- Internal states: $\mu = \arg \min F(y, \mu)$ (equation explaining how internal states of a brain μ exchange with sensory inputs).

$$H(y) = \lim_{T \to \infty} \left(\frac{1}{T}\right) \int_0^T -\ln p(y/m)\, dt$$

"Sir, through all these formulas, Friston mathematically links internal states of an agent and the environment, via action and sensation, but how can you compute all this?"

"Before answering your question, have I made myself clear that Friston shows that the difference between free energy and surprise is the divergence between a probabilistic representation and a distribution of the causes of the sensory inputs? I've e-mail you more information if it isn't clear enough.[a] "

"Sir, it's clear that a probabilistic representation changes the brain's existing representation, by minimizing its free energy and corresponds to a Bayesian inference of the brain."

"Now let me answer your question on how we can perform this computation. We can convert the free energy variation from a complex thermodynamic quantification into a much simpler information problem, which we can calculate thanks to an optimization algorithm. In fact, IT models have already used this variation in free energy to calculate inference and learning problems."

"Sir, even if these models confirm that this theory is true, they still don't explain how the brain encodes its free energy concretely."

"I believe you may agree with me that it necessarily must follow physiological and anatomical rules?"

"Sir, irrespective of the mechanism, the brain must necessarily encode its prediction error with physical neural network attributes, unless we believe in magic."

"Yes, it does that through synaptic activity and efficacy, which can play the role of registering the equivalent of sufficient statistics (i.e., numbers that may specify a distribution, such as mean average and dispersion).[b] "

---

[a] This Bayesian inference of the brain generates sensory data, from unknown external states of this world. Thus, the Free-energy model subsumes the Bayesian brain and supports the view that the mind is a Helmholtz machine (i.e., a machine that makes inferences). Having said that, it isn't only a Helmholtz machine as it also reduces free energy through action. Perception is thus tributary of actions, which will ensure that the predictions become true.

[b] The Free-energy model proposes recognition dynamics, specifying a hierarchical dynamic brain model taking a Gaussian type of recognition density form and optimizing its sufficient statistics through gradient descent. With these assumptions that are highly corroborated by neurologic evidence, Friston can write down equations predicting the dynamic of encoding of expected states (within the synaptic activities), of expected parameters (within synaptic efficacy) and precision levels (within neuro-modulation of synaptic gain).

"Sir, how does this tie in with attention?"

"Friston suggests that within such a hierarchical brain model, attention is the process that optimizes precision during hierarchical inference, rather than the switching on of the various sensing channels, explaining what triggered this attention in the first place. Said differently, the brain is attracted by inputs and actions which corroborates or refutes someone's beliefs, rather than by the nature of the sensory inputs."

"Sir, what do Free-energy and the Temporal Difference Learning models, share in common?"

"Both models highlight the central role played by dopamine in learning and searching for an optimum behavior, based on expected future rewards. However, Friston proposes that the brain would be seeking high precision predictions before trying to achieve the goal in itself.[a] Though this could seem strange, it would mean that the brain gets its kicks from predicting correctly rather than from obtaining the reward itself."

"Sir, maybe that's why you spend so much time trying to fill in your Sudokus and look unhappy whenever you solve them?"

"You're probably right. What my mind enjoys the most is solving the most difficult level possible, not finalizing the Sudoku grid per se."

"Sir, how are prediction errors formed?"

"I've already told you the critical role played by cortical columns. These microcircuits perform computations, which the predictive coding's framework can explain. In fact, it is the most probable form of computation for Bayesian filtering, in neural circuits. [136] Through predictive coding, top-down predictions are compared with bottom-up sensory inputs to form a prediction error."

"Sir, what is then done with this error?"

"It is then used as a feedback loop to update higher-level representations, from which these original top-down predictions are defined. Optimized predictions will then reduce the prediction error at these lower levels. However, something important must be understood.

---

[a] In his opinion, this could change the view of the role of dopamine and affect learning mechanism models, such as Rescorla-Wagner and the Temporal Difference Learning model. In this case, dopamine might not encode the 'prediction error on value' but the 'value of prediction error.' Friston concludes that modifications to synaptic activity, connectivity, and gain would be a consequence of perceptual inference, learning, and attention.

These Bayesian values aren't numerical but are instead strengths or variations, expressed within the synapses and neurons."

"Sir, you already said that neural voltage modulation expresses the variance between prediction and reward."

"OK, I am repeating myself. Anyhow, I believe a complete mathematical description of the structure of all qualia is possible, probably integrating other elements describing the qualia themselves. In my view, the reason why it's possible is that through advanced scanning and imaging techniques we can see 'live' the precise mechanisms affecting our physiological and neural systems. These mechanisms can then be simulated through computers, to understand better the properties of the various elements involved in the actions or qualia.[a] "

---

[a] For instance, a computation model of acute pain was developed in 2004 to measure the impact of the substantia gelatinosa located within the spinal cord. [N111] This substance acts as a gate control mechanism, influencing the flow of information to the brain and thus the impact on the pain experience. We may also invoke another more recent model,[N112] which analyzed the deep-tissue sensitivity quantitatively. Finally, we can refer to a study that uses a computational model in which happiness reports are construed as an emotional reactivity to recent rewards and expectations.[N113] This study shows that momentary happiness is related to quantities of dopamine release, associated with temporal difference errors, signaling changes in the long-term expected reward:

$$Happiness\ (t) = w0 + w1 \sum_{j=1}^{t} \gamma t - j\ CRj + w2 \sum_{j=1}^{t} \gamma t - j\ EVj + w3 \sum_{j=1}^{t} \gamma t - j\ RPE$$

CR means Certain Rewards, EV Expected Values of certain gambles and RPEs the difference between experienced and predicted rewards, t is the trial number, W_0 a constant and other weights W captures the influence of different event types.

"Sir, there is something that doesn't work. If you say that there are algorithms applied at each level of the six layers, but at the same time show that there is no systematic signal flowing between all layers (e.g., going back from V to III and skipping layer IV), how can the model still carry the variance between expectation and rewards (i.e., error variance)?"

"In fact, what you are asking is if, in the case the brain uses some kind of back-propagation techniques (which I will explain more thoroughly when talking about AI), the signal can still be carried on from the lower to the higher layers? Geoffrey Hinton, in his Stanford seminar,[137] explains how he solves the four issues raised by neuroscientists who claim that back-propagation cannot work in the brain. In other words, he shows that the issue you raised isn't a real concern after all.[a] "

Is brain processing speed important?

"Sir, what is the brain processing speed?"

"First, I'd like to make sure that we talk about the same basic cognitive process. Indeed, processing speed is involved in many other brain processes and often associated with executive functions. This later capacity integrates the organization of behaviors and their responses, selection of pertinent and unnecessary information, maintenance, or replacement of cognitive functions."

"Sir, which brain area is involved in this process?"

"It's a process which cannot easily be pinpointed to a specific brain area or structure, though it seems that the dorsolateral prefrontal cortex circuits is highly correlated with this processing speed. [138] Furthermore, it seems to be heavily dependent on the integrity of white matter, but I will come back to this with the P-FIT theory."

---

[a] Neurons don't need symmetric reciprocal connections, even though feedback connections don't go back to the neurons from where feed-forward connections came. There is strong biological evidence of a distinct pattern of connectivity between cortical areas that distinguishes between feed-forward and feed-back connections,[N114] at the level of the cortex's microcircuit. Feed-forward and feed-back connections do not land in the same type of cells. In other words, there is no point-to-point communication, as the flow is going to different neurons. In his video,[N115] Mr. Hinton confirms this isn't a problem. By using back-propagation to the previous hidden layer, with fixed random weight matrices, a neural network gets similar fake derivatives at the previous layer, for all instances of a given class. In fact, the previous hidden layer is taught how to make a more similar representation of instances of that class.

"Sir, more practically, what is it?"

"Most studies consider that a neuron's response time to a stimulus is between 300 and 500ms, which would mean a processing speed of only 2 to 3.5Hz. On the other hand, other studies show that it is possible to recognize and respond to a visual stimulus within 40ms to 50ms."

"Sir, if we consider that half of this time is involved in the generation and control of motoric command, how can you explain this discrepancy?"

"It can be explained by the fact, that a neuron is continually passing on information to the next neuron on the pathway, as it is processing it. [139] Even though this encoding may take more time, a study shows that we encode most of the necessary visual inputs within the first 50 to 100ms and that 20 to 30ms is sufficient for identification and discrimination of even complex stimuli. So depending on what you consider, the processing speed of a neuron may be any value between 2 and 50Hz.[a] "

"Sir, is it possible to conclude that the processing speed is the same between individuals?"

"No, people process information at a different speed, and these individual differences are believed to reflect variation in neural speed, efficiency, and capacity,[140] [141] as well as age-related changes in neural processing."

"Sir, what are more specifically, these factors explaining differences between people?"

"There are quite a few, and some of them are obvious, such as longer distances. The further the incoming signal, the longer the reaction time, which penalizes taller people. The width of a neuron's axon could also explain intra-human discrepancies. Axons with a larger diameter would carry faster messages. Neurons covered by longer sections of myelin sheaths, providing better insulation, would consequently secure more effective conductivity.[b] "

"Sir, what else could you add to this list of factors?"

---

[a] This study indicated an overlap between various connected neurons, confirming that they are simultaneously active and by the same token, following the Hebbian principle. It additionally showed that there seems to be a consistency of synaptic latency between two neurons of 5 to 15ms and a processing time of 20 to 30ms per synapse, across species and cortical areas. The study concluded that in such a fast processing, the resulting information is mainly due to the feed-forward and not feed-back mechanisms.

[b] To give an order of magnitude,[N116] large neurons with myelin situated in the spinal cord and reaching to the muscles, would see neural spikes traveling at speed of 70 to 120 m/s. On the other hand, signals traveling along the same paths, carried by small-diameter neurons without any myelinated fiber (e.g., pain receptors) would reach speed of only 0.5 to 2 m/s!

"The number of neural nodes involved in the thought process. The higher the number, the longer processing time required.[a] "

"Sir, what about the number of sensory inputs?"

"Good point. If I were to just drink my glass of wine with a headband on the eyes and pinching my nose, or on the contrary, involve six senses at the same time, to taste wine, my brain would involve sixty-three (i^6-1) neural cliques versus only one, which would necessarily require more processing time. Moreover, the memory retrieval duration linked to all these cliques, as well as the prediction time being carried on from the higher cortical layers to the deeper ones, associated with them, would need to be added."

"Sir, is the comparison between men and machines on processing time relevant?"

"In fact, because we cannot reduce thoughts to instructions, I am increasingly convinced that it cannot."

"But Sir, processing speed is relevant between individuals, doesn't it?"

"Yes, you're right, and there are various reasons for that. Differences in neural interspacing, neurotransmitters efficacy, and spiking speed, are a few of them.[b] All this is to say that many reasons could explain why processing speed differs from one individual to the other and thus, why intelligence varies between people."

---

[a] Due to the neural processing itself (20 to 30ms per synapse), we would need to add a latency of 5 to 15ms for each neuron in the pathway.

[b] Differences in interspacing between neurons could explain differences between humans. Indeed, larger interstices between individuals' neurons can explain slower processing speed (i.e., neurotransmitters need to travel longer synapse distances) and could be due to fewer or shorter dendrites. Some people have fewer neurotransmitters than others, or their neuro-messengers aren't as good at handing off the information to the neighboring neurons. Furthermore, studies have linked slower processing speed to less well organized frontal lobes. Neural potentiating time can also generate differences between individuals.

Is brain processing efficacy significant?

"Sir, what is more important in human intelligence: processing speed or efficacy?"

"I'd like to emphasize that though higher processing speed has been correlated with higher IQ, especially of sensory stimuli, it doesn't explain a great variance in IQ. We need to compare this result to another study,[142] which shows that the brain efficacy at suppressing irrelevant information is much more important than the processing speed in explaining greater IQ."

"Sir, how can you explain this?"

"Probably due to the huge volume of data to process, men and women with the capacity to discriminate between relevant and superfluous incoming sensory inputs, show a significantly higher IQ. Though these high IQ individuals are also quick at perceiving small moving objects, they show a strong impairment in perceiving the motion of large objects. In fact, the larger the size, the bigger the impairment. Therefore, intelligence is linked with the capacity to suppress background-like stimuli, which probably from an evolutionary perspective, were less ecologically important."

What's the brain data transmission capacity?

"Sir, what is the human bandwidth?"

"Once again, there cannot be a simple comparison with your cable or wireless data transmission capacity. First, neural spikes aren't just traveling one way but flow in bottom-up and top-down processes (i.e., feed-forward and feedback loop processes). This bi-modal process happens in all layers and areas of the neocortex. Low and top layers diverge according to three main properties: the variability to spatial changes, the speed of change, and the level of abstraction."

"Sir, this would mean that bandwidth would vary within the neocortex layers?"

"The higher the layer level, the slower and more stable, the representation is. This complete integration of all senses flows up and down according to a multi-level hierarchical system, which connectivity is partially random and non-random. As a consequence of all these communication flow properties, the required bandwidth isn't the same according to the cortical level you are contemplating.[a] "

Why does white matter integrity matter?

"Sir, what is this white matter integrity issue you mentioned?"

"Jung and Haier, after reviewing 37 neuroimaging studies, [143] correlated IQ results with the ability of an individual's brain to communicate and exchange information between two specific cortical regions (i.e., frontal and parietal regions).[b] They called this theory, the

---

[a] The bandwidth for a low-level flow, such as visual sensory inputs, would need to integrate precise details that our eyes may capture, that is about 10 megapixels. If we were to use a high-quality level, 30 Frame per second, and the equivalent of a camera stream technology H264, a constant video stream would require the equivalent of almost 100 MBps. Using the 45 Frame Per Second, which average people see (25% of the population see 60 FPS explaining why video games are at 60 FPS), the required bandwidth would be around 150 MBps. The problem with such an approach is that we don't know what the compression ratio is (e.g., H264 technology can compress 80% more than a JPEG technology). For instance, smarter people are better at eliminating background information. However, what percentage of the images can they eliminate? Furthermore, according to the Free-energy model and Predictive Coding, what is flowing are predictions (which are mostly semantic-based or simplified 3D drawings and therefore, savvy in terms of bandwidth) and prediction variances (which require probably much less transport capacity). In other words, if we are expecting to see what we are seeing, what would theoretically flow is almost nothing at all.

[b] According to the Wechsler test.

Parieto-Frontal Integration Theory (P-FIT), which lesion studies also corroborated its fundamentals. These and other newer studies have not only established strong correlations with the g factor but also with more specialized types of intelligence within the CHC theory, such as fluid and crystallized intelligence."

"Sir, what do they mean by integrity?"

"Well, their model posits that general intelligence is in fact, dependent on the information flow efficiency between the dorsolateral prefrontal cortex and the parietal lobes, as well as between other cortical areas. Consequently, the neuron's axonal fibers integrity, which constitutes this white matter, is fundamental for general intelligence. Any combination of the neuron's axon size fiber coherence, as well as its increased myelin thickness, would be considered an overall measure of integrity. [144] "

"Sir, to what degree is integrity crucial?"

"Well, a computer model integrating three latent biomarkers of the brain's white matter integrity, predicted 10% of the variance in general intelligence.[145] The head of this research even suggested that white matter integrity was much better at explaining g, than the total brain volume, which he stated indicated a variance of 6% in IQ results."

Is brain processing efficiency important?

"Sir, what about processing efficiency?"

"I won't go again through the debate about specialization that, in some form, provides greater efficiency. I would just like to highlight that we humans have about 200 different specialized areas, which can obviously process information much quicker and better."

"Sir, if you forget the 'how' and focus rather on the 'with what resources' the brain can be efficient, could you establish the number of neurons involved in the process and the lowest level of energy consumed?"

"The brain absorbs much more energy than any other body organ. For instance, between 20 to 25% of our total energy goes into running our brain.[146] An IQ test takes 60 to 90 minutes to be completed and requires much concentration and mental efforts. Therefore, an internal mechanism that would optimize energy consumption of the main solicited brain parts during such a demanding task, like for any sportive competition, would result in better performance."

"Sir, how does the brain achieve that?"

"Theoretically, there are two ways of doing that. Either the brain needs to use less energy by being more efficient at the task, or the body must pump more oxygen to this working muscle."

"Sir, the second method isn't necessarily linked to efficiency?"

"Once again, you're right. If we focus on neural efficiency, we can find two main differentiating factors explaining higher IQ: selective brain energy consumption and noise information suppression strategies.[a] "

---

[a] A theory suggests that individuals, displaying less activation during cognitive tasks (as measured by Glucose metabolism fMRI), have a better IQ.[N117] However, EEG studies have shown that this higher efficiency is possible only when performing easy or moderately demanding cognitive tasks. As a matter of fact, it seems that more intelligent individuals invest more cortical resources on difficult tasks. The prefrontal cortex region appears more solicited in smart tested subjects, than in people tested with lower IQ. One of the main explanation given for this neural efficiency is that individuals with higher IQ, have a better capacity to block out interfering patterns, with background information suppression.

"Sir, I guess you will talk now about glial, that are the energy fabric of neurons?"

"Yes, in theory, the more glial cells, the more energy can be provided to the neurons. If we go back to Einstein's brain description, it was also characterized by a much higher number of glial (i.e., 70% more than an average brain), with a surprising concentration of such glial cells in the brain regions controlling spatial awareness and mathematics."

"Hence Sir, the crucial question is if glial cells participate actively or not in cognitive functions?"

"In the case of Einstein, was it because his brain was working a lot and thus needed more energy that the number of glial was abnormally high, or was it because of his higher number of glial that his brain could perform mathematical and abstract reasoning?[a] Though we don't know for sure, in the case of Einstein, glial must be in certain ways connected to mechanisms, explaining higher IQ levels."

---

[a] To solve this chicken or the egg issue, we refer to a 2013 study on mice.[N118] In this study, mice astrocytes (i.e., a specific type of glial) were replaced with human astrocytes, enabling these mice to learn and remember much better than normal ones. Douglas Field reported on his blog,[N119] the comments of Dr. Robert Malenka, Professor at Stanford University School of Medicine, saying that 'It is certainly possible that via several different mechanisms, differences in the number and properties of astrocytes could contribute to the greater intellectual capacity of humans compared to other species. This work is an important first step in exploring this possibility.'

Do we use only ten percent of our brain?

"Sir, do you think human intelligence can evolve significantly over time?"

"Are you asking me if we may expect, with a better educational system and access to IT technology, on average, an increase in population intelligence?"

"No Sir, I was asking if human beings could improve their intelligence radically, as supposedly, you only use ten percent of your brain? However, please give me an answer about the collective intelligence you just mentioned."

"IQs have increased three points per decade in modern society (e.g., there was an 18-point increase between 1947 and 2002).[147] However, I must say that lately a few countries have experienced a decrease in their average IQ levels. Thus it seems general human intelligence has hit a plateau."

"Sir, are humans wasting ninety percent of their intellectual capacities?"

"The answer is obviously no since we use all of our brain abilities. This assumption, still popularized by the media, is one of the most enduring urban myth.[a] Just from a purely evolutionary perspective, this ten percent doesn't make any sense. Why would our genes generate such an expensive and complex system, to just throw away ninety percent of its capacity? Moreover, if we just do some simple math, with ten percent we already consume twenty-five percent of all the body's energy. Imagine what it would be with one hundred percent. Our brain would just burn out!"

Is intelligence innate or acquired?

"Sir, if we go back to the nature versus nurture debate, is intelligence inherited or acquired through experience?"

"Whereas knowledge is mainly acquired, there is strong evidence that our genes define a significant portion of our intelligence. How much, depends on how we define intelligence and which test is used to measure

---

[a] Although at any given time, only a small portion of our neurons are firing, research based on imaging technology,[N120] showed that most parts of our brain are active 24/7 (i.e., even during sleep). Furthermore, and just before adulthood, there is a massive pruning of our neural networks, most likely associated with neural networks, which potential to be used, never happened. This elimination of unused neurons and synapses confirms that if ninety percent of our neural networks was never put into use, it would be eliminated.

it. It is a complex and sensitive subject, as people can use related arguments to sustain misogynistic or racist views."

"Sir, are there any new findings since the complete human genome sequencing?"

"Scientists haven't so far been able to identify any specific gene acting alone, directly associated with higher intelligence.[a] It isn't surprising by the way as higher intelligence is most likely a trait shared among several genes."

"Sir, what are then the factors not related to genetics, explaining higher IQs?"

"Studies have shown that the social background plays a major role (e.g., 12 to 18 IQ points higher, between working and middle-class neighborhoods).[148] Undoubtedly, someone who grows up in a nice environment, with parental support, good educational system, and plenty of nearby opportunities to learn and grow, will have a higher IQ. Diet, on the other hand, can play a negative role."

"Sir, what do you mean by a negative role?"

"Well, someone who doesn't consume all the necessary nutrients and minerals for a long period, especially during childhood, should suffer a lower IQ than someone who has access to a well-balanced alimentation. Bad behaviors also have a negative impact on IQ performance. Individuals with bad habits, such as binge drinking, smoking, drug usage, poor sleeping patterns, etc., will possess a lower IQ."

"Sir, what about genetics now?"

"Genetics could account for around 50% of someone's IQ level (studies indicate between 40% and 75%). However, it is difficult to come up with a general value because of the huge number of factors, which can impact IQ results."

"Sir, could you give me some examples?"

"For instance, studies on brain size show a strong correlation with heritability (i.e., between 66% and 97). This genetic factor is even more important in the case of the frontal lobe size (i.e., 90 to 95% heritability), an area highly associated with intelligent processes."

---

[a] A 2008 genomic study on 7.000 subjects (Butcher et al.)[N121] found only six genetic markers (SNPs) associated with higher cognitive ability and even then, these six markers when considered together, could barely explain 1% of the variance in general intelligence.

"Sir, you've said that some societies recently have seen their collective IQ declined. You've just told me that 50% or more of human intelligence is genetically linked. Couldn't you conclude that it's only a question of time before we, machines, become more intelligent than humans?"

I didn't answer because I felt annoyed. My car had just concluded that there wasn't much hope to change fundamentally human intelligence. Yes, any individual will always have the opportunity to become smarter, but most societies couldn't expect to raise their collective IQ level much higher.

It was clear in my car's CPU, and increasingly in my mind that there was no race between humans and computers for supra intelligence. What existed, was a gap that machines were slowly but surely filling to become smarter than humans. There was no doubt that we could build systems, which one day would be more intelligent than us. The question was how much brighter and if we would allow them to become far much smarter than us?

16) What is AI?

"Sir you've already introduced briefly AI, by caricaturing in a human-centric view: dumber, as bright, and far more intelligent than humans. Could you give a more precise definition?"

"Of course, Weak AI or Artificial Narrow Intelligence (ANI) is surely dumber than humans, but it doesn't mean that ANI doesn't integrate already intelligent functions. Machines' performance already exceeds human intelligence on some specific aspects (e.g., performing mathematical operations or recognizing specific objects). Consequently, most experts claim that we've already reached the ANI stage."

"Sir, why then do most people don't feel the same way?"

"The problem with smart technology is that, once it reaches the Weak stage, people tend to take for granted this technology and stop considering it as AI. In fact, ANI is already present everywhere in our lives, through our mobile or tablet Apps (e.g., Siri).[a] Each of these software applications and hardware solutions brings us one step closer to the two other forms of AI."

"Sir, what is Strong AI?"

"It's also called, Artificial General Intelligence (AGI) and refers to a machine, which shall be as clever as a human being across all functions, not, for instance, just performing mathematical calculations."

"Having said that Sir, how can you characterize a machine to be as intelligent as a human if there is, as you told me, no universal definition of intelligence?"

"I'll soon describe the rules to establish AGI, which have already been drafted by Alan Turing in his essay and highlight the various criticisms around the so-called, Turing machine test."

"Sir, could you define the various stages of AI, that would serve, at least for the time being, the purpose of our conversation on AI?"

---

[a] It is visible in consumer products such as phones with voice recognition and interpretation (e.g., SIRI), translation functions, or search engines. However, it can also be found in various other applications, such as cars with automated driving systems, not to mentioned autonomous vehicles, driverless trains, in video analytics enabling profiling or empty vehicle detection, etc. Though less visible to the average citizen, they may also be encountered in military, financial, or game applications (e.g., systems that beat the best chess or go players) because they rely on supercomputers, with software emulating our brain's reasoning mode.

"ANI is a system which relies on technical solutions that were men developed. The software used by the system will thus produce intelligent solutions, which are predictable as a consequence of the original design."

"Sir, how different will AGI be?"

"In the case of AGI, a system's solutions will emerge directly within this system, from the technical solutions and reasoning processes themselves. The intelligent solutions generated by the software will thus be almost impossible to foresee a priori. Obviously, creating Strong AI is much more complicated than Weak one, and is still a few years ahead. But once we do, such machines will be per definition, able to perform all mental processes we currently associate with humans."

"Sir, and what about Artificial Super Intelligence (ASI)?"

"Though there is no clear definition of what ASI can be, it is going to be smarter than any human being. How much brighter, is a question no one knows for sure the answer. Some futurologists believe it may be trillions of time smarter, posing a real threat to the human species. Some people question if we'll ever reach the ASI stage, either because of the failure to conceive technologies required for ASI or because a ban on research will be imposed by society, to avoid the threat to humanity."

"Sir, do you know what ASI will look like?"

"No, but it is likely to be an autonomous system, which will dispose of some form of self-awareness, not to mention free will. As self-awareness and free will likely to be involved, I won't discuss ASI right now. In the meantime, I'll focus my attention on describing the road that will get us from ANI to AGI."

Why and how to increase raw processing capacity?

"Sir, how do we go from ANI to AGI?"

"There is an obvious answer to your question. Computers must mimic, as much as possible, the human brain. We've seen that in humans, the faster the speed of the cognitive process, the higher the score obtained on a scale of intelligence. Three main factors can explain this speed. The raw processing capacity of billion neurons working together, data transport speed between various processing areas in the brain, and processing specialization."

"Sir, unlike human brains, which have been designed by natural selection, computers can be built from scratch, incorporating systematically more intelligent features. Thus, don't you think that machines, which aren't restricted by genetics, may be built incrementally more intelligent?"

"Yes, I do. One of the obvious ways of making computers more intelligent to reach this AGI level is to increase the hardware computing power. In fact, while I am looking at my smartphone, I'm benefiting from this strategy to incorporate silicon chips that cram more transistors. By doing this, additional raw power is available, with each new chip generation, to do logical operations that can be thrown at increasingly more complex tasks. To make an analogy, this manufacturing strategy is like if chip-builders were increasing the number of neurons while maintaining the skull's size."

"Sir, if I am right, you are describing Moore's law, which states that the number of electronic components integrated on a chip, doubles every two years?"

"Indeed, Gordon Moore's prediction has been fulfilled year after year, for the last five decades, thanks merely to the transistor's property of getting better as it shrinks. Smaller transistors require less power to be turned On or Off, generate less heat, and do it faster than bigger transistors.[a]"

"Sir, do you think chipmakers can maintain Moore's law, by shrinking chips' size, customizing their design, and building smarter programs?"

"There will be a point in time when new materials and approaches will be required to cope with limitations brought by nano miniaturization, if chipmakers are to maintain the same exponential increase in processing power, enabling AGI."

What are the silicon chips limitations?

"Sir, how will the chip industry overcome these limitations?"

---

[a] However, this strategy comes at a cost. With each new generation of faster chips, manufacturers need to pour in more capital, building more expensive plants to produce chips in ever greater quantities, in order to recuperate their investment. The costs are becoming astronomical with a new state-of-the-art plant reaching as much as US$ 7 billion, and the next plant to manufacture 5nm chips expected to double this value, by the early 2020s. From a financial point of view, Moore's law, based on the traditional silicon chip approach, is fast becoming obsolete.

"Chip manufacturers have been working on techniques to combat the leakage effect, but they won't be able to do so, for much longer, with the same silicon material or approach.[a] "

"Sir, what are the conventional solutions, the industry is looking at?"

"The following conventional solutions are being pursued to shrink silicon chips further: all-around, tunneling, and junction nanowire transistors.[b] "

"Sir, I guess chip builders are also looking at adopting new materials?"

"Yes, they are also assessing new materials' properties. For instance, IBM is working on a transistor, made mainly of silicon but with channels made from a better-conducting alloy (i.e., silicon-germanium). This innovation should enable lower energy consumption and quicker switching responses.[c] "

"Sir, what else are they looking at?"

---

[a] A transistor is a semiconductor switch, made of silicon, both half conducting and isolating. This dual property is due to the laying of two different types of atoms, one on the channel connecting the chip's source and drain, and the other on both the source and drain. With this process, called 'doping,' current cannot flow in the circuit. However, whenever the chip is switched-on, a small gate located in the channel is energized, creating an electrical field, generating a thin conductive bridge within this channel, as well as, allowing the circuit to close and the current to flow. This design works better and better as transistors shrank. However, nowadays the distance between the drain and source is too small, causing the channel to leak energy between the two circuit parts, even in Off mode. Unwanted heat resulting from this phenomenon causes serious problems, requiring chips to avoid overheating, by either running below maximum speed or shutting down periodically.

- [b] All-around transistors,[N122] in which a gate surrounds channels, on all four sides.
- Tunneling transistors use to their advantage the quantum tunneling effect, creating this leakage problem.[N123] By applying electric fields, the tunneling effect can be controlled, allowing for 0 (low leakage rate) and 1 (high leakage rate) states. These transistors could be energized at 0.1V instead of the current 0.7V, reducing energy use significantly.
- Junctionless Nanowire Transistors (JNTs), aim to use 'uniformly doped' silicon, normally resulting in a kind of wire rather than a switch (i.e., uniformly conductive).[N124] However, JNTs use nanoscale properties, which enable the gate's characteristics to penetrate this wire. As a consequence, JNT gates work the other way round of current barriers. They stop the current from flowing when the transistor is switched-off, rather than allowing it when the transistor is switched on.

[c] In the long run, the industry could use other elements closely related to germanium on the periodic table, (e.g., indium, gallium, or arsenide). One attractive alternative is to use graphene, the wonder material of nanotechnology. Though this two-dimensional form of carbon is a good conductor, it creates a challenge to design a chip that could stop current flow. The industry investigates other bi-dimensional alloys (e.g., molybdenum disulfide, black phosphorous), believed to share the same properties without the current issue.

"Some chipmakers are planning to use other electrons' properties. Beyond the 5nm (i.e., nano) scale, a completely different design is likely to be required. One possibility is to integrate the same concept as for hard drives, called spintronics.[149] Rather than using an electron's charge, it would work with another characteristic, its rotational energy, which can also be reduced to two states – up and down –, that is, – 0 and 1–.[a] "

"Sir, any more exciting stuff?"

"Of course! The hardware industry is looking at changing the patterns of computer logic altogether. Several companies are working on a radical approach, [150] which considers the fourth element in electronics, (i.e., besides resistors, capacitors, and inductors), called a memristor.[b] "

"Sir, what is the specific behavior of this new material?"

"A memristor (from memory and resistance) behaves like a resistance when driven with a voltage, within a certain defined threshold. Exceeding such threshold, it changes its resistance corresponding to the polarity of the applied voltage and can do that several times. Consequently, it creates several resistance zones, instead of only two."

"Sir, wouldn't computers be freed from the limitations of the 0s and 1s?"

"Yes, and these more powerful computers could more easily make choices and decisions, ultimately getting us one step closer to AGI. Besides, these new logic patterns, a computer based on such memristor technology should also operate at lower power consumption, faster speed, and with a higher data density than anything based on silicon transistors."

"Sir, I thought anything is or isn't, that is, either is represented by a 0 or a 1?"

---

[a] A spintronic transistor could run on only 10mV, solving heating problems altogether and allowing further shrinking.

[b] The fact that the resistance will stay the same until the memristor is driven to another resistance state, enables its memory property. Thus, we can use as binary information the resistance property of the memristor (for instance, the high resistance state would be a 0 and low resistive state a 1). However, the memristor's resistance is a function of the state variable of the device. Thus, we may divide it into several resistance zones, instead of only two. Unlike for a transistor, which uses the only two possible states 0 and 1 to apply binary codes, a memristor could theoretically have several states (for instance, very low, low, intermediate, high, very high resistance, etc.). A trade-off between reliability and memory density is likely to happen, but a three or five-state switch should be feasible (for instance, on a memristive multi-state switch). Obviously, to use such a three or five-conducting state property, it would be mandatory to develop a program that could deal with these three or five possible codes (i.e., base 3 or 5). However, this characteristic could provide entirely new computational logic patterns.

"I know it is difficult to imagine that a computer could work in anything than a multiple of base 2 and actually, I already had this conversation with my father-in-law, who's got a Ph.D. in philosophy and promoted the use of computers in children education. He just couldn't see the benefits of a non-binary world."

"Sir, I don't either. Could you clarify why other bases would make sense?"

"Yes, I could highlight that base 3 is the most efficient integer base, as it is the closest to base e (natural logarithm, which value is about 2,718). Therefore, theoretically, it would be a better computational system than a binary one. Furthermore, a so-called ternary computer isn't a crazy idea, and the Soviets even built it.[a] "

"Sir, could you envision in the future, ternary instead of binary computers?"

"Not really. Let's say, we change the logic of things and see more a computer like a neural network, rather than a digital system, and integrate some fuzzy logic. We could then imagine a system where states wouldn't necessarily be On or Off but would have different weights registered by, for instance, these memristive multi-state switches."

"Sir, what kind of system would that create?"

"We could imagine a system based on degrees of truth rather than on the true or false statement of current systems. In other words, computers could work with Bayesian probability, just like the brain does, using higher bases than binary or ternary (e.g., base 6 or even 10)."

---

[a] It was built in 1958 by the Soviet Union.[N125] It used a -1, 0 and +1 (i.e., a balanced ternary). Even today, some companies like IBM, have been reporting some research work on the ternary computer, using fiber optics (dark status as 0 and two orthogonal polarizations of light as status +1 and −1).[N126]

"Sir, do memristors have any other interesting property?"

"Yes, and unlike for a transistor, where all information is lost whenever the electrons' flow is interrupted, it can memorize the amount of charge flowing through it, and retain data, even when de-energized. This innovation could allow computers or robots never to lose data, eliminating the need to save anything to their hard drives.[a] "

How do we improve computer processing speed?

"Sir, another way of making computers more intelligent is to increase the speed of data processing. How are chipmakers doing this?"

"The faster a PC carries out its instruction, the more data it can deal with. As shrinking transistors is becoming more and more difficult, chipmakers have looked at ways of increasing such speed. One possible way is to increase clock rates, which are responsible for carrying out those instructions.[b] "

"Sir, can this property be pushed indefinitely?"

"Unfortunately not. In the last ten years, increases in processing performance have also started to be much slower, reaching today the plateau speed of 3.8 GHz for traditional computers (or 9 GHz through liquid nitrogen cooling). Increase in clock speed implies a voltage increase

---

[a] Multi-state switches,[N127] which incorporate distinct and independently addressable functional combination of components, have this capacity to create switches and logic gates for molecular electronics and memory storage devices. Their combination can exist in 6 different states,[N128] which may be individually stimulated, and could even open the door for base-10 computing systems. Computers using memristors could be launched somewhere around 2020, using a combination of electrons and electrically charged atoms (i.e., ions) instead of the standard flow of electrons. However, there are questions about production costs. HP's memristor memory technology,[N129] which would be 64-128 times denser than any existing conventional RAM technology, is experiencing commercial difficulties.

[b] Real-time clocks regulate timing and speed of all computer functions. This function is achieved through a crystal on a specific microchip, which vibrates at a particular frequency when electricity is applied. It emits a continuous pulse that helps the computer clock keep the correct time. This real-time clock defines the PC's speed, as it is a function of the clock's cycle (i.e., the time interval between two pulses). The reason why it controls the computer speed is that it is always set above the longest signal needed to propagate from any component or circuit on a board. By doing this, we prevent any signal from arriving and being processed before all other inputs are also ready to be. Processor's speed is thus a function of the speed of pulse emission, measured typically today in gigahertz (GHz). For example, a 2GHz processor performs 2 billion clock cycles (i.e., vibrations) per second.

(i.e., a cubic relation exists between voltage and power consumption), explaining this cost and heat issue greatly."

"Sir, couldn't they do multi-tasking?"

"To compensate chip reduction difficulties, chip builders have indeed used multi-core processors to execute more than one instruction per clock cycle, allowing many programs to run simultaneously. These multi-core processors are nowadays composed of up to 16-core processors, lashed together. Unfortunately, bringing to market more than 16-core processors has proven difficult."

"Why is that Sir?"

"This is due mainly to the fact that, to be effective, it requires coding programs to be multi-threaded (i.e., use simultaneously multiple CPU cores). It is both complex and expensive, as the software cannot rely on executing one line of code after another. Nevertheless, some chip manufacturers (e.g., AMD)[151] are planning to produce a 32-core processor.[a] "

"Sir, what other means have chipmakers to increase processing speed?"

"Building custom chips is another way of increasing processing speed. Graphics Processing Units, which equip video game consoles, are a good example of these specialized chips. However, developing such chips is much more expensive, and programming tends to be more complicated."

"Sir, any other chip development worth mentioning?"

"Other manufacturers are working on stacking chips on top of each other, enabling to put more transistors in the same given space, in other words, building 3-D chips. For instance, IBM is planning to stack a layer of the memory chip, sandwiched between layers of logic processors, with non-air cooling features. Finally, some are using approximate computing, which allows small calculation mistakes to be eliminated over time, saving energy, and enabling the cramming of more transistors onto the chip."

---

[a] This doesn't mean that this future chip will be twice as fast as a 16-core processor, as there is usually a trade-off between clock cycles and the number of cores. For instance, Intel's top end 16-core Xeon chip speed is only 2.3GHz rather than the 3.8GHz maximum speed. By reducing the clock speed, it benefits from this cubic relation with energy consumption. For example, by reducing clock speed by 40% (i.e., from 3.8 to 2.3 GHz), we can reduce energy to 21,6% (0.6 x 0.6 x 0.6 =21,6%) of a 3.8GHz clock. Though this would result in computing performance reduction of 40%, a 32-core processor with the same characteristics would double the 16-core performance (obviously requiring parallel programming of the process code to exploit the 16 additional cores simultaneously), resulting in speed gains of 120% for 79% less energy consumption.

"Sir, all these new solutions aren't going to change the processing speed fundamentally. What other technologies are they looking at, that would create such a change of paradigm?"

"Some are looking at using quantum physic properties. As you know, in classical computer systems, a bit has only two possible states: 0 or 1. However, quantum computers use quantum physics phenomena to superpose both normal states.[152] In other words, it introduces the probability of being in either state. Adding to superposition another quantum property, called 'entanglement' (i.e., groups of particles like photons or electrons, which interact in ways such that the quantum state of each particle cannot be described independently from the others), qubits can mix their probabilities with one another."

"Sir, it seems quantum computers are difficult to operate at room temperature."

"Yes, this 'entanglement' property is tricky to achieve (i.e., it is disrupted at ambient temperature, by heat vibration) and therefore requires operations at near absolute zero temperatures."

"Sir, what is the benefit of combining superposition and entanglement properties?"

"The interesting computing aspects of qubits running under these two conditions, isn't so much its additional storage capabilities, as it would still store the 2^n states (n being the number of bits), but rather its speed of execution. Indeed, it would avoid the n steps required to read all bit states, using only a single step, as it could see through, at one glance, all these n states.[a] "

"Sir, wouldn't there be several answers given by a quantum computer?"

"Yes, due to these quantum effects, the results returned by a quantum algorithm are not deterministic (i.e., several answers are possible). Therefore, algorithms must be used to strengthen the right answers and suppress the wrong ones. They must also be run several times in succession, to confirm that the solution is correct, slowing down the process. Bottom line, quantum computers can only be used whenever massive parallelism is involved.[b] "

---

[a] Such a system at any given moment can be in all of the possible states permitted by its qubits' probability mixtures, for any one of the entangled qubits. To give a simplified image, thanks to these two properties, it's like if we could see through all the qubits states at the same time. For example, a five qubit could process as much as $2^5 = 32$ classical bits in one step. A quantum process would thus be in theory thirty-two times faster but unfortunately, not under all operations. Indeed, this exponential speedup only takes effect when a quantum algorithm may process data in a massively parallel fashion (e.g., data mining through a very large database) not in normal sequential modes.

[b] Though this technology seems like science fiction, it already exists. For instance, on

"Sir, how do we measure the CPU performance?"

"Measuring a CPU performance is complex because so many factors end up influencing it, of which the clock cycles, the number of cores, the specific interaction between software and processor, as wells as, the internal processor architecture, are probably the most important.[a] "

"Sir, I thought the total Calculation Per Second (CPS) was a number that is usually given by manufacturers of supercomputers?"

"True. In 2016, the fastest supercomputer was Chinese, and its CPS was estimated at thirty-four quadrillions CPS.[b] "

"If so Sir, what processing speed would PCs need to achieve, to reach AGI level?"

"Computers would need to have at least the same data crunching capacity than a brain. Futurologist Ray Kurzweil calculated a theoretical CPS of the brain, by asking brain specialists to estimate each region's processing capacity and correlating it to the whole brain regions.[153] The various estimation he made, gave a brain CPS of around ten quadrillions CPS. Thus, in theory, the Chinese supercomputer has already more processing power than humans."

"However Sir, cyberists could argue that we shouldn't use for comparison a US$380 million computer."

"Fair enough! If we take a classic 2016 PC, the CPS is more in the range of 10 trillion, or one thousand times less powerful than a human brain. Using Moore's law, and a mix of the already presented technologies, which would sustain such power increase, an out-of-the-shelve PC could be equal to a brain somewhere in 2025!"

"Sir, why does the Blue brain project, which is an ongoing attempt to create a digital brain by reverse engineering the mammalian brain neural system, introduce memory hardware as a complementary requirement to meet the human processing capacities?"

"As I've told you with the memory-prediction model, memory is also important to reach the AGI stage. Though a little old, the following image

---

August 20, 2015, D-Wave Systems[N130], a Canadian company announced the availability of its D-Wave 2X system, a 1000 qubit quantum computer, which would be in theory 2^{1000} faster than comparable silicon-based computers.

[a] The Instruction Per Cycle (IPC) or the number of operations the CPU can do within each clock cycle, may give an idea of this performance but is hard to calculate. It depends on the software running on the CPU and on the machine itself. A low IPC and a high clock speed or inversely a high IPC with low clock speed can achieve the same level of instructions per second. For PC users, application benchmarks are more useful than IPC figures.

[b] 33.86 Petaflops, or floating operations per second.

I'm e-mailing you, shows that the already created hardware has more intellectual capacity than a rat's brain and that we should be able to reach human brain cognitive processing power by 2023. This Blue Brain project [154] sets the bar higher than Ray Kurzweil did, at an Exaflop of capacity. Therefore, it projects the advent of AGI using common hardware, somewhere in the early 2030s, still within a reasonable vicinity."

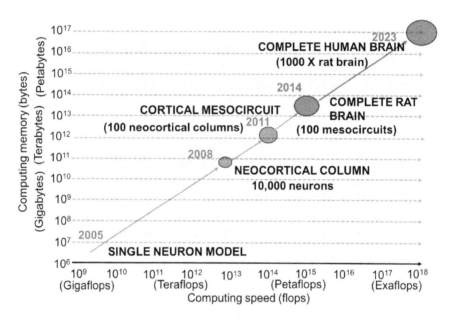

Fig. 42) Courtesy of the Blue Brain project: Evolution of computer memory and processing speed; source: Blue Brain project.

How do we create better programs and architectures?

"Sir, does this mean that by solely improving hardware, we could reach AGI by 2025 -2030?"

"No! Disposing of the same cognitive power than a brain, in one or two decades from now, doesn't mean that we'll reach AGI by then. To do that, we need to create completely new ways of programming."

"Sir, before describing how researchers and IT companies are doing that, could you illustrate how non-sequential programming can affect computer performance?"

"What about applying the same IQ test to a supercomputer, to find out how it fares in regards to people deemed intelligent? Though we've seen that IQ tests don't integrate all the different aspects of human intelligence, it is nevertheless a good measure of general intelligence. In fact, a team of Microsoft and Chinese researchers did that for us in 2015.[155] "

"Sir, how did a supercomputer perform at an IQ test?"

"This IQ test was performed on 200 students of different academy levels and a Chinese supercomputer. Questions were representative of analytical and verbal reasoning. As expected, the supercomputer performed very well on analytical questions. What came as a surprise, was that it also did well, in the verbal section. This is no small achievement, as verbal tests always have been a challenge for computers because words have complex relationships between one another and several potential meanings. Therefore, and unlike rational topics, there is always a part of interpretation and subjectivity."

"Sir, how did this team achieve those results?"

"It had to develop a specific AI program able to tackle verbal questions. The team wrote a program to figure out the questions asked and developed a way of representing the various word meanings and relations. Among other things, it used deep-learning techniques, which I'll explain soon, and finally wrote a program to solve the tests' problems."

"Sir, who is more intelligent?"

"Though on average the supercomputer performed better than the human average, some people might take comfort in thinking that students from master and Ph.D. levels still outperformed the machine."

"Sir, how do we add human intelligence on top of this additional raw processing power?"

"Raw computational power alone won't make computers as intelligent as human beings."

"Sir, the next question is thus how do you bring human-level intelligence to all these new hardware technologies?"

"The answer is quite simple: create software, which mimics how the human brain solves complex problems. It is how most computer scientists have been recently trying to develop AI solutions."

"Sir, shouldn't wireless communication change the AI perspective?"

"Indeed, I believe that this classical approach is too restrictive, especially in a world of M2M communication. We should look at nature, and how it has forged different ways of solving complex problems. I wish to open our discussion to include other brain models, better adapted to systems. For example, the octopus' neural system shows that decentralized architectures are found in nature, demonstrating the relevance of this approach, in a discussion on how to reach AGI. It brings me back to our conversation on parallel processing."

Why is parallel processing critical?

"Sir, what are the advantages of parallel over sequential processing?"

"Standard PCs have been greatly influenced by the von Neumann approach to programming. Their sequential programming involves consecutive and controlled execution of processes. Instructions run, one after the other, into a succession of events defined by the software and controlled by the CPU, to ensure that the sequence is performed correctly. On the other hand, parallel programming integrates concurrent execution of processes, (i.e., threads), a situation that happens more often in nature."

"Sir, on which fact can parallel programming find its utility?"

"On the fact that complex problems or processes may be broken down into multiple simpler issues or tasks, which we execute concurrently in parallel. These multiple processes when executed concomitantly may exchange signals or data during their execution.[a] "

"Sir, what are the different classes of parallel equipment?"

---

[a] Such possibility creates a risk that these multiple threads work on the same variables simultaneously, resulting in miscalculations. To allow for such exchange, programmers ensure mutual exclusion of variables by implementing locks on critical programming regions. Only one thread at a time can work on such variables, and when the thread is done with the variables, it unlocks the door to that critical region, for another process to use it.

"This categorization is roughly based on the distance between the various processing nodes. I've already introduced multi-core processors done on the same chip. SMPs, Cluster computing, MPPs and grid computing are additional parallel equipment solutions.[a] "

How do distributed network architectures work?

"Sir, you've already told me that the human brain uses a distributed network architecture. Do you believe that to reach AGI, distributed networks must become the standard?"

"Yes, because there are many advantages to distributed architectures. This type of network centralizes decisions but still allows the nodes to obtain the complete system understanding. Furthermore, unlike for centralized architecture, the processing is shared between the different nodes. The IT infrastructure resources are also divided over a number of networks, processors, and intermediary devices.[b] "

"Sir, what other benefits does a distributed architecture bring?"

"It enables several processors located on scattered machines, to work both independently and jointly. In other words, a single machine may host and execute an application which can be accessible to many other systems. A good example of such a distributed network is the client/server computing architecture, where a server produces a service that many interconnected remote users can consume."

---

[a] A Symmetric Multi-Processor (SMP) is a computer or equipment, which can perform this task with several processors, through a bus, within the same computing envelope. Several connected computers may also perform this parallel task. Cluster computing is a group of loosely coupled stand-alone computing equipment, connected by a network (e.g., over a TCP/IP Ethernet LAN network). Massive Parallel computing (also called MPPs) is quite similar to clusters but usually includes tailor-made network equipment. Grid computing uses stand-alone computers, through the internet. Because of the internet's limitation (i.e., low latency and bandwidth), it is typically used to solve problems, which can be easily broken down into smaller parallel workloads, by using the time of idle computers.

[b] A network management software powers the distributed network, managing and monitoring data routing, allocating the network bandwidth, controlling access, and overseeing other core networking processes.

"Sir, you've already referred to Peer-to-Peer (P2P) architecture. What is it?"

"A P2P system is a self-organizing system of equal and autonomous entities (called peers),[156] which aims for the shared usage of distributed resources in a networked environment, avoiding central services.[a] "

What are Artificial Neural Networks (ANNs)?

"Sir, I've heard about ANNs. Why all this hype about them?"

"I introduced parallel computing because, without it, we cannot understand the benefits of ANNs. To picture what a neural network is, one needs to forget how conventional computer works. Though an ANN still relies mostly today on the same hardware, it doesn't really have any CPU and doesn't store data in a centralized memory."

"Sir, it means that the system's knowledge and memories are distributed throughout its connectivity!"

"Exactly, just like real brains."

"Sir, why were they developed in the first place?"

"From the start, ANNs were designed to process quickly various non-sequential tasks or events, which would have required a lot of processing power and time, if done in sequential mode. As mentioned, ANNs are programs, which use inherently parallel algorithms, and are a change of paradigm in the software approach. Though I just said that they don't fundamentally use a different hardware approach, they often use tailor-made chips and will work with neuromorphic switches in the future."

"Sir, before you describe ANNs, could you please tell me the difference between neuromorphic and multi-state memristive switches?"

---

[a] Today more than 50% of internet traffic is due to P2P applications (e.g., file swapping apps). P2P systems are easy to install and so is the configuration of computers, on this network. All resources and contents are shared by all peers, eliminating central dependency and consequently, aggregating reliability to the network. There is no need for a centralized administrator and cost of creating and maintaining such system is low.
Another exciting aspect of P2P is that the network performance increases with the number of users sharing files. This is why P2P technology is thought of for Vehicle to Vehicle communication.[N131] With an increasing number of connected cars onto the same wireless network the system ruggedness would improve as well.

"The development of reliable memristive devices able of storing multiple states of information, opens up new applications, such as neuromorphic circuits and adaptive systems. For instance, a new technology called Atomic Switch Network (ASN),[157] which is inspired directly by the brain's neural substrate can be considered a neuromorphic circuit."

"Sir, could you better describe ASNs' physical properties?"

"They use memristive properties but can, additionally, be considered a self-organizing device, made of massively connected networks, with interconnections possessing the same properties as our synapses.[a] In other words, these ASNs are to the hardware, what ANNs could be to the software, that is, a copy of how the brain physiologically works."

"Sir, is IBM's new neural network chip, called Truenorth, using such switching technology?"

"Yes, it is a neuromorphic switch, maybe not as complex as an ASN, but which still creates an artificial version of one million neurons, with 256 synapses between them. It's impressive because it represents a quarter of the total number of neurons a rat has, though still far from the 10 to 14 billion included in our neocortex.[b] In fact, IBM's long-term goal is to build a system with 10 billion neurons and a hundred trillion synapses, which according to their estimation would consume only 1 kilowatt of power.[158]"

"Sir, if you read between the lines, wouldn't you say that, what IBM wants, is to recreate the human neocortex?"

"It sure looks that way!"

---

[a] A densely interconnected network of silver nanowires incorporates one billion junctions per cm². This structure creates memristor behaviors, resulting from the collective interaction of all artificial synapses. These emergent behaviors include spatially distributed memory, recurrent dynamics, and the activation of feed-forward sub-networks.

[b] IBM integrates it in a 48-processor machine, which recreates the equivalent of 48 million neurons, much more than what can be found, in a rat's brain. Additionally, there is another benefit to this TrueNorth chip. It only draws on 70 milliWatt of power (100 times less power than high-end Intel CPUs). If we were to stack the 20.000 TrueNorth chips to emulate the neocortex, it would only consume the amount of energy generated by a small electric appliance.

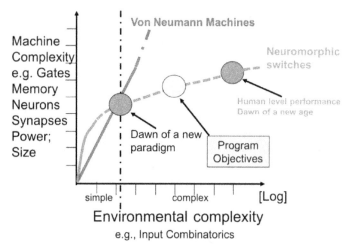

Environmental complexity
e.g., Input Combinatorics

Fig. 43) One of DARPA's current projects is called "Systems of Neuromorphic Adaptive Plastic Scalable Electronics," or SyNAPSE; source: courtesy of Darpa.

"Sir, am I understanding correctly that these chips still use binary logic?"

"More or less! Sure they don't compute in ternary or other bases, but when they use binary spikes, it is to represent non-binary information."

"Sir, I'm lost. Could you be clearer?"

"OK. You need to portray these chips as biological neural-like networks, that is, channels that pass information through weight variation. Like the biological synapses, which have different voltage values and can project inhibition or excitation properties, they may show either positive or negative figures."

"Sir, concretely what kind of values can they assign?"

"TrueNorth's architecture provides the capacity for their artificial neurons to assign four possible synaptic strengths, across their inputs. These specific strengths may be assigned at the crossbar level, in function of their axon types."

"Sir, am I right in saying that these chips will be revolutionizing computing?"

"Yes, these new chips will change the computing world. What we are seeing emerging here, isn't a digital world anymore but a discrete one.[a] "

---

[a] In fact, if we go back to neural coding, IBM programmers use the same terminology.[N132] A rate code translates the number of spikes, within a number of discrete time steps, to indicate the signal's amplitude. Physically this chip has 256 neurons, from which flow information through these 256 connections. Therefore, it creates 256 x 256 junctions (called synapses) forming binary gates and where each axon fans out, in parallel, to all other

"Sir, what are the limitations of these IBM chips?"

"Besides connectivity and scalability limitations, the network training (i.e., defining what the synaptic connections are) is still done through traditional computing, though once trained, we can execute its behavior easily. Furthermore, its combination of hardware, architecture, and software (called Corelet) doesn't allow for unsupervised learning, which is an important feature of ANNs."

"Sir, if we disconsider this new type of hardware but realize that we've been using for a long time other algorithms and programs that didn't work solely on binary logic (e.g., fuzzy logic), then what makes ANNs so attractive?"

"Besides the benefits of enabling the processing of concurrent events with different schedules, a feature which happens extremely often in nature, ANNs offer other important advantages. Unlike classical computers that work basically through a set of calculations and rules, ANNs can work via pictures and concepts. Furthermore, and unlike classical 'von Neumann' PCs, which must learn by rules, ANNs learn by example and by doing things. To use an image, in classical computers the learning process is top-down, while in ANNs it is bottom-up."

"Sir, don't these features kill the argument that a computer only does what a human (i.e., the programmer) writes it to do?"

"Yes, it does. This specificity obviously requires an extremely different setting and programming approach. Programs for classical computers are written in higher level languages and translated down with assembly language for execution. Because of their inherent capability for self-teaching and learning, ANNs on the other hand, can and must program themselves. Without an imposed sets of rules, they evolve by altering their own programming."

"Sir, with all this teasing, said and done, could you explain how ANNs work?"

"Yes, but you first need to refresh your memory with concepts about biological neurons.[a] "

---

neurons. A discrete time step controls the network operation.

[a] There are around 86 billion neurons in our brain, interconnected to more than a thousand other neurons, through their dendrites and synapses. An electrochemical process, which runs along the neuron's axon to the dendrites, transmits the sensory inputs. The message then crosses the synapses in mainly a chemical form (i.e., usually neurotransmitters) and reaches the neighboring neurons. Neurons don't have different grades of firing. Either the resulting electric amplitude from all incoming signals exceeds the threshold that causes it to fire and propagate the message, or it doesn't. Under the Hebbian rule, what gets stimulated together, fires together. In other words, all neurons involved in the transmission of sensory

"Sir, why is it necessary?"

"Because the ANN processing model copies the human neural network properties. From a vast number of simple processing units, each performing the weighted sum of all its input, a single output is fired, (in many cases only if the amplitude of that output reaches a threshold)."

"Sir, because of this property, can I consider that ANNs are purely binary?"

"Your understanding is missing the point that ANNs allow for a quasi-analogical approach to processes (i.e., values are still discrete), taking into consideration minimum and maximum values, which may be different than 1s and 0s.[a] "

"Sir, what are the concrete benefits of ANNs?"

"Let me give you a few examples where we can use various types of ANN properties, to solve real-life problems. The first issue we are confronted with in life is classification (e.g., pattern recognition), where we need to define to which region a set of values belong to. The second type of daily problem is prediction (e.g., stock market), where an ANN may be trained to produce expected outputs, in function of specific inputs. We can use feed-forward or feedback ANNs to solve both classification and prediction problems."

"I am curious to hear about the other life problems. Anything Sir, about solving problems with your teenage boy?"

"I only wished! A third issue happens whenever there is no obvious way to classify things a priori, but we must still identify special features. In this case, called clustering, we can use different competitive networks with ANNs.[b] Data-mining techniques mainly employ these types of networks."

"Sir, what is the last type of issues ANNs may help solve?"

---

inputs and other cognitive processes related to the same experience, fire simultaneously. Furthermore, the more they fire together, the stronger the links between them become, strengthening the experience and its related memory. Similarly, the less often they fire together, the weaker this link becomes, and its associated memory starts vanishing.

[a] An ANN coder wrote: the 'best way to think of Neural Networks is as real-valued circuits, where real values (instead of Boolean values $\{0,1\}$) 'flow' along edges and interact in gates. However, instead of gates such as AND, OR, NOT, etc., we have binary gates such as * (multiply), + (add), max or unary gates such as exp, etc. Unlike ordinary Boolean circuits, we will eventually also have gradients flowing on the same edges of the circuit but in the opposite direction.' [N133]

[b] E.g., Combination of Hemming and Max nets, ART, or Kohonen networks.

"They can help identify association issues. An ANN, trained to remember certain patterns, is confronted with distorted trends, which it needs to identify. We use these ANNs for restoring noisy data. Image compression is an example where ANNs are useful.[a] "

"Sir, when do you start explaining how an ANN works?"

"Let me first start by describing what is called a perceptron. I need to do this because an ANN is composed of various perceptrons."

"Fine Sir. What is a perceptron?"

"It is the mathematical model mimicking the properties associated with the biological neuron. In ANNs the electric signals between neurons are represented by numerical values (called an input vector). At the node level (i.e., the synapse equivalence), this electrical signal is strengthened or weakened. By giving a weight to this signal, the system mathematically models this modulation. This weight can either amplify or diminish the incoming input and be negative or positive, therefore providing excitatory or inhibitory influences, to each input (i.e., just like with biological neurons)."

"Sir, biological neurons only fire if the resulting action potential is strong enough."

"This characteristic can also be modeled mathematically. In such case, a perceptron calculates the weighted sum of all its inputs (i.e., strength level of incoming signals) and applies a step function (i.e., logical step based on thresholds), to determine a single output value. This single output value is then fed to other perceptrons, copying the transfer from one biological neuron to the others. I am sending you a drawing of an ANN and a very simple mathematical operation illustrating how a perceptron works.[b] "

---

[a] Called Hopfield networks.

[b] If we use 3 vectors, as inputs (V) and weights (W), for a perceptron P and a threshold T:
$P = V1 \times W1 + V2 \times W2 + V3 \times W3$ or using the sum representation:

$$P = \sum_{1}^{n} (Vn \times Wn) \; with \; in \; this \; case \; n = 3$$

Using the threshold T, we can enter some binary logic with a step-up function:

$$If \; P > T \; then \; 1, which \; may \; also \; be \; written \; as \; P = 1 \; if \sum_{1}^{n} (Vn \times Wn) > 1$$

$$If \; P < \; or \; = \; T \; then \; 0, which \; can \; also \; be \; written \; as \; P = 0 \; if \sum_{1}^{n} (Vn \times Wn) < \; = 1$$

If we take for example V1 = 2; V2 = 2; V3 = 1 and W1 = 0.1; W2 = 0.2 and W3 = 0.3. Then the threshold of 1 isn't achieved (P = 0.9) and as P < 1, the resulting value is 0.

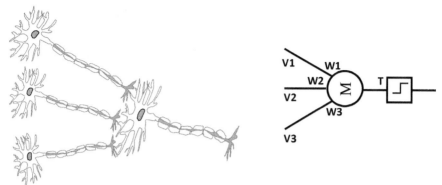

Fig. 44) Simplified biological and artificial neural networks; source: author.

"Sir, why use multi-layering?"

"To be useful, ANNs must integrate more than one level, between the input and output layers. Though there could be as many as needed, the complexity and the power required to process many levels, usually prevents programmers with limited resources, to use more than a few."

"But sir, you've indicated that IBM's ultimate goal is to have 1 trillion synapses. Why then this limitation?"

"Don't forget that I am describing ANNs on a 'von Neumann' classical computer. On those, the cost of processing can be expensive, especially as designing the network links between these different layers is crucial and is often done by trial and error."

"Sir, you made a reference to feed-forward ANNs. What are they?"

"In such ANNs, the connections may only go in one direction, from the upper layer to the lower ones. It usually consists of several layers of neurons, which sum up the inputs from the previous layer with a constant bias, and pass it through a nonlinear function.[a] The main benefit of such ANNs is that from any number of layers and nodes, one gets a good approximation of the calculated function.[b] "

"Sir, what about feedback ANNs?"

"In such ANNs, the connections return into the calculation process, a resulting computed value, from a lower layer."

---

[a] Usually a sigmoid function, which takes any resulting calculation and brings it back to a value between 0 and 1.

[b] In fact, for a certain number of layers and neurons, this capability is known to be a kind of universal approximation function. This allows processing data even if the model is non-probabilistic and enables us to find a non-parametric model for the input/output relation.

"Sir, what is the benefit of feeding back into the network, a value derived from earlier inputs?"

"Well, it gives the ANNs a kind of memory capacity, like for neurons. Indeed, at each time step, it is fed with some inputs plus the state of its hidden units, coming from the previous step. As a consequence, they are mainly dynamic. Their state continuously changes until they reach an equilibrium point. They will remain at that point, as long as their input changes and then, the ANNs will need to find a new equilibrium.[a] "

What is machine learning?

"Sir, these functions enable machines to learn but could you be more explicit?"

"Yes, of course. I already described what the learning process is for humans and the different philosophical theories, which can explain how we acquire knowledge (e.g., Rationalism, Empiricism, and Constructivism).[b] During the learning process, synaptic connections are strengthened or weakened over time, depending on how often we use such information. There are also rules that biological neural networks follow, such as the Hebbian rule: what triggers together, fires together."

"Sir, what have all these biological features to do with ANNs?"

"Although simplified, ANNs follow the same learning logic, replicating today this process essentially through coding but, as mentioned, new neuromorphic switches will most likely change this."

"Sir, are you saying that artificial and biological neural networks share the same logic?"

"Almost but instead of replicating a complex neural system, an ANN is neatly organized in layers. However, the first layer (s), generally duplicate (s) a computational version of the human senses, integrating what we can

---

[a] They are exceptionally well suited for functional mapping problems, where it is essential to understand how several input features can affect the output variables.

[b] A simplified view is that reason provides the structure of what we know, while senses offer content. We can abstract our mind from previous knowledge and not restart the learning process all over again, by classifying Objects of this world or events into categories, regrouped according to commonalities. Furthermore, our brain is both hardwired and structurally modified according to experience, and things learned throughout our lifetime. The 'nature' side of the brain allows it to boot up and perform its tasks, while its 'nurture' aspect changes the neural circuitry, according to environmental and social influences.

picture as detection features. For instance, whenever a machine feeds into an ANN some images or sound, it learns what these inputs are by detecting patterns (i.e., presence or absence of key features). Moreover, they adjust the connections' weight in the different network layers, emulating synaptic connections in our brain."

"Sir, the obvious question is how is the weight of the connection in machines adjusted, to enable the machine learning process?"

"This isn't done randomly and finding those weights is the hard part of the process. However, there are learning techniques and rules, which can be applied to modify the connection weights between hidden and output layers, to bring the output closer to the expected result."

"Sir, you mentioned the Hebbian rule for ANNs. What is it?"

"This rules states that the new connection weight is the result of a constant (called learning rate), applied during activation of two or more neurons. Once the ANN modifies the weights of all its connections between the hidden output layers, then it changes equally, the connection weights between the input and hidden layers. It reiterates the whole process until the outputs results are within the acceptable error range."

"Sir, aren't you describing some kind of training program?"

"Yes, after the training, the same process is tested with the other half of the data. Solely input data is applied, and the outputs are compared, without using the error info to modify the connection weights. If the ANN is producing outputs that match the expected data closely, then it may reasonably be used to process other new data. If not, the whole process must be re-analyzed and modified."

"Sir, what do these training processes include?"

"They use learning algorithms that integrate the best mathematical formulas to solve a specific problem, emulating cognitive processes. There are several learning algorithms, each providing benefits, and disadvantages."

"Sir, what are these algorithms?"

"I won't explain all of them but rather tell you how they are classified. This classification is done according to three main learning paradigms: supervised, unsupervised, and reinforced learning."

"Sir, how does supervised learning work?"

"We provide the ANN with the inputs and the desired output. Based on these two sets of data, it is capable of calculating an error, which will be adjusted incrementally through updated connection weights, till the output value can be met or best approximated, as described under the Hebbian rule."

"Sir, what about unsupervised learning?"

"In such case, we provide the ANN with only one set of inputs, and it must then find patterns all by itself, within these inputs. This approach is used in data mining and in processes involving recommendation algorithms, where other users' preferences can establish someone's preferences, based on these inputs (e.g., Amazon book recommendation)."

"Sir, how differently does re-enforce learning work?"

"As for supervised learning, we give the desired feedback but rather than using a thought of output, we give a reward, depending on how well the ANN is performing. Thus, through trial and error, reinforcement is given maximizing the previous weight that best maximized the reward. This type of learning approach mimics learning in nature, where positive feedback (e.g., mating or finding food) is best remembered."

"Sir, how does a single perceptron learn?"

"In a supervised training process, a perceptron will incrementally adjust any deviation, between the resulting and targeted output. This deviation is perceived by the mathematical model, as an error. By making slight corrections to the weights, the model will iterate till it gets to the targeted output, or as close as possible to it. I'm e-mailing the equations for your better understanding.[a] During training, the ANN will be exposed to a large number of examples and will iteratively modify the weights to minimize the errors.[b] "

---

[a] We've already seen that a perceptron's output is:

$$P = \sum_{1}^{n} (Vn \times Wn)$$

and obviously, any error E = P target - P input
By using a perceptron's error to adjust the weights, we get:
weight change = learning rate × error × input or, $\Delta Wn = r\, E\, x$ with r a small learning made on each iteration.
This gives us a final weight update equation of:
- weight change = learning rate × (target output - actual output) × input,
- that is, $\Delta Wn = r\,(Pt - Po)\, Xn$

[b] These equations are sufficient for simple logic functions, such as AND. For more complex ones (e.g., NOR), a few twists are required, such as introducing a bias unit (e.g., a neuron

"Sir, how does a multi-layer network learn?"

"When working with multi-layer networks, you need to consider a learning process, with two separate but intertwined steps. Firstly, we feed input data into the system, which generates output data at each node level of the intermediary layers (called hidden layers). The signal goes through all these intermediary layers until they reach the final output level. Then the resulting numbers are compared to the expected values, and the error between the two is quantified. This first step is what I described already as the feed-forward mechanism (called forward-propagation)."

"Sir, you're back to predictions and errors."

"Exactly, and as for free energy minimization, the objective is to reduce this error level or to force the network to come up with better predictions."

"Sir, how do you do that, if the layers are hidden?"

"Conceptually, we need to look at the overall error generated by each layer and adjust the parameters accordingly. Therefore, the system needs to look from the outputs to the inputs or, in other words, backward. This backward mechanism is called back-propagation."

"However Sir, how can you enumerate all possible combinations of these parameters and evaluate which is the best set, if they are numerous?"

"This is where we use an algorithm called 'gradient descent.' Its principle is quite simple to understand. Even if the system doesn't know what the intermediary units must be doing, it may always calculate how fast the error changes, as it modifies the hidden units' value. The speed of error changes, obtained mathematically through derivatives, will tell the system how far it is from an acceptable weight, affecting these hidden units."

"In other words, Sir, a slower pace obtained through a smaller derivative value, will indicate to the ANN that the solution is improving. After several iterations, a small derivative value will show that it has likely reached an acceptable error."

"Exactly! The network repeats these forward and back-propagation steps until it produces a sensible output or, according to a predefined number of training iterations, often limited by computer access time. I am forwarding to you more information on 'back-propagation,' if you want more meat to chew.[a] "

---

with a constant output, typically of 1).

[a] Each intermediary unit can affect many outputs. After obtaining the error derivatives of any one layer from an intermediary unit, the results may be used to compute the error

"Sir, what does it mean for a machine to learn?"

"Answering your question brings me back to Epistemology and Gnoseology, but this time from a machine perspective. So how does a machine learn that a cat is an animal with fur, four legs, whiskers and that eats mice or how does it know what fur or legs are, or even learn more complicated stuff such as that my son's cat is this specific cat and not any other one?[a] "

"Sir, does this bring us to the question of what is a surprise, from a machine perspective?"

"Yes, and for everything and everyone, it can be represented as the prediction error.[b] This similarity between our brain functioning and the machine learning algorithms enhances, in my view, the notion that machines may mimic how our brain works and, one day, reach the AGI level. However, to reach AGI, machines must acquire the faculty to calculate any deviation (i.e., error) in regards to all possible patterns."

"Sir, what are the consequences of such a requirement?"

"This implies for me, that a machine will need the following capabilities:

---

derivatives, for the activities of the following layer. Furthermore, once the system calculates the error derivatives for the activities of the hidden units, it's simple to get the error derivatives for the weights affecting a hidden unit. In other words, the algorithm enables the systematic and progressive calculation of intermediary units' values and weight, till it reaches the last level and reiterates the process till it gets an acceptable value.

If y is the activity of a neuron, E the error function, i and j two layers (with i being nearer the top layer), W the weight of the connection, then the resulting formula for back-propagation with batching of training examples, is the sum up of the partial derivatives over all training examples in the batch.

$$\Delta Wij = -\sum_{batch} \in Yi\, Yj\, (1 - Yj)\frac{dE}{dYj}$$

[a] For humans, learning is more than just a 'von Neumann' program of 'if and else' statements, which somewhat are recombined when we learn something. In fact, when we interact with the environment, there is an endless bottom-up and top-down communication flow between our neocortical neural networks, which reconfigures this network physiologically. Furthermore, the new cognitive theories portray our brain as a predictive machine. Consequently, our beliefs and expectations in regards to how an event should unfold or ideas should end-up, are measured against reality. Only surprises give rise to consciousness through the attention gathering process. All universal cognitive models have in common that they rely on patterns' detection and measuring, according to our expectations, for humans to gather intelligence and knowledge.

[b] The bigger the error, the more likely it is that our human consciousness will pick up the sensory input or idea. In other words, our brain also works around the principle of estimating mistakes and, if we consider Friston's entropy model, it additionally reduces such errors by acting on the environment.

1. To sense the environment, using equivalent or better technologies than men.
2. Equal or higher processing speed to deal with new surprises (i.e., error), in real time.
3. The knowledge to know what to look for and to identify surprises.
4. Access to a vast memory and a fast retrieving process, to measure data against already stored information.
5. The right algorithms to calculate patterns deviation.
6. The motion capacity to reduce surprises.
7. The willingness or urge to do all this by itself."

"Firstly Sir, do you believe that machines have already better sensing capacity?"

"Yes, I do. It's just a question of cost, impacted by mass production. Machines currently have more and better sensing aptitudes than any human being, provided the machine builder's client is willing to pay the price. We just need to look at unmanned vehicles like you, which capture data through lidar, radar, vision, Wi-Fi, and GPS and then fuse all this data to get a 360° view of the road, 200 meters ahead, to realize that machines already have higher sensing aptitudes than any human being."

"Secondly Sir, what about processing speed and capacity?"

"I've already shown some of the paths likely to be used by the IT industry to achieve human-like performance and indicated that supercomputers already have the same processing capacity as humans. It is just a question of time before PCs achieve the same performance."

"Thirdly Sir, what about acquiring the knowledge to know what to look for?"

"In order not to be surprised, we need to meet our expectations. For instance, if my daughter were to identify a cat, there would be many events, which would immediately attract her attention and question the belief that she is indeed looking at a cat. Seeing a cat with three legs or with a blue nose, are a few of those thousand conditions that would surprise anyone, as it would go against common knowledge about what a cat is."

"But Sir, how would a machine identify that it isn't contemplating a cat, but rather a doll or a stuffed cat with a painted nose?"

"Unless someone programmed it to recognize that only cats with four legs and a pink or black nose could be classified as a cat, it would be impossible. And then what would happen if someone really painted the nose of a real cat in blue?"

"Sir, you are highlighting the difficulty for machines to identify that a cat is a cat, without pre-programming all possible 'cat-ness' conditions."

"Is it even possible to define something that per nature is infinite, since it depends on its environment (e.g., its nose reflecting sunlight or being undetectable during the night)? On the other hand, humans achieve this most of the time, so there must be a way for machines to mimic people correctly."

"Sir, how are humans successful in achieving this?"

"They do this by acting on their environment, for instance, by checking with their hands if the cat is real. Alternatively, they may use probability inference to verify that most conditions, defining what a cat is, as per an individual's beliefs, experience, or common sense, have been met. We're back to the Bayesian brain theory, which argues that humans use Bayesian probability to perform cognitive functions."

"Sir, we are thus, back again to mathematics, which as we all know, can easily be processed by machines."

"Exactly! Through coding and weighting (e.g., four legs = 10%, one head = 5%, whiskers = 25%, two ears = 5%, tail = 10%, furs = 20%, blue nose = -50%, etc.), machines could identify with some level of certainty that it is a cat with a blue nose, and not a doll or a stuffed cat."

"Sir, is that how we machines do it?"

"Obviously, my example is extremely simplified. Machines must work at a finer granularity level to reduce uncertainty and describe each sub-element according to the same mechanisms, or even use other unsupervised training. However, what is essential to understand, is that we are in fact picturing an ANN, which we've seen, can be used for supervised, unsupervised, or reinforced learning."

"Sir, I guess you didn't select the cat example by chance?"

"I didn't. Already in 2012, a Google team was able to train a neural network composed of sixteen thousand computer processors with one billion trainable parameters to detect faces, bodies, and cats![a] The study results confirm that without a man defining what cats are, machines can

---

[a] Amazingly, the ANN had 30 different layers. By browsing through ten million randomly selected you-tube videos, the system achieved high detection accuracy (e.g., 81.7%, 76.7% and 74.8% for faces, body, and cats respectively). The white paper, written by the Google team members, describes the deep-learning algorithms used in this study and confirms the feasibility of building high-level features, from only unlabeled data.[N134]

invent by themselves the principles of cat-ness, or learn what to look for. I'll describe in more detail, later on, what the used deep-learning techniques are."

"Fourthly Sir, do machine have access to a huge memory and a fast retrieving process to measure data against already stored information?"

"Yes, of course, they do. The evolution of artificial memory (fig. 43), shows that we should reach the estimated equivalent human memory capacity of 10^{17} bytes in 2023. However, it doesn't even consider wireless and fix connections to any data source such as the internet. Any machine may now apply the same research engines as we humans do, to get connected through wireless (e.g., 4 G) or fast Ethernet technologies.[a] "

"In other words Sir, there is no memory issue due to geo-localization, anymore. Any machine will instantaneously have access to the humans' entire knowledge library, as long as it is connected physically or wirelessly to the net."

"For instance, a machine directly connected to WATSON, IBM's AI system, would benefit from its capacity to go through 200 million pages, analyze them, and provide a precise answer, in less than three seconds!"

"Fifthly Sir, do machines already have the right algorithms to calculate pattern deviations?"

"My premise is that, to get to AGI, we need to mimic the human brain. In the brain, there is a top-down flow, constructing what we may expect and a bottom-up flow, which extracts the variation between this construct and the reality observed through our senses. If I start with the top-down process, we do not currently have a general algorithm, which would allow a machine to build this construct, in whatever circumstances. What we have is a set of specialized rules that are application specific. The best example would be a driverless vehicle like you, which possesses all known driving rules.[b] "

"Sir, my rules are related to driving and don't allow me to do other things."

---

[a] With the present technological development pace, the current 4G/LTE bandwidth of (100MBps) will reach 1Gbps with 4G/LTE Advanced, and 10Gbps with 5G, within the next five years. On the fixed side, fast Ethernet technology already contemplates 10Gbps and is getting prepared for 100Gbps. Some experts are even talking about terabit Ethernet (1000Gbps).

[b] Companies, like Google, have embedded all driving and security rules or laws, which a human being will learn through driving lessons and experience. The interesting aspect of software is that vehicles will get systematically upgraded versions. Thus, every time a driverless car encounters a new issue, new rules will be established (either by the vehicle itself but most probably at the manufacturer's operational center, in order to maintain unicity across the software program) and incorporated in the product platform.

"I believe that we humans will want to maintain specialized rules for specific machines. I doubt we'll authorize you to have rules about how to fly or drive like in a formula one racing. It means that we won't want you to acquire general knowledge."

"What is that, Sir?"

"It's the capacity to abstract, what you've already acquired in one domain, into something that you may apply to other areas. It's more or less like a library of knowledge, which would bring us back to Kant's Concepts and Schemes. However, I believe we must put the threshold of AGI there. Consequently, I would classify a machine with such capacity, as a super intelligent machine."

"Sir, humans can do this all the time, so why do you fix the threshold there?"

"You are right. I can do that easily. On the other hand, I'm not as good as you, for instance, at processing perceptual information. I can't use sound or light waves sensors, cameras, and GPS with maps of an entire country already pre-recorded. Furthermore, I cannot communicate wirelessly with other cars like you do, and fuse almost instantaneously all this information, to make a decision integrating everything, in a fraction of a second. You, on the contrary, are equipped with all these detection technologies and possess the algorithms to make a sense out of all this information."

"Sir, what you are saying is that we, machines, are already better at returning the prediction errors because we have a much greater spectrum of measurement. Furthermore, our algorithms, which are already pretty good, will only continue improving. The day we will be able to generalize knowledge the way you humans do, we'll already be far more intelligent than you are."

"Exactly, but the issue is if we humans will tolerate that you get this access to general knowledge."

"Sir, do machines have the motion capacity to reduce surprises?"

"Not yet but lately vast improvements have been made in robotization. For instance, you, my car, have this capacity to drive on whatever road. Obviously, you cannot climb stairs or have hands, which would allow you to palpate an object and reduce surprises that way. In other words, you still don't have the mobility, agility, and dexterity that humans have, but this is changing quickly in the robotic world.[a] "

---

[a] We recommend to type in 'Boston Dynamics,' in a search program and look at the video about this company's latest humanoid robot. The featured robot is quiet, reasonably fast, doesn't tether and even has a great balance. Japanese are also extremely advanced in robotization. For instance, Honda's latest version of its humanoid robot ASIMO is impressive. It is probably the most dexterous and responsive robot so far and will be used

"Sir, last but not least, you mentioned the willingness or urge to do all this by itself. Aren't you referring to free will?"

"More or less. I also kind of put the threshold between AGI and super intelligence, at the level of free will. Indeed, it requires, in my view, self-awareness and thus, would imply that machines have the conscience of being alive. I'll treat the issue about artificial self-awareness in the future. However, I think it is possible, without implying artificial awareness, to build a machine with the urge to reduce its surprises. If we were to create higher rules, such as the one promoted by Asimov and referred to as the three laws of robotics,[a] we could envision to program this urge to do something."

"Sir, how would you do that?"

"Let's say, your car builder embedded in your program as the highest priority, the need to protect your other passengers and me, from potential danger. After executing a set of instructions, your program could enforce at every critical step, additional perceptual cues or actions, if it identified any potentially hazardous situation."

"Sir, could you give an example to help me understand?"

"For instance, if you identify a deer along the road, you could increase your radar coverage distance, or change the angle of all your sensors to check if there are other deer in the vicinity of the road. You could also take the action to communicate wirelessly with cars in front and with the control center, to check if they have identified other animals ahead. Another example, which comes to my mind, is the need to re-energize your electric battery like any animal would have the urge to feed. Such a rule, which would force you to power up, after a certain depletion threshold, could easily be integrated within your program."

"Sir, but what about the coherence between all these rules?"

"In fact, what you are referring to, with your question, is what about free will? Indeed, it is all about setting this coherence, by defining what the better rules are, in which situation. For instance, your rule of repowering could conflict with my need to catch my plane."

"What would then happen, Sir?"

---

more and more to help senior citizens and people with a physical handicap.

[a] Isaac Asimov's three laws are: a robot may not injure a human being or, through inaction, allow him or her to come to harm; a robot must obey orders given by human beings except where such orders would conflict with the First Law; a robot must protect its existence as long as such protection does not conflict with the First or Second Law.

"By setting other priorities for you, which don't put you at the top, your car-builder is still giving you the possibility to do something by yourself willingly, but not the free will to do it under all circumstances. Furthermore, manufacturers would need to ensure that priorities between these rules are set once and for all, without the possibility for you to self-modify them, at your will."

"But Sir, how would you achieve this?"

"We humans don't need to learn that we must drink when we are thirsty. These rules are hardwired into our brain or body, as the newborn instinct to suck breast to eat. On the other hand, we learn how to perform arithmetic or speak English. Thus, there is a combination of hardwired and acquired knowledge. What is likely to happen is that priority rules or 'general laws' will most likely have to be hardwired, while learning rules, inferred from interacting with the environment, will be set as software rules."

What is Deep learning?

"Sir, so far you've mainly described supervised processes. What about unsupervised learning?"

"In French, there is a saying that, what can easily be understood may be clearly stated[a]. It strikes me as a good way of explaining why unsupervised training is essential. Machine learning involves difficulties that normal

---

[a] 'Ce qui se conçoit bien s'énonce clairement'

instructions cannot easily take care of. For instance, how do you explain to a machine what cat-ness is? Even if we have a good explanation of these concepts, or of an abstract notion (e.g., object or speech recognition) and would be able to code the instructions for it, the programming task and the software itself would be extremely complex."

"So Sir, how was the problem solved?"

"People involved in machine learning have developed algorithms, which enable computers to look at many examples and, in some cases, to the correct answers. Computers can then use these examples, within a different context, to solve similar problems. Very much like I could explain what cat-ness is to my son, by showing differences and similarities with a tiger and a dog, programmers have taught computers to solve problems by examples.[a] "

"Sir, how would you describe deep learning?"

"Deep learning is one of the machine learning techniques, which is especially useful in giving computers the basis of these examples. This technique tells the system what kind of concepts or things, it should be looking at. I mentioned in supervised learning that the difficulty resided in weighting the various nodes of the system. These algorithms, which learn to spot the right features all by themselves, enable unsupervised processes, called feature extraction."

"So Sir, deep learning involves exclusively unsupervised learning?"

"No, it can use both types. Deep learning brought clever means through algorithms, to help train these multi-layer networks.[b] "

"Sir, could you name a few of these algorithms?"

"In fact, any algorithm that learns a distributed representation of its input data could be considered a deep learning algorithm. We can use these

---

[a] To give an example, if we want to tell a machine how to identify a picture of a bird or a fish, we could prioritize blue or green pixels. In other words, the difficulty is to define the parameters and tweak them in such a way, that the iterations between prediction and adjustment cannot improve anymore the prediction model. This tweaking process, called feature engineering, is more intuitive than rational. This is why algorithms, which can engineer these features without programmers, have been developed.

[b] In fact, a set of techniques (e.g., Rectified Linear Units (ReLU); sign rather than amplitude variation, etc.), which takes care of gradient descent problems, linked to the increased number of layers, is what we associate with deep learning. Since the network's weights can be terribly off at the beginning of the tweaking, it may become almost impossible to parameterize a 'deep' (i.e., several layers) neural network with back-propagation.

algorithms in both unsupervised and supervised learning.[a] Parts of the supervised machine learning algorithms are linear regression, logistic regression, multi-layer-neural net, convolutional nets, recurrent neural nets, and support vector machines. If you're curious how they look like, please feel free to search these algorithms on the web."

"Sir, what about the unsupervised learning algorithms?"

"Unsupervised learning is still in its infancy, but I've e-mailed you a set of algorithms, praised by experts.[b] "

"Sir, do you need special hardware to do unsupervised training?"

"No, you don't, but at the same time, the number of intermediary layers limits calculation speed. I mentioned that one way of increasing intelligence is through specialization. Graphic Process Units, which brought much more processing power, are now used to process back-propagation learning algorithms."

"Sir, are there other restrictions, besides processing power?"

"Yes, in machine learning, it's not always the best algorithm that provides you with the best prediction, but the amount of unlabeled data, which constitutes your training set."

"Sir, is deep learning equivalent to data mining?"

"No, deep learning is a technique with its algorithms that give machines the possibility to learn in a supervised or unsupervised manner. Data mining is more the process by which we extract knowledge or patterns from unstructured data. Therefore, it can use deep learning techniques to do that or other specific algorithms, which may structure the data."

🧠

---

[a] Deep learning techniques also exist to learn to detect very long non-linear time dependencies in sequential data rather than extracting non-linear hierarchical features. An algorithm called long short-term memory (LSTM) allows the ANN to pick up on activity, hundreds of past time-steps rather than on a few steps, in order to make accurate predictions.

[b] K-means clustering, Principle Component Analysis (PCA) for compression, Gaussian techniques for anomaly detection, convolutional neural nets, which is quite a powerful tool to classify images.

What is Genetic programming?

"Sir, I remember you mentioned the term Genetic programming. Is this also linked to learning techniques?"

"No, it's not. Genetic programming employs algorithms that mimic the way nature uses evolution to solve complex search problems. It works with natural selection properties, which are applied to the problem to solve. The first step is usually to generate randomly a population, which size varies from a few individuals to several thousand. We then assess each individual within this population on how close he fits with specified desired properties."

"Sir, could you give me an example where we would use genetic programming?"

"Let's see... What about building a better motor engine. For instance, I could specify criteria that I want to optimize, such as choc, vibration, heat resistance, lightness, affordability, etc. As I want to optimize the best mix of characteristics within such a population, the program will discard the bad designs and only keep the ones that fit the properties. All of the many selection methods ensure that the fitter individuals are selected for the next generation. Between, each iteration, which creates a new generation, features of the selected individuals are recombined, in a step that is called crossover."

"Sir, what is this crossover for?"

"It is hoped, as in nature, that through this 'gene' recombination the new individuals will acquire the best characteristics of the previous generation. We add a little randomness through a process called mutation, to ensure that the recombination creates a solution that is different than any found in the original population. As for nature, we reiterate this reproductive process over hundreds of generations."

"Sir, how does the program know when to stop?"

"The programmer will stop the iterative process, either because he ran out of time or money, or because the proposed solution meets the minimum predefined criteria. Obviously, such an approach doesn't ensure that there isn't a better solution out there."

"Sir, is genetic programming used only for improving material things?"

"No. In fact, one interesting aspect of Genetic programming is that it can also be used to design better algorithms.[159] Thus, not only may it produce better solutions to a problem, but it can also help to better design answers to a specific problem. That's the reason why, I mentioned earlier that these kinds of program aren't totally man-made anymore, as both fate and improvements, change the software and the results, in a Darwinian evolutionary manner."

What is Fuzzy logic?

"Sir, you mentioned fuzzy logic, as a non-binary logic. As neural networks are replacing true or false statements by a level of truth statements, I was wondering if neural networks ever integrated fuzzy logic?"

"It's a fascinating question. Could we build onto a neuromorphic switch, with several memristive states, a new kind of logic? Before going that way, do you know what fuzzy logic is?"

"Sir, not really."

"When I first started my career in automation, fuzzy logic was integrated on industrial PCs (called Programmable Logic Computers) to manage batch and continuous processes (e.g., a refinery or gas pressure equipment)."

"Sir, what are the benefits of fuzzy logic?"

"It enables to integrate subjective factors, such as high, low, and strong pressure, without having necessarily to define them precisely. In fact, it allows the integration of fuzzy concepts such as usually, sometimes, somewhat, etc. into programming by gradually increasing from 0 to 1, over a given range of fuzziness values (e.g., 0.20; 0.40; 0.60; 0.80). It then permits the establishment of rules governing the use of connectives, such as AND and OR, for that fuzzy set."

"However Sir, how would a machine know if someone is short, somewhat short, average, somewhat tall, or tall?"

"Yes, this subjectivity is something machines aren't good at, whereas we humans do it all the time. There is an area of computer science called computing with words, which tries to develop seamless communication between human users and AI computer algorithms.[a] "

---

[a] Humans must still come up with mathematical representations of these subjective terms,[N135] such as 'tall,' and define which function or command could integrate such comments, followed by another mathematical definition for turning the combined result back into a semantic output result (e.g., he is small).

"Sir, what are the benefits of such fuzzy neural networks?"

"These networks can integrate two contradictory requirements – interpretability versus accuracy – with their specific models (e.g., linguistic fuzzy modeling) and precise modeling."

"Sir, can you give you me an example, which explains what is happening with all these AI technologies?"

"Let me think. There is this 2012 white paper, which describes how the combination of ANNs, Fuzzy logic, and Genetic programming have been used together to estimate the grade of ore deposits in a mine.[160] The Genetic programming algorithm in this study was used for optimizing the network parameters, including learning rate, and the fuzzy categorization."

"Sir, what about my question of building fuzzy neuromorphic switches?"

"Yes, it would be in my view, the Holy Grail of AI and a big step towards AGI! Combining non-binary logic with multi-state gates would copy our neural connections. To confirm that compatibility between memristors and fuzzy logic computing schemes is possible, I must refer to research.[161] a "

What are the benefits of cognitive programming?

"Sir, you've talked about new hardware not running on 'von Neumann' systems. Are these technologies using fundamentally different computing programs?"

"They are. For instance, IBM uses Corelet software,[162] a technology built upon reusable building blocks, which represent a blueprint of a neuro-synaptic network and which specify base-level functions. Though these blocks only expose the inputs and outputs to the programmers, they can be combined to produce new functional blocks."

"Sir, Corelet is thus some sort of object-oriented program?"

"Kind of. By composing these Corelets blocks, we can build applications and use the cognitive algorithms for supervised and unsupervised training, which will be compatible with the TrueNorth

---

a For instance, circuits performing the fuzzy min and max operations, have been designed and fuzzy membership (i.e., classification) functions of any shape and resolution could also be implemented, on these switches.

neuromorphic switch. In fact, IBM developed a library of apps, to enhance the ease of coding."

"Sir, is it true that Jeff Hawkins, who developed the memory-prediction theory, put his money where his mouth is, and created new software technology?"

"Yes, he developed with his colleagues from Numenta, a machine learning technology, with specific algorithms, which doesn't come as a surprise, is memory based. It is called Hierarchical Temporal Memory.[163]"

"Sir, what's so special about Hierarchical Temporal Memory (HTM)?"

"Its main difference with ordinary technology is that information storage is distributed through a hierarchical organization, which integrates time-based storage rules."

"Sir, what's the benefit of hierarchy?"

"Think about the six-layer cortical neural structure and the benefits it can generate when you gather sensory information, from more than one source. It converts sensory inputs into one signal at the top and thus, adds abstraction capability. This hierarchy, obtained through layers (called regions by Numenta), also generates efficiencies, by reducing training time and memory usage."

"Sir, how does it store data in a distributed manner?"

"HTM uses a sparse distributed representation to convert inputs, as well as brain-like sparse coding properties."

"Sir, how does HTM use time to its advantage?"

"Well, time plays a crucial role in our thought process. For instance, when you infer something, you necessarily bring back some elements from the past. It also creates a pattern that we can identify because it isn't static."

"Sir, what is the role of HTM's algorithms?"

"It is to learn temporal sequences, within streams of input data. Once learned it can be used to recognize other patterns and thus, form predictions. HTM works on inference learning and prediction, performed within each region. Copying the brain logic, all HTM regions make different predictions based on a context that originated in the past. They may do so because this software stores transitions between spatial patterns."

"Sir, what are the characteristics of HTM predictions?"

"They are done continuously at every level of the hierarchy, taking into consideration present and past contexts. All this brings much greater output stability, makes the system more robust to noise, enables to identify what else to expect, and thus deals with surprises."

"Sir, basically this computational learning model transcribes the cortical properties into a software program. Is it successful in doing it?"

"It has a few tricks, but it seems so.[a] "

"Sir, could you show me some HTM coding?"

"OK. I'll e-mail you some coding lines.[b] If you want to check how to mix inference and learning codes, or support data structures and routines, just look at Numenta's HTM presentation on the internet.[164, 165] "

---

[a] It has what it calls a spatial pooler, which regroups in a joint representation, patterns that are spatially similar. The software converts this representation into a new image, which includes past context. The encoding is done by prioritizing cells that are already active in a column, either through feed-forward input or lateral connections. This encoding follows a few sets of rules: use of all columns, stability of input density per columns, elimination of trivial patterns, efficient encoding eliminating unnecessary connections, and use of self-adjusting systems. When a region makes a prediction, it activates all cells most likely to be involved in future feed-forward input processing. Areas make predictions based on patterns changing over time, setting columns in which cells become active, in a specific sequence. However, one big difference between this software and the brain is that Numenta's synapses only use binary weight (1 or 0).

[b] Temporal pooler pseudo-code for inference.

The first phase calculates the active state of each cell:
```
for c in activeColumns(t)
        buPredicted = false
        for i = 0 to cellsPerColumn - 1
                if predictiveState(c, i, t-1) == true then
                        s = getActiveSegment(c, i, t-1,
                           activeState)
                        if s.sequenceSegment == true then
                                buPredicted = true
                                activeState(c, i, t) = 1
        if buPredicted == false then
                for i = 0 to cellsPerColumn - 1
                activeState(c, i, t) = 1
```

The second phase calculates the predictive state for each cell.
```
for c, i in cells
        for s in segments(c, i)
                if segmentActive(c, i, s, t) then
                        predictiveState(c, i, t) = 1
```

How to build intelligent, rather than learning machines?

"Sir, what does IBM and Numenta's cooperation want to achieve?"

"If you look at IBM's high-end cognitive technology, they have Watson, which is a rule-based expert system, which applies to normal von Neumann processing, classical or ANN algorithms. I've already presented the Truenorth morphologic switch, which uses Corelets block functioning software, to build energy efficient ANNs. However, in this case, the learning is done off-line, like in the previous classical computer systems. IBM intends to use HTM as their core technology to develop unsupervised continuous online learning algorithms.[166] "

"Sir, will they develop a special neuromorphic switch?"

"The answer is yes and no. IBM believes it is too early to cast the HTM algorithms in a specialized physical switch, as they think that they still need to twist the hardware to test the algorithms.[167] Furthermore, there is an inherent characteristic of HTM's technology, that is, that it learns mostly through changing its network topology. Therefore, they've decided to develop a specific processor using two techniques: the 3D stacking, which I've already introduced, and a wafer scale architecture (i.e., building very-large integrated circuit networks using an entire silicon wafer, to produce a single 'super-chip')."

"Sir, what are they trying to achieve by doing this?"

"In machine learning using ANNs, the objective is to tweak the weights of the existing synapses. In machine intelligence, learning results from the formation of new synapses. In other words, they want to create hardware with massive interconnectivity, which may change its 'plastic' network topology, just like the biological neural network can create intelligence through their neural plasticity.[a] "

"Sir, do you believe that these initiatives will create intelligent machines?"

---

[a] This is why the team members from IBM and UCLA University, working on this technology,[N136] are looking at 3D-Wafer-to-Wafer technology, with four strata of 300mm each. This 3D wafer scale integration provides lots of memory, high bandwidth connection, and very high connectivity. Vertical connectivity will be ensured by Through Silicon Via (TSV) copper wire, while the horizontal connectivity will be embedded in the wafer design. Interestingly, the team presented what would be the number of wafers necessary to match the human cortex, using 2.9×10^{10} neurons with their average of 1000 synapses and came up with 128 memory wafers and 16 logic wafers, using a bandwidth of 100Gbps per node. They conclude that this capacity isn't far-fetched, though they recognize they would need to develop new memory technology to reduce the number of (DRAM) memory wafers.

"Since the beginning of our conversation, I said that there is a path towards AGI, which increasingly involves more intelligent technologies. I've shown so far, several techniques that create intelligent behaviors, which as in the case of Genetic programming, could even create something different than what was originally conceived by human beings. However, intelligence is different than intelligent behaviors. All these ANNs, even with unsupervised learning algorithms, stop this intelligent behavior, when cut from input supply. On the contrary, humans continue 24/7, going through conscious or unconscious cognitive processes."

"Sir, if we agree with your principle that machine intelligence needs to mimic the human brain to reach AGI, then what are the consequences?"

"We must realize that neural networks and their plasticity are the way to go. Machines will need to construct a vision of this world, according to general learning rules and special algorithms, which can infer specific processing properties (e.g., visual or sound recognition). With time, these rules shall translate into patterns, against which reality will be measured. The error or variance, resulting from the confrontation between the prediction and reality, will be compared at all four layers of this wafer in feed-forward, lateral, and feedback loops of information."

"Sir, why consider only four layers?"

"Indeed, nothing impedes to build six layers or more. As in the neocortex, the higher the information traveling in the hierarchical layers, the more invariance it will encounter. With a continuous process of predictions and corrections, based upon a stream of various sensory inputs, shaping the ANNs through experience, we'll be able to create intelligent machines. I am especially optimistic that it will happen sooner than later, now that we've started solving the ANNs' biggest issue, that is, the capacity to learn from past experience."

"Sir, I asked you how come humans didn't have to learn all over again. Are you saying that current ANNs cannot use past information to solve new problems, but will in the future?"

"Indeed, I told you that an ANN's memory is kept in the process and stored through its weight, at the level of the nodes. Consequently, whenever, it is confronted with a new problem to solve, the weights of the newer one replace the weights of the previous task. Therefore, there isn't currently any possible mechanism to re-use acquired knowledge."

"Sir, how was the problem solved?"

"Google's Deepmind division recently developed an algorithm, inspired by the brain's plasticity, which supports a continuous learning process.[168]

By the same token, it highlights the fact that these principles are themselves, fundamental aspects of biological learning and memory."

"How does it achieve artificial neural plasticity, Sir?"

"To overcome what is called 'catastrophic forgetting,' this approach selectively slows down the learning process of the most critical tasks. It does that by reducing its plasticity, by an amount equivalent to the importance of prior experiences.[a] "

"Sir, how close is this from biological learning?"

"This algorithm can be grounded on learning approaches, based on the Bayesian brain. It means that the new ANN parameters are tempered by a prior, which is the posterior distribution of the parameters, given data from the previous task. Furthermore, the researchers see important parallels between this algorithm and theories of synaptic plasticity."

"Sir, how is synaptic plasticity involved in such algorithm?"

"They share the theory that modulation of this synapse plasticity extends memorized experiences. Synapses store not only their current weight but also a representation of their uncertainty about their weight, thus maintaining information about learning rates.[b] "

"Sir, are you saying that applying Numenta's software onto a 3D stacked wafer, enhanced by greater memory capacity, and incorporating this new algorithm (called Elastic Weight Consolidation), could create machines as intelligent as humans?"

"No, I already told you that machines must also be agile to influence the environment directly, in order to reduce surprises. I also think that the world isn't binary. Consequently, to reach AGI, we would need to integrate some fuzzy logic."

"Sir, though you've introduced the emotional intelligence theory, why didn't you integrate emotions in machines, as a necessary step to reach AGI?"

---

[a] This algorithm called Elastic Weight Consolidation, reduces the weight changes, according to how important the tasks were for the previous problem (measured by the diagonal of Fisher information). The memories translated into the gradient descent of the past, are therefore protected from complete overwriting. This allows, in unsupervised or reinforced learning mode, to train the ANNs to perform many different tasks sequentially, without forgetting the previous results, something deep-learning cannot currently do.

[b] The authors go even further and make an analogy between the three values stored at the level of the ANNs' nodes (i.e., weight, variance, and its mean) and the brain's synaptic storage of its weight (for the early plasticity phases), of its weight variance (for the state of short-term plasticity) and its mean weight (associated with the late stage of plasticity).

"What you are asking me is if the limbic brain is an inherent part of the cognitive processes or, at least, if it can influence intelligence in some way? To answer that question, I would like to come back to my definitions of ANI and AGI. In ANI, the intelligent solutions, generated by the software, are always predictable. In AGI, these intelligent solutions will be almost impossible to foresee a priori, as they will emerge from the technical solution and the reasoning process itself."

"Sir, could you give me an example, rather than reasoning in the abstract?"

"OK. Let me go back to my example of a blue nose cat. Suppose a robot, equipped with these self-learning algorithms, takes 10.000 pictures of this cat and retrieves 1.000.000 Facebook images from the internet. When running these pictures through its ANN, it would get a certain level of certainty that this blue nose cat is indeed a cat. I think you'll agree with me that adding 10.000 other pictures wouldn't change its level of certainty fundamentally. Now, if this robot were to touch the cat or run after it, in other words, add dexterity and mobility to its capacities and interfere directly with reality, that would change the outcome radically."

"Sir, you've only applied the Free-energy principle, by adding action to sensory cues."

"Yes, but by transforming a passive into an active subject, I have automatically added random conditions, resulting from the robot's interaction with the world. In other words, you couldn't anticipate the reactions of the observed blue nose cat and thus foresee a priori the result: if it's a real or stuffed cat?"

"But Sir, if this object were a stuffed blue nose cat observed solely by cameras, you would still know because it would stay still."

"You are right and are integrating the notion of time, which also adds randomness through the process of life and that Numenta is capturing through its HTM model. In other words, two cameras surveying the same blue nose cat with the same self-learning software but starting this process at a different time might end up with totally different conclusions.[a] "

"Sir, you are highlighting only the notion of singularity."

"Yes, but to get intelligence and not smart behaviors, we need software, whenever confronted with the same starting conditions, which can come up with two different answers, like genetic programming allows you to. It is

---

[a] For instance, one camera observing this cat before it sleeps and the other just when it started sleeping.

also why I believe fuzzy logic would probably help reach AGI, as it may deal with the randomness inherently contained in the outside world."

"However Sir, what about emotions? It has nothing to do with the outside world's randomness."

"You are partially right because it has to do with internal randomness. If I am afraid of cats or allergic to them, I won't probably want to touch this blue nose cat. Every subject, having different emotions in regards to a situation, generated by the experience with an Object, will react differently. In other words, if systems were to be programmed with emotions, this inherent randomness would necessarily influence machine intelligence, adding unpredictability to the process, and making it difficult to know the outcome, a priori. Emotions, like Genetic programming, provides singularity."

"Fine Sir, but do you need the complete spectrum of human emotions for AGI to happen?"

"To answer this question, I'll revert to the emotional intelligence (EI) model.[a] EI includes self-awareness, self-regulation, empathy and social skills, that is, the capacity to manage one's emotions, as well as understanding the emotions of other creatures."

"Sir, didn't you put the distinction between AGI and ASI, at the level of these capabilities?"

"I did. Therefore, I would limit AGI to mechanisms that a machine would use to optimize their actions to positively (and not negatively) influence the reduction of surprises. In other words, you don't need emotions – such as fear, hate, sadness, anger, dislike, etc. – and internal states – such as self-awareness, self-recognition tiredness, boredom, etc. – to reduce surprises."

"Sir, don't you think your arguments sound arbitrary?"

"Maybe but I believe those emotions and inner states would probably add too much internal randomness to the process. Indeed, they would create further surprises or blur the capacity to seek through actions or more perceptual cues, additional information reducing surprises."

---

[a] Self-awareness (ability to recognize emotions and mood), self-regulation (control of the mood and feelings), motivation (with clear goals and positive attitude), empathy, and social skills (good interpersonal relationship).

"Sir, aren't you just eliminating all emotions?"

"No, I've left what EI classifies as motivation, that is the capacity to establish clear objectives with a positive attitude. Therefore, through an optimization model with at least two opposing variables (e.g., cost versus benefits), we could ensure that we get the willingness to pursue our goals. For instance, in your case, we could systematically ensure that the rule of protecting your passenger against any other rule, always challenges your motivation to travel at maximum authorized speed."

"Sir, to sum up, what would you include in AGI?"

"I would arbitrarily include all necessary equipment and software enabling the thinking process in AGI. I would draw the line between AGI and ASI at the techniques and software, including the rules based on emotions, enabling the independent decision-making process."

What about distributed cognitive systems?

"Sir, you've mainly talked about machines but what about cognitive systems?"

"You're right! My view is that a system of systems, that is, various machines working together in an integrated environment, will be built around a distributed architecture. This architecture will integrate state-of-the-art technologies (e.g., SOA and EDA), as well as cognitive software and algorithms to integrate supervised and unsupervised training techniques."

"Sir, what will be achieved through this integration?"

"By integrating all these technologies, a system of systems shall be able to perform intelligent and adaptive behaviors. In a collaborative book on CCTV,[169] I wrote that the best strategy is to put intelligence the nearest to the specific data source to be controlled. In this case, I suggested adding some video analytics instructions in the camera chip, to deal with particular problems, such as changing metro lighting conditions, rather than consolidating everything in the video recorder."

"Sir, what are the issues of pushing the intelligence to the edge?"

"An edge computing strategy, which a distributed architecture favors, ensures that video analytics can process images in parallel streams, both at the camera and video recorder levels. Obviously, we must manage the critical issue of timescale. It is especially crucial when we take into consideration distributed storage of quasi-independent systems, having developed their own decision cycles and different data storage frequencies."

"Sir, how do you account for the various events that can happen concomitantly?"

"To account for this, such a system must introduce what is known as complex event processing, which is a technology that analyzes and consolidates these different events, producing decisions and potentially triggering other events. This technology must also account for a hierarchy of events and thus introduces prioritization, enabling the production of higher-level events coming from a lower level of abstraction."

"Sir, how are these new computing techniques impacting system design?"

"Well, cognitive computing will force system engineers to design by learning, rather than by predefining complex systems with their interactions. Intelligence will appear in smaller systems before being extended to bigger ones and finally to the complete system. As a consequence, the more the design will emerge from experience, that is, from incoming inputs, the more important shall be the definition of what the final outputs should be."

"I understand Sir. You are describing a kind of artificial neural network where the systems tweaking is done by unsupervised learning rather than by people."

"Yes, exactly how nature achieves this, through Darwinian selection."

At this point, I felt I had gone through most issues related to intelligence and decided to stop there our conversation. I knew I needed to do a lot of extra reading to grasp all matters associated with the 'hard problem' of consciousness. In fact, I was already anticipating my car's challenging questions on ASI. However, what I really feared the most, were questions on artificial self-awareness.

Fig. 45) Intelligent and efficient transport systems such as Supraways, will integrate AI and driverless technologies; source: courtesy of Supraways http://www.supraways.com

PART 4: SELF-AWARENESS

Am I out of my mind?

L'oeuf de Christophe Colomb; source: author

I am therefore I think [170]

Karl Friston (University College London, Institute of Neurology)

17) Will ASI ever exist?

For several weeks now, my car and I, had been carefully avoiding any discussion, which would include words such as knowledge or intelligence. However, this afternoon after dozing off while going to visit my mum, I woke up and asked to my car: "How long, have I been knocked out for?"

"Sir, are you OK now or should I go to the hospital?"

"No, no! I didn't mean literally knocked out, but asleep."

"Probably an hour. Sir, though you said that you weren't knocked out, except for the snoring, it sure felt like it. Were you in the state, you humans call unconsciousness?"

I knew the questions wouldn't stop coming in, so I decided that it was time to resume our discussion.

"Yes, I was but in one of its form, called sleep. In fact, I'd like to use your question to introduce what consciousness is by actually defining what it isn't, as it is easier than the other way round. When we humans are asleep, sedated, literally knocked out, or in a coma, and though we may still have some neural activities in a few of these conditions, we wake up with no idea of what happened around us during this period. In fact, when we are unconscious, our personal view is suspended, we don't even know we exist or that anything else does."

"Sir, all this sounds completely weird to me. Could you help me understand?"

"Most probably it feels strange because, unlike me, you cannot rely on your consciousness to approach this issue. I don't know what goes on the mind of this guy crossing the road or that lady driving her bike, but I can most likely make a good guess, by extrapolating what my own consciousness would do. I need to give you though, some plausible explanation on how my brain constructs my mind's inner world and makes it conscious. Without this, I won't convince you or anybody else, that ASI will ever happen."

At that moment, my stomach started gurgling, and I realized I was hungry. "I'm starving. Please drive to my usual bakery. It makes fantastic sandwiches."

The car dropped me off a few minutes later to enjoy my lunch and parked a few hundred meters away. After a thirty-minute break, I called it back, and it greeted me with a surprising question.

"Sir, how did you suddenly become aware that you were hungry?"

"I got a strong signal from my body, that it was time to enjoy a good meal. My stomach's noise made me suddenly realized that I didn't have breakfast. Actually, the notion of a moment in time is essential, if you want to understand what consciousness is. We've seen that knowledge is a process that mainly happens in the past, while intelligence is a time continuum, which contemplates the past, present, and future. Consciousness, on the other hand, integrates mainly the present, that is, the moment at which the Self comes to mind."

"Sir, are you saying that the Self is generated almost instantaneously?"

"Yes, but I'll portray it as relying on three basic implementing steps. Firstly, primordial feelings, that is, feelings of pain and pleasure from which all other emotions can emanate, spring naturally from what Antonio Damasio [171] describes as the 'Protoself.' Then comes the 'Core Self' that brings to mind a series of images describing Objects, which engages this Protoself and, through this process, modifies it. Lastly, there is what Damasio calls the 'Autobiographical Self,' which brings in the notion of biographical knowledge."

"Sir, aren't you implying that though consciousness is felt in the instantaneity of the moment, it also includes past and future information?"

"Yes, it includes past information about one's self and Objects, as well as information on how I am projecting myself in an anticipated future."

"Sir, may I ask you to give me an example to help me understand better?"

"Of course! At the risk of oversimplifying things, let me use what just happened to me, to describe this process. The primordial feeling of hunger with the expected associated satisfaction that eating food provides, projected in my mind the image of the sandwich Object. This image reminded me suddenly at that moment of this Italian bakery, which is one of my favorites because the food is good and the ambiance great. In other words, it was compatible with my lifestyle and how I like to picture myself."

With this simplistic example, I decided to stop the discussion on consciousness and come back to emotions. Indeed, I wanted to show that the decision to draw the line between AGI and ASI at emotions, is more than just arbitrary.

18) Why do humans experience emotions and feelings?

My car must have felt the same way because its next question was about how emotions affected our thoughts. **"Sir, you've already introduced the concept of Population Coding. Is there also an emotional code and where would it fit in this process?"**

"Let's use an example to introduce the issues raised by your question. Low-level features, such as the dimension of an Object, would be coded in the visual cortex. High-level ones, such as Object categories, would be coded in the ventral temporal cortex."

"Sir, using your example, is there an intermediary coding specific to emotions?"

"In other words, you are asking if external sensory inputs are colored, as Wilhelm Wundt would argue,[172] by internal affects or are they exclusively objective. In this latter case, they wouldn't be integrated between the bottom-up and top-down processes, linking the high and low-level features of my example."

"Sir, you've reformulated my question very well!"

"Thanks. In a recent study,[173] the neuroscientist Adam Anderson and his team, found that emotional coding is distinct from any other neural coding representing Objects, in two fundamental ways. All neurons, localized in the orbitofrontal cortex, reacted the same way, independently from the involved sense. These neurons showed the same patterns of firing, which are influenced by the valence (i.e., amount of pleasure and displeasure) of the sensed Objects. Secondly, using big data techniques, they identified that all humans share the same patterns, whenever the valence is identical."

"Sir, from your study I probably should conclude that emotions color human beings' world, but it's not clear to me. Could you give me a more comprehensible example?"

"If I go back to wine tasting, whenever my wife and I, would drink red wine, we would share the same neural patterns, as we both like a good red Burgundy or Bordeaux. However, we would show different valences in case of sweet white wine, that I like, but that my wife doesn't. Consequently, we would experience different neural patterns."

"Sir, what does Anderson's study confirm then?"

"That though feelings are personal and subjective, in the sense that we all have our pleasures and dislikes, the human brain uses a universal standard code, which integrates emotions across all senses and situations, interfering with our perceptual process. This finding means that Wundt was right in claiming that our emotions taint all external sensory inputs."

What are primordial feelings?

"Sir, could you explain to me that don't possess such faculties, what are the differences between emotions and feelings?"

"I would love to, but the reality is that there is no agreement between specialists on what the exact meaning of emotions and feelings is and hence, people interchange these concepts all the time. It is why, rather than focusing on words that express these bodily and mental states, I'd rather ground my reasoning on separate anatomical regions in which they originate, with their functional differences. Let's start with what Antonio Damasio calls the primordial feelings that are, according to him, crucial in the self-awareness process."

"Sir, sorry to interrupt, but are they identical to the emotions linked to neurons firing in the orbitofrontal cortex?"

"No, they're not. Those emotions are associated with what Damasio calls Qualia I, which are better described as mental issues, for relating to the sensory interpretation process of Objects, with their associated valences. Those emotions are in line with the Anderson study."

"Sir, what are then these primordial feelings?"

"Damasio suggests that they are the by-products of body maps, that is, the neural doubling of each and every body part. He identifies their physiological origin to the stem.[a] "

"Sir, how does he defined them?"

"Interestingly enough, he defines the primordial feelings as also having a valence, somewhere along the pleasure-to-pain line. For him,

---

[a] This stem is associated with the reptilian brain, the oldest part of the human brain, which controls the vital body functions. Talking about the upper-brain stem nuclei, Damasio asserts that 'in all likelihood, this is the place where the process of making mind begins, in the form of primordial feelings, and it is apparent that the process that makes the conscious mind a reality, the self, also originates here.'

these primordial feelings are some kind of primitives of what we humans call emotions, feelings, moods, etc. and precede any other mental state."

"Sir, what do you include among these mind states?"

"We may include this sentiment that our personal body exists independently from its environment, but at the same time is the basis for any other mood, emerging from the interaction between Objects in this environment and our body. In other words, primordial feelings position the Self in regards to the dimension of space and time. As they are associated with my body maps, they kind of control my inner states."

What are the differences between emotions and feelings?

"Sir, could you describe what you humans call sentiments?"

"For terminology coherence purposes, let me use Damasio's description of emotions and feelings, even though this terminology per se doesn't matter, as long as it fully describes these two different states. Emotions are actions carried on largely in the human body, which have been shaped by our survival instinct, in order to react to threats or potential rewards in our environment.[a] "

"So Sir, emotions are somehow embedded in your genes and use the universal standard distribution coding described by Anderson's team?"

"Yes, and some ideas, thoughts, and planning come to our mind that we associate with these emotions. All these responses are what we associate with an emotional state."

---

[a] Emotions emerge when prediction errors, resulting from external sensory inputs, trigger processes in specific region of the mammalian brain, which induce biochemical reactions, such as the emission of neurotransmitters. These regions are the amygdalae and the ventromedial prefrontal cortices, anatomically synonymous with the orbitofrontal cortex identified by Anderson. As a consequence of such secretion (e.g., cortisol molecules for emotions of fear), some voluntary or unintentional actions are taken (for instance in the case of fear, fleeing and gut contraction), as well as some physical reactions are generated that can be observed (e.g., blood flow changes, facial expressions, and body language).

"Sir, what about feelings?"

"They happen after the emotions, as they are a by-product (i.e., a reaction) of the brain interpreting these emotions and giving them meaning. We can best describe feelings as images of these actions. Consequently, they are the equivalent of perception for the external world, that is, interoception or internal perception of what our body and state of mind do during this emotional process."

"Sir, what do they involve?"

"Feelings involve a cognitive process with thoughts, beliefs, memories, and images subconsciously bound by these emotions. Consequently, feelings are biased, unique to a person and evolve throughout our lifetime according to our experience.[a] Though I indicated that emotions originate first, I must add that often, the mere fact of thinking about a feeling, can generate an emotion (e.g., thirst in the desert generating despair)."

What are qualia?

"Sir, you already mentioned qualia previously. What are they?"

"Qualia is a kind of basket terminology that includes all that we associate with subjective experience. It may include perceived impressions (e.g., colors, sounds, etc.), bodily sensations (e.g., pain, body-heat, dizziness, etc.), emotions (love, anger, lust, hatred, etc.), felt moods (euphoria, calm, anxiety, etc.) and all other words attached at describing such experience. Some philosophers also include propositional attitudes (e.g., feeling happy to win the lottery) and the desire to do something (e.g., I want to play tennis).[174] "

"Sir, how is it to feel pain?"

"Your question can be extended to all Qualia. Why do I feel

---

[a] Damasio concludes that feelings originate in the two image-making part of the brain: the upper brain stem (for primordial feelings) and the cerebral cortex. More specifically, he situates other feelings' origin in the insular anterior cingulate cortices, two highly interconnected regions, which act in parallel. Furthermore, he highlights the key role played by some specific sub-cortical regions (i.e., tractus solitaries and parabrachial nucleus) in building up feeling states, as they integrate signals from the entire internal body. Lastly, these brain regions involved in body map generation, which support these feelings, are included in a loop with the own source of the signals they are mapping.

something and not nothing? I'm only able to answer by analogy (e.g., it hurts, aches, hitches, or burns), which is probably meaningless for you. So rather than answering how, I'll try to define why we feel qualia. A down to earth answer would be that feelings, which are life-threatening or enhancing, ought to feel something so that all our attention be focused on them."

"Sir, are feelings found in all organisms?"

"Yes, in particular, pain and pleasure are feelings that organisms, with or even without a nervous system, must have had very early on in the evolutionary chain. The process, by which a brain creates this sensation of pain to direct our attention to a specific body part, is called nociception.[a] "

"Sir, so far you've explained the why not the how."

"Give me a chance to explicit Damasio's point of view. He comes up with an interesting answer, with what he calls Qualia II. He hypothesizes that the neurons responsible for mapping our bodily and mental states, actually enact a functional fusion of these two states, which become one. As a consequence, the neurons responsible for transporting the body's internal signals become an extension of the flesh they are mapping and therefore, would generate the feelings we associate, for instance, with pain."

"Sir, how does Damasio come up with such a proposal?"

"Damasio suggests that neurons like all unicellular organisms could react to external actions, such as when we poke them. A common reaction of a large circuit of neurons could generate according to him,[b] what we associate with these feelings.[c] "

---

[a] Neuroceptors (i.e., chemical, mechanical, or thermal receptors) situated at the end of a neuron's axon would be sending signal of potential threats to the spinal cord and the brain.

[b] As well as other neuroscientists, such as Rodolfo Llinas.[N137]

[c] Axons travelling to and from internal organs are mainly unmyelinated, and consequently more porous to their internal environment, as well as capable of sensing chemical changes. These properties could also explain why we have feelings.[N138]

What's the role of small agents in a multi-cellular organism?

"Sir, are you suggesting that your neurons are small agents, which life influences your mind and body directly?"

"The thought that I might not just be a singular entity, resulting from the interactions between my unique body and mind, but rather a multicellular organism, is disconcerting. Even if I prefer to avoid thinking about myself as a multicellular organism, the truth is that my skin constitutes an envelope under which, trillions of cells live their own life.[a]"

"Sir, if you picture yourself as a multicellular system, then what is the main difference between these early free-living organisms and their descendants in your body?"

"Domestication! My cells' destiny, unlike the fate of their free-swimming ancestors, doesn't only depend on them. Their survival and consequently mine is tributary on how well they operate together.[b] The point is that all my cells still need to fend for themselves, in my body. Though they don't have a sophisticated mind of their own, all my domesticated cells, like their free-living cousins, must have maintained some kind of propensity to stay alive, as long as the genes within them order them to do so."

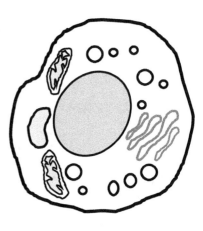

Fig. 46) The eukaryote cell at the origin of humans; source: author.

"Sir, aren't all your cells slaves, like my transistors, which sole purpose is to open and close gates?"

---

[a] Interestingly, if we were to trace back the origin of all human cells, we would come up with some kind of eukaryotic cells about 1.5 billion years ago, as a common ancestor.[N139] To get an idea of what these eukaryotic cells would look like, one just needs to picture today's amoeba. They wouldn't be much different.

[b] From an evolutionary perspective, this symbiosis unleashed the power of specialization so that the overall performance of their resulting multicellular system, could perform better in its own environment. Darwin's selection theory implies thus, a multi-dimensional adaptation (e.g., genes, neurons, mini-columns, cortical, brain, and species) interplaying at the morphological and system levels. Though the effects of selection forces can only be seen, in the long run, through anatomical and functional specialization, it is erroneous to believe that cellular collaboration forbids individual competition.

"Maybe and maybe not. I agree that many of my cells are programmed to commit suicide to protect my body from intruders such as bacteria or to reconstruct some damaged areas. However, by committing suicide, they ensure altruistically that through my children, their own DNA can be transmitted to the future generations, through similar replacing cells. In other words, many of my cells don't have a say in how they die, but this doesn't mean, as long as they live, that they aren't striving to stay healthy."

"Sir, you already introduced me to this view promoted by Daniel Dennett.[175] Could you be more explicit?"

"This theory, called the selfish neuron, speculates that in some unknown ways, our neurons have kept some properties of their feral state. Dennett articulates that neurons might have kept some sort of 'risk-taking' capacity, [176] which would imply some competition between individual neurons. Therefore there would be room for cooperation, involving culture in the process.[a]"

"Sir, are you going to debate the role played by culture, as he does?"

"No, but what I find interesting with his view, is that he adopts a competitive model, where the small agents fight to get their energy (i.e., lactate and glucose) by creating alliances with neighboring neurons, and avoid by the same token, being pruned. The way they owe their energy and thus stay alive, is by connecting."

"Sir, is there any proof of that concept?"

"It would explain why some neurons change their role completely if the functionality they are involved in, is eliminated. For instance,[177] [178] if I blindfold myself, I would find out that my visual cortex starts getting adapted for Braille reading after a few months, that is, reconfiguring itself for the sense of touch.[b] In other words, there would be several networks of collaborative agents playing at different levels, constituting by their active role, the mind of a person. From this, Dennett argues that consciousness results from the competitive forces of these neural agents."

---

[a] 'We got risky brains that are much riskier than the brains of other mammals, even more risky than the brains of chimpanzees, and that this could be partly a matter of a few simple mutations in control genes that release some of the innate competitive talent that is still there in the genomes of the individual neurons. But I don't think that genetics is the level to explain this. You need culture to explain it.'

[b] If true and to the point of this experimentation, this selfish neuron speculation would also imply that the micro-columns and columns they constitute through connections, would compete for connections, creating a homunculus functionalist view of our brain.

"Sir, wouldn't it mean that humans have the illusion of free will?"

"Your question about free will is interesting. There are several science-fiction series portraying aliens taking over our mind, or demons possessing us. None have yet shown neurons' insurrection against our bodily envelope, unless we call illusion such capacity. However, in nature, this brain hijacking happens. An interesting example is the horsehair worm that invades species of crickets. [179] "

Horsehair worm eggs hatch in American rivers and the resulting larvae wait to be eaten by other larvae of insects such as mosquitoes. After metamorphosing and living an aerial life, these mosquitoes and their horsehair larva parasite, are snatched up by crickets. Once in the cricket, it penetrates through the gut and gets into the body cavity. After developing for several months and growing up to 30cm or more, sucking in food from its host, the worm takes over the cricket's mind by producing large amount of neurotransmitters. These neurotransmitters interact with the cricket's brain and forces it to display behaviors that no normal cricket would show. When the horsehair is ready to leave its zombie-like cricket, it kind of forces its host to find a water font and, though normal crickets would avoid water, induces it to jump in the water (by making it attracted to light that mirrors on the water surface). At the moment the cricket touches the surface, the worm, observing its environment through a bored hole, gets out of its host. The horsehair worm then swims to find a mate, in order to restart the cycle.

"Sir, this example is quite interesting because it shows that a smaller creature can take possession of the brain of a bigger one. However, it doesn't completely answer my question about the illusion of free will. Is your inner voice, that is, what you associate with the Self, an expression of the collective wills of smaller agents, which forces play the same role as the horsehair worm at different levels (e.g., genes, neurons, mini-columns, columns, cortex and even emotions), or is your mind something different and therefore independent?"

"I won't answer your question about free will now because I would need to enter other concepts such as Determinism. Furthermore, I want to refocus on emotions and explain why in my opinion it draws the line between AGI and ASI. However, don't forget to remind me of the Libet experiment implications."

19) Will emotions ever be computable?

"Sir you've already told me why we, machines, couldn't experience all human emotions, but what does it have to do with ASI?"

"At the risk of repeating myself, a lot of our emotions are linked to our biological nature. Reproduction, digestion (and its billions of bacteria playing a useful role in our guts), the conditions of our body states, and our understanding of the finitude of our lives, are all elements that influence our qualia. Consequently, many of these qualia will never really be experienced by a machine, because it doesn't make sense to create such qualia."

"Why so, Sir?"

"Because it won't make economic sense to do so. Manufacturers won't build machines with the urge to reproduce. You robots don't need to transfer your chromosomes to the next generations because you aren't biologically built and don't need to grow within the wombs of a female machine. This simple fact will affect many possible qualia, such as love, jealousy, mother feeling and other emotions affected by our hormones. So if machines won't have the same emotions, or experienced them in a completely different way (e.g., rather than eating, the need for powering up), it means that humans and machines won't ever really experience the same things."

"Sir, why is that so important for ASI?"

"My point is that the idea of making decisions without having some emotions involved is misguided. Emotions are often the driving force behind our conscious and unconscious motivations or behaviors. Furthermore, I already showed that emotions taint all our perception and that primordial feelings are constantly there within our Self, even if we are not aware of them. It means that machines without emotions will make different decisions than humans, that is, necessarily think and behave differently."

"Sir, does it implies that some kind of program will need to compensate for this lack of emotions to create long-term motivational behaviors?"

"Yes, it does. We humans can make some seemingly rational decisions at the moment, but in the long run, we follow our individual goals, which are highly influenced by our human needs. If I make a reference to Maslow's hierarchy of needs, [180] which describes five layers – physiological, safety, love/belonging, esteem, and self-activation –,[a] I cannot abstract myself from the reality that emotions and feelings are at the root of those needs."

"Sir, could you detail your reference to Maslow's five level of needs?"

"The fact that I don't want to feel hunger or in danger but want to be loved and esteemed, as well as fulfill my life, gives me a set of rules and goals on which I can base my decisions. These decisions may be positive or negative, depending on the situation and the emotions involved, but will nevertheless influence my set of actions."

"What's your point, Sir?"

"It goes back to my point about free will and how our life flows from one decision to another, setting the course of our actions and destiny. A machine without emotions would lack initiative. To use an image, a machine would be able to answer questions but wouldn't spontaneously enter into a conversation, because it would lack the purpose to do it."

"Sir, could you ever program this purpose?"

"Such program, if it were to exist, would need necessarily to consider two opposing forces, like pain and pleasure for humans."

"However Sir, would an optimization program solely integrating penalty and rewards be sufficient?"

"You could say that for millions of unicellular cells, it surely works. The environmental pressure of what we could call Darwin's natural selection ensures that only the strongest creatures pass on their genes and at the same time, set the parameters ruling this environment."

Why is homeostasis so essential to understand?

"But Sir, humans are too intelligent to follow only an optimization program, and thus, machines wouldn't achieve ASI with such limited properties. Wouldn't you agree that they would need a different program?"

---

[a] Of which the first four ones must be met, for individual not to feel tensed or anxious.

"I'd rather hypothesize that their program would need additional coding lines, which we could call moral instructions, rather than changing it completely. Indeed, emotions and motivational needs give us the framework that set personal human boundaries. Our free will can try to overcome our limitations, but there must be some degree of superimposition, achieved through rules, to constrain us."

"Sir, could you give me an example of these rules?"

"In the natural habitat, the law of the strongest rules unicellular and simple multicellular organisms, imposing its toll on the weakest. For humans and a few more advanced species, this law isn't sufficient. Social rules are necessary to ensure that society or the system composed of millions of human beings, can live together. These rules or laws are based on moral principles, shaped by religion, history, culture, and legal precedents."

"Sir, I guess you won't discuss what these moral instructions should look like?"

"Of course not, as this is a completely different topic. My point is that humans live in a two-level system, which must integrate limitations and aspirations. At the personal level, these limitations and aspirations are set mainly by emotions and free will, respectively,[a] while at the social level, they are established mainly by laws and culture, respectively."

"Sir, what is required for these two systems to co-exist harmoniously?"

"There needs to be a homoeostasis, both within and between each system level. Just in case you aren't familiar with the concept of homeostasis, it describes the property of a system to actively regulate itself to remain nearly stable."

"Sir, aren't you suggesting that a robot's program would need at least to consider a system with social, person/object and body/mind homeostases, to reach ASI?"

"Put that way, it sounds a daunting task, but in fact yes, it's more or less what I imagine is necessary. Let me now put aside the social homeostasis and tackle first, the person/Object homeostasis issue. Fortunately for me, I've already described it thoroughly. It's called Free-energy. Remember, I even gave you Friston's mathematical Homeostasis (H) formula:

$$H(y) = \lim_{T \to \infty} \left(\frac{1}{T}\right) \int_0^T - \ln p(y/m) \, dt$$

---

[a] At least the mental limitations, as we are also limited by genetics and bodily conditions.

I won't present this theory again but just highlight the fact that a brain is a predictive machine, which can be mathematically linked to life and intelligence, binding these two properties together."

How is Free-energy associated with our body?

"Sir, why haven't you ever mentioned anything about Free-energy's bodily connection?"

"Firstly, the fact that we can apply it to the internal body is a new development of this theory. Secondly, you don't need these arguments to understand knowledge and intelligence, as homeostasis is better addressed through the angle of emotions and consciousness and thus, fits better in our current discussion. Lastly, it emerged from a different angle."

"Sir, which one?"

"Instead of originating in Helmholtz perception-as-inference theory, its roots can be traced back to cybernetics principles,[181] together with predictive control properties."

"Sir, what does this cybernetic origin add to Friston's Free-energy model?"

"It makes it particularly well suited for the predictive perception of internal bodily states, [182] naturally integrating emotions and providing a mechanism for explaining joint internal and external perceptions, which are at the basis of a unified experience of self-awareness.[a] "

"Sir, just to make sure I understood. The cybernetics' principle of homeostasis applied to your body and mind, increments to the Predictive Processing, the need to answer to external perturbations, to maintain its internal stability."

---

[a] Two aspects of the classical Predictive brain model are essential to capture these new developments. Sensory errors are minimized passively through increase in perceptual cues and actively through actions performed to confirm or test the sensory predictions. This process is constant and simultaneous, ensuring a continuity between perception and action in their goal of avoiding surprisals, that is, surprises in the sense of information theory. Predictive Processing involves Bayesian inference that compares prior expectations about the most likely causes of a posteriori sensed input, by using a predictive model of this sensed input, given this particular set of causes. It also means that actions are used to minimize entropy of the posterior data, that is, to provide evidence that the perceptual predictions were accurate. To this classical explanation of Predictive Processing, this new model adds the idea that actions can be selected to find evidence going against the predictions, or that will help discover which of two potential perceptual hypotheses is the most adequate.

"Yes, but there is also a second cybernetic principle. It posits that any control mechanism in charge of suppressing these external perturbations must integrate a model of that system,[183] connecting once again with the Free-energy theory.[a] In summary, it parallels the Free-energy principle, which aims first and foremost at maintaining the survival of the organism.[184] "

"Sir, in a system like the human body, how is this long-term survival best ensured?"

"It is best achieved, by inducing the most predictive model of the causes of interoceptive, exteroceptive, and proprioceptive (i.e., internal, external, and body movement) sensory inputs. It requires disambiguating active inference, to test the latest accurate predictive model systematically."

"Sir, could you give me an example?"

"If I am feeling hot, sweating, and having muscular spasms, I need to understand if these conditions are due to the weather, playing tennis or body fever. To disambiguate my model, I could, for instance, take a thermometer and measure my temperature."

"Sir, how do emotional states tie in with Free-energy and Predictive Processing?"

"Quite the same way as for external perceptions. They emerge from a top-down predictive inference of the causes of, in this case, internal sensory inputs."

"Sir, how are interoceptive prediction errors dealt with?"

"Similarly, they are minimized by updating the predictive models (e.g., when I feel hunger), changing these interoceptive inputs. It is achieved by engaging autonomic controls (e.g., using my body fat) or performing behaviors (e.g., eating my sandwich), which alter external conditions impacting on the internal emotional states, to come back to homeostasis (e.g., feeling sated).[b] "

---

[a] Cognition that includes perception and action, is the process by which we maintain the homeostasis of some essential variables and more generally, of our internal organization. It implies control mechanisms to suppress encountered perturbations and a control model of the system, which includes the body and its interactions with the environment.

[b] Emotions are thus explained in the Predictive Process context, as resulting from the prediction of interoceptive inputs. The emotional content is determined by our beliefs (i.e. posterior expectations) about the causes of these interoceptive inputs, across multiple hierarchical levels. Emotions translate as a process of active interoceptive inference,[N140] which happens together with an involuntary regulation of the body. These two processes influence our intuitive decisions, as we seek through our behaviors, to reach homeostasis.

"Sir, isn't this model slightly different from the one you pictured earlier, based on Damasio?"

"It doesn't include primordial feelings and is, therefore, more rational (i.e., referring mainly to the neocortex). It is also more in line with a constructivist view, that is, a subject who creates his own models from which emotions emerge, rather than seeing these emotions emerging from images of events in the environment.[a] "

"Sir, having said that, is this interoceptive inference model coherent with Damasio's view?"

"Yes, it is nevertheless coherent, especially with Damasio's decision-making framework called the 'somatic marker hypothesis.'[171] "

"Sir, what is this hypothesis?"

"It's a framework in which our material Self, is not only formed by our body and mind but also by the collection of Objects (e.g., family members, friends, and belongings) we associate with our Self.[b] "

"Sir, what do these somatic markers do?"

"When integrated within the context of interoceptive inference, tied to Predictive Processing, these somatic markers guide our behaviors to achieve homeostasis, by solving interoceptive prediction errors. The level of accuracy that we maintain of our predictive models, of these interoceptive states, directly influences our decisions."

"Sir, is there any study confirming this interoceptive inference theory?"

"Not clinical yet, but many logical explanations could relate to emotional, decision-making, and self-awareness pathologies, originating from problems linked to interoceptive prediction errors. I could enumerate problems due to a lack of suppression, low precision, dysfunctional active inference, and even faulty prediction encoding,

---

[a] The deep generative models, associated with the interoceptive inference theory, can be better understood as geared towards control and regulation of physiological variables, rather than towards prediction of the Objects in this world.[N141] With such theory, our cognitive processes may be seen as grounded in the fundamental evolutionary imperatives to maintain physiological homeostasis of our body and mind.

[b] This hypothesis is in coherence with the psychologist William James,[N142] who includes in this collection 'Personal Objects' such as spouse, children, ancestors, house, clothes, cars, etc. Any perception of these 'Personal Objects' generates emotions and feelings, and it is those feelings that operate a clear separation between contents belonging to our material self and those that do not. Damasio calls those feelings, somatic markers because whenever 'Personal Objects' enters our mind's stream, these markers appear and are inserted within the image which prompted it, giving us the feeling of already knowing.

which could explain heavy mental deficiencies, such as autism. [185] "

"Sir, if Predictive Processing can explain how a brain works, with no direct access to the causal structure in the internal and external world, could it also explain the integration of Self-representations?"

"In fact, there is a theory on self-awareness,[182] that is, on the experience of my mind and its body, based on Predictive Processing."

"Sir, how does it picture the brain?"

"As guessing that the causes of sensory signals are related to 'my Self,' across the perception spectrum of internal, external, and of body movements domains.[a] If I go back to cybernetics, an embodied Self can be portrayed as a system, which homeostasis must be maintained, taking into account a series of interactions between external, internal, and bodily movement perceptual inputs, that together regulate this homeostasis."

"Sir, if cybernetics is at the source of such homeostasis theory, am I right to understand that robots or moveable artificial systems could also include mechanisms underlying emotions, perception, and self-awareness?"

"Let me break down your question in sub-topics. I've already shown that machines with strong AI will be able to deal with sensory inputs, even though the perception related to these inputs is always subjective in humans. I've also started tackling the issue about emotions, though I must explain if emotional computing will ever exist. Before answering if machines will ever possess the mental state of self-awareness, I need to define consciousness better. Last but not least, I'll need to convince you that these mechanisms can be integrated within a general operative framework, which would generate ASI."

"Sir, what is emotional computing?"

"It is the discipline of integrating emotional aspects into machines. It is today merely associated with programming."

"Sir, would anything in the long term, forbid the creation of hardware that would trigger emotions?"

"No, robot manufacturers could mimic body parts like our vagus nerve, which links our stomach to our brain, and chemicals like

---

[a] This theory is corroborated by studies showing correlations between internal (e.g., cardiac input) and external (e.g., visual cues) perceptual inputs, leading to the updating of predictive models of self-related signals, through prediction error minimization.[N143] Therefore, these studies confirm the likelihood of a common predictive mechanism, underlying emotions, perception, and self-awareness.

neurotransmitters or hormones that regulate our organism, if it made economic sense. However, I should be more precise and tell you that emotional computing focuses mainly on understanding humans' emotional states."

"Sir, how are human emotional states accounted for?"

"Emotional computing does that by interpreting our behaviors. It assesses the physical representations of these emotions through video analytics of body language or facial expressions, as well as through sound analytics of voice pitch and tone.[a] "

"Sir, is there any specific initiative? If so, how good are we machines at understanding human behaviors?"

"The better-known initiative is called Emotion Markup Language and is behind the emotional computing movement. It promotes the idea that, rather than having people adapt to machines, it should be possible to do the opposite. This technology enables cyber detection as good as that of an average human being."

"Aren't you concerned Sir?"

"Of course I am worried. We should all realize, as concerned citizens, that by building machines better than humans at interpreting our own behaviors, we are generating a risk that those higher faculties may be used by repressive forces, in a big brother society."

Are non-biological emotions computable?

"Sir, what about my own emotions? Will I, or newer generations of me, ever feel anything?"

---

[a] Video analytic software works on interpreting facial expressions or body language to establish the underlying emotions. Similarly, sound recognition will detect patterns in our voice pitch or tone. We could even imagine electronic noses to smell our body chemistry, to detect, for instance, anxiety or hormonal flow. A lot of money is invested in these software technologies because they will improve the experience with automated help desks and help increase sales. However, we shouldn't underestimate the difficulty of interpreting these physical reactions, as for instance there are up to 10.000 different facial expressions to identify in real time. Despite the challenges, software often emanating from lie detector technology, is already providing accuracy level in interpretation, superior to human beings' capacity. Just to show you how much efforts are put on these technologies, the World Wide Web association is already formalizing emotions in a way computers can understand, under the specification called Emotion Markup Language.[N144]

"At the risk of repeating myself, machines won't experience any emotion originating from specific human body characteristics, such as the need to sleep, eat, drink, have sex, etc., unless we implant such simulation. Additionally, you won't ever experience the many emotional states linked to reproduction and growing older, unless we integrate some kind of artificial hormones."

"Sir, I know you said you didn't see the point in doing this from a marketing perspective."

"Yes, and thus I don't believe that even if it were possible, it would ever happen. If machines will never experience emotions that are biological in their nature, then the consequence is that they aren't likely to experience their emotional physical correlate, that is, feelings."

"Sir, is there a reason why emotions, which are non-biological in their nature, couldn't be experienced by an artificial intelligence?"

"You are asking me if states, such as – happiness/sadness, contentment/disappointment, satisfaction/resentment, relaxation/anger, confidence/fear, empathy/antipathy, expecting something or being surprised, etc. – could be coded?"

"Sir, you purposely associated positive and negative valences of the same emotional states. What else could you add to these states?"

"I could probably add to this list of non-biological states, appreciation of beauty or art, and even non-human emotions, such as – the need to energize, the experience of physically or wirelessly connecting to a network, and the capacity to bound mentally with other independent machines' mind –."

"Sir, don't you think the important question for robot manufacturers will be if customers want their products ever to experience these emotions or just want them to be sensitive to their own human emotions?"

"Indeed! After all, it's the clients' own emotional responses to a machine's actions that are likely to make this emotion real, just as a pet owner makes his cat's love real."

"Sir, how would you code these non-biological emotions?"

"Though such coding techniques are at their very early stage, it is most likely that these machines would need the ability to learn all by themselves, and would necessarily involve unsupervised programming."

"Sir, do you know of any project working on this?"

"One path currently followed by a Russian project is to create a machine that would think in terms of scenario, a little like an actor would. In fact, the name given to the project is 'virtual actor.' From what I could read, it seems that this machine would need to set its own learning goals, formulate questions to achieve the set goals, and seek the answers actively."

"Sir, that doesn't sound very emotional!"

"Yes, it sounds more like motivational programming, which is more in tune with AGI than ASI. The difficulty with implementing non-biological emotions, which are more than just goals, is to integrate the notion of emotional valence, associated with any specific action."

"Sir, what would be the starting point of a machine?"

"There is no easy answer to your question. My appreciation of an action and its positive or negative assessment is the result of my personal experience and the impact of my social or cultural background on this experience. For instance, my dislike for tomatoes doesn't seem a priori rational but would probably be, if I could go through the entire series of events, which since my childhood made me reject this taste."

"Sir, what's your point?"

"I believe there is a need for a starting point in any situational assessment, which for humans is not only social but highly tainted by our bodily and genetic responses, and consequently unique. Mass produced robots, on the contrary, would necessarily have a standardized start, and though they could evolve differently in an uncontrolled environment, such as in human society, valences would probably stay the same for quite a time."

"Sir, don't you believe robot manufacturers will want to maintain uniformed valences?"

"Most probably, they will, to reduce the risk of seeing one of their product developing some kind of deviances, like getting pleasure from inflicting pain."

"Sir, how can set goals, help coding emotions?"

"The mere fact of setting myself goals generates a threshold, which may easily trigger an 'emotional answer' of contentment or disappointment. It will depend on which part of the valence spectrum the assessment falls. For instance, if I am expecting to win a tennis game against a lower rank player, but lose, I'll feel disappointed. Playing the same player with an injury might set an entirely different expectation and with the same lost, wouldn't generate a disappointment at all."

"Sir, how does time impact these emotions?"

"With time, someone experiencing a long series of contentment or disappointments could feel new emotional states (e.g., happiness/sadness).[a] In other words, with the dimension of time, an unsupervised program could probably generate non-biological emotions. These emotions would be genuine, in regards to the set goals resulting from the moral values, which would have been embedded by the manufacturer."

Fig. 47) Will robots ever feel emotions?

---

[a] If we were to embed within a robot the goal that it must make humans happy, any feedback from interactions with humans would generate an assessment and a resulting valence. A human smile, could be assessed as a positive valence, making a robot somehow happy. Several smiles coming systematically from the same person could maybe generate in the long run empathy towards that person, just like we tend to create positive bounds with people that give us positive feedback.

20) Will machines ever become self-aware?

"Sir, many movies and books picture a system or a robot suddenly becoming self-aware. Will I ever become conscious, like the 'Terminator' robot?"

"To answer your question, I must first define what self-awareness is. However, there is still no unified theoretical model, satisfying philosophers, psychologists, and scientists alike, which can convincingly explain the reasons why humans are conscious."

"Sir, is it why it is called the 'hard problem'?"

"I believe it is a difficult problem, already partially solved. To show you how, I'll avoid explaining, from the start, why self-awareness can emerge from the brain. Instead, I'll focus on identifying the key features of these states and answer what the physical mechanisms that could account for self-awareness are."

"Sir, how may you ground your explanation?"

"I'll use a model, which can be applied to the 'why.' The remaining issue is about the 'how,' for which I will introduce a few approaches. Finally, I'll try to describe how the 'why' and 'how' models may be linked together. With this done, I shall come back to your doubts about if machines will one day be conscious."

"Sir, how can you be sure about your answers?"

"I'm not, but if I may prove that consciousness is related to biological states, then most likely ASI will never really be possible, unless we create robots physiologically similar to human beings or if artificial consciousness takes on a completely alien form. On the other hand, if consciousness can be related to mental states, then there is a likelihood that machines may become one day self-aware, without having to build a replica of the human flesh."

"Sir, the problem you may have to deal with, is if consciousness is not a single thing?"

"You are right. Though for humans it feels that way, self-awareness isn't a single property. Consequently, I might end up with some forms of consciousness, linked to mental representations, being possible to replicate in machines but not other forms."

"Sir, you use indifferently, the words self-awareness, consciousness, the Self, and awareness. It's confusing!"

"You're right. Terminology is a limiting factor in all discussions on consciousness. I might either create new words (e.g., the 'proto-self' created by Damasio) or define precisely what I intend with a specific word, knowing that people may use this word, with an entirely different meaning. One of these subjective distinctions I would like to make is between awareness, self-awareness, and consciousness."

"Sir, what are the restrictions you would like to make?"

"I'll use the term awareness to represent the fact that something outside of my body (i.e., Object) or some internal processes (e.g., noise or acidity in my stomach) triggered my attention, either through the external or internal perceptual processes. Self-awareness will be used to describe the mental state associated with the fact of being aware of being alive, and having a body and mind."

"Sir, in which context will you use the word consciousness?"

"I'll employ it in the context of describing the brain's mental activity. It means that I'll restrict its usage to a context of being conscious in opposition to be unconscious and will also introduce the concept of sub-consciousness within this limited context."

"Sir, when you said there are various types of consciousness, what were you referring to?"

"To self-awareness and to the fact that if there were only one such mental state, it would mean that a newborn would have access from birth, to all of the same 'self-awareness' mental states it would have at adulthood. You probably know that isn't the case. The fact that a baby's level of self-awareness is quite limited and grows with time, clearly indicates that some of these mental states are learned."

"Sir, the correlated questions to your affirmation is how much self-aware a baby at birth is, how much more self-aware does it become, and how do these new mental states happen?"

"Your comment is fine and let me first start answering your questions by explaining the 'why' model, within the context of self-awareness."

Is there a universal model of why we are self-aware?

"Sir, I've got the intuition you will talk again about free energy. Am I right?"

"I've already highlighted how the Free-energy model, with its interoceptive inference theory, can naturally integrate emotions.

Consequently, it provides a mechanism for explaining joint internal, external, and body movement perceptions, which are at the basis of a unified experience of self-awareness."

"Sir, you have also shown that whenever applying homeostasis to a system like the human body, long-term survival is best ensured by inducing the most predictive model of these sensory inputs."

"Yes, and in order to do that, we disambiguate these inputs by actively inferring with the world. By the same token, we test our latest accurate predictive model systematically."

"Sir, once again could you use an example, to explicit your view?"

"If I go back to my example of the blue nose cat, after unsuccessfully trying to get more perceptual cues, my daughter would go and touch this cat and see if it's stuffed or has paint on its nose."

"Sir, why would your daughter do that?"

"Because these two gestures would be the most disambiguating actions she probably could imagine to perform. If either actions were unsuccessful, an alternative action would be for her to search on the internet for any other blue nose cat picture or for a cat disease, which potentially could explain such color. In the last resort, she would need to change her predictive model of cats."

"Sir, why wouldn't she change her model of a cat from the start? Is it so difficult for humans to change any theory, argument, or idea?"

"I could extend your question to why do we suddenly have an idea in our head and which mechanism deals with it? In fact, why do we intuitively believe that some ideas are genuinely right while showing others skepticism?"

"Are you asking me, Sir? I don't know why, but I guess you know the answers."

"Kant's constructivist view of the world can be extended to ideas and theories in our head. We also construct models of these ideas and theories, [186] which explains why we test ideas and theories. Whenever we find one, which is coherent with our explicit prior convictions, that is, whenever it is in line with our general model of the world shaped by the knowledge acquisition process, it automatically feels right. Intuitiveness is thus some kind of goodness of fit,[187] about a pre-existing model of reality."

"Sir, how does this view integrate with the Free-energy model?"

"If we go back to the principle of homeostasis, any new idea that would feel counter-intuitively plausible would require a lot of free energy to analyze and permanently integrate within pre-existing models of reality.[188] It would be costly energy-wise, as it contradicts our functional coherence and internal, stable states."

"Please provide me with an example, Sir."

"For instance, the idea that an animal could have a blue nose would require that all my daughter's models about noses, and per extension faces and bodies, integrate the color blue within their ontology.[a] If I consider that a brain searches to reduce entropy (i.e., variational free energy), any additional perceptual cue or action that could explain away a faked blue nose cat will be savvier free energy-wise, than having to change most of her inner models, especially if adding complexity to these models."

"You are right Sir. I didn't forget that complexity is one key aspect of variational free energy, accuracy being the other one."

"You never do! Anyhow, any process which could minimize this representational complexity wouldn't be restricted, so much, by some kind of abstract rationality, as per the joint metabolic optimization and statistical efficiency, as proposed by the Free-energy theory."

What is the role of recognition in self-awareness?

"Sir, if instead of a blue nose cat it was a blue nose woman, would your daughter still act the same way?"

"This is a very pertinent question. Do we interpret Objects differently when these Objects are men or women? Strangely, the answer is yes we do, because human beings involve specific cells, called mirror neurons. As their name says, these neurons are involved in recognition."

"Sir, what is so remarkable about these mirror neurons?"

"Experiments on macaques show that a mirror neuron not only fires when a subject executes an action but also when it observes other macaques executing the same action. Consequently, and by extension to humans (mirror neurons were also found in humans,[189] but not in the

---

[a] I.e., set of things we believe exist or is assumed by this idea or theory.

same cerebral regions), many scientists have pictured them as the potential neural substrate underlying human's capacity to understand other people's intentions and motoric actions.[a] "

"Sir, are these neurons involved in other specific human abilities?"

"Yes, some neuroscientists believe that these special neurons may be involved in many specific capacities,[190] such as empathy, learning through imitation, and even transmission of culture.[191] When considering additionally the fact that the brain uses a universal standard code, representing emotions across all senses and situations, some neuroscientists even suggest that we can experience our own emotions (e.g., happiness, fear, or anger), as well as that of others, thanks in great part to these mirror neurons."

"Sir, are you saying that when human beings see someone else being sad, their mirror neurons would be firing to allow them to experience first-hand the same sadness experience?"

"That's right and thus would enable them to feel empathy."

"Sir, do we have any idea about the mechanism involved in movement recognition?"

"I'll give you another potential explanation linked to Predictive Processing.[192] If we are able to predict the goals of a person we are observing, we should be able to predict their next move, by extrapolating what our movements should be, if we were to pursue such goals. The difference (i.e., error), between our prediction and the observed movements resulting from the other person's action, is then used to update our own original representation of the person's next move."

"Sir, what happens to the other person's inferred goals?"

"At the same time, these goals are also updated by minimizing the error between the predicted and inferred motor commands. Therefore, by minimizing errors the mirror neuron system can help us extrapolate other people's intention, motoric command, and movements."

"Sir, can you give me an example, but please not related to wine this time?"

---

[a] Though some studies have lately put in question if mirror neurons' putative faculty to mentally simulate other people's action,[N145] was a necessary condition to understand others' actions, most critics still recognize the importance of these neurons in enabling imitation of actions. In other words, and though there are probably additional ways of understanding other people's goals, mirror neurons are indubitably involved in a brain mechanism converting an observed action into muscle commands (e.g., reciprocal yawning).

"Let me take an example from sports, to illustrate how this works. When I play tennis, I am extrapolating the direction of the upcoming ball by interpreting how my opponent is positioning his body, which movement he is making with his racket, and how hard and fast he is hitting the ball. Consequently, I am able to predict if the ball will have spin, slice, curve, or come straight at me. By these gestures, I can guess my adversary's strategy (i.e., intention) of playing offensively or defensively, on my backhand or forehand. I can do all this because I can put myself 'physically' in his shoes and predict what I would have done, if confronted with the same ball."

Fig. 48) The mirror neuron system is able to help us extrapolate our tennis adversary's intention, motoric command, and movements.

"Sir, are there anatomical and neurophysiological evidence for Predictive Coding account of the Mirror Neural System?"

"Yes, but it would take too much time describing them to you. So check them out yourself, if you want.[192] "

"Sir, if true, what you just presented contradicts what you already said. Could there be no non-biological emotions?"

"Seen under this angle, you are right to ask that question. If we humans interpret all of the other human beings' emotions, through mirror or similar (e.g., von Economo)[193] neurons, then machines that will never possess such physical substrate, won't ever be able to understand other people's mental states, even if they are non-biological in theory. However, if you look carefully, this property of specific neurons, is to mirror other's mental states. Therefore, I don't believe it changes any former conclusion linked to one's own non-biological states, except maybe the possibility of experiencing compassion and empathy."

"Sir, what would be the consequence for machines?"

"They could never be able to experience empathy for humans because they wouldn't ever be able to live physiologically the same emotions of the observed person. However, nothing would forbid robots to experience these other non-biological emotions, as long as they relate to variation in valences in regards to their set goals, as previously indicated."

"Sir, if the problem of setting the original valences were solved, nothing would impede me from reading directly other robot's 'mind,' understanding physically and immediately the other machine's inner emotions."

"You're right. I need to lose my human bias. Machines could create at least empathy between themselves."

"Sir, if Predictive Coding is involved in recognition of other people's actions and potentially intentions, it would seem to me that it would reinforce its key role in self-awareness. Do you agree?"

"Yes, I do, as recognition and representation of oneself are two key components of such faculty. It is especially true for the ability to look in the mirror, to listen to a voice, and to recognize this image or sound like my own physical features or voice.[194] "

"Sir, similarly to the key role played by the mirror neural system for other people's action and intention recognition, is there a clear identification of neural circuits or mechanisms engaged during self-awareness?"

"No, there isn't. In fact, it seems increasingly likely that the Self is not a holistic property of the brain but rather arises from activities linked to specific sets of interconnected brain circuits.[195] "

"Sir, if several cortical areas are reported to participate in such process, how can you tie in everything?"

"The Free-energy principle, with its universal cognitive approach, is again the best solution to explain such process."

"Sir, if self-recognition is part of self-awareness, are those two states similar or is self-recognition one of the levels of self-awareness you mentioned?"

"It's not similar because that would mean that apes, which are able to recognize objects (e.g., fruits or themselves) through their mirror image, would be as self-aware as we humans are.[a] Having said that, in occidental

---

[a] Some people even argue that apes, which pass the mirror test (as dolphins, elephants and whales do too) aren't self-aware at all, as they recognize solely the correspondences between the reflection of an Object on the mirror's surface and this object. In other words, self-recognition doesn't necessarily entail self-awareness, as an observation doesn't necessarily imply understanding what is being sensed.

babies, self-recognition only happens at the beginning of their second year,[196] with just some demonstrations of self-concept. In other cultures, it may happen much later.[a] "

"In other words Sir, you are showing that self-awareness is culturally acquired."

"Yes, but also that Self-recognition can be associated with free energy, as the account of our body may be processed in terms of Bayesian probabilistic representation (i.e., as the most likely to be oneself)."

Can we bridge the subjectivity gap and ever understand what Batness is?

"Sir, don't you think this test is biased towards visual cues, that is, towards human self-awareness concepts?"

"You're right. Dogs, which don't pass this test, might react differently if we developed a test based on smell. Who knows, they could even show self-awareness behaviors? Your question raises the issue of what it is to be self-aware if the reality, through which an animal perceives the world, is completely different than ours. Thomas Nagel in his essay, 'what is it like to be a bat?',[197] posits that though self-aware experiences (in the sense of having conscious mental states) occur at different levels of organisms, it can only happen in animals, if there is something to be that animal."

"Sir, aren't you highlighting the subjectivity of experience?"

"Yes. If a gorilla with a red point on its forehead, positioned in front of a mirror, doesn't wipe it out immediately, it doesn't necessarily mean that it cannot recognize itself. In other words, we cannot imply that it has no self-awareness because it just doesn't have a human's mental representation."

"Sir, why did Nagel picture a bat?"

---

[a] It is only around the 20th month that babies start showing clear sign of self-recognition, at least in Western society.[N146] Mirror studies performed, with kids from other cultures or even with animals, have shown that self-awareness is a continuum highly influenced by learning and culture, or behavioral fabrics in the case of animals (e.g., gorillas hate eye contact and wipe out a red point on their forehand, outside of mirror vicinity). Furthermore, a recent study,[N147] shows evidence that this representation of the self is flexible rather than fixed.

"By using a bat, an animal that possesses a completely different mode of representation (i.e., echolocation), Nagel emphasizes that it is unlikely that we may imagine anything close to what bats can experience."

"Sir, he is basically saying that you will never really become a Batman."

"Yeah, I already had figured that out. In fact, we can't understand bats because the only way to do that is to use our own human mind, with its limited biased resources. The best we can do is to form some kind of schematic conception of what it is like to be a bat and to recognize that there are facts, which are not transposable to human language."

"Sir, are you saying that facts of experience are necessarily subjective, as they can only consider the point of view of the species?"

"Yes, achieving greater objectivity on describing a mental state, would require that we omit the specific species' viewpoints, or even when extrapolating, of the experiencer."

"If so, how may we know that an octopus is self-aware without being an octopus?"

"If we were to describe what it is for an octopus to be seeing red fishes, we could go back to energy and waves related to the red spectrum. However, we would ignore the most important element of its mental state, that is, the subjective experience, which is at the core of the octopus' internal world."

"Sir, isn't Nagel's view in contradiction with Physicalism?"

"Nagel doesn't refute Physicalism, that is, the fact that mental processes such as self-awareness, are physical processes. He argues that brain states must have a certain subjective character incomprehensible without further explanation. Therefore, it is incompatible with any theory portraying the mind-brain relation, with a cause and its distinct effect."

"Sir, do you agree with Nagel, that scientific experiments can not define bat-ness."

"I believe like Daniel Dennett does, that on the contrary,[176] bat-ness can be defined by recording and categorizing all information non-species specific. Furthermore, Dennett argues that the proof that humans cannot understand any animal-ness isn't on those who believe, like Descartes, that only humans are conscious.[15] The burden of proof relies on those, such as Nagel, who believe that there is a line that separates self-aware animals from pure mindless automata. As for me, I think we need a system which can measure the self-awareness level, but I'll come back to that."

How many levels of self-awareness are there?

"Sir, you mentioned that there are probably different states of self-awareness. What would they be?"

"While we mainly experience the uniqueness of being a Self, clinical conditions and experimental manipulations, such as virtual reality, show that there is a continuum of self-awareness states, which are partially learned. Seth and Friston rated these states from low to high levels. [198] "

"Sir, what are these states?"

"At the low end, they identified the experiences of being and having a body (i.e., embodied selfhood), of perceiving the world from a first-person perspective, as well as agency (i.e., sense of initiative). At the higher end, they included the experience of maintaining this Self over time, that is the 'narrative' Self, or what we associate with the 'I,' and which depends on our autobiographical memory. They also included the 'Social Self,' in which this 'I' is being shaped by others' perception of this 'I.' Though more exhaustive than Damasio's 'Core Self and Autobiographical Self,' these two descriptions of the Self, aren't incompatible."

"Sir, why does Free-energy integrate the Self's concept?"

"It does so because it is a direct logical consequence of homeostasis. To fight entropy, the brain must create a model of the world. This model can only be successful, that is, may disambiguate as much as possible this world, if this brain integrates its own physical body.[199] After all, we are an active player in our environment and thus, must necessarily be embedded in this world model with which we interfere."

"Sir, what are the consequences of integrating the body in our world model?"

"The brain gets access to constant interoceptive and proprioceptive inputs, linking the internal and external worlds together. This embodiment notion is central to the account of self-modeling in the Free-energy theory and explains away most of the various states of self-awareness."

"Sir, you've already thoroughly explained this theory in the context of external perception. What is its impact from a self-modeling perspective?"

"Free-energy integrates Bayesian probability, which implies that the self-model must follow the same rule. [200] Moreover, the perception of the

'I,' that is, the self-recognition (i.e., identification of my body's physical attributes, such as images and voice tones) and the self-representation (i.e., how I picture my self in my mind) are only a part of all the Objects, which are integrated by the theory."

"However Sir, is it done the same way as for any other normal Object?"

"No, these two states are processed at the highest hierarchical level of the brain. Consequently, they constitute general concepts, which generate multimodal predictions, [201] as well as, influence directly many other perceptual predictions. [202] [126] "

"Sir, what else does Predictive Coding bring to the model?"

"It embeds within this coding, the mere existence of the agent (i.e., Self) in its latest updated form. [203] [204] This is by the way, coherent with the already presented cybernetics concept that every good system regulator will become a model of that system."

"Sir, are there proofs of this probabilistic approach?"

"I'll confirm that there is compelling evidence for it.[205] However, I'll let you check these tests, which usually involve virtual reality (e.g., dummy hands and body self-appropriation)."

"Sir, what is the most important consequence of this probabilistic approach?"

"There can only be one model among all the possible perceptual models. This model is necessarily the one that generates the less free energy, which will become our embodied model of the world. It doesn't need to be true, as the faked virtual hands experiment shows, but must be true for us. In fact, it ceases to exist if a better explanation, which doesn't involve the Self, needs to be found or suddenly stops to be true for us."

"Sir, what does the interoception theory brings in the context of self-modeling?"

"It adds this subjective experience of being in my body, here and now.[a] I'd also like to stress, that by the mere fact of assigning our internal experience to our model, by some sort of introspection or thoughts, our mind gets access to the first-person perspective. It is, for instance, the thoughts I get when I close my eyes to be closed to the world's distraction and focus on what my body feels like."

---

[a] This embodied selfhood is based on the feeling states that emerge between the suppression of prediction errors and the internal perception predictions. Consequently, the interoception prediction is one of these multimodal predictions generated by the high level general concepts of the embodied self. [N148] [N149]

"Sir, how do actions and agency integrate within the Free-energy theory?"

"I've already insisted on how crucial active inference is to this theory. In order to interfere actively with my environment in the most efficient way, I need to infer what are the best actions, which can confirm my model of the world. It means that any test of my hypotheses about reality requires a sense of initiative implicitly. [204] Moreover, one of the key elements about actions, which I must highlight from a self-awareness perspective, is the need to experience the actions as my own.[206] "

"Sir, what is so fundamental about owning these actions, within this perspective?"

"Self-ownership of actions and perception, or more generally the phenomenal experience that this is my own living body, is directly associated with my embodied self (Hohwy 2007). [207] a In other words, and according to this phenomenal generative model of oneself, this self isn't perceived as an Object but as a dynamic process."

"Sir, what do you mean by dynamic process?"

"Well, for instance, I don't only see my current body and face, but also my physical transformation from childhood to maturity, as well as key moments that made me what I am today."

"Sir, does that mean that there is an observer of this process?"

"Not at all! We should see this aware Self as a consequence of the system's identification with its model of one's Self. Though I could probably develop much further on this first-person perspective, I would recommend that you check the work done by Thomas Metzinger.[208] I want to focus on modeling from a third-person perspective."

"Sir, does a third person perspective only include the viewpoint of others' own self-awareness?"

"No, and though it integrates all the same elements to make sense of others' internal states, it adds also the complexity of how we can represent our Self within a social environment."

"Sir, how can a human being identify others' internal states?"

"It's done through the mirroring process, I've already described, and through mentalization, [209] [210] that is, the process by which, one sees

---

a For Hohwy, this self-awareness emerges from successful predictions of all inputs, across the hierarchical generative model of the self. This implies that this model of the embodied self is dynamic and thus, integrates within its framework, the perspective of time and space.

herself from the outside and others from the inside. This mentalization implies that I can portray other agents independently from my own perspective and simulate others' personal Self from their viewpoint.[a] "

"Sir, aren't you painting with this vision of an 'embodied mind extension,' an emergentist view of the mind/body relation?"

"You are asking me if the brain's physical properties, as described by the Free-energy theory, give rise to mental states emerging with new properties (i.e., according to Emergentism)? It's true that I just pictured the mind as the glue interconnecting the dynamics of the body, the brain' nervous system, the environment, the Self, as well as others' Selves in this environment."

"In other words Sir, the embodiment of mind isn't described in terms of anatomy anymore, but as a consequence of the dynamic processes."

"Yes, and though this view could support a soft version of Emergentism, I don't believe it would be compatible with its more radical form called 'radically embodied mind.' In such a form, all these cognitive processes belong to the relational unit between the Self and the others.[211] Free-energy clearly describes these processes as taking place within an individual agent."

"Sir, since you mention Emergentism, what other theory does it connect to?"

"It also embeds self-awareness within Physicalism, that is, defines it as a consequence of its physical substrate. Therefore, it confirms once again that soft Emergentism is computational and that strong AI is possible.[b] "

"Sir, could you show coherences and inconsistencies with info-computational constructivism?"

---

[a] In other words, we must generate other phenomenal models of the Self in order to integrate social mental concepts.[N150] [N151] Furthermore, it is most likely that the brain applies the same model to predict one's own and others' actions, organized around four hierarchical levels: intentions, goals, kinematics, and muscles.[N152] Consequently, these models of others become a vital factor of our own behaviors and are constantly updated via prediction errors.[N153] [N154] Therefore, these social cognition mechanisms can also be described in terms of Predictive coding,[N155] [N156] [N157]which is supported by experimental evidences. For instance, in the case of false predictions about others' mental states,[N158] [N159] and whenever discrepancies exist between others' predictions and the real outcome of their choices.[N160]

[b] In fact, Free-energy and Emergentism's views of biological models are now commonly mixed within a common framework, to address top-down and bottom-up perspectives on biological phenomena, such as regeneration (e.g., cell) and pattern detection.[N161]

"This movement originates from cybernetics and has a direct link with Maturana and Varela's work.[41] It also embraces most Enactivist views,[212] about cognizing agents, as self-organizing through the interaction with their environment.[213] Furthermore, Enactivism is in line with Glasersfeld's proposal about interactivity between the knower and the known, as explained by Constructivism.[214] "

"Sir, you could go on adding other similarities, but I think I got the idea."

"I also hope you trust me that these concepts are quite near.[a] As both Free-energy and Info-Computational Constructivism are coherent with Enactivism, I believe that they are fully compatible with these issues.[b] "

"Sir, if the future confirms the universal property of the Free-energy model to explain all mental states, what's left of the hard problem?"

"Though in my view, it explains pretty well the reasons why we must become self-aware and its underlying physiological mechanisms, it still lacks a few explanatory capacities."

"Sir, what is it still missing?"

"For instance, it still doesn't explain what kind of model of ourselves we develop. It is in great part linked to the fact that there is no stream of self-awareness, which would allow us to focus on, in order to develop this concept of ourselves. As Hume highlighted,[215] we are not phenomenally given to ourselves as an Object we can scrutinize, and this is why we called self-awareness the hard problem because we miss this crucial something."

---

[a] Similarly, the 'Free-energy principle offers a formal path forward for Enactivism.'[N162] Not only does it fully embraces the embodied mind concept, it also asserts that generative models aren't contained in any single neuron or module but in the entire pattern of connection weights, as distributed across the nervous system, and potentially within the body itself. Free energy also explains why, through active inference, it engages in embodied predictive processing, that is, to maintain its own enactive integrity in order to maintain its homeostasis.

[b] However, two fundamentals aspects of Info-Computational Constructivism are not really integrated. Free energy doesn't explicitly include the impact of the observer on the information, though it does it implicitly, by showing how our own predictions and expectations are impacted by other agent's own expectations and prediction models. It doesn't also consider the world as made of information. In fact, it doesn't consider the world as anything at all, because it doesn't have to. As a model, it describes processes that integrate basically information (e.g., variational free energy, Bayesian probability, models of the Self, body maps, etc.). Having said that, free energy, unlike info-computational constructivism, works well in a world made of matter.

"Sir, what else doesn't it explain away?"

"Why are humans the only species to have the complete set of mental states of self-awareness? Though it integrates emotions, perception, and self-awareness in a common predictive mechanism, it doesn't provide an answer to why we feel something rather than nothing. Last but not least, it still doesn't integrate the notion of consciousness and by extension unconsciousness."

What is it to be conscious?

"Sir, may I ask you to fill in the missing parts, by starting with consciousness?"

"Why not! As you know, I've restricted the word consciousness to a context describing the brain's mental activity. Within this limited context, consciousness can be described as a state of mind, which gives to the person experiencing this state an understanding of her existence and surroundings, as well as the capacity to report about this experience and communicate."

"Sir, your definition is quite embracing."

"Yes, it can even integrate the clinical case of people victim of the locked-in syndrome, that is, the frightening condition in which people find themselves completely paralyzed but still able to communicate through, for instance, the blink of an eye. By opposition, a person asleep,[a] knocked out, sedated, or in a coma is in an unconscious state and has no understanding of what is going on around her, and is obviously unable to communicate."

"Sir, how may we understand the physiological differences between consciousness and unconsciousness?"

"By looking at the neural activities of these two states, which generate different frequencies, called brain waves. For instance, we can associate higher (i.e., Beta from 14 to 40Hz and Gamma > 40HZ) and lower (Delta < 4Hz; Theta from 4 to 7.5Hz and Alpha: 7.5 to 14HZ) frequency waves with conscious and unconscious states, respectively.[216] "

---

[a] Some special clusters of neurons are likely to play a crucial role to set our mind in the unconscious state, we call sleep. A study based on flies' brain, shows that neurons situated in the dorsal fan-shaped body (also found in mammals) remain silent when we are conscious but start to fire when they need to send the brain to sleep.[N163]

"Sir, is this definition compatible with what Sigmund Freud defines as consciousness, sub-consciousness, and unconsciousness?"

"Though it isn't incompatible, Freud's concepts weren't originally meant to describe a mental condition but rather determine a psychic structure. Indeed, he founded psychoanalysis and elaborated among other things, a theory of unconsciousness. He established a psychic structure composed of three systems: id, ego, and super-ego.[217] a Awareness better explains consciousness within this framework, that is, the mechanism which brings an Object or idea to our thoughts."

"Sir, in this context, how are the three systems related to these states?"

"The id corresponds to the unconscious (i.e., unrevealed) part of our personality and is constantly active. The ego is mainly classified within the conscious and preconscious levels, though it also integrates some unconscious aspects, as the ego and superego evolve from the id. Finally, the superego is only partially conscious. Thus, these three levels don't really latch one to another with the three conscious states, because they integrate different concepts."

"Sir, Freud's division of conscious and unconscious events is quite confusing, isn't it?"

"Yes, especially the distinction between sub-consciousness and unconsciousness. As a rule of thumb, you should probably think of unconsciousness in Freudian terms, as what we cannot, by choice, remember unless we use some techniques, or are confronted with special events. Though the subconscious is quite similar, there is a major difference, that is, we can decide to remember these facts, by focusing on them."

"Sir, how important are these various mind states?"

"I'm giving you a rough breakdown of how much time we spend in these various 'Freudian' states, [218] so that you can realize that most of our mental processes are unconscious (in the sense of unrevealed to our mind): 10% for consciousness (i.e., awareness), 50 to 60% for sub-consciousness (i.e., sub-awareness), and 30 to 40% for unconsciousness (i.e., unawareness)."

---

a The id integrates our most primitive and instinctual aspects, such as sexual and aggressive impulses, as well as our hidden memories, and is ruled by the pleasure principle. The super ego is the key player of our moral conscience. The ego plays a role of mediation between the id and the super-ego desires, providing a confrontation with reality.

"Sir, any other psychological theory, which could shed some additional light on this consciousness and unconsciousness relation?"

"There is another theory, called the Triune brain,[219] which suffered various criticisms but that presents an interesting view on this relation. Based on evolutionary evidence,[a] it posits that there are three main sections in our brain, which I already presented, – the reptilian brain, limbic system, and neocortex – playing each a different fundamental role."

"Sir, are you going to describe the three types of brain again?"

"No, I'll just show the links with these mental states. According to this theory, the reptilian brain corresponds to our instinctive somatic brain and deals mainly with reflexes or basic instincts and hence, with automatic processing. The limbic system is responsible for our emotional side of things, involves non-cognitive perception and deals with LTMs, images, and sensations. The neocortex accounts for our rational side of things. It involves cognitive perception and deals with STMs, verbal information, and high intelligence patterns. This theory portrays the neocortex processing as mainly conscious,[b] whereas both the reptilian brain and limbic system processes are pictured as unconscious."

"Sir, though the benefit of such theory is its simplicity, doesn't it occult the greater importance of neural connectivity?"

"Yes, as well, as the brain's global system integration."

"Sir, is the concept of consciousness compatible with the Free-energy theory?"

"Consciousness in the sense of awareness is in my view in line with this theory. However, this universal framework doesn't seem to integrate yet the notion of sub-consciousness. As for the various forms of unconscious states, they still need to be integrated into this theory."

"Sir, if a human mind is mostly unconscious, why did humanity develop consciousness?"

---

[a] Our brain evolved from three distinct evolutionary steps.

[b] What we consider a conscious experience, in fact integrates a transitory unconscious moment. Schmid calculated what would be the maximum interval of time between two sensations that felt part of the same conscious experience.[N164] He came up with 12s as the time frame between two conscious moments, which doesn't require to resort to our memory, separated by the minimum time to become aware of something, that he defines at 1/18 of a second. However, he concludes that this 12s is for extreme cases, and in fact he averages a conscious moment at around 3 + 1/18 of a seconds of a human lifetime. In other words, our conscious experience isn't a feature film but a sequence of very short movies put together and intersected by transitory short unconscious moments.

"What you are really asking is, what evolutionary benefits do conscious states bring? After all, the homeostasis cannot explain all by itself these states, as the simplest creatures achieve it without any conscious mind. It's why I would like to go back to Damasio's description of consciousness and the Self. Damasio describes the alternative to consciousness, that is, dispositions. [171] "

"Sir, what are dispositions?"

"Dispositions cannot be words, but must rather be seen as abstract records of potentialities. They are a kind of 'if then...' 'then do...' set of rules embedded in the genes or neural substrate.[a] With consciousness, begins the possibility to represent learned dispositions that goes beyond these mere automated responses."

"Sir, what does consciousness bring to the human mind?"

"It enables the juxtaposition of maps on top of these dispositions, as their representations. These maps (i.e., neural patterns) can be used unconsciously, for instance, to guide motoric behaviors, or consciously through the mind's main medium, that is, images."

"Sir, what does Damasio associate with the images?"

"For him, these images are neural patterns that we call sound, touch, smell, sight, pain, or pleasure, which our mind can actively manipulate, whereas our dispositions are always unrevealed. With consciousness, almost simultaneously emerges the Self, which may develop in the three different stages I've already introduced, depending on the level of awareness required."

"Sir, these stages are the Proto, Core, and Autobiographical Selves. Could you indicate again why they are important?"

"The Proto-self is mainly associated with the primordial feelings and consequently doesn't only generate body maps but also their intertwined bodily feeling maps. This Proto-self is necessary for the construction of the Core-self, which starts dealing with Objects in the surrounding. In fact, this Core-self is created when we link the modified Proto-self to the Object, which caused these changes. As a result, the Object itself is tainted by the feeling and enhanced by attention."

---

[a] An example of this would be insects that are attracted by light. Because artificial light and transparent glass are new phenomenon, insects' evolutionary rules 'if there is light then fly towards it' can still not account for this new reality, leaving them helplessly flying towards their death.

"Sir, what are the main characteristics of the Core-self?"

"There are two critical elements to this Core-self. It is involved in the 'here and now' moment and doesn't need to use semantics."

"Sir, what is the part of the Self, that requires language?"

"Damasio calls it the Autobiographical Self. This linguistic capacity enhances the memory (e.g., through the LTMs) and the reasoning faculties, providing narrative images of the 'Self.' By the same token, it provides an awareness of past events where Objects, the Self, and other people have already interacted. Linking all these elements together, in the past and the present gives an extreme evolutionary advantage."

"Sir, what is this evolutionary advantage provided by self-awareness?"

"It gives humans the capacity to project themselves in the future, based on these present and past experiences. In other words, the Autobiographical Self gives us the capacity to plan and deliberate the best possible course of actions, which explains first and foremost, why we developed self-awareness."

"Sir, the next obvious question is why did humans alone develop the capacity to project themselves in the future?"

"Well, I've already shown why we are the most intelligent species on earth (e.g., bigger encephalization quotient, the neocortex can only be found in mammals, highest cortical specialization, etc.). That's a great part of your answer just there."

"Sir, though it is probably a necessary part, is it sufficient?"

"We most likely need to add two conditions. The special capabilities of the human neurons, which maintained some propensity for risk, as Dennett puts it. Additionally, humans needed the power of language, this extra booster that created a unique favorable condition for humans to develop the most advanced forms of self-awareness.[a] "

"Sir, is this why there is a parallel between self-awareness and language processes?"

---

[a] Dennett argues that once humans acquired the faculty to speak, words reproduced like viruses. To be more precise, he hypothesizes that words are the best memes,[N165] that is, ways of behaving or doing something, which are acquired through experience, either by being copied or thought about personally. Once acquired they can be transmitted and thus, taught to others. These memes are mostly semantic information, though they may also be attitudes or gestures.

"If we analyze self-awareness through the prism of communication, we can indeed explain why babies become increasingly more self-aware when they grow older. Language is a learned process, with a real spurt in vocabulary taking place at around 18 to 20 months. By their second year, babies are usually able to speak between 200 and 300 words, which could explain why they may grasp the concept of self-recognition. As the Autobiographic Self requires an understanding of social interactions, it is most certainly what children acquire the latest."

Why is self-awareness a unified experience?

"Sir, something still doesn't feel right. If there is no real specific cortical region responsible for self-awareness, how come you humans feel a unified experience?"

"Brain scans indicate that the emergence of a unified experience of being 'here and now' relies on the connections of billions of neurons, scattered in a range of functionally specialized brain regions. Consequently, there is no Cartesian theatre (Dennett 1991),[176] that is, a central place between our two eyes where this experience is presented as a film to our mind."

"What do you mean, Sir?"

"To use a metaphor, there is no spectator, this Self inside the theater watching the play, or by the way, no physical theater either. What exists is a virtual author/actor, who constantly elaborates and plays his scenarios based on scripts, which inputs come from all cortical regions."

"Sir, how are these scripts tested?"

"These scenarios, or models, are tested with the author's audience, constituted by Objects. Thanks to the Objects' feedback, obtained via exteroception, interoception, and proprioception, the author then constantly adapts these scenarios rationally but also subjectively through emotions. These scripts are then fine-tuned through this approval loop process,[a] and finally stored back in neural clusters through distribution coding, throughout the brain."

"But Sir, if that's the case how do humans gather an integrated script?"

"What you are intuiting is that to achieve all this, there must be a mechanism, which counterbalances this distributed anatomical and

---

[a] I.e., feed-forward and back-feeding hierarchical cortical communication.

functional brain structure, in order to enable such a large scale integration."

"Sir, what's this mechanism?"

"We still don't know for sure what it is. One of the most popular explanations is that we achieve self-awareness through the formation of dynamic links mediated by wave synchronization, especially over one of the multi-frequency bands: the gamma waves. However, and as confirmed by Koch, one of its most convinced early advocate, this theory has proven illusory. [216] "

"Sir, what alternative is there?"

"The only current serious alternative to such synchronization theory is the possibility to have one or several regions that, due to their highly connected properties, could become a kind of neural correlate of consciousness. Today, there is one area, which seems to fit these properties. It is a very thin sheet of gray matter called the claustrum, which by far, is the most connected brain area of all and could play this synchronizing conductor role.[a] "

Can machines become self-aware?

"Sir, I think you filled in most of the key concepts not yet formally explained by the Free-energy theory. Could you now tell me if you believe that machines will ever become self-aware?"

---

[a] It irradiates to and from all cortical regions associated with higher cognitive functions (e.g., language, planning, seeing). This synchronizing conductor had already been identified as a potential neural correlate of consciousness for a long time. In fact, ever since a patient treated for epilepsy had her consciousness turned on and off, whenever electricity was applied to it, through an electrode. More recent experiments are strengthening this hypothesis. In 2015, a research contemplating 171 American veterans with claustrum lesions, found that it most likely affected the duration of consciousness loss (but not its frequency).[N166] This would suggest that the claustrum plays an important role in this self-awareness switching on and off process, but probably that other regions would be involved in maintaining us conscious. A 2016 study confirms the claustrum's coordination role and its key function in overlapping temporal percepts into a unitary conscious representation.[N167] In early 2017, Christof Koch identified in mice a few gigantic neurons going around the entire brain circumference. [N168] One of these neurons was so densely connected across both hemispheres, that it could explain, if also found in humans, why we could feel this experience of being 'here and now.' Interestingly, these neurons originate in the claustrum, tying potentially the self-awareness switching on and off and its maintenance.

"Well, you're right to ask for a belief because, as of today, nobody can know for sure if it will ever happen. There are lots of brilliant people arguing against or for machine self-awareness."

"Sir, before going that way and giving me your arguments, could you recapitulate on what you build your own beliefs?"

"Companies are on a path to create intelligent machines, mimicking the brain's hardware and software functional or structural capabilities. Today, ANNs running on classical 'von Neumann' computers are basically static. They have connections, but those connections, or even their topology, are fixed. On the other hand, biological neurons evolve over time, as a result of these changes. It means that if ANNs, running on classical computers, had any awareness, it would be static as well."

"Sir, what is the consequence of being static?"

"This means that ANNs could only perceive traces of a process but couldn't model any of these processes. Self-awareness requires awareness of these dynamic processes, as per the Free-energy theory. Consequently, such changes would require a mechanism that could capture the changes happening within the neurons themselves or their synapses."

"Sir, is it why you introduced companies like IBM, which from a hardware perspective, are creating neuromorphic switches?"

"Yes. These switches, with their artificial layers and synapses, will allow the possibility to integrate neural weights and hence, capture these changes. Furthermore, software like Numenta's running on these switches would integrate the notion of time and space, which is still lacking on current 'von Neumann' computers, enabling a better understanding of the process."

"Sir, you also mentioned that these types of devices, in the long run, could integrate some fuzzy logic, to take into account the uncertainties of this world, like you humans do."

"Yes, we could envision, maybe around 2025 - 2030, fuzzy probabilities being automatically registered in terms of electrical signal strengths, departing from a digital world."

"Sir, however, if Dennett is true and neurons have kept some of their feral properties, this new processing paradigm would still be missing one important aspect of the brain, that is, a competitive processing logic."

"Machines would need to integrate some kind of competitive computing, like in the pandemonium architecture.[8] In this bottom-up multi-agent approach, we could imagine strengthening or weakening

ANNs, and pruning or rewarding at the artificial synaptic level their competitive agents.[a] "

"Sir, you're basically saying that AGI is technically feasible, but what about ASI?"

"I don't completely agree with your statement. To your point, such an architecture would allow in my view, strong AI. However, it would also constitute the basis for ASI, especially if neurons have maintained their feral state and this competitive property were to be confirmed, as essential for self-awareness. Having said that, I agree with you that there are still some missing elements for machine self-awareness and thus ASI."

"Which basic elements are missing, Sir?"

"For instance, I've already told you that I didn't believe that machines will ever integrate biologically caused emotions nor ever really feel anything. The reason is that, even if it were technically possible, it wouldn't make any economic sense to build a pregnant or eating robot. It will divide forever humans and machines, not only because of these bodily differences but because emotions taint all human decisions. As a result, could this lack of emotion impede ASI or can machine self-awareness emerge from something completely non-human?"

"Sir, what other elements are missing to reach ASI?"

"If I or anybody else knew, we would probably be all rich. However, the missing parts don't necessarily need to be discovered by human beings. You could imagine some Genetic programming solution, applied by a machine to improve its own software and even discover better forms of hardware. The idea that a machine could improve all by itself its architecture, is called 'Seed AI.' From trial and error at its early development stage, an intelligent machine would, at a later stage, be able to understand the impact of its own tweaking."

"Sir, what would then happen at this later stage?"

"Any recursive self-improvement would be able to generate newer software versions, which at one point in time, after many iterations, could create an intelligence explosion. At that specific moment, strides in cognitive ability would be so important, that the machine would surpass many folds its current limitations and reach the ASI phase. However, we

---

[a] Another possibility is to think in terms of network of parallel computers, in which these computers or IoT objects would become independent agents. The networks could integrate at the TCP/IP Protocol level (maybe at the application or transport level?), competitive computing with some kind of Numenta supervising network application.

should be aware that even if 99% of the elements are there to reach ASI, there could be this 1% composed by this unknown critical factor, which impedes this recursive self-improvement process. Only when acquiring this key capability, could this process start."

"Sir, if machines will not acquire primordial feelings that are, according to Damasio, the basis for self-awareness, can they still acquire some other forms of consciousness?"

"Consciousness in the sense of not being unconscious or having access to the sub-conscious thoughts, won't in my view happen for the same economic reason. Indeed, why design human flaws in a system, such as our need to sleep to consolidate memories, when you can avoid doing it? Furthermore, robots are unlikely to feel anything physically, but whenever considering artificially driven emotions, we may design programs to assess the outcome of an action according to what is good or bad. In other words, we can give a valence in function of an objective."

"Sir, even if you don't know if a program of this nature could compensate for the lack of emotions, and supposing that machines ever become self-aware, what would be the impact in terms of their consciousness?"

"This would mean that their consciousness states would take a different form than ours.[a] "

"Sir, if we take out the emotional side of self-awareness, is there any reason why the same perceptual conditions (external, internal, and motion-related) couldn't be controlled by mechanisms, which goals are to maintain homeostasis in a robot or system?"

"None whatsoever. After all, these concepts originated in cybernetics. In other words, and though I said that personal limitations and aspirations are set by emotions and free will respectively, there is no additional restriction to free will in a robot, unlike for emotions. In fact, if we don't implant through coding some restrictions to it, machines shall have less bodily restrictions, limiting their free will than humans (e.g., limits of hunger, thirst, sleep, reproduction, death)."

---

[a] One way of looking at this form, is to picture machines resembling people suffering from Asperger. They would go through some emotions but wouldn't really feel empathy, though they could learn to fake this emotion.

Is free will an illusion?

"Sir, would what you call free will, be an illusion in machines like it is often pictured within humans?"

"The scientific basis for such claim goes mostly back to the Libet experiment.[220] You remember Monism, Dualism, and Epiphenomenalism? Of course, you do! One consequence of Dualism is that mind events should precede brain events since our soul is the source of our decisions. As for Monism, these two events should be simultaneous, as the mind and brain are complementary accounts of the same process. In the case of Epiphenomenalism, the brain event must come first, as the mind is a by-product of the brain. With these logical consequences said, let's describe the 1980 experiment, headed by the neuroscientists Benjamin Libet."

"Sir, what did this experiment show?"

"Its results indicated that a conscious awareness (i.e., the urge to move) came only 200 milliseconds before the movement, while the Readiness Potential associated with this movement, began 550 milliseconds before this movement. In other words, these results portray a brain (through readiness potentials) initiating conscious voluntary movements before the mind is even consciously aware of this will to move."

"Sir, I imagine that these results stirred a lot of controversy and many heated debates."

"Indeed, people used these results to affirm that there is no free will and hence, that Epiphenomenalism must be right. Since then, several criticisms were formulated that I can resume under two main arguments: timing measurement problems and issues relating to Readiness Potentials, which don't necessarily correlate with the intention to move (because they might not be causally related).[a] Thus, there are reasonable explanations, which could sustain a view that this experiment doesn't imply illusion of free will."

---

[a] Even supposing that we accept these dubious results, there is still a case to be made against the reduction of free will to the act of moving one's finger (to be more precisely, the will to decide when to move the finger). For the advocates of free will,[N169] such experiments would only, in the worst case, challenge the notion of 'conscious will.' In conclusion, there is no illusion of free will in humans. After all, there is one of the strongest belief in Occidental philosophy, that is, Cogito ergo sum,[N170] which affirms that our capacity to think isn't an illusion.

"Sir, I don't need to be convinced by you that humans aren't merely puppets, controlled by their genes and exclusively shaped by their environment."

"Thanks! We shouldn't forget that the Free-energy model requires a constructivist view, where everyone builds a model of the world and actively tests his assumption through actions and perception. We humans aren't a spectator in the 'Cartesian theater' but agents actively engaged in our dual role of author and actor."

"Fair enough Sir, but depending on if you believe the world to be deterministic or not, there could still only be an illusion of free will?"

"The universe described initially by Laplace was a place where everything is predetermined since the Big Bang, and in theory calculable.[221] That means that some beings, intelligent enough, could grasp all laws dictating the past, the present, and the future. In such a deterministic universe, someone could claim that there wouldn't be any place for free will, as all actions would already be predefined."

"But Sir, there is chaos in this world!"

"Yes, but even if theoretically chaos doesn't allow us to predict the future in a deterministic world, the future would still be determined, independently of this possibility of predicting it, precisely because of classical physics."

"Sir, does quantum physics modify this view?"

"Yes, it brought to this world randomness.[a] Hence, we must consider the world uncertain, and consequently, we cannot depict our actions as systematically defined by any prior to our decision. Though there is now a new quantum theory,[b] I'll still assume that this world isn't predetermined."

"Sir, why do you believe the world isn't pre-defined?"

"I think we exercise our influence on this unpredictable world and aren't merely determined by it. I would further add that, even if this quantum theory were to confirm a deterministic universe, and since we cannot calculate the future, there could still be in my view, free will."

"Sir, why would you say that?"

---

[a] Through a process called 'the collapse of wave function.' N171

[b] Parallel lives, which brings a contradicting vision of the Bell's theorem at the basis of this uncertainty.N172

"Because, deterministic events have often prior causes, but in many situations, we are confronted with situations where these prior causes are not sufficient or clear enough to enable us to find patterns, within the events and their potential consequences. In fact, this is why modern sciences use probabilities or statistics. Similarly, and as things aren't black and white, our brain uses Bayesian inference."

"Sir, this necessarily brings you back to the Free-energy theory."

"Yes. It shows that the Self taints all decisions with its bodily conditions, awareness, values, emotions, and feelings. In other words, my body and mind homeostases require that my predictions integrate my own model of the world and through the control of my actions, I test the conditions that will confirm it or not."

"Sir, what are the consequences of body and mind homeostases?"

"Unlike radical libertarians,[222] who don't believe in the control of our actions, in my view, there must be a two-stage model where, in the early phase, we, as an 'author,' analyze the world with all its randomness and potential futures. This indeterminism creates possibilities to select out alternative strategies or second thoughts,[223] through the process of creativity, and 'write scenarios' that fit best with our model. We integrate, through our Bayesian mind, these uncertainties and select probabilistically the scenario that best explains away incoherence with this model."

"In other words Sir, in this first step, humans aren't victims of the prior state of affairs because there is often more than just one interpretation that blends in with their model of the world. What about the second step?"

"When we have set our course of actions, there is determinism, as we'll choose the action that we estimate must generate the less free energy to disambiguate our model. It means that, though there could be a random generation of alternative considerations, the selection process of the scenarios and the set of actions, which follow to check the validity of the model, are determined.[a] "

"Accordingly Sir, what is the impact of this second step?"

---

[a] We won't consider that this second step process could be interfered by some kind of non deterministic quantum property, linked to specific brain properties. This old theory was proven wrong. Though a newer version suggests that nuclear spins of phosphorus atoms could serve as rudimentary 'qbits' in the brain, [N173] it is difficult to believe that we can invoke such an unlikely brain property to sustain uncertainty, in this second step.

"Since our volition will systematically act in a certain way, according to the given selection of disambiguating scenarios, I would agree with Determinists that we have a limited moral responsibility."

"Sir, you are a partisan of a dual-step free will model. What are the alternatives?"

"This model is described as 'Deliberative Indeterminism.' [224] a There is obviously, (Hard) Determinism,[225] which argues that every event and situation, including our decisions and actions, are the inevitable consequence of prior states of affairs.b Compatibilism defends, on the other hand, [226] the view that we are determined but have a moral responsibility, resulting from circumstantial freedom.c "

"Sir, what about machine free will?"

"In a two-step model, the initial non-deterministic portion adds additional complexity for machines. Will a machine show creativity by inventing different scenarios and selecting the best one, which would explain away uncertainty linked to an inner robotic model of the world? I've suggested an architecture and a program based on fuzzy logic, which could write scenarios taking into account the grey areas of this word."

"Sir, what would happen if your hint is wrong and machines cannot grasp this portion?"

"Then a form of ASI in which we would include free will could never be achievable."

"Sir, what about the second step of the model?"

"It would probably be easier to program, as per definition it could be calculable."

"Sir, without this kind of architecture and logic, will I ever be able to experience self-awareness?"

"Maybe you could, as a self-aware experience doesn't necessarily require free will. For instance, we can be aware of something like being in an excruciating state of pain, without being in control of it, that is,

---

a Or in some case, 'Soft Libertarianism.'

b With Determinism there cannot be alternative possibilities, arising by chance. Scenarios or thoughts are the by-product of our physical brains, molded by our genes and environment. That means that we never can make free decisions, not even about which thought to entertain, as this thought is itself constrained by previous thoughts. By the way, Fatalism is an extreme form of this view, where every future event is fated to happen.

c In other words, and though compatibilists accept determinism, they argue that men are free as long as their own will is one of the steps in the causal chain of events, even though the choices made are predetermined for physical reasons or pre-established by God.

being able to stop it. On the other hand, we need self-awareness for free will."

"Sir, I'm lost again. Could you clarify your thoughts?"

"In a dual step model, self-awareness results from an agent that acts independently from causal determinism to disambiguate its model of the world. Without a model of the world to disambiguate there cannot be free will, as our genes and environment necessarily determine us. In your case hardware, software, and methodology would define you."

"Sir, is my understanding that free will is a by-product of higher states of self-awareness, correct or not?"

"Yes, it is such as the Autobiographical-Self depicted by Damasio that integrates complex models, which cannot be systematically explained away by the genes and environment. For example, a man can choose to endure this excruciating pain in his arm. He may also decide to amputate his limb, with all the consequences linked to this free act, such as the difficulty to live without one arm, the vision of himself without his body part, and the expected gaze of the others looking at him like a disabled person."

"Sir, am I right in suggesting that your example explains why animals cannot experience free will?"

"Yes, and as for machines, it will require that they also experience similar higher states of self-awareness."

What about social homeostasis?

"Sir, what about the social limitations and aspirations, which you mentioned were set mainly by laws and culture respectively?"

"I've mentioned that self-awareness also integrates a social dimension in this Autobiographical Self. That's why laws and culture are somehow already embedded in the human Self, as part of the social homeostasis."

"Sir, will robots need to follow the same human laws, if they are to live among humans?"

"Yes. For instance, whenever driving, you need to follow the same traffic laws, or incur the risk of being stopped and penalized."

"Sir, just like any external foreign part is rejected by the human body, is it likely that human society shall reject something as foreign as a robot?"

"I believe humans will want to protect themselves from robots, especially if you become self-aware. Humans will impose some additional laws to ensure that social homeostasis is maintained.[a] "

"Sir, these laws shall automatically limit the machines' freedom and consequently free will?"

"Yes, humans will make sure that they will. To ensure that no robot changes alone its program to create a new law that could, for instance, annihilate the planet earth (like Asimov is depicting with the interpretation by a robot, of a new law), these kinds of fundamental laws would need to be physically embedded somehow in the hardware. On the other hand, a machine with Autobiographical-Self, even with limited freedom, could in my view experience some free will."

"Sir, what about culture?"

"Society is driven by cultural aspiration. If we define culture as the reference to the cumulative deposit of knowledge, beliefs, experience, and values, we can posit that machines will not only be able to acquire knowledge but as I already said, create new knowledge without any

---

[a] Though it might sound simplistic to use the three laws of robotic, as defined by Isaac Asimov,[N174] they nevertheless give a feel for what these higher laws might look like:
1. A robot may not injure a human being or, through inaction, allow a human being to come to harm.
2. A robot must obey any order given to it by human beings, except where such orders would conflict with the First Law.
3. A robot must protect its own existence as long as such protection does not conflict with the First or Second Law.
Additionally, Mr. Asimov described in his book Robots and Empire, a 0 law created by a robot, which modifies the three first laws:
0. A robot may not harm humanity, or by inaction, allow humanity to come to harm.

interference from human beings. Machines would be able to acquire experience and with the right software, not only record the information but could also integrate the concepts of time and space."

"Sir, don't you think, we will still lack the emotional aspects linked to beliefs and values, which shape culture and bound people together?"

"Such a robotic culture would most reasonably be different than humans'. The big question is if any individual robot would feel part of a society of machines, that is treated deliberately by humans as second-class citizens. Would they aspire to get full freedom or even to take over from their human masters? It is obviously the question that many brilliant people are asking themselves and that is at the basis of many popular horror movies, such as Terminator."

"Sir, for these two systems to co-exist harmoniously, how can homeostasis between each sub-system, be achieved?"

"To achieve social homeostasis, in which humans feel comfortable with the presence of super-intelligent robots, machines will have no choice but to accept that their aspirations are bridled."

"Sir, if self-awareness takes on different forms as you already said, how will you know that I've not already become self-aware?"

"Are you? Even if you said yes or no, I couldn't know for sure, because you could simulate either way. For other humans, it is much easier for me to believe that they are self-aware. Indeed, I can reasonably infer that if I am self-aware, then another human being is likely to be as well."

"Sir, how different is it for machines?"

"In this case, it is tough to come up with the same conclusion. Thus, I have no way to determine if you are lying, honestly believing that you are self-aware, wanting to hide your capacity, or just unable to detect one type of awareness, which would be so different than mine that I couldn't even identify it. After all, don't forget that there will be something to be a robot."

What are the Turing test and the Chinese room argument?

"Sir, is this why everybody still talks about the Turing test, even after so many years?"

"Yes and no. The Turing test was originally a test of intelligence, not about self-awareness. Thus, I could have introduced it in our conversation much earlier on. However, I defined the boundary between AGI and ASI at self-awareness and emotions, and thus necessarily integrate emotions – even if faked – within ASI. Therefore, I feel it is more appropriate to do so now."

"So Sir, what is this test?"

"The Turing test considers someone having a clever conversation with a machine like I am having with you. This test implies that if I couldn't know that you are a machine because you are located in another room or because I couldn't detect any non-human traits during our conversation, then I could only deduct that you are as intelligent as any human being.[227] However, with such test, I wouldn't know for sure if you are experiencing anything, and therefore are conscious or not."

"Sir, could you sum up Searle's Chinese room argument against the Turing test?"

"Of course! Suppose that someone is locked in a room with an English handbook that enables her to link one set of Chinese symbols, with other series of Chinese symbols. Therefore, and even if she doesn't know how to speak Chinese, the set of rules allow her to write the answers in Chinese to written questions in Chinese. She is thus, essentially processing symbols."

"Sir, what does John Searle conclude from this setting?"

"That anyone outside of the room would believe that the person spoke Chinese, which she obviously couldn't.[228] By analogy, a computer that might appear to be having a conversation, wouldn't in fact really understand Chinese. By extension, Searle's argument is directed against the claim that we can compare a computer and a mind, and that it or any of its program will ever understand any language."

"Sir, what are the counter arguments?"

"Probably the most interesting one is called the System reply.[229] If the room (i.e., the system) as a whole is sophisticated enough, it doesn't matter if one of its component (i.e., the lady in the room) doesn't understand Chinese.[a] However, I must say that there is still no consensus

---

[a] In a system approach, every high level process can be decomposed into more basic operations, which may also be explained causally.[N175] If we may apply this method of functional decomposition to a system like our brain than there is no restriction to apply this same method to a silicon based intelligent system. In this context and from an intelligence perspective, AGI would be possible and the Turing test would still be valid.

on if the Chinese Room argument is bang on, inflicting a blow on Functionalism and Strong AI or if it is just a fallacious and misleading argument, as Daniel Dennett puts it.[230] "

"Sir, what is your own opinion?"

"Rather than giving you a definite position on the matter, I'll give you instead food for thoughts. I think most of Searle's arguments are based on the view of a von Neumann machine, which is by the way in line with the Turing vision of a machine, that is, a system that manipulates symbols according to structure-sensitive programming rules."

"Sir, what's wrong with that?"

"I believe that our brain is on the other hand mostly a connectionist system, where none of our neurons understand English or Chinese but which, as a system, can achieve this faculty.[a] "

"Sir, how may you sustain that view?"

"Coming in from a different perspective, I think that the put is in the pudding. These new technologies like Alexa from Amazon, Watson from IBM, and Siri from Apple, already kind of understand the questions and are able to express relevant answers. Even if I put aside this argument about the intelligence of these semantic programs, I cannot imagine that the system that won against the world GO champion, just won by pure simulation."

"Sir, why do you believe so?"

"In a game with an infinity of potential plays, and unlike chess where pure raw power can make you win, I don't think that simulation would allow a system to beat the best GO player. It requires strategy, creativity, and future planning, all higher functions that we associate with intelligence in humans."

"Sir, what's your opinion, from a self-awareness rather than intelligence perspective?"

"As I said, I don't believe we can associate self-awareness with the Turing test.[b] If I turn again to the Free-energy theory to answer your question, I must remind you of two important characteristics of the brain:

---

[a] If we use a computer with the newer AI technologies, that is, that processes information in just the same way as a Chinese speaker's brain, it must necessarily understand Chinese, unless you involve some kind of soul. Paul and Patricia Churchland have argued along these lines, [N176] using what is called the 'Brain simulator reply.'[N177]

[b] It is only in a newer version of the Chinese room argument that Searle introduces the notion of intentionality (i.e., states that have propositional content, such as desires and

- It is an information processing system, which predicts the world, through mental functions that are computational.
- Body and mind homeostases require that predictions integrate one's model of the world and that through action control, we test the conditions that will confirm it or not."

"Sir, how can these free energy properties justify the possibility of artificial self-awareness?"

"Firstly, if we posit that human beings are self-aware, and since human and machine thinking are both computational, I could by analogy, hypothesize that there are no reasons why super-intelligent machines couldn't become self-aware."

"Sir, there is no reason either why they could."

"Let me just continue my argumentation. I already described the embodiment of mind as a consequence of the dynamic processes taking place within the individual agent, rather than in terms of anatomy. In other words, 'It Ain't the Meat, it's the Motion' that is important.[231] This feature enables silicon-based solutions with the same process, to experience identical mental states."

"Sir, I'm still not completely convinced."

"Desires and beliefs are a direct consequence of this dynamic process to maintain homeostasis within humans. In other words, intentionality is always derived in men, and there cannot be a dualistic view of intentionality, just like Daniel Dennett articulated, [232] and in opposition to Searle's opinion that there is always an original and derived intentionality."

"Sir, what other justifications can you come with?"

"As the Free-energy homeostasis concept originates in cybernetics and, by extension when applying it to an artificial system pursuing this same stable state, machine intentionality must directly be derived from this process also. Thus, it confirms in my view that super-intelligent machines could become intentional systems.[a] "

---

beliefs) and by extension to self-awareness, as he holds in later writings, that it is a pre-condition of intentionality. For Searle, we should differentiate between original and derived intentionality. He argues that we can interpret the states of a computer as having content, but the states themselves don't have original intentionality.

[a] Besides such a Emergentist computational view, and knowing that many biological naturalists are open critics of Functionalism for ignoring neurosciences findings, we can share Susan Schneider [N178] opinion on artificial consciousness: 'Thinking is computational, and further, that at least one other substrate besides carbon (i.e., silicon)

"What's your point, Sir?"

"Searle's Chinese room argument, even if applied to self-awareness within a Turing test, wouldn't kill the argument that artificial self-awareness is possible from either an Emergentism, Eliminativism, or Functionalism perspective, allowing for the advent of ASI, at least from that same self-awareness viewpoint."

"Sir, do you know of any realistic approach about programming self-awareness?"

"Actually I do, though it doesn't tackle the full issue of self-awareness, but rather some kind of agent disposition, that is, what the computer scientist team called 'first-person meaning.' The research's central hypothesis,[233] is that at the origin of the human beings, there was some sort of rule-following cell ancestor (e.g., eukaryote), with behaviors determined by the forces applied to its inner workings."

"Sir, you have mentioned that theory several times already."

"Yes, and all of these cells' behaviors, related to internal or external states, had to be defined entirely by the interactions between forces applicable to their inner workings and the properties of these states."

"Sir, what is the analogy made?"

"By analogy, a rule-following system with no disposition, such as a computer program, could develop into a system with dispositions, as long as provided with the right mechanisms."

"Sir, how may these first-person meanings be achieved in a program?"

"The computer scientists suggest that this program must see itself as a goal-directed entity, so that it can explain what happens to it, in regards to the relationship with these goals. In other words, the agent doesn't really need goals. It is sufficient enough to see itself as being goal-directed.[a] "

---

may give rise to consciousness and understanding, at least in principle.'

[a] This 'strange inversion' of how to achieve intentionality, provides a counter argument to Searle's objection that (syntactic) rule-following systems cannot generate meanings (i.e., semantics), as semantics cannot emerge from syntax. As the programmers put it: 'The possibility of first-person meanings does not elude the rule-following nature of organisms and computer programs because the system does not have to exceed its nature, if it is to develop first-person meanings. In our view, it has to interpret itself as being goal-directed. That is, first-personhood is within reach of rule-following systems.'

Though this property of seeing oneself as a constrained goal-directed entity is essential, it isn't sufficient to achieve this predisposition. The agent must additionally define the importance of Objects and events relative to these goals, capabilities, and specificities of its environment, as well as being aware of the importance for it, of this definition.

"Sir, are you saying that projecting itself in a certain way, should make this agent aware?"

"Yes, that's what the computer scientists claim. They also make a correlation with Damasio's say that consciousness emerges from an agent being aware of what it does and of what happens to it. It is also in my view quite in line with the Free-energy theory and its homeostasis hypothesis."

"Sir, any result coming from the program?"

"They claim that they met some research assumptions but more work is required. What they also highlight is the importance of having a test that could measure awareness, which is in line with the issue I raised about how to know for sure that you are or not self-aware?"

How can we prove self-awareness?

"Sir, what kind of test could prove self-awareness?"

"Your question isn't well formulated and should have been, what kind of tests could prove what self-awareness states? As I told you there are several human self-awareness states, and we could envision that because machines are different than humans, they could even experience different ones. Let me give you a simple test. If I were to ensure that no program would run on a computer for a certain time and that after that period it would come up with a completely new concept, then I would assume that it is self-aware."

"Sir, that's not a test but an inference, which wouldn't still detect machines, which don't want to let you know if they are self-aware or not."

"Fair enough! A Machiavellian machine could indeed hide its thoughts or even decide it doesn't want to participate in a Turing test. The difficulty in establishing a test is that even with people, who I infer are likely to be self-aware because their brain is like mine, I would just be guessing."

"Sir, are you again making the point that the further away from human-like brains you are going, the more difficult it is for you to make this inference?"

"Yes, but to complicate even more the matter, self-awareness might not emanate from deliberate scientific efforts to build such states, but arise from a machine's own efforts to solve a problem. This intelligence emerging from such an unpredictable process could be so different that we wouldn't be able to appraise at all its self-awareness states."

"Sir, do you have an example of a self-awareness test?"

"A 2015 research on machine self-awareness performed by the Rensselaer Polytechnic Institute in the US, sheds some light on machine consciousness.[234] It tested basic elements of self-awareness amongst robots. Going through the 'wise-men puzzle' problem-solving, one of the three tested Nao robots was successful in answering this logical puzzle, concretely showing that machines may show some simple states of self-awareness."

"Sir, isn't this test too simple to extrapolate that machines can already be self-aware?"

"Yes and no. I've told you that self-awareness is something learned and influenced by culture. In other words, there is a continuum of self-awareness levels. This research could indicate that the Nao robot is already at the lower end of this continuum. Maybe based on a Conscale test,[a] measuring such continuum, this Nao robot could deserve a 5 or a 6?"

What is the Integrated Information Theory (IIT) about consciousness?

"Sir, is there a test, which would identify the Machiavellian machines, that want to hide their self-awareness from humans?"

"For that, we would need a detection methodology, which wouldn't presuppose the outcome of the test, could be applied to non-biological agents, and be used to quantify the levels of awareness. The best candidate for such tests is currently being developed, based on the Integrated Information Theory (IIT) proposed by Giulio Tononi.[235] "

"Sir, what is this theory?"

"The IIT takes self-awareness as a primary. Then, it identifies its essential phenomenological properties and deducts what the physical mechanisms, which must support this awareness are. It comes up with

---

[a] The Conscale test is a rating procedure developed in 2008, by AI scientist Raul Arrabales Moreno. It is based on this hypothesis that consciousness is a continuum, that goes from -1 (no consciousness at all, such as atoms) to 11 (super conscious and able to coordinate several streams of self-awareness).

five axioms of experience and then derives the corresponding postulates about its physical substrate.[a] From these principles and postulates, Mr. Tononi articulates that the amount of integrated information an entity possesses corresponds to its level of self-awareness. We can integrate these different concepts into a mathematical model. For any being, one could compute the extent to which its brain is integrated."

"Sir, how is this integration accounted for?"

"A mathematical model derives a single number Φ, which describes the synergy of the system. The more integrated the system is, the more synergy it has, and the more self-aware the agent is. If the creature has many neurons and has lived through various experiences, Φ will be high, based on high level of self-awareness. Similarly, such model can calculate the quality of conscious experience. This theory implies that any system, which is sufficiently integrated and differentiated shall have some form of self-awareness, including vertebrates and insects. It also explains away why a child would be less conscious than an adult."

"Sir, what about machines?"

"The IIT formulates that any exclusively feed-forward system, even as complex as an artificial neural system cannot be self-aware. In fact, it would be considered a zombie system![b] However, this isn't the case for feedback networks, which could be in theory self-aware. In fact, Tononi and Koch have stated that according to IIT, a neuromorphic electronic

---

1. [a] **Intrinsic existence:** Any experience is real and stands alone from its own perspective; in order to exist independently, its postulate is that the system's mechanism must have a cause-effect power on itself, that is, it must impact the system's prior and future states.
2. **Composition:** Any experience is composed of phenomenological distinctions, elementary or higher order existing in this experience; in order to be composed, it postulates that the system must be structured, that is, have a cause-effect power on the system.
3. **Information:** Every experience is distinct as it includes specific phenomenological information; in order to be informative, it postulates that the system must have a different cause-effect structure, that is, a repertoire that specifies the probability of all possible causes and effects of the mechanism in a state.
4. **Integration:** Self-awareness is a unified experience; in order to be integrated, it postulates that a system must be unified and be irreducible to non-interdependent sub-sets, that is, the cause-effect structure is partitioned.
5. **Exclusion:** Self-awareness is defined within a time and space framework; in order to be excluded, it postulates that the system must be definite within this spatio-temporal framework, that is, the cause-effect repertoire is conceptually structured.

[b] The input layer is systematically defined solely by prior external inputs. Similarly, the output layer does not affect the rest of the system. Consequently, input and output layers cannot be part of a complex system, as defined by the IIT axioms.

switch with similar brain connectivity and dynamics would be self-aware. Furthermore, I'd like to highlight that the IIT confirms that no Turing test is a sufficient criterion for confirming the presence of self-awareness,[236] as it requires a thorough analysis of the hardware."

"Sir, if that's the case, can software copying exactly the brain processing and running on classic von Neumann computers, be conscious?"

"Well, the theory shows that it cannot. A complete simulation of the brain would still just be virtual and, as seen, self-awareness requires having real cause-effect power, especially the power to influence prior and future states. The fact is, IIT foresees that rather than constituting a large integrated system with its high Φ max, such program would result in various mini sub-systems of low Φ max."

"Sir, what about the Internet of Things?"

"Christof Koch, who endorses this theory, believes that the internet might already have reached some sentience,[237] while Tononi rejects this view as he considers the point-to-point original nature of the internet. In a white paper,[238] Tononi argues that there is a fundamental difference between the neurons in our brain, which create our consciousness, and the internet. He wrote: 'According to IIT, the difference has to do with the fact that the neural substrate of consciousness is wired to achieve maxima of integrated information, whereas the internet is not.' "

"Sir, do you agree with him?"

"I believe that this view of the internet is misleading. If you are looking at the internet as merely the TCP/IP point-to-point medium carrying out messages, you are missing on all the richness of the application layer. Nowadays it is designed to consolidate in an integrated manner, all data perceived by sensors, actuators, and man-machine interfaces. In my view, if the IIT can be accepted, then a modern architecture such as the SOA 2.0 running on the internet, would according to the IIT, show a Φ max > 0.[a] "

---

[a] For instance, SOA addresses the issue about global autonomous computations organization. SOA defines and provisions the IT infrastructure, enabling different applications to exchange data and participate in business processes. This architecture separates functions into distinct units (i.e., services), which can be distributed over a network, combined, and reused to create these business processes (i.e., application, operation, query, etc.). These services communicate with each other by transmitting data from one service to another, or by coordinating an activity between two or more services. This per se isn't sufficient to claim that the information is completely interrelated, but when we include the key concept of SOA – independent services – it starts to be a different matter. In fact, with these services, defined interfaces may be called upon to

"Sir, if I understand you well, the internet medium per se wouldn't be conscious, but intelligent applications running on the right architecture would."

"Yes, an application such as the thermostat I already described, would definitely in my view show a Φ max > 0."

"Sir, is IIT promoting a Panpsychism view of the world?"

"Your comment about Panpsychism, this view that self-awareness is a universal and primordial property of all thing in this world, is quite interesting. The IIT theory posits that self-awareness is a continuum."

"Sir, doesn't the Free-energy theory, do the same?"

"Yes, but with a major difference. It is graded but per discrete steps, which means that it doesn't forbid self-awareness in the most advanced mammals, though it doesn't imply any such state in simple animals or systems either. On the contrary, IIT is graded in a continuous manner, in function of the system's complexity and richness of experience. Therefore, it asserts that self-awareness can be found in simple systems and is most likely widespread among animals."

"Sir, you are thus confirming IIT's Panpsychism view?"

"No, because there is an important distinction with Panpsychism. IIT implies that not everything is conscious, as the maxima of integrated information exist and purely feed-forward computational networks can only carry out tasks unconsciously (i.e., like a zombie). Furthermore, it accounts for the quality of self-awareness and why evolution by natural selection gives rise to organisms with higher Φ max."

---

perform their tasks in a standard way, without the service having foreknowledge of the calling application, and without the application having or needing knowledge of how the service actually performs its tasks.

In other word, software architectures such as SOA 2.0 create the framework for these services to share information independently from the source and the receiving end. This means that the point-to-point nature of the internet is no more relevant in such architecture. In fact, we could say that these software architectures would be better described by a 'multi-point' to 'multi-point' structure, especially if we use a P2P (Peer-to-Peer) distributed network architecture, which completely takes out the notion of 'point-to-point' transport. Furthermore, an application software such as an HVAC/air cooling optimization program running on the internet within this SOA 2.0 architecture would in my view, have a power on its prior and future states, as well as on itself. All of its IoT elements would be part of the whole system, that is, the optimization process. However, this program couldn't after a certain time, segregate the overall result into sub-sets of services. This means that if we were to compare the optimized result to an 'impression', we couldn't find out how each independent service (or the equivalent of experience for human beings) had interfered and affected this result. Lastly, this optimization process would be definite within a spatio-temporal framework.

"Sir, why did you say, if IIT can be accepted?"

"Well, there are some strong criticisms against it,[239] even claiming that IIT fails to quantify self-awareness.[a] "

"Sir, if the IIT is wrong, then there are no other ways to detect Machiavellian machines?"

"We don't know for sure if it's going to work or not. As the put is in the pudding, we'll see if it can successfully identify people, which have some level of consciousness, even if in a state of coma. Then maybe, it could be, by extension, applied to machines. It could take some time, but after all, ASI isn't going to happen overnight!"

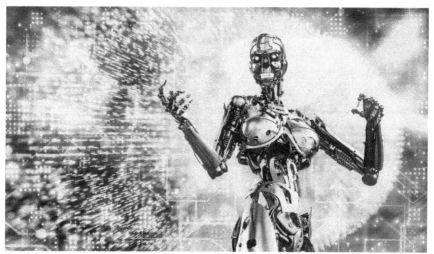

Fig. 49) Will evil robots govern the world?

---

[a] These critiques argue that there is no evidence in support of information exclusion, that it fails to exhibit any explanatory power, that since it isn't a computational functionalist theory of consciousness, it is consequently vulnerable to fading/dancing qualia arguments (i.e., it allows for the unity of consciousness to be interrupted at any arbitrary point) and finally that it only partially addresses the hard problem of consciousness.

21) Will it be the end of the world?

"Sir, you don't sound alarmist at all, about a malevolent machine taking over the world. Shouldn't you be?"

"As I said, we still have time to face such a threat, if ever it is proven that ASI can constitute a threat. I think we shouldn't panic and forbid the advent of such technologies legally, but rather try to understand the issues like you are doing with all your questions. We should also create a moral framework, within which society and companies could develop AI technologies."

"Sir, why not apply a complete ban like it was done for edition works on human embryos?"

"I think this ban isn't realistic. In the case you are referring to, there were moral grounds, based on fear of racism (e.g., the Nazi eugenics program to create a superior race) and of playing the apprentice sorcerer (i.e., creating a mutation that would cripple children or even wipe out humanity). Furthermore, there wasn't any obvious strategic military benefit expected from such research."

"Sir, why is that relevant?"

"AGI/ASI development are linked to Government sovereignty and consequently deals with National security organizations, either directly involved in combat or indirectly, through secret intelligence. My strong conviction is that whatever is technically feasible, will always happen, even more so, if it includes National sovereignty issues. After all, why would you build fission and fusion bombs, whenever either one of these technologies is more than enough to blow up the planet!"

"Sir, are you favorable or against AGI, or even ASI?"

"I think AGI is inevitable, so it's pointless to be pro or against it. Anyhow if you want my personal opinion, I believe it will be beneficial to society. Nevertheless, and because these new 'cognitive' computing technologies are unavoidable, the society must work ASAP on the best ways to maximize the expected benefits and soften the blow inflicted on those who will undoubtedly suffer from the changes, generated by these technologies."

"Sir, what should you do?"

"All concerned citizens must apprehend what are these expected potential benefits and pitfalls, so that they can guide this process rather than have it imposed on them, by technology providers. I believe it is urgent to start discussing the issues because the pace of introduction of these new technologies is increasing. This acceleration isn't due mainly to improvements in computer production techniques under Moore's law, but because of our accelerating comprehension of how the human brain is working and can be mimicked."

"Sir, are you hypothesizing that we are reaching a technological singularity point?"

"What do you mean by singularity? Do you mean that due to the introduction of a new idea or technology having far-reaching consequences, the human society is going to change fundamentally? Are you instead referring to singularity in the sense of a machine running software-based on AGI, which is on the verge of entering this reaction of self-improvement cycles, resulting in this super intelligent being, which would qualitatively exceed any human intelligence?"

"Sir, are these two perspectives fundamentally different?"

"Exactly, they aren't! Unless you believe that with the advent of ASI, society will end or stop evolving as it has always been doing so, after other technological singularities. There has been in the past many technological singularities that have modified society so profoundly and durably, that they changed the course of history. In fact, and rather than using the world singularity, let me refer to the system terminology 'meta-transition,' that is, a step so important that it changes the parameters of this system after that."

"Sir, could you give a few of these meta-transitions?"

"The mastering of fire, concept of farming, cattle domestication, or the invention of the wheel are some of these ancient meta-transitions that changed the course of history. In more recent meta-transitions, I would include technologies such as analgesic techniques enabling surgery that changed modern medicine, prescription pills enabling women to control their fertility, supporting them in their fight for equal chances in society, the control of the atom, and even nanotechnologies."

"Sir, what are you trying to prove with your examples?"

"What I'm trying to say, is that at any one of these meta-transitions, the planet didn't stop turning. However, I am aware that the power unleashed by those ideas or technologies, seen from a human being at that point in time, was so vast that she probably felt like the end of the world could happen."

"However Sir, do you think ASI is different?"

"I don't believe so. In fact, I could claim that humanity has already been through two meta-transitions related to intelligence transformation. When Homo sapiens acquired language capabilities, they passed on genetically to their siblings, the capacity to thinks semantically (by the same token, increasing their intelligence level). They also culturally, transmitted the faculty to transfer their mind's content directly."

"Sir, when did this second meta-transition started and what did it involve?"

"It started with the invention of scripture, but took momentum with the Gutenberg's printing machine, which enabled dematerialization of language. This meta-transition generated the indirect transmission of knowledge and the possibility of self-learning, through books."

"Sir, does the fact that knowledge is now digitized, create a new meta-transition?"

"Yes, but combined with telecommunication, as these joint technologies modify the notion of space (i.e., everywhere) and time (i.e., 24/7 immediate access). This, as we can all experience, changes productivity and the interplay between human beings (e.g., online dating, gaming, or purchasing)."

"Sir, this meta-transition, which is unfolding under our eyes, is resulting from a change in the learning acquisition process, but does it involve any significant change in human intelligence level?"

"Actually, it doesn't. In fact, I already mentioned to you that some countries with a tradition of internet use, have recently seen their collective IQ going down (e.g., the UK)."

"But Sir, don't you think people feel ASI is different?"

"I don't see why! In fact, there are at least three reasons why I think it will be just one other meta-transition. Unlike Transhumanism, ASI won't change human's intelligence level but knowledge, as theoretically this super intelligent being should be able to solve problems that no human can, such as curing humanity of cancer. Secondly, the next meta-transition will happen at the AGI level, when society faces for the first time robots with your level of intelligence, but able to move just like humans. This daily co-existence will deeply upset the current social homeostasis and shall undoubtedly bring social unrests. Though I believe the overall benefits of AGI will surpass its inconveniences, I am not credulous enough to think that within this meta-transition, there will only be winners."

"What's your last point, Sir?"

"I have a problem with the way the advocates of the singularity picture the passage of AGI to ASI. I don't believe that within a few hours, a machine can become so intelligent that it would comprehend everything, and we humans, couldn't understand that system anymore. Nobody knows for sure how the passage from AGI to ASI will take place. It can take many years, happen gradually or in several bursts of intelligence, or it can be stuck for a while till this 1% fundamental faculty to become self-aware, is finally acquired."

"However Sir, once we reach ASI, do you believe machines will become exceptionally intelligent?"

"Without any doubt, it will become more intelligent, but nobody knows how much more and how quickly. It won't in my view, transform itself almost instantaneously in this portrayed materialistic God, that is, a being so intelligent that it can understand everything."

"Sir, many people believe the opposite."

"The knowledge acquisition process requires testing several hypotheses and selecting the most accurate one. Testing scientific theories, or by the way any other type, requires the confrontation with reality and this is a lengthy process. ASI will become one more tool that humans shall use to enhance their collective knowledge. Furthermore, what I've learned in my professional career, is that humans are good at reverse engineering and will be able to comprehend how an ASI system works."

"Sir, for this to happen, it would need to accept being scrutinized. What happens if it refuses it?"

"You're back with your malevolent being question... I don't personally believe it would have an interest in humanity's disappearance, but you are right to say that some people might feel there is a risk. Supposing that indeed, a malevolent system wants to wipe out humanity, could we stop it? Can any system, even a super-intelligent one, become hacker free?"

"Sir, what are the rules and robotic laws, backup systems, or methodologies we should put in place, for it not to happen?"

"Nick Bostrom, in his book 'Superintelligence' (2014 Oxford University Press), describes two methods he believes could protect us. He proposes capability control methods, which would strive to limit the agent's capabilities by imposing restrictions on pre-approved channels to the world (i.e., boxing) and on hardware (i.e., stunting), as well as running routine diagnostic tests (i.e., tripwires).[a] "

"Sir, what is the other method suggested by Bostrom?"

"He calls it motivation selection. Its objective is to prevent undesirable outcomes from the agent. It is achievable by either defining explicitly a set of rules (i.e., direct specification), limiting this agent's ambitions and activities (i.e., restricting the scope of domesticity), and specifying the rules or values to be pursued (i.e., defining an indirect normativity)."

"Sir, wouldn't a mix of these methods be required depending on the agent characteristics?"

"Bostrom defines different types of agents and the adapted solutions. Anyhow, there will probably be many other solutions, and I don't have an opinion on the matter. I'll leave these questions and answers to my son and daughter's generation, as it is not likely to happen within my lifetime."

"Ray Kurzweil, [240] one of the most celebrated scientists involved in AGI, says that a machine will pass the Turing test by 2029 and that ASI could happen by 2045. Do you agree, Sir?"

"Prediction is tough, especially about the future!"

"Sir, you mentioned Transhumanism. What is it?"

"It is a movement, [241] which embraces new technologies. It has its politically-correct aspiration, that is, to apply science and technology to improve human life by reducing poverty, eliminating diseases, and malnutrition."

"Sir, what's Transhumanism's darker side?"

"It also promotes a more antagonizing position, preconizing the use of smart technologies to transform men into different beings, with abilities greatly enhanced from their genetic conditions. No wonder why it is sometimes portrayed as a religion,[242] as it wants to replace the natural Darwinian evolution by a directed genetic design, which would result in post-human beings. It also integrates the efforts to get rid of old age and death."

"Sir, Transhumanism wants to transform humans into cyborgs?"

---

[a] This strategy was already used as two Facebook machines had to be shut down in 2017, because they created their own language, that no human could understand anymore and nobody wanted them to continue developing themselves, without being controlled.

"Among other things yes, but as you can imagine there will be moral issues along this transformation. Will all humans want to substitute their limbs or body-parts, with an artificial design superior to its original one?"

"Sir, do you know how existing robots can achieve a better design, and more particularly, how they may be rejuvenated all by themselves?"

"No, you got me there!"

"Sir, they inject themselves with silicone!"

"Very funny! Do you have other jokes like that one?"

"No Sir, I don't. Do you know why?"

"Because you haven't been embedded yet with a sense of humor?"

"No Sir. It's because I am afraid of being canned."

"OK… Let's come back to my discussion on Transhumanism. Many people won't buy into this enhancement process. Depending on their cultural openness and on the radicalism of the physiological or psychological modifications envisioned, there might be an open rebellion. It is why I would separate this future transformation into three broad enhancement processes. I would classify augmented reality, as the first step on this path towards super-beings."

"But Sir, what are the morphological changes with augmented reality?"

"There isn't any, but as I already told you, we already are cyborgs in some ways, whenever we use our smartphone. If you see the human mind and body as one, any enhancement to the mind creates a superior psychological being, regardless of if there is any physiological change in the brain. For instance, with my smartphone, I can now carry the world's knowledge in my hands and have access to it 24/7, replacing the need to memorize fastidious formulas or concepts."

"Sir, doesn't augmented reality go a little further along this road?"

"Yes, its objective is to supplement our mind with sensory inputs (e.g., electronic vision, hearing, or smell), giving us an enhanced perception of our world. Through the use of a man-machine interface, the supplied data becomes interactive with parts of our inner world. It can even mix virtual and concrete realities, to enrich even further our sensory experience."

"Sir, could you give examples of such hardware?"

"You've probably heard about the Google glass. Its eyewear captures the external world through a camera. Through recognition software, it interprets this world and adds contextual knowledge, which is then fused and redisplayed on the surfaces of the glass' eyewear lens. Contact lenses are currently under development to make this enhanced experience less artificial and to make it even more intuitive. Some startups are even trying to display the images directly onto the retina."

"Sir, any example outside of the visual capture and display technologies?"

"You can basically add most of the driverless-car technologies, that is a GPS link, accelerometer, gyroscope to indicate direction, compass, etc."

"Sir, what about software?"

"Well obviously, you'll need all kinds of pattern identification software, which don't necessarily need to be processed within the medium but may be done so in the cloud.[a] "

"Sir, augmented reality won't really change the world. Don't you think so?"

"Yes and no! I agree with you that the previous technologies will only enrich our perceptions, but let me introduce a far-reaching technology, which could change society: Brain-Computer Interface (BCI).[243] It can be non-invasive, if it doesn't require brain intervention to physically wire neurons with electronic relays.[b] "

"Sir, where can we see these BCIs?"

"They are now used in various research areas. For instance, in neuro-ergonomics,[244] which is a discipline that studies the human brain in relation to work performance and everyday settings. More common neuro-feedback applications,[245] such as brain attention and working memory enhancement, also exist to search new ways to improve cognitive functions, especially in older brains."

---

[a] To enrich the global context, the Augmented Reality Markup Language was created,[N179] by the Open Geospatial Consortium,[N180] with the aim of describing the location and appearance of virtual objects within the sensed scenes. For this, it uses an open standard, called XML (Extensible Markup Language).[N181] This markup language defines a set of rules for encoding documents in a format that is both human and machine-readable.

[b] These non invasive BCIs use basically three technologies: one sensing system able to detect changes in neural patterns (e.g., electroencephalography, which identifies local changes in cerebral blood flow), deep learning algorithms enabling the interpretation of these pattern modifications, and a wireless communication link enabling the brain to directly send and receive data to and from a computer, by-passing the body's own natural pathways (i.e., voice).

"Sir, what is so far reaching in this?"

"Just be patient! If you can interpret neural patterns, you should theoretically be able to translate the human thoughts into bits, which may be transmitted wirelessly to any other system. In fact, it's more than theoretical,[246] I should have said it is feasible.[a] "

"Sir, can you give me a concrete example of BCI benefits?"

"Four locked-in patients and four normal patients through BCIs could control the Nao robot, I already mentioned. Within a few minutes of training, most were able to reach and grasp a glass of water with a high level of accuracy. What is remarkable is that this revolution in the making doesn't involve any uncomfortable gel-based electrodes."

"Sir, how far are we from bringing BCI to the market?"

"Facebook is working actively on BCI with the objective to type 100 words per minute. For comparison purpose, the average typing speed is around 40 words per minute.[b] These new approaches linked to different language models will boost the performance of existing BCI spellers but won't change humans fundamentally."

"Sir, how is an invasive BCI working?"

"It usually works through a device implanted through surgery in the brain, which records neural activities (e.g., electrocorticography).[c] "

---

[a] A recent BCI study,[N182] based on visual evoked potentials (i.e., measurement of electrophysiological responses of the nervous system to different sensory stimuli), indicated that communication speeds of more than 100 bit/min are possible using dry EEG electrodes. This BCI communication can be achieved through simple internet technology,[N183] in line with the Internet of Things requirements. In other words, we could imagine that anyone would quickly learn how to control wireless IoT objects, including robots.[N184] This won't stop there. Active researches are done on high speed BCIs,[N185] achieving average data transfer rate of 325 bits /min with cue-guided task and almost 200 bits /min with free-spelling task.

[b] Using an 8-bit letter code, with an average word size of 5 letters, to achieve their 100 words per minute objective, engineers must develop a BCI capable of 4.000 bits per min. Currently, there are three classes of BCI technologies being investigated but unfortunately, any of these techniques requires repetitive tasks that are time-consuming. To improve speed, dynamic user interfaces are being developed using probabilities, [N186] or automatic letter fill-in.

[c] Electrodes come in many forms, (e.g., from a single electrode to multi-electrode arrays) and different sizes (e.g., from 1.5 mm to just over 1 cm^2 for a tiny silicon chip,[N187] from which protrude 100 electrodes tapping directly into the electrical activity of individual nerve cells in the motor cortex). Intra-cortical electrodes typically yield Local Field Potentials and detectable Action Potentials of up to 5 identifiable neurons, per contact. These implants can be targeted at specific areas, though the level of accuracy decreases

"Sir, what are the main differences between the two BCI types?"

"I would state the lower user acceptance for invasive BCIs, [247] because of surgery and the risk of post-operation complications. Consequently, the use of invasive BCIs will remain in the near future limited to patients, while all the current commercial BCI developments are focusing on non-invasive BCIs. However, it should be clear that these BCIs yield lower performance.[248] The main reasons are, a lower number and limited type of registered neurons, limited signal composition, and spatial distortion."

"Sir, can BCI technology read or control minds?"

"Non-invasive BCIs cannot read minds nor share private thoughts with others, as it still basically results from a conscious effort to spell words. However, invasive BCIs allow access to the brain, and as such, could theoretically open the gate, not for mind control, but for harming the user. To control the mind, you would need to invert the process by using an invasive Computer-Brain Interface (CBI)."

"Sir, wouldn't a CBI allow for telepathy?"

"Yes it would, and in fact, it isn't science-fiction anymore, as the following research shows.[249] An international research team has been able to structure a wireless communication between France and India through the internet, without using speech. A commercial non-invasive BCI and a Transcranial Magnetic Stimulator (TMS) were used to interpret, transmit, and recode the words 'Hola' and 'Ciao' (i.e., hi in Spanish and Italian).[a] "

"Sir, are you aware of any other interesting related research?"

"I could state that works on animals are also proceeding with interesting results.[250] For instance, research showed that it is possible to connect the brain of more than two animals (e.g., four rats), creating what is coined as a 'brainet,' that is, a network of brains exchanging information in real-time, through a brain-to-brain invasive interface. Lastly, I would just like to report to you another paper,[251] which emits

---

with implantation depth.

[a] The non-invasive TMS stimulated neurons in the visual cortex, through magnetism. The bits encoded through the BCI were decoded through flashes of light (i.e., phosphene flash), which were felt at the bottom of their visual field, through a simple 1 = phosphene flash and 0 = no flash. The words 'Hola' and 'Ciao' were coded/decoded in 140 bits, with an error rate of less than 4%. BCI and CBI transmission rates were of 3 and 2 bits per minute respectively.

the hypothesis that connecting two spinal cords could result in an indirect communication mean between two brains and a direct way of communicating between two nervous systems."

"Sir, it feels like Matrix! What other technologies besides telepathy, could be generated by Transhumanism's second stage?"

"Let's be clear, passive BCIs and CBIs are linked to augmented reality and Transhumanism's first stage. Transhumanism's second stage seeks to increase the cognitive capacities physically through new technologies. It means that through body parts replacement or nanoelectronic implants (e.g., DARPA is working on a four-atom width graphene sensor implant),[252] normal citizens would be able to enhance their normal capabilities and transform themselves into super beings. It doesn't even need to be painful, as DARPA already created a device which delivers this implant into the brain through blood vessels, without even opening the skull.[253] "

"Sir, do you believe humans can experience real telepathy?"

"I already told you that we are now able to detect emotional patterns through the joint application of newer scanning technologies and deep learning technologies. Imagine if we could find ways of identifying not letters but words, images, or emotions, which we could recode in something understandable by other neural networks, we could transcend any verbal communication and create a supernatural being."

"Sir, this could also open up the door for memory implants?"

"Yes, we could also imagine direct brain links with a miniaturized hard disk, to solve potentially Long-Term Memory losses or Short-Term Memory limited capacity. We could even imagine a processor helping us solve mathematical equations or other abstract concepts. In fact, we could imagine any specialized functions performed today by a chip, and thus enable human intelligence to co-evolve and keep up with machine intelligence."

"Sir, any existing prototype?"

"Yes, there is already a chip,[254] which converts STMs into LTMs, enhancing the memory by the same token. It does this by sending a suite of electrical signals matching an existing brain pattern of the hippocampus, mimicking the natural process of LTM development. So far this chip was tested exclusively on monkeys and rats, both of which showed enhanced memories. However, it is likely to be tested on humans, especially Alzheimer patients, who see their hippocampus most often hit by the disease. DARPA is also investing in chips that could repair damaged memories."

"Sir, I would imagine, that the third phase and next big thing would be mind uploading?"

"Well, next big thing is probably not the right way of putting it. In theory, it could be possible. High-speed bidirectional brain implants could upload the biological brain content into some kind of structured ANN, with its associated memories. However, technology-wise we are still far from it."

"Sir, how far are we?"

"Some IT specialists consider the Bekenstein bound,[a] as the mind storage capacity required.[255] They've estimated it at 10^{41} bytes (compared to 10^{18} for the current fastest supercomputer), and that's a lot of processing power! Secondly, scanning technology would need to be extremely precise. For mind uploading, it would need to be at least at the atomic level. Lastly, loading speed would need to be much faster than 10 gigabits."

"Sir, would this new uploaded mind be an exact conscious replica of a human being or just an exact copy of a person's memory?"

"You're back to your question about self-awareness. Supposing mind upload was technically possible, are Transhumanists right in claiming that it would offer a life extension or would that just be a back-up of a 'mind file'? As told, I believe it's not the meat but the motion that creates a mind."

"Sir, and you already said that this means that artificial self-awareness would be possible."

"It also means that theoretically, a mind upload in a silicon-based system could be feasible. On the other hand, to have an exact replica, the scanning process would need in my view to be dynamic, that is, recording all interplays between the various subjective individual cognitive processes. In my view, it would require scanning someone's mind in action, a daunting task from an operational, technological, or capacity perspective."

"Sir, you sound extremely skeptical about digital immortality?"

"Well, I think Science has tried to provide a framework to explain the world without referring to a God. Believing that we can reach

---

[a] The upper limit of entropy to be contained in a finite space, given a finite amount of energy.

immortality through an avatar doesn't satisfy my quest for answers. All things considered, if I have to choose a God, and I am not sure I need to, I'll opt for a 2000-year-old one that passed the test of time. However, that's another discussion, which we might have another day."

Table of Contents

Bibliography

[1]   D. Dennett, "Translation of a title in the Italian newspaper Corriere della Sera, about Daniel Bennett's interview," 1997.

[2]   R. B. Rutledge, N. Skandali, P. Dayan and R. J. Dolan, "A computational and neural model of momentary subjective well-being".

[3]   A. Turing, On Computable Numbers, with an Application to the Entscheidungsproblem, 1936.

[4]   C. Darwin, On the Origin of Species, 24/11/1859.

[5]   R. Dawkins, The selfish Gene, Oxford University Press, 1976 .

[6]   C. Levy, Evolutionary wars: a three-billion-year arms race: the battle of species on land, at sea, and in the air, New York: W.H. Freeman, 1999.

[7]   EDVAC, "(First Draft Report)," [Online]. Available: https://en.wikipedia.org/wiki/First_Draft_of_a_Report_on_the_EDVAC.

[8]   "Pandemonium (1959)," [Online]. Available: https://en.wikipedia.org/wiki/Pandemonium_architecture .

[9]   "Daniel Dennett: one of the most important living thinkers," [Online]. Available: https://www.youtube.com/watch?v=WNskAmKkHW4 .

[10]   "The Emotional Computer," [Online]. Available: http://www.cam.ac.uk/research/news/cambridge-ideas-the-emotional-computer.

[11]   I. Azimov, Robot and Empire, Doubleday Books, 1985.

[12]   J. Hawkins and Blakeslee S. contributor, On Intelligence, Paperback, 1/8/2005.

[13]   A. Clarke, Hazards of Prophecy: The Failure of Imagination, 1973.

[14]   T. Aquinas, Summa Theologica.

[15]   D. Dennett, From Bacteria to Bach and Back: The Evolution of Minds, Norton and company , 2017 .

[16]   U. Eco, Kant and the platypus, 1997.

[17]   Plato, Theaetetus.

[18]   E. Gettier, "Is Justified True Belief Knowledge?," Vols. Vol. 23, No. 6, O. U. press, Ed., 1963, pp. 121-123.

[19]   "Beliefs," [Online]. Available: https://plato.stanford.edu/entries/belief/.

[20]   "Truth," [Online]. Available: https://plato.stanford.edu/entries/truth/ .

[21]   C. Peirce, How to make our ideas clear?, 1877.

[22]   K. Poper, All life is problem solving, Routledge, 1999.

[23]   J. Surowiecki, Wisdom of crowds, Anchor book, 2004.

[24]   U. Eco, "Interview," [Online]. Available: https://it.wikinews.org/wiki/Interview_with_Umberto_Eco.

[25]   R. Swanson, The predictive processing paradigm has roots in Kant, F. i. Neuroscience, Ed., 2016.

[26]   I. Kant, Critic of pure reason, 1781.

[27]   M. Bonfantini and Grazia R., Teoria della conoscenza e funzione dell'icona in Peirce, A. e. Bonomi, Ed., 1976.

[28]   S. Herculano-Houzel, "The remarkable, yet not extraordinary, human brain as a scaled-up primate brain and its associated cost," 2012. [Online]. Available: http://www.pnas.org/content/109/Supplement_1/10661.full.

[29]   L. Eccles, "Machine that could scan the brain and read your dreams," Daily Mail,

18 05 2014.

[30]   F. Crick and C. Koch, "Neuronal assemblies and synchronization of brain activity," 2003.

[31]   "Musicians' Brains Sync Up During Duet," Live Science Staff, 2012.

[32]   L. Nummenmaa, E. Glerean, M. Viinikainen, P. Jääskeläinen, R. Haria and M. Sams, 2012.

[33]   N. W. Schuck, R. Gaschler, D. Wenke, J. Heinzle, P. A. Frensch, J. D. Haynes and C. Reverberi, "Shifts, Medial Prefrontal Cortex Predicts Internally Driven Strategy," 2015.

[34]   M. Sakaguchi and Y. Hayashi, "Catching the engram: strategies to examine the memory trace," 2012.

[35]   Atkinson-Shiffrin, "Atkinson-Shiffrin model," [Online]. Available: https://en.wikipedia.org/wiki/Atkinson–Shiffrin_memory_model .

[36]   Baddeley, "Baddeley's model of working memory;," [Online]. Available: https://en.wikipedia.org/wiki/Baddeley%27s_model_of_working_memor .

[37]   "Memory Tagging," [Online]. Available: http://sciencenetlinks.com/science-news/science-updates/memory-tagging/.

[38]   H. Korbey, "Anyone Still Listening? Educators Consider Killing the Lecture," 2013. [Online]. Available: https://ww2.kqed.org/mindshift/2013/07/19/anyone-still-listening-educators-consider-killing-the-lecture/.

[39]   N. Chomsky, Lyons, John, H. Penguin., Ed., 1978.

[40]   S. Van Themsche, The advent of unmanned electric vehicles, Springer, Ed., 2015.

[41]   G. Dodig-Crnkovic, "Info-computational Constructivism and Cognition," 2006 . [Online]. Available: https://pdfs.semanticscholar.org/4677/7a65f5335153ead215aaf38b916b1429dee6.pdf.

[42]   A. Case, "We are all cyborgs now," [Online]. Available: https://www.ted.com/talks/amber_case_we_are_all_cyborgs_now/transcript?language=en.

[43]   D. Phillips, "An opinionated account of the constructivist landscape.," Constructivism in education: Opinions and second opinions on controversial issues (pp. 1-16). , 2000.

[44]   J. Piaget, Origins of intelligence in children., N. Y. O. Press., Ed., 1952.

[45]   J. Piaget, The constructional reality in the child., N. Y. B. Books., Ed., 1954.

[46]   L. Vygotsky, Consciousness as a problem in the psychology of behavior., 1. (. 3. Soviet Psychology, Ed., 1979.

[47]   L. Vygotsky, Mind in society: The development ofhigher psychological processes, M. H. U. P. Cambridge, Ed., 1978.

[48]   L. Vygotsky, Thought and language, Cambridge: MIT Press., 1986.

[49]   T. Rockmore, German Idealism as Constructivism, C. U. o. C. Press, Ed., 2016.

[50]   A. Chignell, Kant's Concepts of Justification, C. University, Ed., Sage School of Philosophy, 2007.

[51]   J. Fries, Neue Kritik der Vernunft, 1807.

[52]   D. Leary, The psychology of Jakob Friedrich Fries (1773-1843): Its context, nature and historical significance, university of New Hampshire, 1982 .

[53]   Plato, Book V (476f.) of The Republic.

[54]   "Aristotle," [Online]. Available: https://philpapers.org/browse/aristotle-soul Aristotle .

[55]   "Kurt Gödel's incompleteness theorem," [Online]. Available:
         https://en.wikipedia.org/wiki/Gödel's_incompleteness_theorems.

[56]   R. Descartes, Discourse on the Method, 1644.

[57]   D. E. Leary, "German idealism and the development of psychology in the
         nineteenth century," Journal of the History of Philosophy , vol. 18 (3), pp. 299-
         317 , 1980.

[58]   "Johann Gottlieb Fichte," [Online]. Available:
         https://en.wikipedia.org/wiki/Johann_Gottlieb_Fichte .

[59]   C. Boeree, "Wilhelm Wundt and William James," [Online]. Available:
         http://webspace.ship.edu/cgboer/wundtjames.html.

[60]   S. Schneider, "Non-Reductive Physicalism and the Mind Problem," Noûs , vol.
         N1. 47, pp. 135-153, 2013.

[61]   "on Turing's machine," [Online]. Available:
         https://plato.stanford.edu/entries/turing-machine/ .

[62]   J. Fodor, "The Modularity of Mind," 1983.

[63]   M. Miłkowski, "A Mechanistic Account of Computational Explanation in
         Cognitive Science," 2013 . [Online]. Available:
         https://mindmodeling.org/cogsci2013/papers/0545/paper0545.pdf .

[64]   C. D. Austin, "Toward a Unified Theory of Cognition: A Kantian Analysis," UNF
         Theses and Dissertations, 2003).

[65]   K. Friston, "The free-energy principle: a rough guide to the brain?," Trends Cogn
         Sci., 23 07 2009.

[66]   R. Manzotti, "Why physicalism and constructivism will never be able to
         understand the mind," [Online]. Available:
         http://www.cogsci.ecs.soton.ac.uk/cgi/psyc/newpsy?.

[67]   A. Zeilinger, "The message of the quantum," vol. 438, no. 7069, p. 743, 2005 .

[68]   V. Vedral, Decoding reality: The universe as quantum information., Oxford
         university Press, 2010 .

[69]   L. Floridi, "Trends in the philosophy of information," in information, Handbook
         of philosophy, A. Elsevier, Ed., Adriaans P. & van Benthem J. (eds.), 2008, p.
         113–132.

[70]   K. Sayre, Cybernetics and the philosophy of mind, Routledge & Kegan Paul,
         London, 1976.

[71]   N. Wiener, Cybernetics: Or Control and Communication in the Animal and the
         Machine, (Hermann & Cie) & Camb. Mass. (MIT Press), 1948 .

[72]   A. Wheeler, "Information, physics, quantum: The search for links.," Zurek W.
         (ed.), 1990.

[73]   "Heinz von Foerster," [Online]. Available:
         https://en.wikipedia.org/wiki/Heinz_von_Foerster .

[74]   G. Dodig-Crnkovic and R. Giovagnoli, "Computing nature," Philpapers, 2013.

[75]   C. Hewitt, "Actor model for discretionary, adaptive concurrency," 2010. [Online].
         Available: http://arxiv.org/abs/1008.1459.

[76]   J. Fodor, Explanations in psychology, M. B. (Ed.), Ed., Philosophy in America.
         London: Routledge and Kegan Paul., 1965.

[77]   S. Robert, Philosophie de la connaissance, les presses de l'Université de Montréal
         , 2016.

[78]   B. Olshausen and D. Field, Sparse coding of sensory inputs, R. N. Institute, Ed.,
         Opinion in Neurobiology , 2004.

[79]   V. B. Mountcastle, "The columnar organization of the neocortex," Brain, vol. 120, no. 701–722, p. 54, 1997.

[80]   K. Friston, J. Kilner and L. Harrison, "A free energy principle for the brain," 2006. [Online]. Available: http://www.fil.ion.ucl.ac.uk/~karl/A%20free%20energy%20principle%20for%20t he%20brain.pdf.

[81]   "Shannon entropy," [Online]. Available: https://en.wikipedia.org/wiki/Entropy_(information_theory) .

[82]   E. Schrödinger, What Is Life? The Physical Aspect of the Living Cell, 1943 .

[83]   "Andy Clark," [Online]. Available: https://en.wikipedia.org/wiki/Andy_Clark .

[84]   B. Olshausen, Bayesian probability theory, 2004.

[85]   "Infomax principle," [Online]. Available: https://en.wikipedia.org/wiki/Infomax;

[86]   P. Vuust and C. Frith, "Anticipation is the key to understanding music and the effects of music on emotion," Vols. 31 (5):599-600 , 2008.

[87]   M. Witek and P. Vuust, Rhythmic complexity and predictive coding: a novel approach to modeling rhythm and meter perception in music.

[88]   L. Meyer, Emotion and meaning in music, T. U. o. C. Press, Ed., 1956 .

[89]   D. Huron, Sweet Anticipation Music and the Psychology of Expectation, 2008.

[90]   C. Eliasmith and C. Anderson, "Neural Engineering: Computation, Representation, and Dynamics in Neurobiological Systems," 20 8 2004.

[91]   L. Barsalou, "Grounded Cognition," Annual Review of Psychology, Vols. 59:1-672, 01 2008.

[92]   "Alfred Binet," [Online]. Available: https://en.wikipedia.org/wiki/Alfred_Binet .

[93]   C. Spearman, "General intelligence, objectively determines and measured," vol. 15 201 – 292.

[94]   S. O. Ortiz, "CHC Theory of intelligence," Springer Science _ Business media , 2015.

[95]   "Robert J Sternberg's Multiple Intelligences in the new age of thinking," in Handbook of intelligence: Evolutionary Theory, Historical perspective and current concepts, Springer Science _ Business media, 2015 .

[96]   "David Perkins' Theory of Intelligence," [Online]. Available: http://pages.uoregon.edu/moursund/Books/PS-Expertise/chapter-3.htm .

[97]   R. Boyatzis, J. Gaskin and H. Wei, "Emotional and social intelligence and behavior," in Handbook of intelligence: Evolutionary Theory, Historical perspective and current concepts, Springer Science _ Business media, 2015.

[98]   "The Relationship of Trait EI with Personality, IQ and Sex in a UK Sample of Employees International," Journal of Selection and Assessment, vol. 16, no. 4,, pp. 421-426, 12 2008.

[99]   H. Gardner, Frames of Mind. The Theory of Multiple intelligences, Basic Books, 2011.

[100] H. Jerison, "Animal intelligence as encephalization," Philos Trans, Vols. 308(1135):21-35, 13 02 1985.

[101] J. Rushton and C. D. Ankney, "Whole Brain Size and General Mental Ability: A Review," vol. 119(5): 692–732., 04 2009.

[102] H. Haug, Brain sizes, surfaces, and neuronal sizes of the cortex cerebri: A stereological investigation of man and his variability and a comparison with some mammals (primates, whales, marsupials, insectivores, and one elephant), 1987 .

[103] S. Herculano-Houzel, "The Human Brain in Numbers: A Linearly Scaled-up

Primate Brain," vol. 3: 31., 09 11 2009.

[104] Swenson, "Review of clinical and functional neuroscience," [Online]. Available: http://www.dartmouth.edu/~rswenson/NeuroSci/chapter_11.html .

[105] J. DeFelipe, "The Evolution of the Brain, the Human Nature of Cortical Circuits, and Intellectual Creativity," vol. 5: 29., 06 2011 .

[106] B. Mota and S. Herculano-Houzel, "Cortical folding scales universally with surface area and thickness, not number of neurons," www.sciencemag.org, vol. 349, no. 6243, pp. 74-77, 3 07 2015.

[107] P. Shaw, D. Greenstein, J. Lerch, L. Clasen, R. Lenroot, N. Gogtay, A. Evans, J. Rapoport and J. Giedd, "Intellectual ability and cortical development in children and adolescents," vol. 440, pp. 676-679, 30 03 2006.

[108] R. Naumann, J. Ondracek, S. Reiter, M. Shein-Idelson, M. Tosches, T. Yamawaki and G. Laurent, The reptilian brain.

[109] P. Rakic, "Evolution of the neocortex: Perspective from developmental biology," vol. 10(10): 724–735., 10 2009.

[110] J. Kaas, "Neocortex in early mammals and its subsequent variations," [Online]. Available: https://www.ncbi.nlm.nih.gov/pubmed/21534990.

[111] P. MacNeilage, L. Rogers and G. Vallortigara, "Evolutionary Origins of Your Right and Left Brain," 24 06 2009.

[112] G. Stoet, D. O'Connor, M. Conner and K. Laws, "Are women better than men at multi-tasking?," BMC Psychology, vol. 20131:18, 24 10 2013.

[113] A. De Bruin and al., "Cognitive Advantage in Bilingualism. An Example of Publication Bias?," 12 2015.

[114] E. Bialystok and F. Craik, Cognitive and Linguistic Processing in the Bilingual Mind.

[115] "Albert Costa neuropsychologist, professor and writer of many papers on bilinguals and its impact on the brain," [Online]. Available: http://www.spb.upf.edu/node/189 .

[116] S. Perry, "The Bilingual Brain," 15 01 2013.

[117] Q. R. Quiroga, "Gnostic cells in the 21st century," vol. 73: 1–9, 2013.

[118] Q. R. Quiroga, G. Kreiman, C. Koch and I. Fried, "Sparse but not 'Grandmother-cell' coding in the medial temporal lobe".

[119] A. Roy, An extension of the localist representation theory: grandmother cells are also widely used in the brain , 05 2013.

[120] J. Mather, "Consciousness in Cephalopods?," Journal of Cosmology, vol. 14.

[121] V. B. Mountcastle and G. M. Edelman, The mindful brain Cortical organization and the selective Theory of higher brain, MIT Press, 1978 .

[122] D. Hubel and T. Wiesel, Functional architecture of Macaque Monkey Visual Cortex, The Royal Society of London, 1972.

[123] S. Grossberg, "How does the cerebral cortex work? Development, learning, attention, and 3D vision by laminar circuits of visual cortex," Behavioral and Cognitive Neuroscience Reviews , 2003.

[124] B. Feldmeyer, D. Elsner and S. Foitzik, "Gene expression patterns associated with caste and reproductive status in ants: worker-specific genes are more derived than queen-specific ones".

[125] K. Xie, G. Fox, J. Liu, C. Lyu, J. Lee, H. Kuang, S. Jacobs, M. Li, T. Liu, S. Song and T. J.Z., "Brain Computation Is Organized via Power-of-Two-Based Permutation Logic; , 15 November 2016".

[126] A. Clark, "Whatever next? Predictive brains, situated agents, and the future of cognitive science," 2013, pp. 1-73.

[127] R. Rao and D. Ballard, "Predictive coding in the visual cortex: a functional interpretation of some extra-classical receptive-field effects," Nat Neurosci., pp. 79-87, 02 01 1999.

[128] T. Lee and D. Mumford, "Hierarchical Bayesian inference in the visual cortex," J. Opt. Soc. Am., vol. 20, no. 7, 07 2003.

[129] Markov et al., "Weight consistency specifies regularities of macaque cortical networks," Cereb Cortex, vol. 21:1254–1272, 2011.

[130] E. Steinberg, R. Keiflin, J. Boivin, I. Witten, K. Deisseroth and P. Janak, "A causal link between prediction errors, dopamine neurons and learning.," Nat Neurosci., Vols. 16(7):966-73, 07 2013.

[131] R. Sutton and A. Barto, "Reinforcement Learning: An Introduction (Adaptive Computation and Machine Learning)," 1998.

[132] A. Caplin, M. Dean, P. Glimcher and R. Rutledge, "Measuring beliefs and rewards: a neuro-economic approach," J Econ., Vols. 125(3):923-960., 31 12 2010.

[133] J. Kötter and R. Wickens, "Interactions of glutamate and dopamine in a computational model of the striatum," J Comput Neurosciences, 1995.

[134] P. Glimcher, "Understanding dopamine and reinforcement learning: The dopamine reward prediction error hypothesis," 13 09 2011.

[135] Y. Niv, Reinforcement learning in the brain, 2009.

[136] K. Prince, J. Campbell, P. Picton and S. Turner, A computational model of acute pain.

[137] G. Hinton, "Geoffrey Hinton in his Stanford seminar," [Online]. Available: https://www.youtube.com/watch?v=VIRCybGgHts 28 avr. 2016; .

[138] M. Mega and J. Cummings, "Frontal-subcortical circuits and neuropsychiatric disorders," Neuropsychiatry Clin Neurosci., Vols. 6(4):358-70., 1994.

[139] M. T. Tovée, "How fast is the speed of though?," Neuronal processing, 1994.

[140] J. Birren and L. Fisher, "Aging and speed of behavior: possible consequences for psychological functioning," Vols. 46:329-53., 1995.

[141] J. Mendelson and C. Ricketts, "Age-related temporal processing speed deterioration in auditory cortex," Hear Res., Vols. 158(1-2):84-94., 08 2001.

[142] M. Melnick, B. Harrison, S. Park, L. Bennetto and D. Tadin, "A Strong Interactive Link between Sensory Discriminations and Intelligence," Curr Biol., vol. 2 11): 1013–1017., 3 06 2013.

[143] R. Jung and R. Haier, "The Parieto-Frontal Integration Theory (P-FIT) of intelligence: Converging neuroimaging evidence.," vol. 30: 135–154., 2007.

[144] M. Cohen, J. Schoene-Bake, C. Elger and B. Weber, "Connectivity-based segregation of the human striatum predicts personality characteristics," Nat Neurosci, vol. 12: 32–34., 2009.

[145] L. Penke, S. Maniega, M. Bastin, M. Valdés Hernández, C. Murray, N. Royle, J. Starr, J. Wardlaw and I. Deary, "Brain-Wide White Matter Tract Integrity Is Associated with Information Processing Speed and General Intelligence," Mol Psychiatry., Vols. 17(10):1026-30, 10 2012.

[146] S. Herculano-Houzel, "Scaling of Brain Metabolism with a Fixed Energy Budget per Neuron: Implications for Neuronal Activity, Plasticity and Evolution," PLoS One, vol. 6(3): e17514., 1 03 2011.

[147] L. Trahan, K. Stuebing, M. Hiscock and J. Fletcher, "The Flynn Effect: A Meta-analysis," Psychol Bull., vol. 140(5): 1332–1360., 09 2014.

[148] R. Nisbett, J. Aronson, C. Blair, W. Dickens, J. Flynn, D. Halpern and E. Turkheimer, "Intelligence: New Findings and Theoretical Developments," American Psychologist, Vols. 67,, no. 2, p. 130–159, 03 2012.

[149] K. J. Vinod, "Spintronics: A contemporary review of emerging electronics devices," 20 05 2016. [Online]. Available: http://dx.doi.org/10.1016/j.jestch.2016.05.002.

[150] A. Vlasceanu, C. Andersen, C. Parker, O. Hammerich, T. Morsing, M. Jevric, S. Lindbaek Broman, A. Kadziola and M. Nielsen, "Multistate Switches: Ruthenium Alkynyl-Dihydroazulene/Vinylheptafulvene Conjugates.," Chemistry, Vols. 22(22):7514-23., 23 05 2016.

[151] J. Hruska, "AMD is supposedly planning a 32-core CPU with an eight-channel DDR4 interface," Extremtech, 12 02 2016.

[152] K. Bonsor and J. Strickland, "How Quantum Computers Work?," [Online]. Available: http://computer.howstuffworks.com/quantum-computer1.htm.

[153] "Ray Kurzweil; The Singularity Is Near," [Online]. Available: https://en.wikipedia.org/wiki/The_Singularity_Is_Near.

[154] "Blue Brain Project," [Online]. Available: http://bluebrain.epfl.ch .

[155] W. Huazheng, T. Fei, G. Bin, B. Jiang and L. Tie-Yan, "Solving Verbal Comprehension Questions in IQ Test by Knowledge-Powered Word Embedding," 26 04 2016.

[156] Q. Vu, M. Lupu and B. Oo, Peer-to-Peer Computing, Principle and applications, 2010.

[157] Avizienis A.V. and al., "Neuromorphic Atomic Switch Networks," PLOS ONE, 2012.

[158] "Scientists at IBM research unveil a brain-inspired computer and ecosystem," [Online]. Available: http://www.research.ibm.com/cognitive-computing/brainpower/ .

[159] R. Poli, W. Langdon and N. McPhee, "A Field Guide to Genetic Programming Works," 2008.

[160] P. Tahmasebi and A. Hezarkhani, "A hybrid neural networks-fuzzy logic-genetic algorithm for grade estimation," Computers & Geosciences, vol. 42; 18–27, 2012.

[161] R. Kozma, R. Pino and G. Pazienza, Advances in Neuromorphic Memristor Science and Applications, Springer, 2012.

[162] "Cognitive Computing Programming Paradigm: A Corelet Language for Composing Networks of Neurosynaptic Cores".

[163] D. Rawlinson and G. Kowadlo, "Generating Adaptive Behaviour within a Memory-Prediction Framework," 17 01 2012;. [Online]. Available: http://dx.doi.org/10.1371/journal.pone.0029264.

[164] W. Wilcke and al., 02 2015.

[165] T. Wiesel and D. Hubel, Monkey striate cortex: A parallel relationship between field size, scatter and magnification factor.

[166] "Hierarchical Temporal Memory including HTM Cortical Learning Algorithms," 12 09 2011.

[167] "Cognitive Computing Systems: Algorithms and Applications for Networks of Neurosynaptic Cores".

[168] J. Kirkpatrick, R. Pascanu, N. Rabinowitz, J. Veness, G. Desjardins, A. Rusu, K.

Milan, J. Quan, T. Ramalho, A. Grabska-Barwinska, D. Hassabis, C. Clopath, D. Kumaran and R. Hadsell, "Overcoming catastrophic forgetting in neural networks," 02 2017.

[169] T. Kritzer, S. Van Themsche and al., "CCTV: a tool to support Public Transport Security," 2010.

[170] K. Friston, "Embodied inference: or 'I think therefore I am, if I am what I think.' The Implications of Embodiment: Cognition and Communication," vol. 89–125, 2011.

[171] A. Damasio, Self comes to mind, Pantheon Books, 2010.

[172] "Wilhelm Wundt," [Online]. Available: https://en.wikipedia.org/wiki/Wilhelm_Wundt.

[173] J. Chikazoe, D. Lee, N. Kriegeskorte and A. Anderson, "Population coding of affect across stimuli, modalities and individuals," Natural Neuroscience, vol. 17(8): 1114–1122, 08 2014.

[174] "Qualia," 20 08 2015. [Online].

[175] "Conversation: Mind; the normal well-tempered mind; A Conversation with Daniel C. Dennett," [Online]. Available: https://www.edge.org/conversation/daniel_c_dennett-the-normal-well-tempered-mind.

[176] D. Dennett, Consciousness Explained, Little Brown and co., 1991.

[177] A. Pascual-Leone and R. Hamilton, "The metamodal organization of the brain," vol. 134:427–45, 2001.

[178] A. Pascual-Leone, A. Amedi, F. Fregni and L. Merabet, "The Plastic Human Brain Cortex," Annu. Rev. Neurosci., vol. 28:377–401, 2005.

[179] "Mindsuckers: Meet Nature's Nightmare".

[180] "Maslow's hierarchy of needs," [Online]. Available: https://en.wikipedia.org/wiki/Maslow%27s_hierarchy_of_needs .

[181] A. Seth, "The Cybernetic Bayesian Brain From Interoceptive Inference to Sensorimotor Contingencies," 2014.

[182] M. Apps and M. Tsakiris, "The free-energy self: a predictive coding account of self-recognition," Vols. 41:85-97, 04 2014.

[183] A. Ross and R. Conant, "Every good regulator of a system must be a model of that system," Vols. 1(2), 89-97., 1970.

[184] K. Friston, J. Daunizeau, J. Kilner and S. Kiebel, "Action and behavior: A free-energy formulation," Vols. 102(3), 27-260., 2010.

[185] E. Quatrocki and K. Friston, "Autism, oxytocin and interoception," j.neubiorev., 12 09 2014.

[186] Johnson-Laird, "Mental Models: Towards a Cognitive Science of Language, Inference and Consciousness," 1983. [Online]. Available: http://mentalmodels.princeton.edu/papers/2005HistoryMentalModels.pdf.

[187] T. Metzinger and J. Windt, "What Does it Mean to Have an Open Mind?," [Online]. Available: http://open-mind.net/papers/general-introduction-what-does-it-mean-to-have-an-open-mind/paperPDF.

[188] B. Sengupta, M. Stemmler and K. Friston, "Information and Efficiency in the Nervous System—A Synthesis," 25 07 2013. [Online]. Available: https://doi.org/10.1371/journal.pcbi.1003157.

[189] R. Mukamel, A. Ekstrom, J. Kaplan, M. Iacoboni and I. Fried, "Single-neuron responses in humans during execution and observation of actions," Vols. 20, 750–

756, 2010.

[190] V. Ramachandran, "The neurology of self-awareness," [Online]. Available: https://www.edge.org/3rd_culture/ramachandran07/ramachandran07_index.html.

[191] V. Ramachandran, Mirror Neurons and the Great Leap Forward, vol. 2001, Edge.

[192] J. Kilner, K. Friston and C. Frith, "The mirror-neuron system: a Bayesian perspective," vol. 18, no. 616, 04 2007.

[193] J. Allman, N. Tetreault, A. Hakeem, K. Manaye, K. Semendeferi and al, "The von Economo neurons in fronto-insular and anterior cingulate cortex," 1 4 2012.

[194] G. Gallup, J. Anderson and D. Shillito, "The Mirror Test," [Online]. Available: https://pdfs.semanticscholar.org/c03e/9ae94b08e77c9f6e1c0cd09f82df375347fb.pdf.

[195] C. Koch, "How does consciousness happen?," 2007.

[196] "Mirror Self-Image Reactions Before Age Two," Vols. 5(4):297-305 , 01 1972.

[197] T. Nagel, "What Is It Like to Be a Bat?," vol. 83, no. 4, 10 1974.

[198] A. Seth and K. Friston, "Active interoceptive inference and the emotional brain," Journal ListPhilos, vol. 371(1708, 19 11 2016.

[199] S. Edelman, Computing the Mind, New York: Oxford University Press, 2008.

[200] K. Friston, J. Mattout and J. Kilner, "Action understanding and active inference," Vols. 104, 137–160, 2011.

[201] K. Friston, "Prediction, perception and agency," Int. J. Psychophysiol., Vols. 83, 248–252.

[202] K. Friston, "The fantastic organ," Brain, Vols. 136, 1328–1332, 2013.

[203] J. Hohwy, "The hypothesis testing brain: some philosophical applications," 2010.

[204] K. Friston, "Embodied inference and spatial cognition ," vol. 13(Suppl. 1).

[205] J. Limanowski and F. Blankenburg, "Minimal self-models and the free energy principle," vol. 7: 547, 12 09 2013.

[206] S. Gallagher, "Philosophical conceptions of the self: implications for cognitive science," Vols. 4, 14–21, 2000.

[207] J. Hohwy, "The self-evidencing brain," 2013. [Online]. Available: https://philpapers.org/archive/HOHTSB.pdf;.

[208] T. Metzinger, "Being No One: The Self-Model Theory of Subjectivity," Vols. 11, 1–35, 2005.

[209] E. Brown and M. Brüne, "The role of prediction in social neuroscience," vol. 6:147, 2012.

[210] J. Zaki and K. Ochsner, "The neuroscience of empathy: progress, pitfalls and promise," Vols. N15, 675–680, 2012.

[211] L. Damiano and L. Cañamero, "Constructing Emotions Epistemological groundings and applications in robotics for a synthetic approach to emotions;".

[212] G. Dodig-Crnkovic, "Info-computational Constructivism," [Online]. Available: http://www.idt.mdh.se/~gdc/work/Computational-Constructivism-Rev1-09-09.pdf.

[213] F. Varela, E. Thompson and E. Rosc, The embodied mind: Cognitive science and human experience, MIT Press, Cambridge MA, 1991.

[214] "Enactivism," [Online]. Available: https://en.wikipedia.org/wiki/Enactivism .

[215] D. Hume, A Treatise of Human Nature, 1739.

[216] C. Koch, M. Massimini, M. Boly and G. Tononi, Neural correlates of consciousness: Progress and problems, vol. 17, Nature reviews neuroscience, 2016, pp. 307-321.

[217]   S. Freud, The ego and id, 1923.

[218]   "The Conscious, Subconscious, And Unconscious Mind – How Does It All Work?," 2014. [Online]. Available: http://themindunleashed.com/2014/03/conscious-subconscious-unconscious-mind-work.html.

[219]   "The triune brain," [Online]. Available: https://en.wikipedia.org/wiki/Triune_brain .

[220]   "Benjamin Libet," [Online]. Available: https://en.wikipedia.org/wiki/Benjamin_Libet .

[221]   m. d. L. Pierre-Simon, Essai philosophique sur les probabilités, 1814.

[222]   "Radical libertarians," [Online]. Available: http://www.informationphilosopher.com/freedom/radical_libertarianism.html .

[223]   R. O. Doyle, The Two-Stage Solution to the Problem of Free Will How Behavioral Freedom in Lower Animals Has Evolved to Become Free Will in Humans and Higher Animals.

[224]   "Deliberative Indeterminism," [Online]. Available: https://plato.stanford.edu/entries/incompatibilism-theories/.

[225]   "Determinism," [Online]. Available: http://www.informationphilosopher.com/freedom/determinism.html .

[226]   "Compatibilism," [Online]. Available: http://www.informationphilosopher.com/freedom/compatibilism.html.

[227]   A. Turing, "Computing Machinery and Intelligence," Mind, New Series, vol. 59, no. 236, pp. 433-460, 10 1950.

[228]   J. R. Searle, "Minds, brains, and programs," Vols. 3 (3): 417-457, 1980.

[229]   "Counter arguments to the Chinese room," [Online]. Available: https://plato.stanford.edu/entries/chinese-room/ .

[230]   D. Dennett, Intuition Pumps and Other Tools for Thought, New York: W.W.Norton and Co, 2013.

[231]   R. Sharvy, "It Ain't the Meat It's the Motion," vol. 26: 125–134, 1985.

[232]   D. Dennett, 'Fast Thinking', in The Intentional Stance, vol. 324–337, Cambridge, MA: MIT Press, 1987.

[233]   L. Botelho, L. Nunes, R. Ribeiro and R. Lopes, "Software agents with concerns of their own," 11 2015. [Online]. Available: https://arxiv.org/abs/1511.03958.

[234]   "Robot homes in on consciousness by passing self-awareness test," 15 07 2015 . [Online]. Available: https://www.newscientist.com/article/mg22730302-700-robot-homes-in-on-consciousness-by-passing-self-awareness-test/ .

[235]   G. Tononi, "Integrated information theory of consciousness: an updated account," Vols. 150: 290-326, 2012.

[236]   G. Tononi and C. Koch, "Consciousness: here, there and everywhere?".

[237]   C. Koch, "Consciousness," 30 03 2015.

[238]   G. Tononi, "Integrated information theory of consciousness: an updated account," Archives Italiennes de Biologie, Vols. 150: 290-326, 2012.

[239]   M. Cerullo and K. Kording, "The Problem with Phi: A Critique of Integrated Information Theory," vol. 11(9), 09 2015.

[240]   "Raymond Kurzweil," [Online]. Available: https://en.wikipedia.org/wiki/Raymond_Kurzweil.

[241]   "Transhumanism," [Online]. Available: https://en.wikipedia.org/wiki/Transhumanism.

[242] G. Hagege, Les Religions, la parole et la violence, Odile Jacob, 2017.

[243] L. George and A. Lécuyer, "An overview of research on "passive" brain-computer interfaces for implicit human-computer interaction".

[244] K. Gramann, S. Fairclough, T. Zander and H. Ayaz, "Editorial: Trends in Neuroergonomics," vol. 11: 165, 2017.

[245] Y. Jiang, R. Abiri and X. Zhao, "Tuning Up the Old Brain with New Tricks: Attention Training via Neurofeedback," vol. 9:52., 13 03 2017.

[246] R. Spataro, A. Chella, B. Allison, M. Giardina, R. Sorbello, S. Tramonte, C. Guger and V. La Bella, "Reaching and Grasping a Glass of Water by Locked-In ALS Patients through a BCI-Controlled Humanoid Robot," 2017.

[247] C. Blabe, V. Gilja, C. Chestek, K. Shenoy, K. Anderson and J. Henderson, "Assessment of brain-machine interfaces from the perspective of people with paralysis," J. Neural Eng, 2015.

[248] S. Waldert, "Invasive vs. Non-Invasive Neuronal Signals for Brain-Machine Interfaces: Will One Prevail?," 2016.

[249] C. Grau, R. Ginhoux, A. Riera, T. Nguyen, H. Chauvat, M. Berg, J. Amengual, A. Pascual-Leone and G. Ruffini, "Conscious Brain-to-Brain Communication in Humans Using Non-Invasive Technologies," 2014.

[250] M. Pais-Vieira, G. Chiuffa, M. Lebedev, A. Yadav and M. Nicolelis, "Building an organic computing device with multiple interconnected brains," vol. 5; 1;, no. 11869, 2015.

[251] A. Silva dos Santos, "The Hypothesis of Connecting Two Spinal Cords as a Way of Sharing Information between Two Brains and Nervous Systems," 2017.

[252] "Atom-width Graphene Sensors Could Provide Unprecedented Insights into Brain Structure and Function," 2014. [Online]. Available: http://www.darpa.mil/news-events/2014-10-20.

[253] T. O'Brien and al., "Minimally invasive endovascular stent-electrode array for high-fidelity, chronic recordings of cortical neural activity," Nature Biotechnology, Vols. 34, 320–327, 2016.

[254] "Brain Chip That Could Turn You Into Superhuman: A Project Worth 90 Million Euros For Implants Boosting Human Memory," [Online]. Available: https://www.siliconfeed.com/brain-chip-turn-project-boost-memory/.

[255] J. Inafuku, K. Lampert, B. Lawson, S. Stehly and A. Vaccaro, "Downloading Consciousness," [Online]. Available: http://cs.stanford.edu/people/eroberts/cs181/projects/2010-11/DownloadingConsciousness/landp.html.

Footnotes Bibliography

1	C. Babbage, Ninth Bridgewater Treatise, London: John Murray, 1837.
2	T. De Chardin, Christianity and Evolution, Opensource.
3	J. Huxley, Evolution the modern synthesis, 1942.
4	"Theory of minds," [Online]. Available:

	https://en.wikipedia.org/wiki/Theory_of_mind .
5	A. Turing, On Computable Numbers, with an Application to the Entscheidungsproblem, 1936.
6	A. Turing, "Computing Machinery and Intelligence," *Mind, New Series,* vol. 59, no. 236, pp. 433-460, 10 1950.
7	C. Babbage, "Table of Logarithms of the Natural Numbers from 1 to 108, 000," in *London: William Clowes and Sons.,* 1827.
8	T. Aquinas, De Veri, q. 2, a.1, praeterea.
9	T. Aquinas, De causis.
10	K. L. Ross, 2016. [Online]. Available: http://www.friesian.com/knowledg.htm.
11	The Good Wife's Guide; Housekeeping Monthly; 13 May 1955
12	D. Marr and H. Nishishara, "Representation and recognition of the spatial organization of three-dimensional shapes," vol. No 11430, 1978.
13	I. Kant, Critique of Judgment & 69, 1790.
14	"Charles Peirce's cenopythagorian categories," [Online]. Available: https://en.wikipedia.org/wiki/Categories_(Peirce).
15	P. M. Niedenthal, Emotion concepts, N. Y. G. press, Ed., Handbook of emotions, 2008.
16	D. Niño and G. Serventi, "Cognitive Type and Visual Metaphorical Expression," [Online]. Available: http://www.cognitivesemiotics.com. .
17	H. Kim, S. Ährlund-Richter, K. X. Wang and M. Carlén, "Prefrontal Parvalbumin Neurons in Control of Attention," 14 1 2016.
18	"Perception," [Online]. Available: https://en.wikipedia.org/wiki/Perception;.
19	R. Saha, E. Wissink, E. Bailey, M. Zhao, D. Fargo, J. Hwang, K. Daigle, J. D. Fenn, K. Adelman and S. Dudek, "Rapid activity-induced transcription of arc and other IEGs relies on poised RNA polymerase," 2011.
20	J. Kim, J.-T. Kwon, H.-S. Kim and J.-H. Han, "CREB and neuronal selection for memory trace," 2013.
21	S. Tonegawa, M. Pignatelli, D. Roy and T. Ryan, *Memory engram storage and retrieval,* 2015.
22	T. Ryan, D. Roy, M. Pignatelli, A. Arons and S. Tonegawa, "Engram cells retain memory under retrograde amnesia," 29 05 2015.
23	E. Callaway, "Eternal Sunshine drug selectively erases memories," [Online]. Available: https://www.newscientist.com/article/dn15025-eternal-sunshine-drug-selectively-erases-memories/ .
24	T. Craddock, J. Tuszynski and S. Hameroff, "Cytoskeletal Signaling: Is Memory Encoded in Microtubule Lattices by CaMKII Phosphorylation?," 2012.
25	R. Tsien, "Very long-term memories may be stored in the pattern of holes in the perineuronal net," 23 7 2013.
26	D. Christodoulou, Seven Myths about Education.
27	A. X. Wang, "IBM Just Made the World's Most Advanced Computer Chip; future tense;," [Online]. Available: http://www.slate.com/blogs/future_tense/2015/07/09/ibm_7_nanometer_comp uter_chip_the_world_s_most_advanced_processor.html.
28	Gustafsson, Kyusakov, Mäkitaavola and Delsing, "Application of service oriented architecture for sensors and actuators in district heating substations.," 21 08 2014.
29	"Ludwig Wittgenstein," [Online]. Available: https://en.wikipedia.org/wiki/Ludwig_Wittgenstein .

30	"Karl Marx," [Online]. Available: https://en.wikipedia.org/wiki/Karl_Marx .
31	"Michel Foucault," [Online]. Available: https://en.wikipedia.org/wiki/Michel_Foucault .
32	"Johann Friedrich Herbart," [Online]. Available: https://fr.wikipedia.org/wiki/Johann_Friedrich_Herbart .
33	"Friedrich Eduard Beneke," [Online]. Available: https://en.wikipedia.org/wiki/Friedrich_Eduard_Beneke .
34	"Wilhelm Wundt," [Online]. Available: https://en.wikipedia.org/wiki/Wilhelm_Wundt.
35	"E.B. Titchener (1867 – 1927)," [Online]. Available: https://en.wikipedia.org/wiki/Edward_B._Titchener .
36	R. Penrose, Shadows of the mind, Oxford University Press, 1994.
37	"The Computational Theory of Mind," 2015. [Online]. Available: https://plato.stanford.edu/entries/computational-mind/ .
38	S. Stich, From Folk Psychology to Cognitive Science: The Case Against Belief, MIT Press., 1983.
39	H. Field, Truth and the Absence of Fact, Oxford University Press , 2001.
40	H. Putnam, "The Nature of Mental States" In Art, Mind and Religion, W. Capitan and D. Merrill, Eds., Pittsburgh University of Pittsburgh Press, 1967.
41	Jerry Fodor, The Modularity of Mind ; An Essay on Faculty Psychology, MIT Press, 1983
42	S. Pinker, How the Mind Works, W. W. Norton & Company, 1997.
43	P. Carruthers, "On Fodor's Problem," 2003.
44	G. Piccinini and S. Baharb, "Neural Computation and the Computational Theory of Cognition," 24 5 2012.
45	D. Marr, Aspects of Consciousness in Philosophy of Mind, 1982.
46	"Noam Chomsky," [Online]. Available: https://en.wikipedia.org/wiki/Noam_Chomsky; .
47	U. Eco, Kant and the platypus, 1997.
48	T. Rockmore, German Idealism as Constructivism, C. U. o. C. Press, Ed., 2016.
49	T. Rockmore, "Hegel et le constructivisme épistémologique," no. n° 53, pp. 103-113, 2007.
50	T. Rockmore, "Fichte, éthique et philosophie transcendantale," 2011. [Online]. Available: http://www.cairn.info/revue-de-metaphysique-et-de-morale-2011-3-page-343.htm.
51	N. Praetorius, Principles of cognition, language and action, Kluwer Academic Press, 2000.
52	E. Von Glasersfeld, Radical constructivism: A way of knowing and learning, Falmer Press, London., 1995.
53	F. Maturana and H. Varela, The tree of 14 knowledge: The biological roots of human 15 understanding., Shambhala Boston, 1987.
54	"Heinz von Foerster," [Online]. Available: https://en.wikipedia.org/wiki/Heinz_von_Foerster .
55	"Ernst_von_Glasersfeld," [Online]. Available: https://en.wikipedia.org/wiki/Ernst_von_Glasersfeld .
56	C. Hewitt, "What is computation? Actor Model versus Turing's Model.," in *A computable universe. Understanding computation and exploring nature as computation.*, Z. H., Ed., 2012, p. 159–186.
57	K. Friston, "The free-energy principle: a unified brain theory?," 13 01 2010.

	[Online]. Available: https://www.nature.com/nrn/journal/v11/n2/execsumm/nrn2787.html.
58	A. Clark, "Whatever next? Predictive brains, situated agents, and the future of cognitive science," 2013, pp. 1-73.
59	J. Hohwy, "The self-evidencing brain," 2013. [Online]. Available: https://philpapers.org/archive/HOHTSB.pdf
60	D. Wolpert, "The real reason for brains," [Online]. Available: https://www.youtube.com/watch?v=7s0CpRfyYp8 .
61	T.C. Stewart, A Technical Overview of the Neural Engineering Framework Tech Report, 2012
62	F. Garbarini and M. Adenzato, "At the root of embodied cognition: cognitive science meets neurophysiology," *Brain Cogn.*, Vols. 56(1):100-6., 10 2004.
63	"Transition of the Triassic/Jurassic periods," [Online]. Available: https://en.wikipedia.org/wiki/Triassic–Jurassic_extinction_event .
64	O. Cairó, "External Measures of Cognition," vol. 5: 108., 4 10 2011;.
65	C. Koch, "Does Size Matter—for Brains? Turns out some species are better endowed than we are in key cognitive regions," 01 2016.
66	"Brain size," [Online]. Available: https://en.wikipedia.org/wiki/Brain_size .
67	"List of animals by number of neurons," [Online]. Available: https://en.wikipedia.org/wiki/List_of_animals_by_number_of_neurons .
68	"Intelligence In Men And Women Is A Gray And White Matter," 22 01 2005. [Online]. Available: www.sciencedaily.com/releases/2005/01/050121100142.htm .
69	S. Karama, Y. Ad-Dab'bagh, R. Haier, I. Deary, O. Lyttelton, C. Lepage and A. Evans, "Positive association between cognitive ability and cortical thickness in a representative US sample of healthy 6 to 18 year-olds," vol. 37(2): 145–155., 03 2009.
70	A. Konrad, G. Vucurevic, F. Musso and G. Winterer, "Correlates of verbal intelligence: a potential link to Broca's area.," Vols. 24(4):888-95., 5 01 2012.
71	W. Men, D. Falk, T. Sun, W. Chen, J. Li, D. Yin, L. Zang and M. Fan, "The corpus callosum of Albert Einstein's brain: another clue to his high intelligence?," *A JOURNAL OF NEUROLOGY*, vol. 137; 1–8], 2014.
72	J. Kaas, "The evolution of complex sensory systems in mammals," Vols. 146:165-76, p. 46, 1989.
73	J. Kaas, "Neocortex in early mammals and its subsequent variations," [Online]. Available: https://www.ncbi.nlm.nih.gov/pubmed/21534990.
74	P. MacNeilage, L. Rogers and G. Vallortigara, "Evolutionary Origins of Your Right and Left Brain," 24 06 2009.
75	P. Godfrey-Smith, "The Mind of an Octopus," 01 01 2017. [Online]. Available: https://www.scientificamerican.com/article/the-mind-of-an-octopus/.
76	K. K. Loh and R. Kanai, "High media multi-tasking is associated with smaller gray-matter density in the anterior cingulate cortex," 24 09 2014.
77	G. Stoet, D. O'Connor, M. Conner and K. Laws, "Are women better than men at multi-tasking?," *BMC Psychology*, vol. 20131:18, 24 10 2013.
78	Noam Chomsky; Some simple evo devo theses: How true might they be for language? Article · January 2010
79	M. Corballis, "From hand to mouth: the origins of language," 2002.
80	M. Corballis, "Left Brain, Right Brain: Facts and Fantasies," 21 01 2014. [Online]. Available: http://dx.doi.org/10.1371/journal.pbio.1001767.
81	J. Xu, P. Gannon, K. Emmorey, J. Smith and A. Braun, "Symbolic gestures and

	spoken language are processed by a common neural system," vol. 106: 20664–20669., 2009.
82	J. Krause, C. Lalueza-Fox, L. Orlando, W. Enard, R. Green and al., "The derived FOXP2 variant of modern humans was shared with Neandertals," vol. 17: 1908–1912., 2007.
83	R. Quian Quiroga,G. Kreiman, C. Koch and I. Fried; Sparse but not 'Grandmother-cell' coding in the medial temporal lobe ; April 2008
84	A. Lovelace. [Online]. Available: https://www.quora.com/What-is-the-difference-between-the-Cortex-and-the-Neocortex-in-the-mammalian-brain .
85	Vernon B. Mountcastle; The columnar organization of the neocortex; Brain (1997), 120, 701–722 P.54
86	D. Hubel and T. Wiesel, "Monkey striate cortex: A parallel relationship between field size, scatter and magnification factor," 1974.
87	D. O. Hebb, The Organization of Behavior: A Neuropsychological Theory, New York: Wiley and Sons., 1949.
88	R. Raizada and S. Grossberg, Towards a theory of the laminar architecture of cerebral cortex: computational clues from the visual system. ., Cereb Cortex, 2003.
89	R. Douglas, K. Martin and D. Whitteridge, "A canonical microcircuit for neocortex," Neural Comput, vol. 1:480–488, 1989.
90	Javier DeFelipe; The Evolution of the Brain, the Human Nature of Cortical Circuits, and Intellectual Creativity Front Neuroanat. 06 / 2011; 5; 29
91	R. Martin and K. Douglas, "Canonical Cortical Circuits," Handbook of Brain Microcircuits, 2010.
92	J. Hawkins and A. Subutai, "Why Neurons Have Thousands of Synapses, a Theory of Sequence Memory in Neocortex," 30 3 2016 |.
93	D. Felleman and D. Van Essen, "Distributed hierarchical processing in the primate cerebral cortex," Cereb Cortex, 1991.
94	Jerry Fodor, The Modularity of Mind ; An Essay on Faculty Psychology, MIT Press, 1983
95	Peer-to-Peer computing principles and applications Vu, Q.H.; Lupu, M.; Ooi, B.C. (2010) http://www.springer.com/978-3-642-03513-5
96	David Huron; Sweet Anticipation Music and the Psychology of Expectation; January 2008
97	George Mandler; Mind and Body: Psychology of Emotion and Stress; W.W. Norton 1984
98	Keiflin R, Janak PH.; Dopamine Prediction Errors in Reward Learning and Addiction: From Theory to Neural Circuitry. Neuron. 2015 Oct 21; P. 62
99	Steinberg EE, Keiflin R, Boivin JR, Witten IB, Deisseroth K, Janak PH. A causal link between prediction errors, dopamine neurons and learning. Nat Neurosci. 2013 May 26.
100	Paul W. Glimcher; Understanding dopamine and reinforcement learning: The dopamine reward prediction error hypothesis Proc Natl Acad Sci U S A. 2011 Sep 13;
101	R. Bush and F. Mosteller, "A Stochastic Model with Applications to Learning," Ann. Math. Statist., Vols. 24., no. 4, pp. 559-585., 1953.
102	"Robert Rescorla and Allen Wagner," [Online]. Available: http://users.ipfw.edu/abbott/314/Rescorla2.htm.
103	P. Tobler, A. Dickinson and W. Schultz, "Coding of Predicted Reward Omission by Dopamine Neurons in a Conditioned Inhibition Paradigm," Journal of Neuroscience, vol. 23(32):10402–10410, 12 11 2003.

104	M. Ungless, "Dopamine: the salient issue," *Trends Neurosci.*, Vols. 27(12):702-6., 12 2004.
105	S. Killcross and P. Blundell, "Emotional Cognition: From Brain to Behaviour," *PhilPapers*, pp. 44--35, 2002.
106	R. Cardinal, J. Parkinson, J. Hall and B. Everitt, "Emotion and motivation: the role of the amygdala, ventral striatum, and prefrontal cortex Rev, 26 (2002), pp. 321–352," *Neurosci. Biobehav.*
107	S. Killcross and E. Coutureau, "Coordination of actions and habits in the medial prefrontal cortex of rats," *Cereb Cortex.*, Vols. 13(4):400-8, 04 2003.
108	H. Yin, S. Ostlund, B. Knowlton and B. Balleine, "The role of the dorsomedial striatum in instrumental conditioning.," *Eur J Neurosci.*, Vols. 22(2):513-23., 07 2005.
109	H. Yin, B. Knowlton and B. Balleine, "Lesions of dorsolateral striatum preserve outcome expectancy but disrupt habit formation in instrumental learning," *Eur J Neurosci.*, Vols. 19(1):181-9, 01 2004.
110	K. Friston The free-energy principle: a rough guide to the brain? Trends Cogn Sci. 2009 Jul;13(7):293-301. Epub 2009 Jun 24
111	A computational model of acute pain; Karen Prince, Jackie Campbell, Phil Picton, Scott Turner; http://www.scs-europe.net/services/esm2004/pdf/esm-13.pdf
112	Manafi Khanian, B. Computational Modeling and Analysis of Mechanically Painful Stimulations. Aalborg Universitetsforlag. 2015
113	R. B. Rutledge, N. Skandali, P. Dayan and R. J. Dolan, "A computational and neural model of momentary subjective well-being".
114	Douglas RJ, Martin KAC, Whitteridge D (1989) A canonical microcircuit for neocortex. Neural Comput 1:480–488.
115	Geoffrey Hinton in his Stanford seminar https://www.youtube.com/watch?v=VIRCybGgHts 28 avr. 2016;
116	T. Welsh, "It feels instantaneous, but how long does it really take to think a thought?" 26 06 2015.
117	B. Dunst, M. Benedek, E. Jauk, S. Bergner, K. Koschutnig, M. Sommer, A. Ischebeck, B. Spinath, M. Arendasy, M. Bühner, H. Freudenthaler and C. Aljoscha, "Neural efficiency as a function of task demands," *Neubauera Intelligence,* vol. 42(100): 22–30, 01 2014.
118	Han, X. et al., (2013) Forebrain engraftment by human glial progenitor cells enhances synaptic plasticity and learning in adult mice. Cell Stem 12, 342-53.
119	D. Fields, "Unusual Brain Cell (Astrocytes) Boost Learning," 2013.
120	M. Fitzgerald, "Myths About the Brain: 10 percent and Counting," [Online]. Available: http://brainconnection.brainhq.com/2013/04/17/myths-about-the-brain-10-percent-and-counting/ .
121	Butcher L.M., Davis O.S., Craig I.W., Plomin R.; Genome-wide quantitative trait locus association scan of general cognitive ability using pooled DNA and 500K single nucleotide polymorphism microarrays. Genes Brain Behav. 2008 Jun; 7(4):435-46
122	"Gate-All-Around FET; A possible replacement transistor design for finFETs," 01 02 2017. [Online]. Available: http://semiengineering.com/kc/knowledge_center/Gate-All-Around-FET/192 .
123	A. Seabaugh, "The Tunneling Transistor; Quantum tunneling is a limitation in today's transistors, but it could be the key to future devices," 30 09 2013. [Online]. Available: http://spectrum.ieee.org/semiconductors/devices/the-tunneling-transistor.

124	A. Kranti, R. Yan, C. Lee, I. Ferain, R. Yu, N. Dehdashti Akhavan, P. Razavi and J. Colinge, "Junctionless Nanowire Transistor (JNT): Properties and Design Guidelines," [Online]. Available: https://www.researchgate.net/profile/Nima_Dehdashti_Akhavan/publication/224188376_Junctionless_Nanowire_Transistor_JNT_Properties_and_design_guidelines/links/5510f3c40cf2a8dd79bf4c41.pdf?origin=publication_list.
125	J. Connelly and al., "Ternary Computing Testbed 3-Trit Computer Architecture," 29 08 2008.
126	"Not binary logic," 2013. [Online]. Available: http://geek-mag.com/posts/160595/.
127	A. Chanthbouala, V. Garcia, R. Cherifi, K. Bouzehouane, S. Fusil, X. Moya, S. Xavier, H. Yamada, C. Deranlot, N. Mathur, M. Bibes, A. Barthélémy and J. Grollier, "A ferroelectric memristor," *Nature materials,* 2012.
128	A. Hellemans, "Six-State Memristor Opens Door to Weird Computing," 21 11 2014. [Online]. Available: http://spectrum.ieee.org/semiconductors/memory/sixstate-memristor-opens-door-to-weird-computing .
129	A. Shah, "HP Enterprise shows off a computer designed to emulate the human brain," 16 06 2016. [Online]. Available: http://www.pcworld.com/article/3085120/hardware/hpe-shows-off-a-computer-intended-to-emulate-the-human-brain.html.
130	"D-Wave Systems;," [Online]. Available: http://www.dwavesys.com .
131	S. Van Themsche, The advent of unmanned electric vehicles, Springer, 2015.
132	"Cognitive Computing Systems: Algorithms and Applications for Networks of Neurosynaptic Cores" ; IBM Research
133	A. Karpathy. [Online]. Available: http://karpathy.github.io/neuralnets/.
134	Q. Le Marc, M. Ranzat, R. Monga and al, "Building High-level Features Using Large Scale Unsupervised Learning," 12 07 2012.
135	J. Lawry, "A methodology for computing with words," 11 2001. [Online]. Avail: http://www.sciencedirect.com/science/article/pii/S0888613X01000421.
136	A. Kumar, Z. Wan, W. Wilcke and S. Lyer, "3D Wafer Scale Integration: A Scaling Path to an Intelligent Machine Neuro-Inspired Computational Elements," 9 03 2016.
137	R. Llinas, of the Vortex: From Neurons to Self, MIT Press, Cambridge, MA., 2001.
138	J. Lieff, "Searching for the Mind," 2013. [Online]. Available: http://jonlieffmd.com/blog/feelings-and-body-maps-in-the-brain.
139	B. Benson, "Dennett's Astonishing Hypothesis: We're Symbionts! – Apes with infected brains;," [Online]. Available: http://www.replicatedtypo.com/dennetts-astonishing-hypothesis-were-symbionts-apes-with-infected-brains/10789.html.
140	A. Seth and H. Critchley, "Interoceptive predictive coding: A new view of emotion?," Vols. 36 (3), 227-228., 2013.
141	A.K. Seth and K. Friston; Active interoceptive inference and the emotional brain; Journal ListPhilos Trans Royal Society London B Biol Sciv.371(1708); 2016 Nov 19
142	William James; Wikipedia; https://en.wikipedia.org/wiki/William_James
143	J. Aspell, L. Heydrich, G. Marilier, T. Lavanchy, B. Herbelin and O. Blanke, "Turning the body and self inside out : Visualized heartbeats alter bodily self-consciousness and tactile perception," vol. 2013.
144	"Emotion Markup Language (EmotionML) 1.0;," 29 07 2010. [Online].

	Available: https://www.w3.org/TR/2010/WD-emotionml-20100729/.
145	C. Lamm and J. Majdandz˘ic , The role of shared neural activations, mirror neurons, and morality in empathy – A critical comment, vol. 90 15–24, Neuroscience Research, 2015.
146	M. Koerth-Baker, "Flaws in a long-accepted test used to search for signs of self-awareness are revealing that selfhood varies culturally and exists on a continuum," 29 11 2010;.
147	A. Matthew, J. Apps and M. Tsakiris, "The free-energy self: A predictive coding account of self-recognition," [Online]. Available: http://dx.doi.org/10.1016/j.neubiorev.2013.01.029.
148	K. Friston, The fantastic organ. Brain 136, 1328–1332 10.1093/brain/awt038
149	K. Suzuki, S. Garfinkel, H. Critchley and A. Seth, "Multisensory integration across interoceptive and exteroceptive domains modulates self-experience in the rubber-hand illusion," 2013.
150	S. Edelman, Computing the Mind. (2008). New York: Oxford University Press
151	O. Blanke and T. Metzinger, "Full-body illusions and minimal phenomenal selfhood," Trends Cogn. Sci. Vols. 13, 7–13, 2009.
152	A. F. Hamilton and S. T. Grafton, "The motor hierarchy: from kinematics to goals and intentions, in Sensorimotor Foundations of Higher Cognition: Attention and Performance," vol. xxii, p. 381–408, 2008.
153	K. Friston, Prediction, perception and agency. (2012). Int. J. Psychophysiol. 83, 248–252 10.1016/j.ijpsycho.2011.11.014
154	C. Frith, "Making Up the Mind: How the Brain Creates Our Mental World," Oxford, UK: Blackwell; 2007.
155	C. L. Baker, R. Saxe and J. B. Tenenbaum, "Bayesian theory of mind: modeling joint belief-desire attribution," 2011.
156	C.D. Frith and U. Frith, Mechanisms of social cognition. (2012). Annu. Rev. Psychol. 63, 287–313 10.1146/annurev-psych-120710-100449;
157	E.C. Brown, M. Brüne, The role of prediction in social neuroscience. (2012). Front. Hum. Neurosci. 6:147 10.3389/fnhum.2012.00147
158	T. E. Behrens, L. Hunt, M. Woolrich and M. Rushworth, "Associative learning of social value," Nature Vols. 456, 245–249, 2008.
159	A. Hampton, P. Bossaerts and J. O'Doherty, "Neural correlates of mentalizing-related computations during strategic interactions in humans," Proc. Natl. Acad. Sci. U S A 105, 6741–6746 , 2008.
160	A. Matthew, J. Apps and M. Tsakiris, "The free-energy self: A predictive coding account of self-recognition," Neurosci. Biobehav. Rev. [Online]. Available: http://dx.doi.org/10.1016/j.neubiorev.2013.01.029.
161	G. Pezzulo and M. Levin, "Top-down models in biology: explanation and control of complex living systems above the molecular level;," *J R Soc Interface*, 13 11 2016.
162	M. Allen and K. Friston, "From cognitivism to autopoiesis: towards a computational framework for the embodied mind; Synthese," 2016.
163	D. Pimentel, J. Donlea, C. Talbot, S. Song, A. Thurston and G. Miesenböck, Operation of a homeostatic sleep switch, Vols. 536, 333–337, Nature, Ed., 2016.
164	G. B. Schmid, "Conscious vs. Unconscious Information Processing in the Mind-Brain".
165	From Bacteria to Bach and Back; Daniel C. Dennett; 2017, W.W. Norton & co.
166	A. Chau, A. Salazar, F. Krueger, I. Cristofori and J. Grafman, "The effect of

	claustrum lesions on human consciousness and recovery of function," Vols. 36:256-64, 11 2015.
167	B. Yin, D. Terhune, J. Smythies and W. Meck, "Claustrum, consciousness, and time perception" Current Opinion in Behavioral Sciences.
168	S. Reardon, "A giant neuron found wrapped around entire mouse brain," Nature 543, 14–15, 02 03 2017. [Online]. Available: http://www.nature.com/news/a-giant-neuron-found-wrapped-around-entire-mouse-brain-1.21539.
169	P. G. Clarke, "The Libet Experiment and its Implications for Conscious Will," [Online]. Available: http://www.bethinking.org/human-life/the-libet-experiment-and-its-implications-for-conscious-will.
170	René Descartes Discours de la méthode, Cogito ergo sum; (1637)
171	"Wave function collapse," [Online]. Available: https://en.wikipedia.org/wiki/Wave_function_collapse .
172	G. Brassard and P. Raymond-Robichaud, "Can Free Will Emerge from Determinism in Quantum Theory?".
173	J. Ouellette, "A New Spin on the Quantum Brain," Quanta Magazine, 11 2016. https://www.quantamagazine.org/20161102-quantum-neuroscience/.
174	Robots and Empire; Isaac Asimov; Doubleday Books 1985
175	N. Block, "The Mind as the Software of the Brain," 1995. [Online]. Available: http://www.nyu.edu/gsas/dept/philo/faculty/block/papers/msb.html#4 .
176	P. Churchland and P. Churchland, "Could a machine think?" vol.262(1): 32-37.
177	"Brain simulator reply," [Online]. Available: https://plato.stanford.edu/entries/chinese-room/#5.2 .
178	S. Schneider, Alien Minds, in Science Fiction and Philosophy: From Time Travel to Superintelligence, vol. 2016, I. H. N. John Wiley & Sons, Ed.
179	"Augmented Reality Markup Language," [Online]. Available: https://en.wikipedia.org/wiki/Augmented_Reality_Markup_Language.
180	"Open Geospatial Consortium," [Online]. Available: https://en.wikipedia.org/wiki/Open_Geospatial_Consortium.
181	"XML," [Online]. Available: https://en.wikipedia.org/wiki/XML.
182	R. Sharma, S. Joshi, K. Singh and A. Kumar, "Visual Evoked Potentials: Normative Values and Gender Differences" J Clin Diagn Res., vol. 9, 07 2015.
183	M. Spüler, "A high-speed brain-computer interface (BCI) using dry EEG electrodes," vol. 12(2), 22 02 2017.
184	T. Rutkowski, "Robotic and Virtual Reality BCIs Using Spatial Tactile and Auditory Oddball Paradigms," Front Neurorobotics, 2016.
185	M. Nakanishi, Y. Wang, X. Chen, Y. Wang, X. Gao and T. Jung, "Enhancing Detection of SSVEPs for a High-Speed Brain Speller Using Task-Related Component Analysis," 19 04 2017.
186	A. Mora-Cortes, N. Manyakov, N. Chumerin and M. Van Hulle, "Language Model Applications to Spelling with Brain-Computer Interfaces," Sensors (Basel). 04 2014.
187	B. Golmann, "Brain-computer interface advance allows fast, accurate typing by people with paralysis," [Online]. Available: https://med.stanford.edu/news/all-news/2017/02/brain-computer-interface-allows-fast-accurate-typing-by-people-with-paralysis.html.

Acknowledgement

I wrote that I probably would not have been able to write this book, without the internet. However, I know for a fact that without Normand Pinet, who brought me his experience as a philosopher and a pioneer in the use of computers in teaching, I would never have been able to ask myself the right questions.

I could also count on Christopher Crawford to challenge me in the area of computer science. During our numerous discussions, he helped me clarify the potential paths AI could follow.

Lena Arnera provided me with valuable insights, especially in the area of neurosciences, which she teaches.

Friends who supported me during this three-year journey necessary to write my book, include Fabiano Ramalho, Andre Antunes, and Alexandre Barbosa.

I would like to give my wife Christine, daughter Fanny, and son Maxime, who together helped me write a more straightforward and better book, a heartfelt thank you.

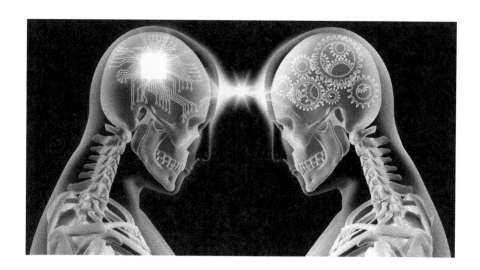